AGAINST ABANDONMENT

AGAINST ABANDONMENT

Repertoires of Solidarity in South Korean Protest

JENNIFER JIHYE CHUN AND **JU HUI JUDY HAN**

STANFORD UNIVERSITY PRESS
Stanford, California

Stanford University Press
Stanford, California

© 2025 Jennifer Jeehae Chun and Ju Hui Han. All rights reserved.

No part of this book may be reproduced or transmitted in any form or by any means, electronic or mechanical, including photocopying and recording, or in any information storage or retrieval system, without the prior written permission of Stanford University Press.

Printed in the United States of America on acid-free, archival-quality paper

Library of Congress Cataloging-in-Publication Data
Names: Chun, Jennifer Jihye, 1973- author. | Han, Ju Hui Judy, author.
Title: Against abandonment : repertoires of solidarity in South Korean protest / Jennifer Jihye Chun and Ju Hui Judy Han.
Description: Stanford, California : Stanford University Press, 2025. | Includes bibliographical references and index.
Identifiers: LCCN 2024036670 (print) | LCCN 2024036671 (ebook) | ISBN 9781503641723 (cloth) | ISBN 9781503642256 (paperback) | ISBN 9781503642249 (ebook)
Subjects: LCSH: Protest movements—Korea (South) | Working class—Political activity—Korea (South) | Precarious employment—Korea (South) | Demonstrations—Korea (South) | Political culture—Korea (South)
Classification: LCC HM883 .C49 2025 (print) | LCC HM883 (ebook) | DDC 303.48/4095195—dc23/eng/20240814
LC record available at https://lccn.loc.gov/2024036670
LC ebook record available at https://lccn.loc.gov/2024036671

Cover design: Daniel Benneworth-Gray
Cover photograph: Chung Taekyong, *Kiryung #073 Seoul Kwangjang Kogong Nongsŏng*, 2008.

CONTENTS

List of Illustrations   vii

Notes on Romanization, Translation, and Use of Hangul   ix

Preface and Acknowledgments   xi

INTRODUCTION
Life-and-Death Protests   **1**

1   **Refusing Precarity**   34

2   **Rituals and Repertoires**   72

3   **Conjuring Solidarity**   117

4   **Caring Infrastructure**   147

5   **Protest as Place Making**   184

CONCLUSION
Hope and Failure   **223**

Glossary   241

Notes   243

Bibliography   271

Index   289

LIST OF ILLUSTRATIONS

FIGURE 0.1. KTX unionists demand direct employment — 3

FIGURE 0.2. KTX unionists perform *och'et'uji* — 7

FIGURE 0.3. Kiryung unionist in a high-altitude-occupation protest — 24

FIGURE 1.1. Selfie from the Kwanghwamun Billboard Occupation — 36

FIGURE 1.2. Ground-level protest camp beneath Kwanghwamun Billboard Occupation — 38

FIGURE 1.3. Public art installation with *Sewol*-ferry life jackets — 41

FIGURE 1.4. Promotional poster for *Sister J* (2020) — 52

FIGURE 2.1. "Kogong'yŏjido," a map of high-altitude-occupation protests in Korea — 92

FIGURE 2.2. Yoosung unionists perform *och'et'uji* — 105

FIGURE 3.1. Kiryung workers Kim So-yeon and Yu Heung-hee on day sixty-five of their hunger strike — 127

FIGURE 3.2. "We want to return to work!" poster for KTX workers, with art by Yi Yunyop — 135

FIGURE 3.3. Ssangyong Motor unionists' protest altar — 136

FIGURE 3.4. KTX workers' encampment inside Seoul Central Station — 137

FIGURE 4.1. Protesters chain their bodies to a makeshift tent — 149

FIGURE 4.2. Catholic Mass in solidarity with *Sewol*-ferry victims, survivors, and families — 155

vii

FIGURE 4.3. Catholic Mass in solidarity with Ssangyong Motor unionists ... 164

FIGURE 5.1. Candlelight Protest, facing north, with yellow-ribbon public art installation ... 191

FIGURE 5.2. Map of public restrooms near the Seoul City Hall and Kwanghwamun area ... 192

FIGURE 5.3. Marchers commemorate the thirtieth anniversary of Lee Han-yeol's death ... 198

FIGURE 5.4. Visitors wrap the "comfort woman" statue in a warm blanket ... 204

FIGURE 5.5. Portrait of Baek Nam-ki on a truck as part of the public funeral procession ... 212

NOTES ON ROMANIZATION, TRANSLATION, AND USE OF HANGUL

Following scholarly conventions, we primarily use the McCune-Reischauer system in this book to romanize Korean words and names of places, individuals, and organizations. However, we use alternative romanizations if they are already widely in use, such as in Hangul (한글; Hangŭl), Seoul (서울; Sŏul), Baek Nam-ki (백남기; Paek Nam-gi), and Kim Jin-suk (김진숙; Kim Chin-suk). In such cases, we provide, in parentheses, the word in Hangul and the standard romanization for reference. These appear only once at their first occurrence in the book. We do not provide the Hangul for place names.

We use romanized Korean words throughout the book because they contain unique and culturally specific meanings and nuances that are important for our discussion, such as *pijŏnggyujik* (비정규직), *nongsŏng* (농성), and *tangsaja* (당사자). We use Hangul throughout the text when we feel that it would benefit readers familiar with the Korean language. We provide the Korean names of organizations in Hangul if we refer to their English name, but we do not romanize their Korean name—for example, Korean Confederation of Trade Unions (전국민주노동조합총연맹). For Korean organizations that already have an official English version of their name or acronym, we do not edit or create our own translations of their name. Please see the glossary. For some other formal groups, like committees and commissions, the Hangul is not included.

Throughout the body of this book, surnames precede given names without a comma for names of Korean nationals unless they publish under alternative names, and we often use the full name throughout the book to minimize confusion between common surnames. All translations are ours, except when otherwise indicated.

PREFACE AND ACKNOWLEDGMENTS

As we were finishing this book, solidarity-protest encampments took center stage in the news. Joining a worldwide movement to call for a ceasefire in Palestine and demanding that the University of California, Los Angeles (UCLA) disclose the extent of its financial investment in Israel and divest, the student-led Palestine Solidarity Encampment at UCLA flourished with mutual aid and community support. There were vigils, rallies, walkouts, and teach-ins all in a concerted effort to draw attention to the genocide unfolding in Palestine, and solidarity became a focal point for much of our daily lives. The timing was uncanny as we were grappling with the repertoires of solidarity in South Korean protest, including the practices of long-term struggle and occupation protest, and soon, we would also be reminded of the enormous cost of engaging in political protest as our students, friends, and colleagues at UCLA and throughout the United States and Canada faced violence, repression, and a range of disciplinary actions and even criminal charges. We continue to be inspired by the extraordinary and profoundly ordinary ways in which powerful protest movements persist.

Our interest in protest cultures converged somewhat unexpectedly in the mid-2000s. Jennifer had recently finished the research for her first book on the turn to symbolic forms of labor organizing among low-paid, precarious workers, and Judy was working on her dissertation on evangelical Christian missionaries and their commitment to growth and developmentalism. It seemed unlikely at first that our research interests would ever converge, but we found ourselves captivated by

xi

several recurring questions over the past two decades: What motivates people to keep fighting even when the odds are against them? How do we go beyond notions of militancy or desperation to explain the various ways in which so many activists *work* to effect meaningful change?

We deeply appreciate all the individuals who generously shared their time and expertise for this project and invited us to countless gatherings, meetings, film screenings, commemorations, and celebrations. Some of our earliest and most influential interlocutors in these discussions were through the Korean Women Workers Association: Maria Chol-soon Rhee, Bae Jinkyoung, Park Jinyoung, and Park Namhee. We could not have produced this book without the critical insights of Aelim Yun, Jeong Jooyeon, Kwak EKyeong, Kim Seungha, Ryu Eunsook, Kim Hyejin, Kim So-yeon, Yu Heung-hee, Kwon Okja, Oh Min-gyu, Lee Taeho, Na Young, Tari Young-jung Na, Nara, Yunjin, Zacchaeus, and Sister Maria (pseudonym). We are especially indebted to Hae-joang Cho Han for her mentorship and for connecting us to the most ideal rental housing that made our stay in Seoul a truly magical experience and Won Jaeyoun, Kim Hyun Mee, Paik Young-Gyung, and Jung Ji Young for their friendship and camaraderie in academia and beyond. Many individuals whose names or voices may not appear explicitly in the book are nonetheless very much part of it, and we are grateful for the many years, even decades, of conversations and debates about activism and organizing.

While we were both at the University of Toronto, funding support from the Social Science and Humanities Research Council of Canada (SSHRC) enabled us to carry out the multiyear research that is at the heart of this book. Special thanks to Patricia Landolt, who went above and beyond, joining Jennifer on a summer field school in Seoul in May and June 2017, immersing students in the vibrant worlds of labor- and social-movement activism. Judy appreciates the generous support from the Academy of Korean Studies Grant for the Korean Government (MEST) (AKS-2011-AAA-2104), which enabled field research especially regarding the religious and urban aspects in this project. Over the many years of field research as well as transcription, translation, and manuscript preparation, we are indebted to the tremendous amount of help we received from Woo Jin Cho, Da In Choi, Ga Young Chung, Ji Hyun

Kim, Garam Kwon, Minyoung Kye, Ji-Won Lee, Juwon Lee, Yurim Lee, Jeongsu Shin, and Wei Si Nic Yiu.

We hold dear the vibrant intellectual community and deep friendships we enjoyed in Toronto, including (but certainly not limited to) Nadine Attewell, Deb Cowen, Cynthia Cranford, Robert Diaz, Fidan Elcioglu, Tak Fujitani, Richard Fung, Mary Gellatly, Evelyn Encalada Grez, Janice Kim, Yangsook Kim, Dai Kojima, Deena Ladd, Grayson Lee, Vinetta Lenavat, Tim McCaskell, Lisa Moore, Nada Moumtaz, Alison Mountz, Vinh Nguyen, Hyun Ok Park, Geraldina Polanco, Thy Phu, Josh Pilzer, Adriana Paz Ramirez, Rania Salem, Andre Schmid, Gökbörü Sarp Tanyildiz, Sohoon Yi, and Lisa Yoneyama.

We have benefited from presenting earlier drafts of several chapters from this book to a variety of academic audiences: Yonsei University's Sociology Department, ChoongAng University's Sociology Department, Cornell University's Labor Relations and International Comparative Labor Department, Dartmouth College's Department of Asian Studies, New Frontiers Seminar at the University of Toronto Scarborough, the Groupe de recherche interuniversitaire et interdisciplinaire sur l'emploi, la pauvreté et la protection sociale (GIREPS) International Symposium at Université de Montréal, McMaster University's School of Labour Studies, Center for Korean Studies at the University of California, Berkeley, Johns Hopkins University's Sociology Department, Mellon Sawyer Seminar at the University of California, Santa Barbara, State University of New York at Oswego's Year of Korea series, the UCLA Anthropology Department's Culture, Power, and Social Change seminar series, the UCLA Geography Department's colloquium series, Nam Center for Korean Studies at the University of Michigan, Institute for Korean Studies at George Washington University, Korea Institute at the Australian National University, Geography Department at Oregon State University, East Asian Studies Center at Spelman College, Center for East Asian Studies at the University of Chicago, Idaho Asia Institute at the University of Idaho, Institute for Korean Studies at Indiana University, Centre for the Study of Korea at the University of Toronto, the Modern Language Association annual meeting in Washington, DC, the Association for Asian Studies annual meeting in Seattle, Washington, and the International Sociological Association for the eighteenth World Congress of Sociology meeting in Yokohama, Japan. We are grateful to colleagues and friends for inviting us to share our work over the years, including Rina Agarwala, Ruth Barraclough, Evelyn Clark Benavides, Kyeong-Hee Choi, Judy Fudge, Immanuel Kim, Seung-kyung Kim, Yang-sook Kim, Byounghoon Lee, Yoonkyung Lee, John Lie, Purnima Mankekar, Jeff Kyong-McClain, Se-Mi Oh, Albert Park, John Park, Youngju Ryu, Sooyoung Suh, Jaeyoun Won, and Carole Yerchowski. In addition, the joint public lecture we presented with GYOPO, a collective of diasporic Korean cultural producers and arts professionals, in Los Angeles in 2019 was pivotal in articulating our central arguments about affect and performance. The opportunity to collaborate with brilliant artists in GYOPO was one of the highlights of this project. Special thanks to Ellie Lee, Jennifer Moon, Audrey Min, Cat Yang, Nancy Lee, Kavior Moon, and, last but not least, Yong Soon Min, who tragically passed away in 2024.

After we moved to UCLA, we found ourselves surrounded by incredibly supportive and generous colleagues in our respective departments, Asian American Studies and Gender Studies, including our chairs Victor Bascara, Keith Camacho, Elizabeth Marchant, Natalie Masuoka, and Sherene Razack. We were able to hold a book-manuscript workshop with thanks to Grace Kyungwon Hong and the UCLA Center for the Study of Women, with staff support from Rosa Chung and Katja Antoine. Grace's unwavering encouragement helped push us through many crucial moments and see this project to the end. We are deeply thankful to Deborah Cowen, Eleana Kim, and Seo Young Park for being our astute and constructive external readers and our colleagues at UCLA—Grace Kyungwon Hong, Namhee Lee, Thu-Huong Nguyen Vo, Zeynep Korkman, and Juan Herrera—for their brilliant feedback at the workshop. Hyun Ok Park has long been an invaluable interlocutor for our work, with her probing insights and indispensable suggestions that helped us sharpen the book's arguments and contributions. Toby Higbie and the Institute for Research on Labor and Employment at UCLA provided invaluable support and resources. Thank you to our friends close and far—Adriana, Eleana, Michelle, Mimi, K-Sue, Eunkyung, Jini, Sujin,

Enji, Laura, Ellie, Grace, Nicole, Sungyun, Rina, Robyn, Rachel, Kim, Ananya, Saba, EKyeong and Hana, Alejandra and Jason, Namhee and Michael, and Kian and Aya—who have supported us in so many ways and cheered us along this long and exhausting journey of book writing.

We extend our deepest thanks to Dylan Kyung-lim White at Stanford University Press for believing in this project and stewarding it to the finish line. Many thanks also to Austin Michael Araujo, Tiffany Mok, Laura J. Vollmer, and Elise Hess. We are grateful to the anonymous reviewers for their critical feedback. Our heartfelt thanks go to Chung Taekyong, Kim Hungku, Lee Yunyop, and Park Eunsun for allowing us to include their amazing photography and illustrations in this book.

And finally, it feels strange to cowrite this acknowledgment and somehow find a way to thank each other for this opportunity to collaborate on something so massive and so meaningful. We are convinced that just one of us could not have taken on this book project single-handedly and feel incredibly fortunate to have our partnership—in research and in life. Jennifer's parents, Kyung Ja Chun and Yang Kog Chun, and Judy's parents, Hui Sook Yoon and In U Han, as well as our sisters, brothers, nieces, and nephews were a constant source of love and support. Puca and George oversaw the start of the research project, and Koga assisted us during our field research in Korea in 2016–17. Aji and Hugo will be happy to have more of our attention now that this book project has come to a close.

INTRODUCTION
LIFE-AND-DEATH PROTESTS

Today marks 4,526 days since we began our struggle. This
place where we are standing . . . has always been the core site
of our fight [투쟁현장]. On the left is the steel tower that we
once occupied, and on the right is the tent encampment that
we have maintained to this day. I can't believe that we are
finally here not to struggle or occupy but to thank you because
our dispute has been resolved. It feels like a dream.[1]

—Kim Seungha (김승하; Kim Sŭng-ha), union head

How do we find the place of freedom? More precisely,
how do we make such a place over and over again?

—Ruth Wilson Gilmore, *Abolition Geography*

KIM SEUNGHA, THE HEAD OF the Korean Train Express (KTX) Crew Workers'
Union (승무원 노조), stood at the base of the steps leading up to the main
entrance of the Seoul Central Station, surrounded by fellow workers
and supporters on what was undoubtedly a momentous occasion. It was
the summer of 2018, twelve years after KTX workers first began their
strike in protest of the unequal and unjust conditions of *pijŏnggyujik*
(비정규직), or what is commonly translated as "precarious," "irregular,"
or "nonregular employment."[2] The union was finally able to negotiate
a collective agreement with the Korea Railroad Corporation (KORAIL;
한국철도공사), and 180 women who worked as crew attendants (승무원)
on the nation's first high-speed bullet train would be directly hired as
KORAIL employees. The details of their reinstatement were still to be
determined, and only a few of the laid-off workers would likely return to

2   INTRODUCTION

their coveted jobs once known as "flight attendants on the ground," but the moment was triumphant. Holding the microphone with tears in her eyes, Kim Seungha addressed the crowd in disbelief. She emphasized the grueling nature of their fight, highlighting the duration of 4,526 days and the many places that they once occupied in protest. Seoul Central Station was not just a train station to them. It was where they had once worked, where they fought to demand justice and dignity, where they slept in tent encampments, and then where they announced the end of their long struggle.

No one could have imagined, including the KTX workers themselves, that when this all began, young, college-educated women, who epitomized the normative ideals of femininity and grace, would launch—and eventually win—the kind of "fight to the death" (결사투쟁) that is typically associated with militant unionism in South Korea. In a much-photographed direct action in 2006, striking KTX train attendants tied themselves to each other while wearing matching, formfitting crew attendants' uniforms consisting of light-gray skirt suits and bright-multicolored neck scarves (figure 0.1).[3] Their leaders shaved their heads and waged long hunger strikes in subsequent years. They fought so hard and staged so many occupations—at the Seoul Central Station, KORAIL offices, politicians' offices, and many other government buildings—that a journalist once quipped that there was not a place that KTX unionists had not at least once occupied. Even as their numbers declined sharply from three hundred at its height to merely thirty-four after an unsuccessful three-year-long workplace occupation, the remaining workers refused to abandon the fight.

In the summer of 2017, after several years of mostly legal battles, the KTX crew union renewed their public-facing campaign in the wake of the nation's largest candlelight protests (촛불집회) and hopeful signs of political change in the air. The largest and most widely heralded protest event in contemporary South Korean history, the Candlelight Protests of 2016–17, helped oust Park Geun-hye (박근혜; Pak Kŭn-hye) from the presidency on charges of bribery, corruption, and abuse of power. Over six consecutive months, an estimated total of eighteen million people took over the streets and public plazas of Seoul's historic central district

FIGURE 0.1. KTX unionists demand direct employment, September 2006. Photo by Kim Hungku.

in peaceful protest every Saturday evening, culminating in a final mass assembly the day after the Constitutional Court of Korea approved the presidential impeachment on March 10, 2017. The KTX workers participated in the Candlelight Protests and celebrated the historic moment, but they refused to accept the idea that the "world had changed" when "nothing had changed for them."[4] They were determined to hold accountable the so-called Candlelight President, Moon Jae-in (문재인; Mun Chae-in), who had made explicit promises as a candidate to address the unresolved grievances of precariously employed workers, like the KTX workers. Their fight would not be just about getting their jobs back; they were struggling for a moral economy that supported life and human flourishing, not a premature death under the crushing weight of debt and shame.[5]

The loss of workers' lives in the context of antiunion retaliation and ongoing labor protests, including for KTX workers, had reached a critical threshold. One of their own union leaders had tragically died by suicide in 2015 after the Supreme Court of Korea reversed the terms of compensatory wages that were previously awarded, and religious leaders were extremely concerned for the well-being of the remaining KTX unionists, which Anglican minister Father Zacchaeus (자캐오 신부) described to us in an interview as having become a "matter of life and death." In the months following the Candlelight Protests, KTX unionists participated in a month-long series of prayer protests, held daily inside the Seoul Central Station, and were accompanied by multifaith leaders from the country's four major religious groups: Protestants, Catholics, Buddhists, and Anglicans. They embarked on an arduous protest procession involving full prostration through Kwanghwamun, Seoul City Hall, and the Seoul Government Complex before reaching their destination, the Blue House. On July 21, 2018, when the KTX Crew Workers' Union finally resolved their long-standing dispute with KORAIL, they took down their protest tent and cleared the area for the last time.

To those who are familiar with South Korea's vibrant culture of labor protest, the details of the KTX union's fight would likely not be surprising. Like in many other labor protests, the KTX unionists engaged in everything from confrontational direct action and occupation of public spaces, just to name a couple, to holding head-shaving ceremonies and prayer protests over the course of their long, protracted fight. Put together, these protest actions and events comprise a remarkable protest repertoire that has taken on urgency and significance in the context of the life-depriving conditions of globalized neoliberal capitalism. Political geographer and abolitionist scholar Ruth Wilson Gilmore refers to the predatory conditions of capitalist domination as the death-dealing forces of an extractive system of racial capitalism that resolves its perennial crises of accumulation and profitability through "fatal couplings of power and difference."[6] In the United States, racism—and its intersectional relations of social inequality and oppression—has functioned as the dominant modality in which minoritized groups, especially Black workers, have been subjected to a premature death. In South Korea, workplaces and labor markets stratified by gender, age, and employment status, among other axes of social inequality, have rendered women workers in precarious jobs, as well as the rural and urban poor, disabled people, and sexual minorities, vulnerable to intensified relations of abandonment produced by labor commodification, which have degraded people's ability to survive, let alone flourish.

Precarity as the index of an unlivable life reverberates throughout the repertoire. Faced with the limits of the law and the violence of capital and the state, aggrieved workers and the people who support their struggles put their bodies and lives on the line, showing what it means to be treated as disposable and what it takes to resist. Protesters hold placards that express the indignity of being thrown in the trash like the ubiquitous single-use paper or plastic cup. Their slogans, chants, banners, T-shirts, vests, and headbands demand the guarantee of their democratic rights—rights that were gutted long before the International Monetary Fund (IMF) bailed out the South Korean currency in December 1997. Yet, more than words and semantics, the repertoire is profoundly embodied and affective. Through performances that circulate and gain traction across disparate bodies, causes, and sites, the repertoire generates intensities of feelings, sentiments, and dispositions that reach beyond a personal grievance or a particular dispute. As "structures of feeling," the repertoire produces "affective elements of consciousness and relationships" that may seem "private, idiosyncratic, and even isolating" but "exert palpable pressures and set effective limits on experience and action," as Marxist cultural theorist Raymond Williams famously elaborates.[7] Concretely identifying how structures of feeling transform collective norms and institutional rules or the relations of domination and subordination that structure everyday capitalist life makes its empirical study elusive, yet to do so, we look closely at the ways in which labor- and social-movement actors in South Korea use protest to illuminate "what is actually being lived, and not only what is thought is being lived."[8]

A book about protest politics in South Korea, *Against Abandonment: Repertoires of Solidarity in South Korean Protest* chronicles the long-term struggles of workers, women, and other minoritized social groups who use protest—and the ability to intensify its affective charge through the choice and combination of tactics, symbols, scripts, and performances in a broader repertoire—to amplify the life-or-death stakes of refusing precarity in the broader political economy. As one of the leading agents of repertoire amplification, workers—many of whom are women in precarious jobs, like the KTX train attendants we profiled at the start of the chapter—spearhead grueling battles that last months and sometimes years with no end in sight. Their labor disputes usually begin with a fairly routine pattern. After joining or forming a union, workers demand collective bargaining as the primary arena in which to resolve their grievances about unfair working conditions and the unjust terms of their employment. Yet as unions representing workers in precarious jobs encounter unyielding opposition and repeated legal setbacks, they face the Arendtian denial of the "right to have rights."[9] They confront the violence of the law itself, which is a vital means for expressing grievances and demanding institutional protection but subjects those who oppose the relentless devaluation of human life under globalization's necropolitical order to a "life of waste and absolute expendability," as Neferti X. M. Tadiar puts it, "making legal disenfranchisement a key process in the production of disposable life."[10]

In response, aggrieved workers turn to protest forms that stretch a sense of time and space. High-altitude protests (*kogong nongsŏng*; 고공농성) are a variation of place-based-occupation protests in which protesters not only go without necessities—like warm and safe shelter, running water and electricity, and often food for prolonged periods—but also endure extreme isolation at perilous altitudes as a way to heighten the stakes of their struggles. The KTX's occupation of a forty-meter-high steel tower behind the Seoul Central Station is one of over one hundred high-altitude occupations that have taken place between 1990 and 2015, demonstrating a sense of embodied and transhistorical connectedness that extends across space (including face-to-face encounters and digital networks) and time (through connections to past and future struggles).[11] Slow-moving and painstaking processions influenced by the Tibetan Buddhist rituals of *samboilbae* (삼보일배), a half-prostration procession, and *och'et'uji* (오체투지), a full-prostration procession, direct one's attention to the spectacle of bodies crawling on the ground. KTX unionists performed a 3.8-kilometer-long *och'et'uji* on the 4,223rd day of their fight as the temperature dipped below three degrees Celsius (figure 0.2). Its

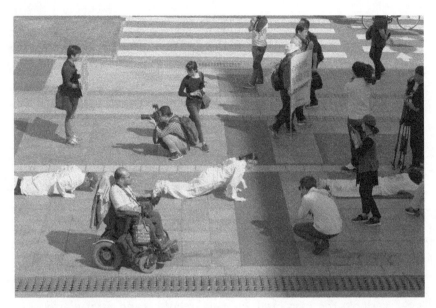

FIGURE 0.2. KTX unionists perform *och'et'uji*, September 2017. Photo by Chung Taekyong.

scale or difficulty might pale in comparison to the five-day-long, fifteen-kilometer *och'et'uji* performed by laid-off Kiryung Electronics (기륭; Kiryung hereafter) workers in December 2014, which marked the end of their decade-long fight, but it was nonetheless an agonizing and sobering display of bodies protesting in motion.

BEYOND DESPERATION

Why, in the face of misrecognition, abjection, and failure, do protesters continue to protest and in ever more desperate registers? One answer to this puzzle, which is often echoed by workers' own words, is that they are, in fact, desperate. After doing everything that they can think of and more, they reach the end of a losing battle having diminished their strength in numbers, punished and exhausted their bodies and minds, and put their livelihoods, families, and futures in extreme peril. The emphasis on workers' desperation is repeated in media accounts of extreme protest practices and in academic literature on South Korean labor protest. Scholars describe the proliferation of high-altitude occupations and worker suicides that followed the so-called IMF crisis as desperate and irrational acts that substitute individualized sacrifice and suffering for more purposive and impactful collective strategy.[12] The "protests of desperation" that Ching Kwan Lee examines reflect similar characteristics, though the tactics of last resort waged by laid-off workers in China's declining industrial rustbelt have more to do with workers' sense of outrage and indignation over disappearing socialist entitlements than the lack of attention to strategic modes of collective action.[13]

Waging uneven contests certainly can push people to engage in desperate acts that may appear to undermine the goals of purposeful collective action. However, the emphasis on desperation as an explanatory lens overlooks the ways in which social relations and cultural processes shape the interior life of a protest repertoire itself—relations and processes that are always nested in the broader power dynamics of fundamentally asymmetrical social-movement contests. It also neglects the significance of interactional dynamics that occur between and among protesters as well as with supporters and the places and spaces of protests, all of which shape the ability of protesters to sustain high-risk forms of collective action against powerful opponents in ways that are more life-affirming than life-depriving.

To understand how protest repertoires have effects that exceed the motivations of an individual protester or even the stated goals of a collective action, we return to a foundational premise in social movement theory. "Rather than seeing social movements as expressions of extremism, violence, and deprivation," asserts Sydney Tarrow, "they are better defined as collective challenges, based on common purposes and social solidarities, in sustained interaction with elites, opponents, and authorities."[14] Prioritizing the forms and patterns of oppositional collective action over their reactionary and often-desperate characteristics has produced a vibrant body of literature that has expanded understanding of how protest movements draw attention to social and political issues, rally advocates and supporters, stoke opposition and intensify repression, and elicit unexpected and often-unpredictable moments of institutional change. However, an Achilles's heel plagues the field of social-movement theorizing when it comes to understanding protest patterns that defy expectation and reason.

As protesters continue to risk their bodies and lives against all odds, the motivations and goals that first animated their struggles—such as the protection of jobs and collective labor rights—remain constant, yet their tactics become amplified by difficult acts of self-sacrifice and suffering. While this disjuncture can stoke concern about the dissonance between means and ends, it can also ignite unexpected connections between previously unrelated groups and intensify solidarity between ostensibly unrelated issues, which can change the course of history. Revolutionary uprisings have often followed acts of self-immolation and death by suicide by political martyrs. The bonds formed between radical activists and religious clergy across a number of different movements waged on behalf of workers, the urban poor, oppressed groups of women, racialized minorities, and migrants and on behalf of the environment, to name just a few, constitute other examples, as well as the unlikely affinities forged across class, nationality, ethnicity, race, gender, sexuality, and religion between revolutionary uprisings against authoritarian regimes and populist rebellions against the global economic order.

PROTEST REPERTOIRES

Making sense of the surprising entanglements of disparate protest acts and actors addresses another lacuna in the social-movement scholarship: the utility of protest beyond strategy. Protest is often treated as a public-facing strategy, a way for aggrieved actors with limited resources and authority to win support for their grievances and demands through public shaming strategies and other forms of external public pressure. Yet scholars have also pointed out that the power of protest does not derive from a single event or even a series or waves of protests regardless of how eventful that historical moment may be.[15] Rather, the contentious-politics tradition highlights the significance of historically durable protest repertoires—mainly in the form of contentious performances—that provide extralegal avenues for ordinary people who lack access to institutional channels to make collective claims against ruling elites, be they landlords, bosses, governments, or multinational corporations. When drama and theater become pronounced in public displays of popular contention, the repertoire operates more like a well-recognized set of performances than a spontaneous response to exceptional circumstances.[16]

While culture is foundational to the doing and feeling of protest, the sociological literature on protest repertoires and contentious politics has devoted surprisingly little attention to cultural processes of meaning making beyond collective-identity formation and discursive-framing strategies. Questions of culture are central in Charles Tilly's field-defining monograph *The Contentious French* (1986), which undertakes a rigorous examination of four centuries of popular contention in France.[17] Yet, over time, his attention shifts to identifying the causal factors that foster variation across different types of repertoires in relation to institutional violence and state regimes.[18] Tilly focuses on issues of performance and pedagogy in his later monograph *Contentious Performances* (2008), but his empirical reliance on the historical archive limits his analysis of how nuanced interactional dynamics, especially between and among protesters and supporters, shape the characteristics and development of the repertoire itself.[19]

The emotional turn in the study of social movements has produced new avenues for examining how the lived experience of protest shapes the internal dynamics of protest repertoires and social movements more broadly.[20] Highly charged feelings, such as anger and indignation, not only affect how blame is allocated and collectivities are formed but can also change the decisions that protesters and social-movement actors more broadly make in the context of opposition, backlash, disappointment, and failure. Deborah B. Gould points to the importance of an emotional pedagogy as "a template for what and how to feel" to help guide social-movement actors to make strategic decisions about protest forms and tactics in emotionally fraught contexts, such as the AIDS epidemic in the 1980s.[21] Similarly, Erika Summers Effler observes that given the inevitable disappointment and exhaustion that many social-movement actors experience when driven by unattainable altruistic goals, such as the eradication of poverty in the case of the Catholic Workers activists, social-movement actors engage in critical forms of emotion work to direct and redirect the negative emotional energy that saturates high-risk collective action.[22]

The interdisciplinary literature on protest in performance studies, anchored in the work of Diana Taylor, further illuminates how the felt and embodied performances produce repertoires that endure across place and time.[23] From the perspective of embodiment, performing protest is less about whether an aggrieved actor achieves their goals against targeted opponents and more about producing and sustaining body-to-body transfers of shared memory and collective knowledge between and among people who perform the protest. For Taylor, a repertoire "lays out the range of possibilities" for encounters to take place between and among disparate social actors and settings, operating more like a scenario with props, place markers, and a cast of characters than a script with a fixed plot.[24] When protests are performed as routine acts of political-claims making, they may seem to operate more like habitual behaviors than creative forms of activity that produce generative encounters and outcomes. Yet regardless of how well developed a repertoire is or how many times a familiar act or scene is repeated, the outcome of any given performance is never fixed or predetermined. The performative power of a repertoire to move people occurs through "reactivation rather than duplication," underscores Taylor, mediating the relational processes that take place between performers and the audience, actors and supporters, witnesses and participants.[25] In effect, by operating as a range or set of actions rather than one-off events, the repertoire creates a medium through which activists and organizers foster translocal and transhistorical circuits of feelings and memories, including through deterritorialized digital platforms and online networks.[26] Protest repertoires thus create the conditions for embodied knowledge to be transmitted across history and geography as vehicles of social transformation.

REFUSAL AND SOLIDARITY AS POLITICAL AFFECTS

In this book, we argue that protest repertoires entail much more than what movements do—or seek or claim to do—in order to achieve their goals. Crucially, they shape *how movements move.*[27] By "move," we refer not only to the flow of bodies in motion across time and space or the feelings and sentiments generated when one is moved emotionally but also to catalytic affects that operate on a different register from emotions.[28] Rather than reside in the interior life of individuals, affect circulates and gains traction between and across bodies and places, movements and atmospheres.[29] We are especially interested in affect as a relational force, echoing feminist philosopher Sara Ahmed, who writes that affect can align "individuals with communities—or bodily space with social space—through the very intensity of their attachments."[30] By generating and animating affective attachments and spatial realignments, the protest repertoires we discuss do more than simply enact a political ideology or instrumentalize a movement strategy. Structures of feeling coalesce around protest repertoires in ways that "envelop political movements and figures," as can be seen in the "atmospheric pressures" surrounding protest practices, such as in the case of long-term tent encampments, high-altitude occupations, slow-moving processions, and prayer protests on the streets of KTX workers.[31] Repeatedly performing acts that reference a modular repertoire of extralegal performances, symbols, and discourses, we argue, generates solidarity as "affect in motion," evoking a sense of connection that ties people, places, objects, and scenes together through shared practices and collective memory.[32]

Analyzing how political affects circulate and gain traction in a broader protest repertoire interweaves the internal dynamics of protest repertoires to the broader political economies in which unequal contests are taking place—a macrolevel context that is often obscured in social-movement scholarship on the internal processes of social-movement reproduction.[33] Precarity is the defining condition of a globalized neoliberal economy that has made life itself the site of relentless capitalist expropriation. Intensified labor commodification alongside broader processes of marketization and financialization have degraded the quality of people's jobs and livelihoods in ways that saturate the atmosphere with feelings of desperation and hopelessness. Also in circulation are intense feelings that compound and contradict each other: anger, shock, betrayal, grief, mourning, courage, audacity, gratitude, joy, triumph, and so on. These catalytic intensities have material and symbolic effects. They create passionate leaders who refuse to submit in the face of intensifying levels of sacrifice and suffering, even as the number of protest participants dwindles and they must continue to fight on behalf of others. These intensities also create devoted supporters who assure the protesters that they are not alone, providing critical forms of physical, emotional, financial, and discursive support. Protests that consist of life-threatening acts by extraordinary individuals are thus simultaneously powered by the affects and relations of solidarity that sustain a collective praxis of refusing precarity.

Drawing on over two decades of ethnographic research, *Against Abandonment* provides a searing examination of the utility—and futility—of protest in challenging the indignity of precarity as a life-depriving system under globalized neoliberal capitalism. In the case of veteran labor- and social-movement activists in Korea, protesters' embrace of drama and ritual has reignited their political passions and spurred them to carry on the spirit of sacrifice and suffering, which animated staunch opposition to decades of military rule and authoritarian industrialization. Younger generations of activists and artists who promote a broad range of social-movement causes—from civic and human rights and social and environmental justice to gender and LGBTQ+ (lesbian, gay, bisexual, transgender, queer/questioning, plus others) equality—have become galvanized as enthusiastic supporters who travel near and far to support spectacular acts of protest. Ordinary citizens new to political activism as part of the massification of public protest have also taken interest in unionized workers and other radical activists that they may have previously viewed as unlawful and violent. While the nature and duration of solidarity vary across different groups of supporters, together they make sure that protesters are not abandoned, despite intensifying internal fragmentation and repeated and ongoing failure. As we show, solidarity itself becomes a defining feature of a protest repertoire that cultivates leadership, strengthens commitment, and fosters alternative ways of caring for one another during seemingly unwinnable fights against precarity.[34]

Tracing the interconnections between protest and solidarity, we argue, in the chapters that follow, that protest repertoires take on a life-and-death character through the labor of refusal. By the "labor of refusal," we call attention to forms and practices of political belonging that locate their legitimacy not in the criteria of legal personhood and liberal citizenship but in the everyday social relations that take shape and form "in memory, in conversation, [and] in sociality," as Audra Simpson puts it.[35] Solidarity is the precondition of sustaining the labor of refusal. Without the creation of robust organizing networks, extensive social-movement know-how, and grassroots communities of mutual aid and collective care, protesters would have to face the conditions of abandonment under precarity alone, vulnerable to institutional neglect and social disavowal as "disposable" and "criminalized" populations. For social movements, this involves the background work of outreach, planning, coordinating, publicizing, documenting, and evaluating, which facilitates the flow of bodies in motion across power-laden geographies—the infrastructural activities of social movements.[36] It also involves the cooking, cleaning, and other reproductive labor involved in caring for people who put their bodies and well-being in jeopardy. This infrastructural and reproductive labor is typically performed by women and thus often devalued, yet it is crucial to the care work involved in sustaining the life of protests and protesters themselves.

The labor of refusal also involves the creative and resourceful work of place making—that is, the use and transformation of the built environment of the city as part of a spatial politics for inclusion and belonging. The work of place making involves planned disruption in commercial and public life, which has been the bread and butter of popular contention. Yet it also entails a relational understanding of space that accounts for the "the contemporaneous existence of a plurality of trajectories; a simultaneity of stories-so-far," in the words of feminist geographer Doreen Massey.[37] Solidarity, in this sense, is not about political ideologies and collective identities that demand likeness and similarity or the "binding together of pre-existing communities."[38] Solidarity itself is immensely productive. It produces new ways of relating and interacting with each other and the diverse places and spaces that organize everyday life through the life-giving activities of social reproduction. Solidarity is something, Gilmore reminds us, that is "made and remade" through "radical dependency"; it fosters new ways of "life and living together."[39] Solidarity is that which can help "find the place of freedom" and do so "over and over again"—in response to Gilmore's query in the opening epigraph.[40]

At the crux of the book is the pursuit of what it means to refuse precarity and build solidarity in times of profound capitalist injustice.[41] The protesters that we follow and the protests they wage are routinely disavowed by powerful individuals and institutions because of who they are and what injustices they seek to redress as minoritized workers, women, and political dissidents. Yet they do not accept their disavowal. Rather, they seek to alter the very grounds on which everyday social relations are produced and reproduced as sites of violence and dehumanization. They refuse their predicament as commodified labor with no institutional protection by inciting affective politics and weaving together solidaristic relations. They refuse the terms of their disposability and abandonment by transforming the labor of social reproduction from a "stifling discriminating activity into the most liberating and creative ground of experimentation in human relations."[42] Some of the risks and harms that accumulate during the course of a struggle may defy common sense, but they inspire new ways of understanding how and under what conditions people take extraordinary risks to transform unjust worlds.

UNDERSTANDING PRECARITY

Precarity has taken center stage in public fights against extreme inequality, corporate greed, government corruption, racial and gender violence, and social and ecological destruction. First linked to the explosion of mass mobilization across western and southern Europe in the context of capital-accumulation crises and neoliberal structural-adjustment policies, "precarity" has come to denote a generalized condition of insecurity and vulnerability propelled by the market-driven processes of privatization and financialization under neoliberal global capitalism.[43] The dismantling of basic labor rights and social protections alongside the decline of government-funded public services have exposed people located on the bottom rungs of the social and economic hierarchies to intensified levels of precariousness, or the generalized state of what Judith Butler describes as an "unlivable" life.[44]

Scholars of the Global South, however, take issue with the assertion that precarity—or, to employ the more widely used term outside the Global North, "informality"—is a new phenomenon.[45] The social compromises negotiated between organized labor and capitalist welfare states after two imperialist world wars created the foundation for a global structure of exclusion and hypocrisy that prescribed a different set of terms for what democracy looked like in the decolonizing world, even when workers were granted similar rights on paper. "Precarity is capitalism's norm, not its exception," asserts Kathleen M. Millar, and the "experience of insecurity, degradation, exploitation and abuse" that corresponds with the fundamental dependence on wage work for one's survival has long pervaded the everyday conditions of work and life for the majority of the world's rural and urban poor.[46]

Notwithstanding the problems with Northern-centric and universalizing definitions of "precarity," precarity provides a useful framework for understanding how people—especially workers located on the margins of globalized neoliberal capitalism—make sense of the degraded social and economic conditions that correspond to intensified marketization and financialization across variegated geographic contexts. We conceptualize precarity not as a direct reflection of objective historical conditions but as a structure of feeling that is produced by the "frequent tension between the received interpretation and practical experience" under the changing institutional and material conditions of capitalism.[47] In places like the United States, where the promise of the American dream was used to justify its position as a global hegemon, one way in which precarity acts as a structure of feeling is through affective attachments to the "good life"—despite the fact that "middle-class" aspirations rooted in the ideology of the self-made, entrepreneurial individual for working people are less and less attainable given the state's disinvestment of public infrastructure and the social rights of citizenship that guarantee labor and welfare protections.[48] In postapartheid South Africa, precarity has become synonymous with the indignity of informality and unemployment in a postcolonial nation that has equated national liberation with the provision of "decent jobs" and "social wages" to oppressed and excluded Black workers.[49]

In South Korea, precarity as a structure of feeling is perhaps best captured in the subjective feelings of devaluation and deprivation that have taken root in the context of heightened economic volatility, deepening income and wealth inequality, and increasing socioeconomic polarization, especially by age and gender. The state-supported liberalization of the Korean economy, which intensified after the 1997 Asian financial crisis and the 2008 global financial collapse, has fueled a widening gap between the rich and the poor, especially the working poor.[50] Income inequality not only is rising in ways that depart from relatively moderate levels that were often heralded during the decades of authoritarian industrialization between the 1960s and 1980s but also, with a sharp rise after 1997 after a sharp decline just prior, has remained at historically high levels. In addition to income inequality, poverty rates are at historic levels. In 2021, income inequality rates were above the Organization for Economic Cooperation and Development (OECD) average and in the top third of all OECD countries.[51] The top 10 percent of income earners accounted for 33.7 percent of the share of income for Korea in 2020, continuing the trend of rising income concentration among the highest earners.[52] Relative poverty rates reveal the extreme difficulty in making ends meet that many individuals with earning levels below the poverty line experience, especially among the nearly 45 percent of the elderly population experiencing poverty-level conditions in 2018.[53]

Deeply entrenched employment-based dualism between *chŏnggyujik* (정규직; regular employment) and *pijŏnggyujik* (비정규직; nonregular, or precarious, employment) has intensified the institutional vulnerability of the poor and low-income population. Although the overall share of workers in nonregular jobs has gradually declined between

2000 and 2020, they comprise a sizable proportion of the total wage workforce at 41.6 percent (8.5 million persons) as of August 2020. The average monthly wages of workers in nonregular jobs are almost half that of workers in regular jobs (51.5 percent), reflecting a significant source of economic discrimination.[54] Workers in precarious jobs and self-employed workers also earn significantly lower incomes and are not covered by basic social-protection schemes, such as employment insurance, which protects working people from lost income due to job loss, illness, and disability. One study published by the OECD found that workers who take minimum wage jobs instead of receiving unemployment benefits are even further disadvantaged since their income levels decline once they are no longer unemployed.[55]

The deprivation of the working poor has become more deeply entrenched as chaebols (재벌) increase their monopolistic control of financial resources across diverse sectors of the economy. Family-owned companies with vertical subsidiaries across diverse industries, chaebols drive investment in research and development, manufacturing, services, technology, housing, entertainment, and infrastructure, to name just a few. The top five chaebols—with the Samsung Group as the most profitable and most infamous—generate over half of the nation's gross domestic product and stock market value.[56] The gradual relaxation of restrictions on chaebol control over the financial sector from the 1980s onward, imposed initially by bans on bank ownership by chaebols, has paved the way for more creative strategies by chaebols to circumvent regulatory controls through a complex web of cross-holder sharing, especially since the mid-2000s. For example, although the Samsung Group owns five financial institutions, their intergroup investments expand across twenty-seven different companies.[57]

Gender inequality pervades all levels of social polarization and social vulnerability, especially when considering the nexus between employment and inequality. For decades, South Korea has recorded the most severe gender pay gap among all OECD countries, with women paid 37.2 percent less than men in 2015, second only to South Africa and India.[58] The growing rate of women's labor-market participation—an increase of nearly eight percentage points from 1980 to 2005—has coincided with their increasing concentration in precarious and temporary jobs.[59] Women tend to be disproportionately represented in nonregular jobs in comparison to men (50.7 percent of women; 33.2 percent of men) and experience even greater income and poverty disparities given their disproportionate employment in low-paid service-sector and manufacturing jobs in small and medium firms.[60]

Rising levels of inequality, polarization, and vulnerability have anchored widespread perceptions of feelings of deprivation and loss across social classes and groups. Hagen Koo highlights contradictory feelings for affluent classes who feel simultaneously privileged and anxiety ridden.[61] They invest in lucrative real estate, both residential and rent seeking, spend enormous sums on their children's private education as well as their own health and well-being, and travel the world in luxury and style as part of the global elite. However, their conspicuous consumption is not just a marker of their class privilege. Koo finds that it produces constant anxiety that they too can lose everything and then be left behind. In contrast, the ranks of the working poor are depicted as having little hope of status mobility. Unable to obtain coveted regular jobs that guarantee a life of security and upward mobility, the working poor struggle to make ends meet, working in precarious jobs with long hours and low wages with no social benefits or social status. They cannot afford to buy or even rent adequate housing in desirable areas, which many view as a prerequisite to any possibility of social and economic security and mobility.

The immiseration of the working poor and the indignity and violence that pervade their everyday life frequently appear in award-winning films and television series, such as *Parasite* (2019) and *Squid Game* (2021) as well as countless other portrayals about class and social inequality in South Korea. Scenes of wealthy and powerful elites behaving as aristocrats and tyrants are juxtaposed against images of the rest, whose life chances seem increasingly circumscribed by prohibited access to wealth, property, job security, and so on. The working poor, as they are portrayed, embodies what it means to experience a premature death, faced with a life of abjection, denied social recognition and political belonging. Interestingly, though, these works of fiction often contain plot reversals in which the seemingly powerless confront the powerful rather than wallow in feelings of powerlessness and hopelessness.

We see a similar reckoning in the aftermath of the *Sewol* disaster in April 2014, which transformed a devastating crisis into a national social trauma. Hae-joang Cho Han traces the trauma to the conditions of organized abandonment under Japanese colonial rule and decades of war, dictatorship, and neoliberalism, and asserts that people continue to operate with a mentality in which they have been "reduced to a refugee status within an emergency state."[62] Rather than take the time to reflect upon what is possible and desirable as part of the collective good in the context of changing historical conditions, the prevailing attitude remains: "Why are you bothering me when I'm just trying to get ahead?"[63] This widespread depoliticization has its limits, however. A decade and a half after the "IMF crisis," a profound political awakening was produced in the wake of the tragic sinking of the *Sewol* on April 16, 2014. As the nation watched the *Sewol* sink over the course of seven hours on live television, taking the lives of hundreds of passengers, 250 of whom were high school students from the same working-class community in Ansan, feelings of shock, disbelief, rage, and grief besieged the nation, "making everyone aware of the fragility of their everyday lives within which a tragedy like this could befall anyone at any time."[64]

The *Sewol* tragedy, in many ways, has come to epitomize the gross neglect of the state, especially the cruel disregard of their own president at the time, Park Geun-hye, in protecting the most fundamental aspects of people's lives and futures. Precarity, in the context of this "disaster of democracy," as Hyun Ok Park puts it, manifests as another facet of the "capitalist unconscious," which is rooted in part by utopian market ideals of freedom as private property and in part by the fallacy of democracy itself.[65]

GENDERING CAPITALISM

In South Korea, the institutional and material conditions that have produced precarity as a structure of feeling operate through the disavowal of the figure of the aspirational worker seeking democratic rights. This figure has been attacked and undermined by state regimes promoting neoliberal policies, even as it is heralded for exposing the contradictions of South Korea's "illiberal democracy" under successive military dictatorships supported by US empire building during the Cold War and ushering in a new historical period of liberal democracy.[66] Using the rule of law to criminalize union militancy provides a potent channel for capital and for the state to remove the threats that organized labor poses to unfettered capital accumulation. Successive liberal democratic administrations with ties to popular movements—including Kim Young Sam (김영삼; Kim Yŏng-sam) (1994–98), Kim Dae-jung (김대중; Kim Tae-jung) (1998–2003), and Roh Moo-hyun (노무현; No Mu-hyŏn) (2003–8)—have justified ongoing labor repression through "the logic of the police, property and the penal code, rather than through deliberative politics," thereby resulting in the systematic dismantling of labor's de jure and de facto collective rights.[67] Consequently, when workers today turn to democratic labor rights that have been codified in the nation's constitution and the National Labor Standards Act (근로기준법) of 1953—legal frameworks that enable labor to challenge authoritarian industrialization—they face a litany of civil and criminal charges for disrupting traffic, disturbing the peace, and obstructing business, all of which can result in exorbitant and debilitating financial penalties and even jail time.[68]

Conceptualizing precarity as labor's disavowal reveals how the degradation of labor rights and social protections under neoliberal technologies of rule should not be understood as an inevitable response to the economic orthodoxy of "free market" capitalism. Building on the groundbreaking theorizing of Gilmore on racism and capitalism, Grace Kyungwon Hong argues that neoliberalism is more aptly understood as a "structure of disavowal" that has occurred in the context of the state's simultaneous promotion of market rule and multicultural democracy in response to worldwide movements for decolonization and liberation in the post–World War II era.[69] The politics of disavowal and disposability that pervade the lives of minoritized groups, both in the United States and globally, reveal the importance of conceptualizing precarity, as well as neoliberalism, in terms of its connections with the social conditions of domination under capitalism. As Jodi Melamed writes, "Capitalism *is* racial capitalism"—that is, the ability of capital to accumulate in the face of perpetual crisis and conflict depends on producing ongoing fictions about "differing human capacities."[70] Yet, like Hong asserts in her focus on the practices of collective care and survival in the writings of Black and other women of color feminists, Melamed argues that there is nothing inevitable or totalizing about the forces of antirelationality that produce asymmetrical geographies of human deprivation and ecological destruction. Rather than accept the "forgetting of interconnections, of viable relations, and of performances of collectivity that might nurture greater wholeness," minoritized subjects can invoke alternative genealogies of surviving disposability and abandonment across the shifting historical temporalities of global racial capitalism.[71] If the production of antirelationality pertains historically to race and racism in the United States, in Korea, they pertain to the inequalities of gender and sexuality that have devalued the lives of men and women workers.

Gender and its intersecting relations of social and economic subordination are particularly germane for understanding how precarity as well as struggles against it have taken root both historically and under contemporary conditions. Korean workers have long fought against labor's disavowal under predatory capitalist regimes that have subjected minoritized workers to a premature death. Key to their struggles has been the cultivation of a repertoire that protests precarity through the use of workers' bodies. Of particular note is the development of a protest repertoire among labor and social movements that has explicitly *defined labor rights as human rights* throughout the twentieth century. Rather than reframe labor issues as community issues as part of a broad-based platform of social-movement unionism—as was the case in similar political economies, such as Brazil and South Africa—Korean workers articulated clear moral critique and strong class identity that challenged the brutal and inhumane treatment of workers as "despised laborers" during the 1970s and 1980s.[72] This critique extends even further back to the period of Japanese colonial rule (1910–45), when Korean workers faced "extreme contingency and precariousness" in the context of their expropriation from the land and the economic compulsion to find work as racialized colonial subjects.[73] Nonetheless, the literature on labor and capitalism in Korea tends to neglect the significance of women workers in contributing to moral vocabularies of labor resistance and class struggle, with notable exceptions.[74] Even though women workers in labor-intensive factories led the movement in the 1970s and 1980s for democratic unionism to assert that workers had the right to live as human beings, not animals or machines, the political nature of their demands became sidelined by a labor-movement history that by and large stressed the numerical strength and structural power of the predominantly male workforce in heavy industries in the late 1980s and 1990s.[75]

Hwasook Bergquist Nam skillfully and movingly addresses this historical absence by examining a century of industrial women workers' labor resistance. Her discussion of intensified proletarianization during the Pyŏngyang rubber factory strikes of 1930 and 1931, which involved more than two thousand workers, both men and women, during Japanese colonial industrialization, is particularly illuminating.[76] These strikes drew fascination from the media at the time because of the widespread practice of factory women who engaged in hunger strikes and other forms of bodily protest, such as perilous occupations. They also captured attention because of the militancy of women factory workers, such as Kang Chu-ryong (강주룡), who spent nine hours on top of a rooftop in protest of the police crackdown on unionized workers. Her protest was prominently reported in the newspapers at the time, though the story remained little known until recently when it became celebrated as the predecessor to contemporary high-altitude-occupation protests, such as the one waged in 2008 by a Kiryung unionist during the course of their grueling long-term struggle (figure 0.3).[77]

As we show in the chapters that follow, women workers with first-hand experiences of violence, death, and grief as well as resistance and resilience have profoundly shaped the affective register of labor-protest

FIGURE 0.3. Kiryung unionist in a high-altitude-occupation protest known as *kogong nongsŏng* near Seoul Station, May 2008. Photo by Chung Taekyong.

politics today. Especially in the current neoliberal political economy in which death and dying have become endemic for precarious workers, the affective power of long-term, sustained protests shows that precarity is always experienced through the grammar of domination and subordination, inequality and injustice, and performed through gendered cultures of resistance and solidarity.

STUDYING PROTEST REPERTOIRES

Against Abandonment examines the life-and-death character of protesting precarity by conducting a relational ethnography of its expression as a historically durable repertoire. Heeding the call by Diana Taylor "to resist the act of turning everything into text or narrative," we approach the study of protest repertoires by examining the affective, embodied, and interactional processes that mediate how disparate people and places come into relation with one another.[78] We document live and ongoing social processes that take form and shape through improvisation and reactivation. Online platforms for livestreaming and social media archives of protest events have further expanded the scope of possibility for ethnographic inquiry by enabling us to examine the relational dynamics among protests that explicitly cite one another and protests and their participants that are digitally networked yet spatially and temporally separated.[79]

A relational approach to ethnography provides a framework for addressing questions of power and positionality in the production of knowledge. By locating individual cases in the wider relations and forces of capitalist transformation, we build on the extended-case-method tradition of global ethnography developed by Michael Burawoy.[80] By treating ethnography as a reflexive, iterative process, the extended-case method pushes ethnographers to identify contradictions and surprises that occur in the field as opportunities to continuously revise theories of capitalism as universalizing but fundamentally contingent and place-specific processes of world-historical change. An intersectional and transnational feminist approach to relational ethnography explicitly connects such contradictions and surprises that are produced through embodied and place-based practice of ethnography not just as violations of theory or expected knowledge but as a "set of processes, procedures, and technologies for decolonizing the imagination," what Chela Sandoval characterizes as a "methodology of the oppressed," rooted in the theoretical and political critiques of US Third World feminism.[81]

Acknowledging how research and researchers are shaped by wider circuits of power and inequality is essential to challenging the production of ethnographic knowledge that relies upon and reproduces colonial binaries between researchers as outside experts and native subjects. Our positionality as Korean/American feminist researchers in a number of interconnected diasporic locations explicitly informs how we have articulated the aims of the overarching research project as well as characterized the expertise of the labor- and social-movement activists who have graciously agreed to participate in the research. In recognition of the central role of South Korean labor- and social-movement activists as knowledge producers, we refer to the individuals who participated in the study through observation and interviews as key interlocutors rather than key informants or key experts whose insights and expertise are abstracted and generalized to represent a community or population devoid of differences and hierarchies. Emphasizing their role as key interlocutors recognizes the coproduction of knowledge through mutual exchange and dialogic conversation about topics of shared interest, given our overlapping spheres of research and activism. Some of our interlocuters are acclaimed authors, public intellectuals, and frequent contributors to public and policy debates, and we view such deep and reflexive engagements with them as critical to understanding how and under what conditions protest has taken on distinct characteristics at the level of the entire repertoire. We acknowledge that our decision to highlight in-depth engagement with several key interlocutors may create the perception that these individuals have a disproportionate influence on the dynamics of the repertoire and our analysis of them. We want to remind readers that our interviews do not reflect a representative sampling of a wide range of voices and experiences. Rather, our focus on depth over breadth seeks to illuminate the relations and interactions that take place in the broader repertoire.

The pursuit of our research as a relational ethnography also situates the study of labor- and social-movement protest in South Korea as part of transnational circuits of theory and knowledge, especially about the similarities and differences of being integrated into global capitalist systems of maximizing profits over people. South Korea is one of the most contentious societies in the world, yet scholarly—as well as public—discussions rarely connect vibrant protest movements occurring in South Korea to the global explosion of protest movements taking place around the world, especially in defiance of precarity. We are careful to avoid the treatment of South Korea or any single national case study as either exceptional or as a bounded comparison to other national units. Rather, we view our "case" through the lens of "minor transnationalism" and "relational comparison."[82] In doing so, we not only challenge the methodological nationalism that has long defined the study of labor and social movements in South Korea but also bring the complex dynamics of capitalist destruction and transformation in South Korea, viewed through the empirical lens of protest and protest repertoires, in conversation with critical theorists of feminism, transnationalism, and racial capitalism among minoritized communities in the United States and the Third World / Global South. By seeking out "submerged perspectives," our research seeks to advance the kind of "decolonial methodology" that Macarena Gómez-Barris calls for—one that moves beyond a "paradigm of mere resistance" and instead reveals the emancipatory potential of "less perceivable worlds, life forms, and the organization of relations with them" in the context of the extractive geographies of neoliberal capitalism.[83]

The book's long-term ethnographic field research begins in the mid-2000s, with the start of two major union struggles in 2005 led by three groups of women: factory workers at Kiryung Electronics, train attendants on the KTX high-speed trains, and cashiers at E-Land/Homever department stores. Between 2006 and 2016, we followed protest actions and visited protest sites, sustaining relationships with numerous labor and movement activists across seniority, rank, and age, ranging from labor and women's movements to LGBTQ+ and disability justice, religious justice, human rights, antipoverty, environmental justice, antieviction, antimilitarism, and peace activism. We attended rallies, strikes, marches, public meetings and commemorative events, mass gatherings, vigils, and tent encampments organized by many key cases profiled in the book.

Between September 2016 and September 2017, we conducted intensive fieldwork in Seoul and around the country. Given the timing of our fieldwork, which coincided with the start and end of the Candlelight

28   INTRODUCTION

Protests, we immersed ourselves in a world of daily protest actions ranging from small to astonishingly large. We attended weekly Candlelight Protest events held every Saturday in Seoul's historic city center over the course of six months, which also sparked a series of conservative counterprotests, known as the T'aegŭkki Rallies (태극기 집회), or Korean national flag rallies. At the same time, we continued to attend smallerscale protests waged by unionized workers, religious activists, evictees, former "comfort women," bereaved parents of the *Sewol*-ferry victims, queer and feminist activists, as well as human rights advocates committed to addressing a variety of social concerns. Our routine site visits and informal conversations helped us produce a curated list of participants for in-depth, semistructured interviews.

Between April and August 2017, we conducted forty formally recorded, semistructured interviews with individuals from organizations that ranged in size, constituency, goals, priorities, program activities, and ideological orientations.[84] We focused primarily on activists that were involved in day-to-day organizing rather than formal leaders and especially sought out interview participants with direct experience performing and supporting protest actions in the broader repertoire. We interviewed well-known organizers of large, national movement organizations, such as the Korean Confederation of Trade Unions (KCTU; 전국 민주노동조합총연맹) and People's Solidarity for Participatory Democracy (PSPD; 참여연대). We interviewed rank-and-file leaders of key unions engaged in long-term struggles at the KTX Crew Workers' Union, the Kiryung Electronics Workers' Union (기륭전자노조), and other unions. We interviewed staff organizers from diverse social-movement organizations, as well as artists, filmmakers, and media producers. Since some of our key interlocutors actively serve as media experts and write articles, reports, and books for public audiences, we included their names and organizational affiliations with informed consent at the time of the interview and again prior to publication. When we felt the purpose of a selected quote was better delivered with anonymity or if the research participant asked not to be disclosed, we used a pseudonym or removed identifying details. Direct quotations from interviews that were conducted and translated by the authors appear throughout the text.

The process of coding interviews was inductive, and we focused on identifying crosscutting themes and interactional dynamics that occur between and among protesters and supporters. We recorded when, where, how, why, and by whom particular protest forms were used and took particular care in trying to capture the embodied and place-based processes that took place. As we noted earlier, it is difficult empirically to examine the production and circulation of affects and feelings, so we tried to do so by asking nuanced questions during both informal conversations and formal interviews that go beyond the oft-repeated explanations. We have provided a glossary of key terms and organizations that appear repeatedly in our book.

In addition to our ethnographic fieldnotes and formal interviews, we built an archive of activist narratives published in books, newspapers, periodicals, blogs, and social media. Korean movement worlds are extraordinarily well documented, both in print and on digital platforms, largely because documentation practices are prioritized in many movement spheres. Activist and independent news reporting and social media as well a vibrant culture of activist scholarship have enabled us to study protest repertoires even while not "in the field" physically in person. Our ability to inhabit and participate in the worlds of South Korean labor- and social-movement activism in person and virtually was critical in carrying out this research. Granted, even when we were technically there "in the field," it would have been impossible to be physically present for all crucial moments at all times.

ORGANIZATION OF THE BOOK

The chapters that follow focus principally on the protests of women workers in precarious jobs, yet as the ensuing chapters emphasize, such practices cannot be understood without attention to the wider social, organizational, and historical contexts in which they take place. While protest politics in South Korea define the geographic boundaries of our empirical lens, we draw on the rich scholarship produced by researchers and practitioners of protest and social movements around the world to make sense of their significance and impact. In particular, we draw connections between protest in South Korea and in social movements studied by interdisciplinary critical scholars in Indigenous, Black, and ethnic studies. These engagements were crucial for moving beyond the normative frameworks of liberal democracy that often narrow the analytic themes in the social-movement scholarship and divorce theorizing from the cultural and political sensibilities of minoritized groups, whether they are women workers in South Korea or members of Indigenous and Black communities in the United States. In doing so, *Against Abandonment* theorizes protest as a political form with far-reaching resonance across history and geography, underscoring its significance for cultivating collective survival, self-determination, and emancipatory transformation.

Chapter 1, "Refusing Precarity," examines the consolidation of a protest repertoire that has become synonymous with the life-and-death stakes of precarity. We begin with a case of a joint hunger strike and high-altitude occupation to illuminate the conflict-ridden terrain of waging such grueling and punishing acts of protest, which we argue have become familiar forms that are repeated, especially by workers in precarious jobs and by laid-off workers in regular jobs that have become mired in long-term fights. We engage with interviews from several key interlocutors who have played important roles in supporting the amplification of the protest repertoire by *tangsaja* (당사자), or directly impacted persons in a dispute or grievance. We find that protesting workers who refuse to surrender in the face of mounting challenges and powerful opponents have reignited support from longtime allies as well as new advocates. They have also redefined public understandings of the connections among precarity, disposability, and death. While the persistence of antiunion sentiment may limit more broad-based support, the vibrant connections between and among labor- and social-movement actors through the amplification of the protest repertoire have revitalized gendered cultures of solidarity for aggrieved workers in neoliberal times.

Chapter 2, "Rituals and Repertoires," examines the interior life of protest repertoires by outlining various and specific forms of protest, such as hunger strikes, high-altitude occupations, long-term tent encampments, and religiously inflected rituals, such as Buddhist prostration processions and street prayer services. By focusing on specific forms of protest in the repertoire, we delve deeper into the interactional dynamics between *tangsaja* and external allies and supporters that have shaped the performative and ritualized aspects of protest repertoires. We pay particular attention to how the temporal duration and spatial practices of long-term struggles have enabled protesters and supporters to link contemporary protest acts to a long history of protesting injustice through the felt, embodied, and place-based nature of protest. Examining the interior life of the protest repertoire through a focus on discreet forms also enables us to account for the contradictory aspects of protests as a formal process—initiated in a context of injustice, grievance, and institutional neglect, escalated through confrontation and conflict, and followed by waning interest and commitment.

Chapter 3, "Conjuring Solidarity," focuses on three interrelated cases of women workers fighting precarity to elaborate how and under what conditions protest repertoires cultivate solidarity as both affect and praxis. By showing how the repeated enactment of high-altitude occupations and Buddhist prostration rituals function as affectively charged protest forms that move people to act in solidaristic ways, this chapter details how solidarity operates as a catalytic force that binds people and worlds together. The chapter shows how political affects charge and animate protest repertoires in ways that circulate and gain traction in the context of compounding feelings of anger, indignation, betrayal, joy, passion, hope, and gratitude as well as create embodied, material, and symbolic connections across different actors and sites. The chapter also highlights the significance of gendering the analysis of repertoires of solidarity to understand how the embodiment of protest is directly relevant to ongoing processes of repertoire amplification.

Chapter 4, "Caring Infrastructure," shifts attention from protest as spectacular public-facing acts to the infrastructural practices of care and support that enable protesters to endure in protracted fights. Long-term tent encampments and many other protest forms rely on bodily deprivation and social suffering, and protesters must find ways to address the stress and discomfort, as well as the despair and misery, involved in sleeping on the streets or camping out in train stations or building lobbies or even surviving atop construction cranes or rooftops. We do not take these challenges for granted. Focusing on the experiences and reflections of two particular activists, we elaborate how protest repertoires rely on the multifaceted nature of caring as both visible and invisible, embodied and cognitive, experiential and reflexive. Building caring infrastructures, we argue, includes the pragmatic skills of coordinating, planning, and publicizing protest events and solidarity actions, as well as the material and immaterial work of taking care of people's physical and spiritual lives in the face of seemingly insurmountable odds.

Chapter 5, "Protest as Place Making," turns our attention to the Candlelight Protests of 2016–17. The Candlelight Protests are commonly heralded as an unprecedented moment of popular history, which attracted broad participation from mothers, seniors, children, and other ordinary citizens who marched in unison for a shared political goal: the ousting of then president Park Geun-hye. Yet a closer look at the production of mass protests as megaevents reveals the significance of the old, well-established, and organized social-movement actors that have developed extensive know-how in assembling, moving, and dispersing protesting bodies across place. This type of know-how is the product of accumulated knowledge and experience among social-movement actors who have staged defiant protests all over the city and country, especially in the last five decades. It has also resulted in creative and resourceful approaches to place making that have become central in articulating a collective politics of belonging in increasingly unequal and polarized capitalist economies.

The conclusion revisits what it means to survive capitalist abandonment by exhausting a protest repertoire. Resistance against precarity and refusal of disposability, which lie at the core of the protests we examine, are not just concerns for job security, a living wage, or social protections, though these aims should not be overlooked or disregarded; they are about defending human dignity at all costs, regardless of what outcome seems likely or even possible, and refusing to abandon one another. The protesters we worked with and have followed refuse to consent to a world organized solely in terms of extractive capital accumulation, socially sanctioned or legalized forms of dispossession, and state violence. They challenge unfair and discriminatory employer practices, repudiate unjust laws and policies, and hold accountable corrupt institutions and leaders, including at the highest ranks of government and business. And even when they are disavowed and criminalized for their refusal, they persist against all odds. By struggling to create spaces of continued resistance and mutual aid, protesters insist on the importance of solidarity and community as foundational to life worth fighting for, even at great personal cost, even without guarantees. These protests against abandonment powerfully resonate with other struggles of generations of racially and politically oppressed peoples and the ongoing work of decolonization and emancipation that insist on building communities of care and life-affirming forms of collectivity.

1 REFUSING PRECARITY

For people who have worked for a long time, they feel deeply wronged when they get fired for organizing a union. They work really hard and do their best with a sense of ownership, but when they are fired, they realize, "Ah, I am like a disposable product to them, like a single-use paper cup." This is a hard thing to accept. If this feeling is shared, then it becomes a collective fight. If it is not, then workers abandon the fight and move on.

—Kim Hyejin (김혜진; Kim Hye-jin), Korean Solidarity against Precarious Work (전국불안전노동철폐연대)

Jeopardizing one's security is always a fraught exercise, but it has particular significance and stakes at this historical moment, because security—or lack thereof—becomes exactly the site where power operates in the wake of the social movements of the post–World War II period.

—Grace Kyungwon Hong, *Death beyond Disavowal*

IN THE WEEKS LEADING UP to the special presidential election following the impeachment of Park Geun-hye, a group of precarious workers who had been participating in the Candlelight Protests grew increasingly apprehensive. From late October 2016 to mid-March 2017, they joined millions of people in the streets and squares of Seoul's historic city center to denounce the widespread corruption and abuse of power that had taken place at the highest levels of government and business. While they too celebrated the "people's victory" that jubilant spring, they understood that formal leadership transitions in government would not guarantee fundamental change in the structural conditions that had stripped workers of their jobs, livelihoods, rights, and dignity over the past two decades. The group had come together in late October 2015 as part of a national ad hoc coalition of workers from ten different workplaces around the country under an impossibly long group name: the Joint Struggle for Abolishing Mass Layoffs and Precarious Employment, Defending Democratic Unions, and Calling the Removal of Park Geun-hye for Union Repression and the Destruction of People's Livelihoods (정리 해고 철폐, 비정규직 철폐, 민주노조 사수, 노동탄압 민생파탄 박근혜 정권 퇴진을 위한 공동투쟁).

Concerned that Moon Jae-in, the presidential frontrunner who would be sworn into office after the special election, would not uphold his campaign promise to end predatory forms of precarious employment, the group decided to take drastic action. On April 14, 2017, six workers representing six different unions climbed forty meters to the top of a ten-story building located next to the busy exit 7 of the Kwanghwamun subway station, surrounded by skyscrapers and billboard advertisements.[1] Each worker carried a sleeping bag, a blood-glucose meter, digestive medicine, a plastic trash bag, and their smart phone. For the next twenty-seven days of their *kogong nongsŏng*, or high-altitude protest, they confined themselves to a cramped and exposed area beneath the massive LED billboard structure affixed to the building's rooftop and occupied the structure without food, running water, or electricity (figure 1.1). They had no shelter from the sun, rain, or cold. Supporters on the ground attempted to send up a canopy for shade on the second day, but the police declared it as unpermitted aid to an illegal occupation and blocked the supply. Things got physical: the police ended up sending three workers to the hospital after they were injured in a fight to get the canopy to the protesters up above, to no avail. All of this was visible to passersby through the presence of riot police next to a large crash pad set up on the sidewalk at the base of the building and a large banner draped across the top of the building broadcasting their central demands: "Guarantee labor rights and protect workers' livelihoods."

South Korean workers' protest repertoires are characterized by high levels of sacrifice and suffering. In addition to familiar tactics of disruption and mobilization, the repertoire includes long-term tent encampments, life-threatening hunger strikes without a planned end,

FIGURE 1.1. A selfie from the Kwanghwamun Billboard Occupation, April 2017. Source: "Kwanghwamun 40m kogong nongsŏng hyŏnjang 'Chigŭm naŭi chujŏkŭn . . .'" [From the Kwanghwamun 40m-high-altitude occupation site, "My main enemy right now is . . ."], *OhMyNews*, April 27, 2017, https://m.ohmynews.com/NWS_Web/Mobile/at_pg.aspx?CNTN_CD=A0002320568#cb.

slow-moving, ritualized processions that go on for hours and sometimes days, and dangerous occupations at high altitudes. What might be overlooked in all this is that the turn to drama and ritual is notably pronounced among workers who have become embroiled in protracted disputes. *Chŏnggyujik,* or "regularly employed workers," fighting for wage increases or against redundancy dismissals are generally more visible in the news, but at the forefront of amplifying the repertoire are *pijŏnggyujik* workers, with nonregular or precarious employment status. Many *pijŏnggyujik* workers have worked for years at the same workplace, oftentimes alongside *chŏnggyujik* coworkers who are paid more for doing similar jobs with job security and company benefits. Thus, when they are fired after forming a union, unceremoniously over text, after having endured both explicit and subtle forms of discrimination and mistreatment, they "feel deeply wronged," as longtime activist Kim Hyejin emphasized in the opening epigraph. They realize that, despite hard work and commitment, their employers view them as "disposable," like a "single-use paper cup." But, this realization does not mean that workers accept their disposability. While some workers might give up and move on, other workers who share feelings of being wronged decide to fight collectively. Through their bodies and the everyday spaces in which they live, work, and play, workers refuse to accept a system that deprives them of their livelihoods and dignity. They protest.

Aggrieved workers' passionate politics were on full display at Kwanghwamun Square in the spring of 2017. To support the perilous *kogong nongsŏng* waged high above, supporters on the ground staged daily scenes of crisis and emergency. After the police blocked their effort to send up a canopy, they set up a street-level protest camp, which displayed solidarity messages and photographs of the workers who were risking their lives in the high-altitude-occupation protest (figure 1.2). They organized concurrent press conferences, street marches, evening cultural programs, and a social media campaign that asked members of the public to join their one-day solidarity hunger strikes. Unions, political parties, and social-movement organizations sent banners expressing their support for the protest action, which were strewn alongside the tent. This solidarity camp was not to be confused with the State-of-the-

Nation Sit-in Protest (시국농성) that workers from this coalition set up in front of the Government Complex in Seoul as their main base camp, located nearby on the northeastern corner of Kwanghwamun Square, throughout the duration of the six-month-long Candlelight Protests. From the twenty-four-hour base camp on one end of the square to the solidarity camp on the other end, protesters urged the public to pay attention to the gravity of labor precarity and the invisibility of their long-term fights for institutional protection against unjust dismissals and antiunion retaliation.

While some passersby from the Candlelight Protests stopped by the tent to learn more about what was happening and express their support, most appeared to be interested in the Candlelight Protests, not this small protest within. Kim Hyejin—who served as the media spokesperson for the emergency-response team and provided direct support for the collective action as a staff leader of the Korean Solidarity against

FIGURE 1.2. Ground-level protest camp beneath Kwanghwamun Billboard Occupation, Seoul, April 17, 2017. Photo by Jennifer Jihye Chun.

Precarious Work—acknowledged that it would be difficult to get public attention while the Candlelight Protests were taking place. The workers occupying the billboard structure were "treated like ghosts," she told a news reporter. "We did everything possible, including putting [workers'] lives on the line, but we could not get people to look at us even just once."[2] The workers occupying the billboard felt similarly too, disappointed by the apparent indifference. One worker said to the press, "We were continually rejected from speaking about workers' issues on the Candlelight Protest stage. . . . It was as if no one wanted to deflate the mood. We remained as isolated as ever."[3] The inability to elicit even a token gesture of support from the KCTU deepened the sense of isolation and abandonment among protesting workers and their supporters.

On the morning of May 10, we stood in the crowd near the solidarity camp beneath the billboard occupation as the feelings of worry, apprehension, sadness, disappointment, care, and dedication permeated the air. Approximately a hundred supporters gathered for the press conference and listened to moving speeches by labor activists and workers, chanting, singing, and pumping their fists in unison. This was a press conference to announce the end of the *kogong nongsŏng*, and afterward, the crowd waited quietly for each protester to carefully make their way down from the rooftop. We spotted two KTX leaders wearing their union vests in the crowd, and later we would learn that they were initially asked to join the occupation and go up to the billboard but had decided not to because of complications around timing and strategy (see chapter 3). Also in the crowd were several reporters and photographers who had been covering the Candlelight Protests in the vicinity. Cameras flashed rapidly each time one of the protesters emerged—weak from twenty-seven days of surviving hunger and cold weather—and exited the building, to be placed in one of the ambulances waiting on site.[4] They would be transported to the Green Hospital, a well-known destination among activists as a hospital that administers treatment for physical *and* emotional trauma related to long-term protests. After the last protester left the site, the crowd that had gathered began to dissipate, with a smaller group of activists cleaning up and dismantling the camp, which we will elaborate on further.

But we want to take a moment first to describe the space of the Kwanghwamun Square, where we had spent a great deal of time over the past few years, an urban space well known for tourism and commerce as well as political gatherings. Since 2014, Kwanghwamun Square has also been a symbol for solidarity and overwhelming grief. Three years prior to the Kwanghwamun Billboard Occupation was the tragic sinking of the *Sewol* on April 14, 2014, that resulted in the deaths of 306 out of 476 passengers on board, the vast majority of whom were high school students on a year-end field trip. Bereaved parents had begun occupying the southern portion of Kwanghwamun Square—just across the street from the billboard occupation—demanding an investigation into the truth of what happened and accountability for all concerned, including President Park Geun-hye, who was famously nowhere to be found during the seven initial hours of "golden time" that would have been essential for a successful rescue operation. The grief and outrage surrounding the *Sewol* disaster were expressed and reinforced through public art and performances in this public space during the Candlelight Protests and beyond. One particularly striking public art installation we witnessed during the Candlelight Protests consisted of 306 bright orange life vests arranged on the ground in rows of eight, each adorned with a yellow ribbon, a button, a candle, a protest sign, a single white chrysanthemum flower, and the number and name of the victim written on the ground in yellow chalk (figure 1.3). As one of our key interlocuters, Kwak EKyeong (곽이경; Kwak I-kyŏng), a labor organizer who began her career as a queer activist, remarked, the *Sewol* disaster created political reverberations far and wide. As she said, "death" became a defining keyword of the time. The *Sewol* disaster continues to serve as a reminder that inequality and injustice permeate everyday life in South Korea, where the poor and workers in the lower rungs of the capitalist economy appear to be abandoned, condemned to die without rescue.

Across the street from the tent structures and public art installations regarding the *Sewol* disaster, the mood was also somber where the Kwanghwamun Billboard Occupation Protest had ended. To decompress and discuss what we had just observed at the press conference and the end of the *kogong nongsŏng* that morning, we made our way to a café

FIGURE 1.3. Public art installation with *Sewol*-ferry life jackets, Kwanghwamun, November 2017. Photo by Ju Hui Judy Han.

on the second floor of a nearby building—adjacent to the building that the billboard-occupation protest had taken place—which overlooked the area where solidarity tents had been pitched. Over the next couple hours, we watched a mesmerizing scene unfold as though in a silent movie. Approximately a dozen people, comprised of men and women wearing union vests, methodically and expertly dismantled the encampment. They looked as though they had done this countless times, working together to fold up large tarps and sleeping mats and load them into the union van waiting curbside to transport the banners, flags, picket signs, leftover water bottles, and various miscellaneous items, such as T-shirts, backpacks, sneakers, and flipflops, that had been left behind. Someone started sweeping the floor, even as another was col-

42   CHAPTER 1

lecting rubbish into a trash bag. Soon, there was no trace of the protest, as if nothing at all had happened there that morning, let alone the last twenty-seven days.

The movements, images, and sounds of this particular day stand out in our memory. Yes, there were many jubilant scenes throughout this extraordinary period of political upheaval, but there was also a deep sense of loss and heartbreak and overall ambivalence. Protests have certainly never stopped, not after independence from colonial rule and not after democratization, and they continue to take place in Kwanghwamun and throughout the country. Protests assemble laid-off and striking workers, people fighting eviction and displacement, activists concerned with environmental, peace, and human rights, and feminist-, queer-, and disability-justice activists, who point out time and time again that we must pay critical attention to the intersection of multiple systems of injustice that produce amplified vulnerabilities. But the majority of these protests and social movements hardly receive media coverage. Many do end up achieving their stated goals, but many do not. Regardless of whether these protests are successful in achieving their goals, though, we are fascinated by the complex and contradictory spaces of protest that reveal the fraught politics of "jeopardizing one's own security" as a site of political struggle, in the words of critical feminist and ethnic studies scholar Grace Kyungwon Hong.[5]

The Kwanghwamun Billboard Occupation Protest ended in defeat. And it would not be the last time workers waged the kind of fight that seemed bound for failure. Why do protesters, especially workers in this book, insist on fighting back when the odds are stacked against them? Beyond the wins and losses, successes and failures of campaign aims and movement goals, what do protest repertoires create, and what difference do they make?

DISAVOWING LABOR

The contrast between the sense of alienation and defeat that permeated the Kwanghwamun Billboard Occupation Protest and the collective euphoria that pervaded the Candlelight Protests reveals significant cleavages in the landscape of solidarity. Once considered foundational to democratization, the militancy of democratic trade unions is often perceived as out of place and out of sync not only by the conservatives who oppose labor rights but also by critics on the left and the center. No longer dominant is the radical political ideology behind the *minjung* (민중; the people) movement of the 1970s and 1980s, which heralded industrial workers, peasants, and the urban poor as the revolutionary agents of change against the mutually constitutive forces of authoritarian repression and capitalist exploitation. Generations of activists have actively engaged in sacrifice and suffering to propel their political claims, but this approach is now frequently disparaged because of the heavy toll associated with it.[6] For South Korea, the so-called traditional protest tradition of *minjung* is associated with a configuration of political power and influence known as the 386 Generation. This is a generation that protested as students in the 1980s and subsequently became political leaders and policymakers in their thirties to shape the country's transition to parliamentary democracy.[7] President Roh Moo-hyun (2003–8) was elected largely due to the support of the 386 Generation, though he later turned against democratic labor. In a cabinet meeting in 2003, Roh reportedly said that the time of using self-immolation or political suicide as a tactic to win (labor) rights has passed, that these are outdated tactics of a bygone era—a comment that incensed the labor movement.[8] Roh Moo-hyun was Moon Jae-in's mentor, himself a former human rights attorney like Roh, also with a record of defending union activists, but this comment by Roh as well as his administration's policy record on a range of social, economic, and environmental issues ultimately led many progressive labor- and social-movement activists to consider Roh antilabor.

The touted protagonists of the Candlelight Protests of 2016–17—versions of which had erupted in 2002 and again in 2008—were also disdainful of the so-called outdated politics of the past.[9] Led by a new generation of internet-savvy, pop-culture-consuming, and globally conscious youth, candlelight protesters tended to eschew the austere and self-sacrificing sensibilities of the political generation that fought against dictatorship, instead celebrating the feelings of joy and pleasure linked to festival-like protests in the new millennium.[10] By "showing the world" what peaceful protest can look like in the streets, candlelight protesters heralded themselves as a new generation, showing their respect and consideration for public space by cleaning up after each mass assembly and minimizing disruption to the functioning of everyday life. Over and over again, South Korean and international media observers have expounded on how these fun, loosely organized, and nonideological protest spaces are radically different from the militant and miserable mass protests associated with middle-aged men wearing their signature red union vests. That is what the Kwanghwamun Billboard Occupation Protest looked like—old and familiar, full of misery and suffering, and disruptive of road traffic and confrontational against police. These political affects would be unwelcome in the Candlelight Protests.

We do not disagree that there are tendencies in militant labor politics that might be considered anachronistic or, more broadly, problematic. We are, however, interested in moving beyond generational explanations to understand why aggrieved actors continue to engage in high-risk protest tactics that consistently fail. Generational explanations, which are all too commonly deployed to dismiss and disparage militant workers, flatten understandings of the social and cultural motivations that fuel protest participation while reproducing normative assumptions about what counts for progress and prosperity and why.[11] In this chapter, we examine how precarity as a structure of disavowal shapes worker-led protests against precarity. Rooted in the disavowal of minoritized workers as human beings whose lives are worth protecting, precarity is experienced through the Agambian formulation of unprotected life as "bare life" in which "one is physically alive, but one's life is politically unprotected."[12] Precarious workers, especially poor and disadvantaged women workers, are repeatedly left unprotected against discrimination and retaliation for exercising their labor rights in their workplaces, in the courts, and in their own representative organizations. In this context, the protests that they enact against precarity intensify what Grace Hong characterizes as the state's selective protection of minoritized life. Protesting workers' consignment to an unlivable life, however, is not the end of their story. Through forms of protest that enact the seemingly impossible, they refuse to accept the legitimacy of a capitalist employment system that devalues their life and labor. By making the politics of life and death itself the basis of their collective political refusal, these protests show that even the failure to achieve one's protest demands can yield significant dividends in purpose, strategy, and lasting impact. By amplifying the life-or-death stakes of protesting precarity, furthermore, aggrieved workers demonstrate that the conditions of precarity itself are akin to social death, eliciting solidarity from labor- and social-movement actors that likewise view the fight against predatory forms of capitalism as a fight for the rights and dignity of oppressed classes. These protests are about refusing precarity and rejecting inequity, and these collectively performed protest repertoires enable workers to "organize against their own abandonment."[13]

We draw on key cases of long-term union struggles waged by *pijŏnggyujik* workers as part of the shifting landscape of labor and social movements more broadly between 2000–2018 to examine the consolidation of a protest repertoire that has made the life-or-death stakes of surviving precarity central to its mobilizing frame. In particular, we draw extensively on in-depth interviews conducted with key interlocuters in the *pijŏnggyujik*-workers' movement, including Kim Hyejin and Kwak EKyeong, as well as Oh Min-gyu (오민규; O Min-gyu), the latter of whom was, at the time, KCTU's director of strategic operations for precarious and unorganized workers. Each individual hails from a different part of the labor- and social-movement sphere: Kim Hyejin as a former student and labor activist from the 1980s, Oh Min-gyu as a former auto union leader and national news columnist on economic affairs, and Kwak EKyeong as a labor activist with a history of queer activism. They continue to be part of movement organizations with different ideological goals, political orientations, and membership constituencies, though sometimes they overlap for moments in large organizations like the KCTU, as is the case for Oh Min-gyu and Kwak EKyeong. And they have participated, at various levels and degrees, in some of the most notable coalitional movements, including the Hope Bus (희망버스) movement for Kim Jin-suk (김진숙; Kim Chin-suk), the People's Committee for the *Sewol*-Ferry Tragedy (세월호 참사 국민대책회의), and the Emergency

Action for Park Geun-hye's Resignation (박근혜정권 퇴진 비상국민행동) during the Candlelight Protests of 2016–17, to name just a few. Each of these individuals also actively contribute to public and policy debates as well as shape discussions about strategy and principles that have guided the direction of the *pijŏnggyujik* workers' movement. In the sections that follow, we draw on case studies and in-depth interviews to deepen understanding of (1) how the protest repertoires of *pijŏnggyujik* workers have changed the public "common sense" about what constitutes precarious work and (2) how the consolidation of a life-or-death protest repertoire led by *pijŏnggyujik* workers has pushed the organized labor movement to be more solidaristic than exclusionary, especially in relation to more vulnerable workers in its ranks. In doing so, we show how protest repertoires often achieve outcomes and produce reverberations that go beyond their intended goals.

FIGHTING PRECARITY

The everyday workings of precarity as a structure of disavowal can be seen in the neglect and abandonment of *pijŏnggyujik* workers during the course of a prolonged union fight. Kim Hyejin has been a leading figure in the *pijŏnggyujik* workers' movement since the 1990s, when understandings of precarious employment and how it perpetuates discrimination and injustice were relatively nonexistent. Her beginnings in the labor movement date back to the 1990s, when the independent union movement was exploding in the Kuro industrial district, which had the highest density of small and medium factories in Seoul at the time. After many subcontracting factories in the area shut down or significantly reduced their scale of operations, especially during the IMF financial crisis, Kim Hyejin shifted her attention to the issue of *pijŏnggyujik*, which was quickly becoming the predominant type of new jobs available to laid-off factory workers, especially groups of older women. When founding the Korean Solidarity against Precarious Work in 2002, she and other activists, including legal scholar and labor activist Aelim Yun (윤애림), sought to build an independent organization that could support the growing number of struggles led by precarious workers as *tangsaja*, or the most directly impacted protagonists of their own fights. At the time, the number of civil society organizations was exploding, yet they actively distinguished themselves from nongovernmental organizations (NGOs)—who tended to operate in conjunction with the neoliberal policies of state agencies—and instead aligned themselves with the struggles of rank-and-file union workers building an anticapitalist labor movement.

Since the early 2000s, Kim Hyejin has witnessed many *pijŏnggyujik* workers realize what it means to be treated as disposable and what it takes to fight against disposability. This realization occurs, she told us in an interview, when *pijŏnggyujik* workers lose their jobs for forming a union and going on strike despite the fact that many have worked for significant periods of time as so-called temporary, or limited-term, contract workers. "Imagine you already have grievances against your company and then one day you get fired because you formed a union," she said. "Workers think, 'I have put in so much work for the company. How can they do this to me?' They feel betrayed." While many workers might move on and find another job, some workers decide to fight. However, because the contractual nature of precarious work often makes collective bargaining negotiations "institutionally impossible," it is "difficult" for workers to "force any kind of response [from targeted opponents] through strength alone." Kim Hyejin elaborated, "Labor strikes typically last only about twenty days or so. It was really unimaginable that a strike would last for over two hundred days. But for *pijŏnggyujik* workers who get fired and kicked out, strikes become really prolonged, and negotiations go for a very long time without resolution. As it gets longer and longer, the long struggle itself makes people think, 'Shouldn't I try to contribute somehow?' and as it gets even longer, I think we talk about it more and more."

As workers begin to exhaust the tactics involved in exposing the conditions of neglect and abandonment during their prolonged fights, time itself becomes a metric for conveying protesters' high level of commitment and resolve. Kim Hyejin recalled when union struggles started to become prolonged: "The Korea Telecom Contract Workers' Union [한국 통신계약직노조] had waged a *nongsŏng* [농성; prolonged protest] that was 517 days in 2001. I remember that number: 517 days. At the time, it was a number that was almost unimaginable. Before that, E-Land workers had also waged a struggle in 2000 that lasted 270 days. That, too, I remember was an unimaginable number at the time."

Yet what was once "unimaginable" has become commonplace. When talking about the struggle led by one of the workers of the Kwanghwamun Billboard Occupation, Lee In-geun (이인근; Yi In-kŭn), from the Cort/Cor-Tek Guitar Workers' Union (콜트-콜텍 기타노동자 노조), Kim Hyejin remarked that she lost count of the total duration because it was so long. At the time, it was reported as "the longest labor struggle in Korean history," lasting a total of 4,464 days for workers fighting to get their jobs back and start working again.[14] However, as we discuss in the introduction and elaborate in greater detail in chapter 3, the distinction of being the "longest labor struggle in Korea history" arguably belongs to the KTX train attendants' union, who signed their collective agreement with KORAIL after 4,526 days. For the record, between 1998 and 2012, there were over 150 cases of union struggles waged by *pijŏnggyujik* workers documented in one study.[15] Not all these cases have resulted in failure; in fact, a strong predictor of success in winning one's union fight is the ability to prevent the fight from becoming protracted.

Precarious workers were early drivers of protracted fights that emerged after 2000. Kim Hyejin remembers vividly the 517-day fight by the Korea Telecom (KT) Contract Workers' Union, which she and the Korean Solidarity against Precarious Work actively supported at a time when few other unions or labor activists paid attention. As the major telecommunications provider in the domestic market, KT faced repeated pressures to liberalize and restructure throughout the 1990s, resulting in the creation of a two-tiered workforce.[16] In 2000, KT management terminated the contracts of seven thousand workers employed under fixed-term contracts, the majority of whom had been employed between two and ten years. After their attempts to join the existing union were rejected by the *chŏnggyujik* workers, who dominated the union's membership, aggrieved *pijŏnggyujik* workers established a separate trade union, affiliated with KCTU's Seoul Regional Branch (서울본부). Striking KT contract workers engaged in many tactics to pressure KT management to address their demand for reinstatement. They shaved their heads, occupied the KT headquarter office, and scaled a city bridge on a frosty winter day to drop a banner with its demands. Legal appeals filed by the union regarding unfair and discriminatory employment practices were rejected by the National Labor Relations Commission and the courts. "The courts held that there hadn't been any discrimination in wages," labor scholar Aelim Yun writes, "instead finding that regularly-employed workers had more responsibility in their jobs, even though the fixed term workers did the same work."[17] The handful of KT contract workers persisted in their fight, and though it ultimately ended without success, it would be remembered as a landmark struggle.

One of the earliest and most grueling long-term struggles waged by women—who are disproportionately employed in precarious jobs—was the unlikely case of home study tutors. Women primarily in their thirties, forties, and fifties, these home study tutors sold educational materials, including textbooks and exercise books, for Jaenung Educational Industries (JEI).[18] As a large private corporation, JEI issued contracts with individual tutors to sell directly to elementary school students but not as direct employees of the company. Given the precarious nature of their employment, which was classified as a form of "special employment" (특수고용), JEI tutors formed an independent union in 1999, the Jaenung Educational Tutors' Union (재능교육교사노조). During the union's first six years, JEI workers won a landmark legal victory for workers classified as "specially employed," including the right to legally unionize and collectively bargain. However, after unrelenting pressure from the company to decertify the union, the Supreme Court of Korea ruled in 2007 that tutors associated with JEI were not legitimate workers protected under the national labor laws. JEI management immediately responded by refusing to recognize the legitimacy of the union and demanding that five thousand tutors withdraw their union membership or face termination.

Twelve women stood up to refuse. In December 2008, Yu Myŏng-ja (유명자) was the first worker to be fired, and the remaining unionized workers were fired by 2010. In protest of the company's intimidation tactics, two JEI union members—Yŏ Min-hŭi (여민희) and Oh Su-yŏng (오수영)—occupied the twenty-meter bell tower of Hyehwa-dong Catholic Church in Seoul, located across the street from the JEI headquarters. There were seventeen attempts since May 22, 2012, to negotiate between striking unionists and JEI, each resulting in failure.[19] Their struggle officially ended on August 26, 2013, when Yŏ Min-hŭi and Oh Su-yŏng came down from the tower after 202 days and were subsequently reinstated after 2,076 days of continuous protest. Although the progressive media reported that this was an important victory for workers in "special employment," the long-term protracted struggle hardly strengthened the overall membership base. In the early 2000s, the Jaenung Educational Tutors' Union had approximately 3,800 members, but over the course of the struggle, that number dropped to twelve.[20] The JEI struggle was nonetheless influential in engaging the support of a new generation of young people, especially university-student activists, for the labor movement led by precarious workers.

Another influential case in inspiring a broader base of social-movement participants to their union fight were the laid-off workers known as Cort/Cor-Tek guitar-manufacturing workers (콜트-콜텍 기타 노동자), herein referred to as "Cort workers." The union fight began in March 2007 after fifty-six out of 160 workers who were directly employed by the company as regular workers were abruptly laid off by Cort Guitars and Basses, one of the world's leading guitar-manufacturing companies. The next month, in April, an additional eight-nine Cort workers were laid off, and union struggles expanded across different locations. As the *Hankyoreh* reported in 2019, "Claiming financial troubles, the company fired its employees en masse and shut down its factory in Daejeon. The guitars that had been made there were transferred to a facility in Indonesia. But the laid-off workers refused to accept the company's claims because of its obvious success: it was one of the world's top three guitar manufacturers, controlling thirty percent of the global market. The workers took their complaint to the courts."[21] While Cort workers were not employed in precarious jobs, for the next thirteen years, Cort workers—like JEI, KTX, Kiryung, and other laid-off workers—became embroiled in protracted legal battles against retaliatory antiunion firings, winning and losing appeals in the lower courts, the Seoul High Court, and the Supreme Court of Korea. Since lower-court rulings are frequently overturned by higher-court rulings and a significant period of time would lapse between court decisions, waiting for rulings and then waiting for appeal decisions made the law and legal proceedings a constantly moving target for labor activists. And even so, in the end, many union leaders would have to accept an agreement that stipulated a partial and cruel compromise—reinstatement for the union members except for the leaders themselves.

While protesting workers rarely regain the jobs that they lost at the outset, the amplification of the protest repertoire in the context of drawn-out and contradictory court rulings helped attract the support of a broader base of labor and social movements. The Cort workers, for instance, relied on music to draw a connection with young musicians and artists, who organized solidarity concerts and festivals through their thirteen-year struggle, including during workers' multiple overseas trips to Germany and the United States.[22] Soon after launching their union fight, the Cort workers built a protest camp in front of company headquarters in Seoul's Tŭngch'on-dong neighborhood, which is in the same district as the Kimpo Airport. Once constructed, the protest camp operated as a multifunctional base camp, enabling workers to do everything from holding strategy sessions and debrief meetings to storing protest supplies and raising public awareness by interacting with visitors who stopped by the base camp to offer their support and encouragement.

Cort workers' union president Lee In-geun—who began working in the Taejŏn factory in 1998 and was laid off nine years later—endured several grueling protests, including a twenty-day struggle during which he fasted on the top of a transmission tower near the Han River in 2008 and a twenty-four-hour-long one-person protest (일인시위) in May 2014. He participated in the *och'et'uji* in solidarity with the laid-off Ssangyong Motor (쌍용자동차) workers in 2015, as well as the Kwanghwamun Billboard Occupation and hunger strike in the spring of 2017, which we discussed at the beginning of this chapter. On April 22, 2019, Lee In-geun and two other union leaders—Kim Gyeong-bong (김경봉; Kim Kyŏng-bong) and Lim Jae-chun (임재춘; Im Chae-ch'un)—signed an agreement in which the company expressed regret for the layoff that took place thirteen years ago and extended an "honorary reinstatement" to the three workers. At the time, Lee In-geun had been on a hunger strike for forty-two days. In an emotional announcement, Lim Jae-chun said, "We've waited thirteen years to get this agreement, to hold it in our hands. I hope this is the last time that struggling workers have to go on a hunger strike. I hope that young people don't have to go on a hunger strike or hold sit-ins on rooftops to demand their rights."[23] Lim Jae-chun would be featured prominently in an award-winning independent documentary film titled *Sister J* (재춘언니), released to critical acclaim in 2020, that chronicled the Cort workers' long fight and its culture of resistance (figure 1.4). Tragically, Lim Jae-chun passed away suddenly from an illness on December 30, 2022, at the age of sixty.

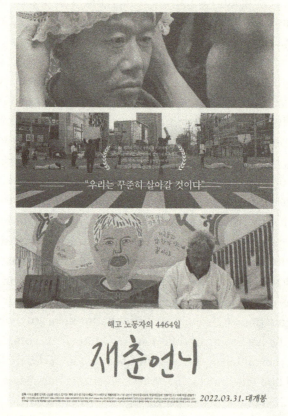

FIGURE 1.4. Promotional poster for *Sister J* (2020), a documentary film directed by Lee Soojung. Reprinted with permission from CinemaDAL.

We would like to discuss one more case of a long-term labor struggle that did not last as long and was relatively lower in profile. It was waged by women who were middle-aged and older, working in precarious jobs that do not connect easily with popular culture or younger students. Hospital aides at the Ch'ŏngju City Geriatric Hospital (청주시노인전문병원) organized a remarkable fight in a publicly managed hospital in the capital and largest city of North Ch'ungch'ŏng Province a hundred kilometers south of Seoul. When hospital administrators began cutting wages and benefits and harassing and intimidating hospital aides who were hired by multiple third-party contractors on an annual-contract-renewal basis, Kwon Okja (권옥자; Kwŏn Ok-cha) convinced her fellow coworkers to form a union and go on strike.[24] She had vowed never to join another union, she recalled in our interview, let alone lead another grueling union fight, because of her previous experience with a failed union struggle at an electronics factory. When asked what led to her "change of heart," Kwon Okja let out a laugh. She recounted the routine insults and derogatory treatment by her supervisors and managers, who scoffed at her and said, "What are sixty-year-old women doing forming a union and engaging in [political] struggle?" So when the working conditions took an even-worse turn—when hospital management abruptly tripled the patient load for hospital aides during the initial stage of collective bargaining negotiations—forming a union and starting a strike did not take much convincing, she said.

When the union fight began to drag on, however, it was difficult to convince fellow union members to persist. Similar to the JEI and KTX cases, the number of active union members involved in the Ch'ŏngju City Geriatric Hospital Workers' Union's (청주시노인전문병원 노조) fight also dwindled over time, in this case declining from one hundred workers at the start to just twenty-three people by the end.[25] To strengthen the resolve of the remaining workers, the union leaders nonetheless maintained a protest base camp for 456 consecutive days (fifteen months) and engaged in a variety of ritualized protests, including performing a *samboilbae* that started and ended at the steps of the city hall. As the union leader, Kwon Okja shaved her head and went on a twenty-eight-day hunger strike that began on the 675th day of their struggle and ended when she was rushed to the hospital. She also attempted, unsuccessfully, to set herself on fire in a self-immolation attempt on February 2, 2016, in which she demanded a meeting with the mayor. It was on July 22, 2016, that the hospital management finally agreed to reinstate the twenty-three dismissed workers that had remained in the union as well as guaranteed significant improvements to their working conditions. Interestingly, when asked what she found to be the most difficult protest tactic, Kwon Okja responded, "Shaving my head." While this protest act is fairly routine for striking male unionists—so much so that hair clippers are a standard part of protest gear—shaving her head was a particularly distressing act especially because of her family responsibilities. By showing up at family gatherings with a shaved head, Kwon Okja not only outed herself as a militant unionist to her husband's family but also transgressed her gendered duties of showing filial respect for her in-laws through bodily care and comportment.

These cases are just a few examples of workers' protests that have changed the structures of feeling associated with precarity. Workers often recount that before they joined a union and participated in a collective struggle, they thought that the discrimination and deprivation they faced in their jobs was simply "natural." According to a survey published in *Hankyoreh*, many *pijŏnggyujik* workers saw themselves as part of the "lower class," or what is popularly referred to as the "subordinate" party in a zero-sum balance of relationship between the dominant *kap* (갑) and subordinate *ŭl* (을).[26] The *kap-ŭl* discourse usefully conveys the consequences of unequal power relations and agency between two parties. As a *Kyŏnghyang sinmun* editorial explains, "In a bilateral relationship, the stronger person who holds the other party's right to live or escape is *kap*; the weak person who has to beg for his or her life is *ŭl*."[27] Another way to capture the meaning of the *kap-ŭl* relationship is to contrast the "99 percent of the people [who] are holding their breath due to the tyranny of 1 percent of the people," referencing the near-total domination that a handful of wealthy chaebols have over everyone else in society.[28] However, despite the inequalities linked to power and status differentials, the *kap-ŭl* dynamic is never all-encompassing. As many of the cases that we discuss show, even if just a small handful of workers persist in their fight, workers can demonstrate that precarity is neither inevitable nor a finished project. "Time may not be on the side of underdogs," explained one union activist during an interview, but the choice by protesting workers to subject their bodies to pain and suffering is a purposive one.

By using protests to reveal the deadly terms and conditions of precarity, workers in precarious jobs have helped change the meaning of *pijŏnggyujik* from one associated with "frustration and abandonment" to one that signifies "revolution and instability."[29] The very fact that some workers refuse to submit to the futility of protesting precarity, even at great cost to their health and well-being, has raised public visibility about the urgency of precarious work as a widespread social problem. This shift must be recognized as a "truly important and valuable achievement," emphasized Kim Hyejin. She elaborated,

> People these days take for granted that precarious employment exists, but early on, when precarious workers first began to organize and fight, people used to ask, "What is precarious work?" Nowadays, everyone recognizes that precarious work is a serious problem. . . . Workers have shown us why precarious employment is wrong and why it is a problem that as a society on the whole we need to address. When precarious workers engage in extreme forms of struggle, like high-altitude occupations, the occupation of stores and workplaces, and hunger strikes, their fights make the issue visible. . . . In this respect, it is an important and valuable achievement that we have public consensus that precarious work should not be normal.

In fact, precarious workers have been so successful in raising public awareness that Oh Min-gyu said to the press that the government wants to do away with the term *pijŏnggyujik* in order to suppress its connotations of "agitation and resistance."[30]

Changing public understandings of precarious work is an important objective and outcome of workers' protests and, more broadly, the communicative work that oppositional social movements do. Through their protests, precarious workers have shown how their refusal to submit is much more than a fight to resolve their individual grievances—it is about challenging the legitimacy of a political economy that treats groups of workers like they are disposable and undeserving of rights. By showing how the fight against precarity is a fight for the rights and dignity of all working people, precarious workers have challenged their own organizations and labor-movement leaders to pay more attention to the importance of more vulnerable workers in their ranks.

REDEFINING THE PRIORITIES OF ORGANIZED LABOR

Since the mid-2000s, struggles waged by *pijŏnggyujik* workers around the country have pressured KCTU, as the nation's representative democratic union confederation, to pay more attention to the collapse of labor rights in the context of widespread labor precarity. The KCTU's decision to publicly oppose the Nonregular Worker Protection Act (비정규직 보호법), which was passed in 2006 and went into effect in 2007, was an important turning point in strengthening the visibility of the *pijŏnggyujik*-workers' movement within organized labor.

Introduced by Roh Moo-hyun (2003–8) and his ruling Uri Party (열린우리당) in 2004, the Nonregular Worker Protection Act was immediately deemed an "unjust or evil law" by precarious workers who had been demanding an end to discriminatory and predatory forms of precarious work. When the Uri Party announced that it would hold a public hearing on the proposed bills related to precarious workers, a group of fifteen people representing different groups of precarious workers—including in-house subcontractors (사내하청), ready-mixed concrete drivers (레미콘 기사), home-based tutors (학습지 교사), caregivers (간병인), and construction workers (건설 노동자)—decided they needed to make their voices heard. Aware that party officials would heavily control access to the public hearing but had "no legitimate right to block their participation," protesting workers performed their opposition by "ripping up" all the written papers that were presented at the public forum while shouting, "When did we ask you to make a law like this?" Protesting workers continued to voice their opposition by occupying the Uri Party chairperson's office, located on the second floor of the building, for the next week.

The passage of the 2006 law was not the first time that the National Assembly of South Korea passed labor-law reforms that were intended to mitigate labor precarity but ended up legalizing the expansion of precarious work across diverse sectors of the economy. The passage of the Act on Protections for Temporary Agency Workers (파견근로자 보호 등에 관한 법률) in 1998 was particularly detrimental as it authorized employers to hire workers indirectly through temporary agencies for the first time "across 197 different job categories," including "work requiring expert knowledge, technology and experience for a maximum of two years."[31] Well aware of the dangerous precedent of this law, workers who had experienced the gross injustice of precarious work during the course of their union struggles came together in 2005 to oppose the passage of the Nonregular Worker Protection Act as part of a cross-sectoral effort.

Before joining KCTU, Oh Min-gyu worked as the policy director of a national coalition of *pijŏnggyujik* labor unions (전국비정규직노조연대회의) between 2004 and 2012, which grew significantly after the sit-in he helped organize in opposition to the passage of the Nonregular Worker Protection Act. During our interview, Oh Min-gyu shared what he felt the broader impact of the *nongsŏng* was in strengthening the *pijŏnggyujik*-workers' movement on a national scale. While the driving force of choosing a tactic is not about strengthening internal solidarity since tactics are always about increasing pressure against targeting opponents to achieve your goals, the *nongsŏng* itself enabled *pijŏnggyujik* workers to cultivate a shared sense of purpose and understanding about distinct challenges and threats they faced. In other words, the *nongsŏng* was really the first time that *pijŏnggyujik* workers "from so many different industries" had the opportunity to talk and gain a better understanding of the nature of their shared struggles, explained Oh Min-gyu. This was partly due to the fact that they were forced to spend twenty-four hours together in a cramped space for an entire week "without being able to drink alcohol" and with little to do except "have conversations." *Nongsŏng* organizers invited legal activists to visit the occupation and discuss in detail what made the proposed law so antithetical to protecting the rights of precarious workers. These types of prolonged protests may not be the only method for prying up lines of communication with opponents, but the use of body-based spatial occupation "is a more intensive way to communicate." Oh Min-gyu elaborated,

> Holding press conferences and delivering position statements—these routes certainly exist for us to get our voices out. But what is traditionally even more important for the South Korean democratic labor-movement tradition is that in *nongsŏng*, we have all that close, physical interaction with one another. People from different workplaces are able to share their experiences with each other, sleep together, eat together, drink together, and they fight together too in internal debates. All this forges camaraderie that's even stronger than family ties. So when you fight, you should fight together. You can tell—there is a qualitative difference between people who have gone through *nongsŏng* together and those who have not. There is such high value in *nongsŏng* demonstrations. They unite folks behind internal goals and strengthen cohesive internal organization.

Another defining moment in which KCTU showed its solidarity through actions, as well as words, was during the E-Land Union's (이랜드노조) struggle in 2006. The E-Land Union struggle was an important case among KCTU affiliate unions for many reasons, including the fact that it was one of the early successful examples of unions overcoming divisions between regular and precarious workers in their membership ranks, as well as organizing workers who were predominantly women in precarious jobs in the service sector. In response to anticipated dismissals associated with the 2006 Nonregular Worker Protection Act, the E-Land Union prepared to launch a strike of approximately 180 dismissed retail and supermarket cashiers and sales assistants working in E-Land stores in July 2007. The majority of E-Land unionists on strike were women over the age of thirty earning approximately 800,000 won a month, well under the average monthly wage. Although workers were technically hired under short-term contracts, most workers had worked continuously for years with little indication that the terms of their employment were finite. Many workers did not regard the company's contracts with much credibility since their supervisors periodically asked them to use their sisters' or friends' name to renew their contracts to get around the provision of benefits. When the management used the rationale that the end of workers' fixed-term contracts meant their employment would be terminated, dismissed workers joined the union's plans to strike.

In preparation for the wave of contract terminations that were likely to follow the passage of the 2006 Nonregular Worker Protection Act, the E-Land Union planned multiple high-profile workplace occupations, including the company's flagship store in the World Cup Stadium shopping complex. During the course of their twenty-one-day occupation, E-Land Union members camped out in the store. They laid mats next to the locked-down cash registers at the front of the store and affixed colorful union banners and posters throughout the store. Prominent political leaders from organizations like the now-defunct Democratic Labor Party (민주노동당) visited the strike site to express solidarity and support for the heroic efforts of the E-Land workers. Progressive left activists from the People's Solidarity for Social Progress (사회진보연대) played a major role in supporting the occupation as outside allies. But most importantly, the strike, occupation, and subsequent boycott had the KCTU's full support for perhaps the very first time. Kim Hyejin explained, "If you look at it from KCTU's perspective, KCTU as a whole completely shut down stores when E-Land and New Core workers waged sit-ins in their stores in 2006 and 2007. We all entered the store and surrounded it, as the entire democratic labor movement declared that precarious employment is an issue that concerns all of us. It was a time we fought alongside each other under this banner." This period was particularly important because it represented a time when KCTU's rhetoric about representing all workers seemed closest to its practice, including providing concrete and material support for precarious workers' independent union struggles as well as sponsoring new approaches to organizing and campaigning.

Since 2006, as multiple high-profile struggles waged by precarious workers were exploding throughout the country, KCTU as an organization began reorganizing its internal operations to more actively support precarious workers. A new precarious workers' division was created within KCTU, which is devoted specifically to supporting the union struggles of precarious workers and actively organizing unorganized workers. KCTU launched a multiyear campaign, including support for twenty-four trained organizers who could be dispatched to its industrial union affiliates to strengthen the capacity of the precarious workers' movement.[32] Union membership rates began to rise, and "the majority of precarious workers' unions were able to use collective bargaining to effectively strengthen job security," explained Kim Hyejin. These shifts have created new opportunities but also differing opinions about how to tackle the problem. These changes have also fomented internal divisions within workplaces between workers with regular employment and those in precarious jobs and organizational conflicts between and across different precarious workers' labor unions. Thus, Kim Hyejin emphasized in our interview that "rather than precarious labor becoming the most pressing problem of the labor movement," meaningful change was thwarted.

One of the major difficulties that the precarious workers' movement faces in the current context is their ongoing marginal status within KCTU as a peak labor organization. As of 2020, approximately 30 percent of KCTU's membership (310,000 out of 1.04 million persons) consists of workers in precarious jobs, with some estimates placing this figure closer to four hundred thousand.[33] This is a significant percentage, and yet the lack of visibility about issues facing workers in precarious jobs creates additional problems within organized labor. Kim Hyejin elaborates,

> Despite the fact that the precarious labor movement has become extremely important, it begs the question, Is it really at the level where the movement as a whole is doing everything possible to strengthen the will of precarious workers? This is not happening. Instead, we are pretty much going about things separately, as if we are each on our own path. Considering this, we are confronting some serious limitations. Institutionally, there has been backsliding in terms of the labor systems since not one of the demands that we have put forward have actually advanced. And because there has been a continual "worsening" of [precarious workers'] problems, there has not been much overall progress regarding precarious labor.

In this context, precarious workers are isolated, left to fight the conditions of organized abandonment without the support of KCTU and the majority of its regularly employed rank-and-file membership base. As of 2020, overall union density for precarious workers remains extremely low at 2.5 percent in comparison to regular workers, whose union density rate is 19.2 percent.[34]

THE MOBILIZING FORCE OF DEATH: OLD AND NEW ALLIES

The deaths of workers—as well as students and political dissidents—have long sparked extraordinary moments of collective solidarity against economic and political injustice in Korea. However, these deaths typically corresponded to individual acts of self-sacrifice by political martyrs, such as twenty-two-year-old Chun Tae-il (전태일; Chŏn T'ae-il), who died by self-immolation in protest of the exploitation of garment workers who toiled in sweatshops in the Seoul Peace Market in 1970, or the wrongful deaths of student activists at the hands of police violence, such as third-year Yonsei University student Lee Han-yeol (이한열; Yi Han-yŏl), who died after being hit by a tear gas canister during the historic June 1987 uprising. During the early 2010s, the phenomenon of group deaths associated with the neoliberal violence of industrial restructuring, financialization, free trade policies, and the generalized emphasis on profit over life created a new affective context that began to revitalize alliances with old social movements and fostered new allies for protesting workers.

In the labor movement, one of the most significant cases of group death was linked to the deaths of thirty Ssangyong Motor unionists over an extended period of time. On April 28, 2009, the day that the Ssangyong Motor company announced the layoffs of 2,646 out of 5,300 workers on the eve of a transnational acquisition by a Chinese automaker, a precarious worker, who was employed by one of the automakers' subcontractors, died by suicide. The following May, a second worker died from a cerebral hemorrhage after the brutal crackdown of the union's seventy-seven-day factory occupation in opposition to the mass layoffs.[35] During the period, workers experienced warlike conditions, which one Ssangyong Motor protester, Lee Chang-kun (이창근; Yi Ch'ang-gŭn), later described as akin to being "thrown into a life-or-death situation, often with no other option but to betray and dupe each other."[36] As the occupation persisted, protesters were locked inside the factory as the company cut off access to power, water, and food. The constant vilification of striking workers in the press fomented internal divisions, putting workers "against one another, the laid-off versus the employed, the dead versus the living."[37] Over time, the number of workers occupying the plant dwindled from the initial high of nine hundred, but approximately seven hundred workers still occupied the plant when riot police were dispatched on the seventy-seventh day to remove all remaining protesters, pouring tear gas from military helicopters, shooting rubber bullets and tasers, and beating down protesters with shields and batons. Much of this resurfaced with the success of the Netflix series *Squid Game* in 2021, in which only two out of the 456 original participants survive a brutal game of life and death. The fictional story was inspired by the real-life experiences of laid-off Ssangyong Motor workers, and Lee Chang-kun writes, reflecting on the parallels between *Squid Game* and his own experiences, "Heart-wrenching desperation, the fear of death, and unending horrors often overcame me throughout the occupation. I still suffer nightmares and flashbacks of the violence and division inflicted upon us more than ten years ago."[38]

Although the militancy of laid-off Ssangyong Motor unionists was well known even outside the South Korean labor movement, the brutal violence and collective trauma that they experienced remained invisible for many years following the union struggle. It was only when more and more Ssangyong Motor unionists continued to die in the subsequent years, either by suicide or due to health complications, that critical attention turned to the collective trauma of surviving—and not surviving—neoliberal labor repression. Quoted in a news article three years after their mass layoffs, Han Sang-gyun (한상균), the former head of the Ssangyong Motor Union (쌍용자동차 노조) and former KCTU president (2014–18), said in an interview, "Many workers and their family died after the strike because they could not see hope in the despair that the company, Ssangyong Motor, locked them in, and also because society did not care and turned away from them. I couldn't read the domestic news section in the newspaper for a while because I was afraid I'd read of another death."[39] Despite the horror of each new death, which in 2012 included twenty-two workers, it was only when protesting workers relocated one of the union's memorial altars to Taehanmun—the eastern gate of Tŏksu Palace in central Seoul, across the street from Seoul City Hall and in between Seoul Central Station and Kwanghwamun Square—that their struggle began to receive more widespread public support.

During the summer months of 2013, the Catholic Priests' Association for Justice (CPAJ; 천주교정의구현전국사제단), known as the "fathers and nuns of the street," as well as other activist nuns and progressive religious leaders were among the most visible supporters of the struggle by laid-off Ssangyong Motor workers. Since their founding in 1974, CPAJ has traveled directly to sites of protest to hold prayer services to offer solace and comfort to protesting publics, particularly in cases where protesters have experienced the loss of life and suffered severe police repression as a result of their collective actions. However, religious solidarity became a less prominent part of the labor movement as unionized workers could rely more directly on their economic power and legal rights during the 1990s. In the context of the rising death toll, however, laid-off Ssangyong Motor workers approached CPAJ and other religious allies to find a protest site in central Seoul to continue their public mourning after suffering multiple attacks by the company in P'yŏngt'aek and feeling pressured by their former coworkers and even their own families and communities. In many ways, the fact that laid-off Ssangyong Motor workers reached out to religious leaders to support their ongoing fight was anomalous. Ssangyong Motor workers could be described as part of the "labor aristocracy," which was severely criticized in the media for pursuing workers' self-interests over the financial well-being of companies. Autoworkers in regular employment benefit from their strategic location in core manufacturing industries and their employment in full-time, regular jobs with an array of fringe benefits, making alliances with social movements less necessary for them than for their *pijŏnggyujik* counterparts. However, the laid-off Ssangyong Motor workers who continued their fight were part of a left-wing political formation within the democratic labor movement that staunchly opposed neoliberal economic restructuring and stood in solidarity with precarious workers. Their refusal to give up their fight created rifts within the union, with coworkers, and in the broader community in P'yŏngt'aek, which essentially operated as a company town. Many workers who participated in the factory occupation chose to go back to their jobs under less secure employment conditions or found other jobs in the industry. Facing relentless harassment and heightened conditions of isolation, laid-off Ssangyong Motor workers attracted the support of a diverse range of social-movement activists, who recognized the moral stakes of their fight.

One of the most unlikely alliances that formed during this struggle was with progressive queer activists. In 2013, the gay men's choir G-Voice traveled to the Ssangyong Motor Union's protest camp in front of their factory in P'yŏngt'aek to support one of the high-altitude occupations that workers had waged during their struggle. During that time, queer activists were waging an occupation of their own in Seoul City Hall in the summer of 2013 to demand that the Seoul city government pass an antidiscrimination ordinance to protect and advance LGBTQ+ rights. While their fights were different, their protest practices shared similarities. When laid-off Ssangyong Motor workers visited the city hall *nongsŏng* waged by queer activists, the latter emphasized the significance of being recognized for the first time on the basis of their queer identities and politics as an equal counterpart in the exchange of political solidarities. Granted, many queer activists were already actively involved in supporting militant labor struggles throughout the 1990s and 2000s but from their positionality as radical students and human rights activists rather than explicitly queer activists who have "come out." For queer activist Kwak EKyeong, who became the director of external relations and solidarity at KCTU after founding and leading the group Solidarity for LGBT Human Rights Korea, the solidarities forged between Ssangyong Motor workers and queer activists helped lay the basis of tackling homophobia within the KCTU, which was undoubtedly a difficult challenge given the patriarchal and masculinist tendencies among the rank and file and the leadership. Inspired by the labor-queer alliances emerging among union leaders and queer activists, Kwak EKyeong helped organize a community screening of *Pride*, an uplifting 2014 British film about the group Lesbians and Gays Support the Miners and their unexpected involvement in supporting the miners' strike in 1984 at the height of Margaret Thatcher's policies of neoliberal austerity.[40]

Kwak EKyeong is an important figure in the converging protest landscape across multiple, intersecting social movements. As one of few out lesbian or gay activists in the labor movement, Kwak is well known for traversing a wide range of spaces related to the queer-labor solidarity movement. She worked briefly on the staff of the Korean Women Workers Association (한국여성노동자회), which was one of the first labor organizations to pay attention to the struggles of precarious workers in the late 1990s.[41] She later found herself at the center of the infamous "*najunge* [later] incident," a direct-action protest that became "emblematic of the political stakes of queer and transgender critique of the Candlelight Protests of 2016–17 and the subsequent liberal government headed by President Moon Jae-in."[42] Kwak EKyeong strengthened KCTU's organizational support of the Seoul Queer Culture Festival that summer in 2017 and has continued to foster queer-labor solidarities.

Immediately preceding the 2016–17 Candlelight Protests, Kwak EKyeong was in charge of the steering committee that organized protests and related activities in support of Baek Nam-ki (백남기; Paek Namgi) throughout the ten-month period (317 days) in which he was in a coma. A longtime activist within the Catholic farmers movement, Baek was struck by a high-velocity police water cannon at a protest on November 14, 2015, and suffered a traumatic cerebral hemorrhage. He fell unconscious and remained on a respirator for ten months, and when, in September 2016, the news started reporting that Baek's death may be imminent, round-the-clock vigils and rallies were organized outside the Seoul National University Hospital not only to grieve and wish him well but to protect his body from being taken by the police for an unauthorized autopsy against his family's wishes. For thirty-seven days after his death, a collective defense of activists and supporters kept the police at bay and thwarted their multiple attempts to execute a warrant to seize Baek's body. The activists received such an overwhelming amount of food and other supplies during this time that they announced at one point that the provisions would be redirected to other protest sites nearby. This intense standoff galvanized the start of the Candlelight Protests of 2016–17 that we discuss in depth in chapter 5.

Across all these different protest spaces, the politicization of death as a mobilizing force created affectively charged bonds that pulsed through protesting bodies, objects, and sites, as we elaborate in greater detail in chapters 3 and 4. While Baek's death mobilized the traditional anchors of the *minjung* movement, what was also unmistakably foundational was the *Sewol* tragedy. Kwak EKyeong said,

> In my perspective, *Sewol* is the defining moment in which "death" became a keyword in Korean society. Really, the keywords for Korean social movements have changed in terms of a before and after *Sewol*. Before *Sewol*, the deaths of Ssangyong Motor workers were also a motivating force. After *Sewol*, there was also the tragedy at Kuĭi Station, which in some ways could be described as a new starting point. Yet, in my opinion, the reason why the Kuĭi Station became such a big issue is because *Sewol* came before it. After *Sewol*, people's consciousness about living in a safe society has become pretty high. People have started to think, "Why are poor people and those who are lower class the only ones to die?"

By using the term "keyword" (키워드), Kwak EKyeong acknowledged the significance of death as an important part of a cultural lexicon for social movements that articulates the relationship between social class and social death. In our interview, she recounted the many cases of workers who have died under tragic circumstances because of dangerous working conditions—both before and since the capsizing of the *Sewol* ferry in 2014. The list included young workers killed in blast furnaces and coal conveyer belts and countless other precarious workers who die every day in machine and heavy industry factories. While acknowledging that unjust, premature death is certainly not a new phenomenon in the country's brutal history of capitalist industrialization and economic development, something had shifted with *Sewol*. The emotional reach of these deaths, even the well-known deaths of the laid-off Ssangyong Motor workers, once seemed limited to the world of progressives and movement activists. It was not until the *Sewol* tragedy, Kwak emphasized, that public feelings were swayed by the terror of witnessing the government's blatant disregard for the safety and lives of its own citizens, even children.

Kwak EKyeong explained how her own job responsibilities at KCTU also shifted in the post-*Sewol* environment. One of her responsibilities at work was to build solidarity for a coalitional effort to demand changes to the labor-dispatch practical training service, which has sacrificed too many young workers' lives. She was also spearheading an effort to raise the national minimum wage to 10,000 Korean won ($8.50). While KCTU has been at the forefront of demanding increases to the minimum wage since the matter became a public issue in the early 2000s, the campaign became explicitly linked to the vulnerability of young workers in precarious jobs who are subjected to extremely low wages or exploited as apprentice workers. The young worker's death at Kuŭi Station was especially shocking because of the brutal circumstances: he was crushed to death, trapped between the oncoming train and sliding safety screen doors he was repairing, alone without a coworker, who should have been there to ensure workplace safety. He was simply named Kim-*gun* in the news media, depicted as a kind of a common man with the commonest name.[43] The contents of Kim-gun's backpack later revealed three unopened instant-ramen bowls, which painted a painful picture of a young worker, just nineteen years old and earning barely a minimum wage, too busy and too poor to afford a decent meal. He was doing hazardous machine-repair work, while formally employed by a negligent third-party labor-dispatch company for one of the world's largest metropolitan subway systems, Seoul Metro.[44]

KCTU, the Arbeit Workers Union (알바노조), and a number of other groups of workers and their advocates led an effort to raise the minimum wage and improve conditions for young workers.[45] To mourn the Kuŭi Station worker's death, protesters held a candlelit memorial procession outside for several evenings, walking silently from Kuŭi Station to Konkuk University Medical Center, where incense was burned at a memorial altar. The site of Kim-gun's death on the subway platform became a place to share public messages of grief and mourning, with single-stem white chrysanthemum flowers, as is the traditional practice, and instant-ramen bowls, snacks, and soda in reference to what was found in Kim-gun's backpack.[46] Hundreds of sticky Post-its covered the glass sliding doors where he died, a practice that has become common since the Post-it memorial following the murder of a young woman in Kangnam in May 2016, just a few months before the Candlelight Protests. There is now a permanent memorial stone plate in place at Kuŭi Station with two sayings. The first is "It wasn't your fault," a rejoinder to those who blamed Kim-gun's death on his own supposed carelessness. And the second is, simply and powerfully, "You are me," a message of identification and solidarity. Standing out from all the other expressions of condolence and grief—such as "We will remember," which alludes to the victims of the *Sewol* tragedy—these two sayings have been repeatedly used at Kim-gun's memorial every year and as a rallying cry for youth labor activism.

GENDERING THE LABOR POLITICS OF GRIEF AND DEATH

The deaths of workers in precarious jobs and of poor and laboring classes more generally, as Kwak EKyeong put it, have long incited affec-tively charged solidarities between and among labor and social move-ment actors. In the Korean women workers' movement, one of the most significant labor martyrs is Kim Kyŏng-suk (김경숙), a unionized factory worker of the YH Trading Company who died at the age of twenty-one during a violent police crackdown of their union on August 11, 1979. The YH Trading Company produced wigs as well as a variety of other prod-ucts for export, such as gloves and electronics. At its height, the factory employed approximately four thousand workers, who were housed in the company dormitory to facilitate twenty-four-hour production sched-ules when needed; however, declining sales, outsourcing and capital flight, and managerial corruption resulted in the announcement of the plant closure in March 1979.[47] YH Union (YH 노동조합) members faced repeated and ongoing retaliation by the company after establishing an independent union and negotiating their first collective bargaining agreement. They also witnessed severe repression against unionized workers at Wonpoong Woolen Textile, Dongil Textiles, Bando, and Chŏngkae Clothing. After learning that their own plant closure could be interpreted as an act of retaliation against the union, YH Union members decided to strike. After being locked out of the factory, they waged a sit-in at the headquarters of the oppositional political party's building.

Pak T'ae-yŏn (박태연), the former general secretary of the YH Union who later became the president of the Puch'ŏn Women Workers' Association (부천여성노동자회), recalled her experience at the time: "There were people who wanted to give up the fight because they felt burdened by anxiety and the long struggle ahead. So, I stepped forward and said, 'We cannot retreat, and if our demands are just, it is the least we can do for our survival.' In front of the members, I announced I would protect our rights with my death, and prepared to immolate myself. Because of this, people were in shock and cried. Then, we decided to die together, and swore to fight until the very end."[48] Pak T'ae-yŏn did not wage a suicide protest that day, but her comrade Kim Kyŏng-suk was found dead after falling from the fourth floor of the building after their occupation was raided at 2:00 a.m. by two thousand riot police wearing steel helmets and wielding clubs and by an additional five hundred police in plain clothes. In just twenty-three minutes, they stormed through the building's doors and windows, hurling smoke bombs while beating up and dragging out all 187 protesters. Pak T'ae-yŏn and other protesters were taken directly to the Taenŭng Police Station, but Kim Kyŏng-suk was rushed to the hospital after being found unconscious on the basement level and pronounced dead at 2:30 a.m.[49] Pak T'ae-yŏn remembers learning about her comrade's death from a torn piece of newspaper in a police bathroom. "If someone had to die, it was supposed to be me," she thought.[50]

Thirty-five years after her death, Pak T'ae-yŏn and the Korean Women Workers Association established the annual Women's Labor Movement Award in honor of Kim Kyŏng-suk to remember the forgotten sacrifices of women workers who have been a driving force of the labor movement. As the former Korean Women Workers Association chairperson Maria Chol-soon Rhee (이철순; I Ch'ŏl-sun) writes, these are workers who "never let the light of struggle die" and "ushered in a

CHAPTER 1

time of solidarity struggle."[51] On November 15, 2016, we attended the third annual award ceremony in an event billed as a "night of solidarity" between *sŏnbae* (선배), or "senior," and *hubae* (후배), or "junior", activists, joining over a hundred people gathered to honor the Ch'ŏngju City Geriatric Hospital Workers' Union and Kwon Okja. The following year in 2017, the KTX Crew Workers' Union would receive the award.

CONCLUSION

In this chapter, we discussed how workers' protests challenge the politics of disposability and abandonment that constitute precarity as social death. "To be ineligible for personhood is a form of social death," asserts Lisa Marie Cacho, which renders people "rightless" in the eyes of the state.[52] Denied basic labor rights and institutional protections on contractual grounds, precarious workers and other workers who have been stripped of their right to have rights under neoliberal employment regimes experience disavowal as more than contractual discrimination and legal exclusion. They experience precarity in terms of loss, humiliation, betrayal, shock, anger, and indignation—all feelings that take center stage in their choice of protest tactics. The turn to protest repertoires that dramatize sacrifice and suffering is commonly portrayed as "extreme" and "desperate," including by workers themselves, who enact dangerous hunger strikes and long-term occupation protests. However, we witnessed over and over in solidarity actions and heard in our interviews from key interlocuters that the protesting workers who push their fights beyond impossible and unimaginable limits have effects that exceed the goals and intentions of their own individual grievances. Workers' performance of life-threatening protests makes visible and palpable the urgency of apprehending precarity as social death, both in the broader public and in their own representative organizations. Workers' politicization of life and death through dramatic protest also activates support from allies, old and new, including progressive religious leaders, university students, young workers, queer-rights activists, and leaders of the women workers' movement.

The optics of social death to challenge the devaluation of workers' life and labor under capitalism have long been a feature of workers' protest practices, extending well before the current neoliberal economic orthodoxy became hegemonic in Korea's political economy in the late 1990s. Situating precarious workers' protests as part of a longer history of struggle for labor rights as human rights sharpens our understanding of the relationship between protest repertoires and moral economies. Moral economies do not exist as nonmarket forces that impinge on the destructive forces of the market or as precapitalist values rooted in solidaristic relations and notions of the common good in the Polanyian sense.[53] What are considered just, acceptable, and dignified forms of work have been deeply influenced by "complex fields of struggle" tied to the development of "particular movements and social structures."[54] By cultivating a shared protest repertoire that resonates between and among workers across history and across different types of employment and sectors of the economy, workers' protests have fueled the emotive core of a moral economy thar rejects the treatment of workers as undeserving of rights and protections by the state, whether in its past authoritarian iterations or current neoliberal visage. Recognizing minoritized workers, such as women factory workers during the 1960s and 1970s, as key drivers of repertoire creation and amplification is indispensable in understanding the afterlives of protests. The women workers' movement commemoration of labor martyr Kim Kyŏng-suk is just one of many significant examples that have shaped the ways in which protest repertoires are celebrated both as an index of workers' commitment to a collective politics of refusal and the relational basis of a shared political struggle in broader labor and social movements.

In the next chapter, we turn our attention to the internal life of protest repertoires and the role of performance and ritual in both shaping political subjectivities and creating embodied interconnections that reproduce moral economies across time and place. While the protests of aggrieved workers have long treated the conditions of life and death as the basis of collective political action, they have not acted in isolation from broader collectivities in struggle that have also used protest as a trenchant form of social and political critique and a basis for creating more solidaristic worlds.

2 RITUALS AND REPERTOIRES

> Unlike in *samboilbae* where you get up right away, you spend
> more time prone on the ground in *och'et'uji*. After one or
> two hours, you have a lot of time to think about things.
>
> —Yu Heung-hee (유흥희; Yu Hŭng-hŭi),
Kiryung Electronics Workers' Union

> *Doing* is fundamental for human beings who learn through
> imitation, repetition, and internalizing the actions of
> others. . . . Performance, however, is not limited to mimetic
> repetition. It also includes the possibility of change, critique,
> and creativity within frameworks of repetition.
>
> —Diana Taylor, *Performance*

PROTEST REPERTOIRES REVEAL A WORLD of contradictions. They produce feelings of isolation, alienation, disappointment, and betrayal, as well as relations of support, reciprocity, interdependence, and solidarity. These feelings and relations coexist and mutually reinforce each other, shaping how repertoires develop as dynamic fields of collective political praxis. For *tangsaja*, who are considered the directly affected party of a grievance or dispute, the experience of injustice can lead to a sequence of acts that "push the limits" of what a single body—typically in concert with other bodies—can physically and psychically endure. By maximizing the limited resources available to them, including their bodies, social relationships, and the built environment, protesters connect their experiences of being treated as disposable to the morally charged world of political critique. They bridge the gulf between their experience of precarity as a structure of feeling and explicit condemnations of the death-dealing forces of globalized neoliberal capitalism. As we discussed in the last chapter, in Korean protest cultures, this political critique is often embodied in the life-or-death stakes of minority-labor politics, which become intensified throughout the course of a union dispute that becomes protracted over time. Protesters use the spectacle of extraordinary sacrifice and suffering to remind democratic publics of the deadly politics of prioritizing profits and wealth over people's jobs and livelihoods.

Performance is the primary modality in which the lived experience of injustice and collective challenges to it take form and shape. Through performance, protesters make visible structures of feeling that exist primarily as symbolic violence—the forceful yet concealed ways in which accelerated processes of commodification and marketization further degrade people's everyday lives and futures. The injustice can be a violation in how workers expect to be treated in the social exchange of labor for a wage or as members of a national political community. The injustice also can be a violation in what it means to be human and live as part of interdependent ecosystems in life. The experience of injustice rarely escalates into a contentious event, as Barrington Moore pointed out long ago, but when it does, it is often expressed through performative practices that have made the body as well as the optics of time, place, and mobility the sites of popular contention.[1] Protest repertoires that have congealed into fairly routine and recognizable practices can seem more habitual than transformative, as in the case of labor- and social-movement actors in Korea over the past two decades. However, performance studies scholar Diana Taylor emphasizes that we need to recognize the creative force of imitation and repetition since performance is inherently about doing, and every act of doing, regardless of how often it is repeated, always "includes the possibility of change, critique, and creativity within frameworks of repetition."[2]

Like performance, ritual is a powerful medium for exploring the physical and metaphysical dynamics of the body as a vehicle for transformation, both at the individual and collective levels. On the surface, ritual is assumed to reflect existing values and beliefs—the practices of the already faithful. However, as Saba Mahmood underscores, ritual may be better understood as embodied pedagogy, a way of using gestures, aesthetic practices, corporeal discipline, and bodily comportment to cultivate one's commitment and devotion to a community of faith in the context of doubt and ambivalence, whether that is to an organized religious tradition or a secular political ideology.[3] As Kiryung union leader Yu Heung-hee remarked, performing slow-moving and physically strenuous rituals, such as *och'et'uji*, for long periods of time gives a person "a lot of time to think about things." The experience of time through ritual can lead to intense reflection about what went wrong and why. It can also shift people's subjective understandings of what abstract ideas, such as liberal democracy, mean, especially when it contradicts one's lived experiences. The adaptation of ritual into protest forms thus can be understood as an embodied practice of cultivating faith in political belief systems that espouse ideas about rights, entitlements, and collective prosperity but often violates those expectations in profound ways.

In this chapter, we turn our attention to the performative and ritualistic elements of protest repertoires and their role in creating the figure of the protester as the embodiment of challenging injustice. We make a distinction between individuals who participate directly in protests and those who witness and support the protest struggles—not to impose narrow or rigid definitions and classifications but because they constitute distinct political subjectivities in the doing, feeling, and witnessing of protest. As a key term in minority rights discourse—especially in disability politics in both Japan and South Korea since the 1970s, when a range of social movements emerged with the aim of combating discrimination and defending minority rights—*tangsaja* commonly appears in political legal studies, where the term refers to the "people or parties directly involved in the matter," particularly in litigations and lawsuits. In activist and protest dynamics, the *tangsaja* is often a very specific category of protest participants, such as workers who were laid off, bereaved families who suffered a personal loss, survivors of state violence, and so on. Joining them in struggle are activists, advocates, and other community members, who nonetheless recognize they are not the *tangsaja*—a category reserved for the very core of a *tangsaja*-led fight. These distinct political subjectivities as well as more pragmatic roles and responsibilities are formed through a long process of learning, building upon, and innovating repertoires of solidarity, which accumulate over time. Though rarely found in official historical archives, these repertoires persist through what Taylor calls an "ephemeral repertoire of embodied practice/knowledge"—that is, performances, rituals, storytelling traditions, and gestures and other nonverbal practices that convey knowledge and transmit cultural memory about alternative ways of being and becoming.[4] They find expression through the art, poetry, and literature of left cultural artists who convey ideas about capitalist exploitation, political repression, and social injustice through aesthetic practices.[5] They evolve and change through interactional dynamics, especially in response to the backlash and repression of targeted authorities, the police, and state actors as well as internal conflict and cooperation between and among protesters and supporters.[6] For example, the choice to engage in an indefinite hunger strike is not one that any protester takes on lightly given the great harm it can do to an individual, but it can also place supporters in a difficult position as they witness such life-threatening acts.

The embodied, subjective, and interactional dynamics of protest raise crucial questions about how protest actors navigate the interior life of a protest repertoire. How does the staging of protest as performance and ritual enable protesters to sustain protest in the face of high levels of opposition and backlash from targeted opponents and the state? What specific forms do protesters choose, and what difference do they make? What conflicts and dilemmas do their choices engender, and how do the people who witness and support protest acts make sense of these tensions and contradictions?

Examining the interior life of protest repertoires shifts the focus of attention from who and why protests take on the characteristics of "life-and-death" dramas, which we explored in the previous chapter, to *how* such protests are able to persist in the context of institutional backlash and historical transformation. Sustaining solidarity between and among protesters and movement actors is an important part of repertoire dynamics. Solidaristic collectivities and identities are forged and reinforced through performance, but at the same time, they can weaken and dissipate when confrontational struggles become protracted to a point of depletion and despair.

In Korean protest cultures, we see a range of performative and ritualized practices that shape how people protest and to what ends. This includes multiscalar occupations of workplaces, city streets, and architectural skylines as well as religiously inflected acts, such as hunger strikes, slow-moving processions, street prayer protests, candlelight vigils and marches, one-person protests, and so on. Through our in-depth discussion of several distinct protest forms, we find that *tangsaja* protest actors, as the directly aggrieved parties, play a leading role in choosing to amplify protest performances and rituals that are extremely risky and often life-threatening. Movement actors are also party to this process of amplification, whether or not they personally support the choice of certain tactics. Activists and supporters perform the emergency care work involved in sustaining the basic needs of protesters as well as the behind-the-scenes work of outreach, mobilization, and communication, as we elaborate on in chapter 4. And they do often participate in the performance itself, joining grueling hunger strikes and ritual processions, for example, though they often—but not always, controversially—defer to the *tangsaja* activists. In many cases, movement supporters help protests sustain their fights by providing the linkages to draw upon the established network of allies and movement histories. It is important, we suggest, to broaden the study of protest repertoires to delve more deeply into the internal dynamics of solidaristic-movement communities in order to make sense of the persistence of dramatic and ritualized protests.

PROTEST REPERTOIRES

In places with a strong tradition of protest, such as South Korea, the protest repertoire does appear to cluster into a "limited number of recurrent, well-defined types."[7] One act of protest typically leads to another, according to Charles Tilly, forming "a class of communications that evolve in something like the same way language evolves: through incremental transformation in use."[8] Yet the literature of collective-action repertoires has paid relatively little attention to the complex relationship between and among protesters and movement supporters, reproducing assumptions that these groups are one in the same. Part of this tendency can be attributed to the focus on processes of collective-identity formation, which can give the appearance that social movements are bounded social formations rather than "clusters of performances," as Tilly emphasizes. Even when protest repertoires appear to take on an autonomous life of their own, there are in fact complex processes that yield familiar outcomes and thus cannot be fully comprehended "without having robust descriptions and explanations of their operations."[9]

During the process of repertoire amplification, protest actors and the people who witness and support their struggles develop shared vocabularies and collective memories that amplify certain types of performances over others.[10] Tilly, however, identifies a "puzzling feature" when it comes to WUNC protest performances—that is, performances that correspond to public displays of worthiness (W), unity (U), numbers (N), and commitment (C). In principle, combining all four types should strengthen the persuasive power of protest performances. However, "as [WUNC performances] increase, they almost necessarily contradict each other."[11] For example, to gain numbers, movement actors strive to mobilize the participation of broad sectors of the population to attend a rally or march, sign a petition, post a social media message, or donate to a cause. Mobilizing the masses, though, often requires appealing to lowest-common-denominator politics in order to emphasize unified displays of collective unity over the "worthiness of difference." We saw how these tensions played out during the Candlelight Protests of 2016–17 when event organizers asked militant protest actors to refrain from standing out as identifiable representatives of specific unions and activist organizations and instead urged them to participate like everyone else as "ordinary citizens." In contrast, strengthening public displays of worthiness (W) and commitment (C) often requires deemphasizing the value of numbers (N) and unity (U). Worthiness is typically displayed by showing "evidence of previous undeserved suffering" through moral symbols and aesthetic markers, the presence of religious and political authorities, and places of historical significance and meaning, while commitment demonstrates "persistence in costly or risky activity, declarations of readiness to persevere, resistance to attach."[12] Thus, emphasizing the worthiness and commitment of protesters can in effect discourage ongoing participation and thus result in decreasing numbers and fracturing unity.

The embrace of grueling and punishing protest acts in South Korean protest repertoires is indicative of these dilemmas and contradictions. Across all the cases we examine, as protesters turn to more risky and life-threatening protest acts in the context of declining participants, there results an attrition of struggles to just a handful of remaining protesters. One way that protest campaigns address their dwindling numbers is by focusing on a different kind of number—the temporal duration of the protest. Counting the number of days that a protest endures effectively deflects attention away from the declining number of actual protest participants. Relatedly, the emphasis on the worthiness of individual protesters who engage in life-threatening protests, such as hunger strikes, often results in an increased involvement and visibility of religious leaders and other political dignitaries, who bring added legitimacy and moral authority to a localized dispute. Religious leaders hold street prayer protests in solidarity and Buddhist-inflected ritual prostrations especially to support protracted labor- and social-movement protests. At the level of the repertoire, ritual action and public performance make explicit connections to past histories of struggle in ways that amplify the worthiness and commitment of protesters who refuse to accept defeat. Worthiness and commitment thus operate in an inverse relationship to numbers and unity, resulting in patterns that proceed from attrition to escalation among the rank and file, followed by a more diversified level of participation among religious activists and other members of the public who interface with the struggle in solidarity. To better understand these internal dynamics, we turn to distinct protest forms in the repertoire.

NONGSŎNG AS PLACE-BASED PROTEST

Nongsŏng is a widely used concept in the vocabulary of protesters in Korean labor and social movements. *Nongsŏng* refers to the spatial tactics that are utilized by a wide variety of protest actors around the world, yet it is a term that defies simple translation across linguistic and historical contexts. The term *nongsŏng* is sometimes translated in the English language as a "sit-in" or "sit-down strike," which refers to a type of protest in which people take over a building or designated area and refuse to leave until their demands are met or until they otherwise decide to end their protest. The term "occupation" is a more familiar term in today's political lexicon given the global diffusion of the protest encampment as a modular strategy to expose the injustice of neoliberal globalization, political authoritarianism, and more. However, unlike the contemporary form of the protest camp, which has "adapt[ed] practices and infrastructures from tent cities, festival cultures, squatting communities, [and] land-based autonomous movements," the occupation protest (점거 농성) by Korean protest actors traces its origins to a civilizational genealogy rooted in ideas of place-based defense and collective survival.[13]

Nongsŏng, which uses Chinese characters (籠城), was used historically to depict a type of crisis when members of the population would lock themselves inside the walls of a fortress (성곽) to protect the community against an external threat, such as a foreign invasion during the five-hundred-year period of Chosŏn dynastic rule (1392–1910). At the time, the premodern architecture of a fortress included the construction of two walls—an inner and outer wall—as a form of double protection against invading forces. When the outer wall was breached, the inner gates could be locked and defended for an indefinite period of time. The historical origin of the term was referenced during a news segment on the YTN television network in 2018.[14] When discussing the workplace occupation of supermarket workers (판매원), featured guest Cho Yun-kyŏng (조윤경) explains, "All people inside the fortress would unite and defend themselves behind closed gates" during the Chosŏn period, "whereas today, *nongsŏng* has changed to mean staying put in one place to express one's demands." In the contemporary case, the supermarket workers, who were predominantly middle-aged women earning minimum wage and working under limited-term employment contracts, locked themselves inside their workplace for the purposes of fighting unjust firing and unilateral layoffs. For them, the decision to occupy their workplace was an act of defense for themselves as the rightful occupants of a place or space. *Nongsŏng* thus enacted a spatial relation of attachment and belonging.

The idea that *nongsŏng* is part of striking workers' transhistorical memory was commonly repeated during our interviews, though few people knew exactly when or where the tradition started. One union leader responded matter-of-factly, with a slight tone of annoyance when asked where the protest practice came from, that setting up a *nongsŏng* is "simply part of our history and tradition." By "our," he invoked the subjective "we" (우리) that is often used by Koreans to denote a shared national sensibility. He emphasized that Korean workers have "always done *nongsŏng* since the very beginning." While this notion masks the fact that "sleeping away from home for weeks, months, and now years at time" is "not a realistic strategy for working mothers and women who are heads of their households," as one feminist labor activist remarked, his statement points to the fact that the tradition of *nongsŏng* is indeed perceived to be common knowledge.

While the term *nongsŏng* defies a specific origin story in the history of Korean social protest, the presence of a *nongsŏng* marks a particular workplace or geographical location as the core site of active struggle— what Korean movement actors refer to as a *hyŏnjang* (현장). Not all workers' protests involve *nongsŏng*. Setting up a *nongsŏng* at a *hyŏnjang* usually occurs in response to an impasse, such as when collective negotiations between a targeted opponent and an aggrieved group breaks down. To escalate the stakes of the conflict, striking workers might barricade themselves inside their workplaces for an indefinite period of time, preparing to eat, sleep, and occupy the place until their demands are met. For occupations that are expected to be protracted, typically due to high levels of employer opposition to unions, striking workers will begin the *nongsŏng* with provisions—as well as contingency plans to replenish when needed—in order to maintain their daily life in places that are not ordinarily designed as residential spaces, such as the floors of factories, retail stores, hospitals, train stations, subway stations, universities, and office buildings. In some cases, their protest results in total shutdowns, with normal routes of entering and exiting blocked by protesters, riot police, or both, as in the case when the E-Land/Homever workers shut down their place of work and led an occupation strike. In other cases, though, indoor occupations permit some flow of normal activities, as was the case for the KTX workers' three-year occupation of the Seoul Central Station and disability activists' decade-long protest camp in the subway underpass at Kwanghwamun Square.

The *nongsŏng* often becomes more elaborate after the experience of repression and violence. Companies that seek to forcefully dismantle a strike barricade or a protest encampment at the workplace usually pursue two avenues: demanding police intervention to break up occupations that they deem "illegal" and utilizing security-service firms (용역업체), which dispatch what protesters refer to as contracted thugs for hire (용역 깡패). The use of violence to drag protesters out of an occupied site can spark a "critical emotional event," in which anger and indignation toward the excessive use of force, especially by the police, ignite a full-fledged "protest spectacle" that manifests into the defense of a long tent encampment.[15] Union banners and flags, amplified sound systems, and other protest-related supplies and equipment are brought in to make the *nongsŏng* an extraordinary political space, albeit temporarily. Internally, the *nongsŏng* site serves as a de facto headquarters, where striking workers can gather every day to set priorities and plan activities on a day-by-day and sometimes hour-by-hour basis.

As a *nongsŏng* becomes more protracted over time, though, it can take the form of an elaborately constructed protest camp, transformed by its multidimensional functionality, which is reflected in the architecture and construction too. Protesters create *nongsŏng-jang* or site to function as both a political space and a place of temporary dwelling where they can not only meet, strategize, and discuss but also eat, sleep, and rest. These practices of "homemaking" are consistent with the historical usage of the term as a defense of domicile. They also reflect the practicalities of waging day- and night-long protests and related activities concerning time-sensitive matters. Organizers who set up protest camps research and determine where the best place to locate an on-site encampment may be, what materials and supplies are required to maintain a continued presence, and how to create a comfortable space for meeting, sleeping, eating, and hosting guests and visitors. Part of this involves finding ways to demarcate the "inside" space from the "outside" space, to use a quotidian example. In most *nongsŏng* sites that we visited, there was such a demarcation. Shoes worn outside would be removed and left outside the indoor space of more private quarters.

The creation of a homelike environment at a protest camp during a long-term struggle enables protesters to greet supporters who visit the protest site as a show of solidarity, much like hosting a friend or colleague at your home or place of work. This can take the form of short, impromptu visits in which visitors spend a few moments keeping protesters company in the context of long and often-idle hours spent defending a *nongsŏng* site. They can also consist of planned and scheduled visits by individuals and delegations from unions, social organizations, or organized groups. During the Miryang encampment (discussed in chapter 4), which was constructed to oppose the building of high-voltage transmission towers, the protesters routinely welcomed visitors from out of town, who came bearing gifts and even treated guests to home-cooked dinners as well as lively speeches and performances.[16] Maintaining a vibrant *nongsŏng* helps build a sense of unity and purpose between and among protesters as well as demonstrates the commitment and resolve of the struggle to allies and supporters who visit to express solidarity in both symbolic and tangible ways.

We visited an elaborately constructed *nongsŏng* site in the city of Kumi in North Kyŏngsang Province where the Asahi Glass In-House Subcontracting Workers Union (아사히비정규직지회) held a rally marking the two-year anniversary of their strike. Union leaders proudly gave us a tour of their encampment space, which consisted of separate sleeping quarters, a kitchen, a canteen, a meeting space in which to greet visitors, and a storage space for union banners, picket signs, amps, and other protest equipment. We were particularly impressed by the high quality of construction and efficient design and layout of the space. During our interview, the union leader, Ch'a Hŏn-ho (차헌호), explained that many rank-and-file workers had skills in production and engineering, given the type of industrial fabrication that their jobs entailed in a glass factory, which made it easy for them to build the encampment structures.[17] They even had a rank-and-file member who was a former chef and knew how to cook for large groups of people. These skills were extremely useful as the union continued to expand and fortify their camp in response to the grueling nature of their union struggle, especially in this notoriously conservative region with a history of dismantling democratic unions.

Located inside the Kumi Industrial Complex, which is dominated by the proemployer Federation of Korean Trade Unions (한국노총), the trillion-dollar Japanese company Asahi Glass relied on in-house subcontracting companies, which hired workers indirectly and paid them minimum wages. When the majority of the workers formed a union within the first two weeks—138 out of the total 170 workers—many of whom were older women workers, union leaders felt encouraged by their ability to win a quick resolution with just three demands: recognize the union, raise the hourly wage from the minimum of 5,580 won to 8,000 won, and change the required work uniforms. However, what followed were years of antiunion retaliation and eventually, termination via text message. One worker explained, "I worked like a machine at Asahi Glass for nine years. I couldn't endure it anymore and formed a labor union, but a month later, I lost my job."[18] As one of only two democratic unions in the area and the first union by any group of workers, let alone precariously employed workers, to wage a strike in ten years, the Asahi Glass union workers faced an uphill battle.[19]

The union set up their strike camp on July 1, 2015, and it was built and rebuilt several times in response to violence by security-service firms and the police. When unionists first set up their strike camp, one hundred people were dispatched by the firm to tear it down. A few weeks later, seven hundred people from the firm were sent to dismantle the camp, which had become more extensive in size and function. Unionists defended their encampment that day for five hours, blocking traffic from all directions and tying themselves to construction forklifts. Four people were arrested and taken to the police station that day.

In cases of highly protracted struggles, some protesters try to maintain multiple sites in open-air locations, such as the street, sidewalk, or public plaza or square, though this depends on the resources available to them. Supported by the Korean Metal Workers' Union (전국금속노동조합), laid-off Ssangyong Motor workers, for instance, were able to set up multiple protest camps throughout their struggle over many years, including one outside the Taehanmun of the Tŏksu Palace in Seoul's Kwanghwamun. That particular street *nongsŏng* lasted approximately a year, as protesters withstood multiple efforts by the police to "clean up" the tent encampment through violent, surprise raids. In the early hours of the morning of April 4, 2013, the Ssangyong Motor autoworkers' tent encampment, including a memorial altar, was forcibly torn down by city workers and security personnel, who took a mere ten minutes to drag out the sleeping occupants and destroy the protest site. The city workers then poured forty tons of dirt to construct planters in its place, making sure a tent encampment could not be rebuilt there. A notorious police chief named Choi Sŏng-yŏng from the Namdaemun Police Station would earn the nickname "Eichmann of Namdaemun" for the violent action he authorized that morning. Today, the enormous concrete planters with flowers and shrubs remain where the Ssangyong autoworkers' *nongsŏng* site used to be. As an interviewee quipped with bittersweet memory, these planters are now famous as the most despised planters in the country.

To maintain an outdoor occupation over extended periods of time, protesters build makeshift shelters, which often become more elaborately furnished in the face of repeated efforts to dismantle them. Interestingly, once a *nongsŏng* takes on the characteristics of a protest camp, the long-term struggle becomes integrally linked to the many activities required to keep the encampment going in the face of human and nonhuman threats. We interviewed one longtime union activist who had participated in multiple factory occupations as a rank-and-file autoworker in the late 1980s and early 1990s and then as a staff organizer at multiple unions, including the KCTU, which is a common trajectory for workers who are fired for leading a struggle and subsequently blacklisted from finding work in their respective occupations. In the early days, workers used to find whatever objects in their vicinity to build and fortify their encampments, he said, which usually made for poorly constructed shelters with little protection from inclement weather, whether the scorching sun, heavy rain, or debilitating cold. But things are different these days, he laughed as he detailed the growing range of outdoor camping equipment that have made long-term occupations relatively more comfortable and more sustainable. One can find affordable and portable camping chairs and tables, he said, as well as padded and insulated sleeping mats, efficient gas burners for cooking, and high-quality tents that are waterproof and windproof. Some protesters even find ways to set up minifridges and small air conditioning units powered by generators or electricity that neighbors are willing to share with them.

As protest encampments drag on for months and years, though, tension does arise regarding the upkeep and cleaning of the space. Throughout our interviews and site visits, especially in mixed-gender protest camps, we often noticed the division of labor between the male union leaders, who did the hosting and greeting, and the predominantly women union members, who did the cooking and cleaning. When the topic came up during informal conversations, such as our stroll around the Asahi Glass protest camp, we were told that yes, men tended to do the constructing and heavy-lifting work, and women tended to be better at preparing meals, but many of the men had also picked up skills during their military service and were more than capable of taking charge of cooking. We also learned that since protest camps usually rely on a time schedule and role delegation, one of the most important tasks is to assign individuals, almost always men, to stand guard and protect the space from the ever-present threat of being destroyed, especially in the middle of the night. *Nongsŏng* sites are never to be left unattended. The space can also become cluttered and messy with backpacks, clothing, and other personal items left inside by the long rotating list of inhabitants. *Nongsŏng* sites can sometimes serve as a resource for temporarily storing people's belongings and protest-related items that are cumbersome to carry around. In fact, one protester that we spoke with expressed regret that she had treated the *Sewol* tents in Kwanghwamun as a de facto locker, a convenient storage space given its central location, especially during the Candlelight Protests of 2016–17. Women participants we spoke with in particular tended to express more dissatisfaction about the housekeeping work, which fell disproportionately on women. It was, according to one interviewee, one of the worst things about long-term encampment—that they had to deal with the chaos and mess of the protest space alongside gendered assumptions about who would be responsible for these problems.

Despite what many recognized as the difficulties of maintaining an encampment, one particularly extraordinary site was constructed and maintained in a highly atypical location in Seoul by social activists who had few ties to the labor movement and were predominantly women. It was a protest camp in Kangnam, led by the labor-health movement Banolim (반올림). Between 2007 and 2018, Banolim activists led a campaign under the name Supporters for the Health and Rights of People in the Semiconductor Industry (SHARPS), which included victims and their families as well as doctors, scientists, lawyers, and labor consultants. SHARPS demanded that Samsung Semiconductor take responsibility for the deaths of semiconductor workers, who were almost entirely young women who died from leukemia and other related diseases they believed were linked to working in Samsung Semiconductor factories. The media commonly referred to the phenomenon as "Samsung leukemia"; however, this term was vigorously contested by health experts associated with the company.[20] The No More Deaths campaign, which was officially launched on November 20, 2007, was originally spearheaded by the father of twenty-three-year-old Hwang Yumi (황유미; Hwang Yu-mi), who died from a rare strain of leukemia after working at Samsung's semiconductor plant in Kihŭng, just south of Seoul in Kyŏnggi Province.[21] When her father, Hwang Sang-ki (황상기), learned that other workers also contracted leukemia at the same factory, he became singularly focused on holding Samsung accountable for workers' wrongful deaths. He joined forces with other patients and their families, as well as activists, experts, human rights organizations, and social-movement organizations to form SHARPS.[22] They faced extreme intimidation and retaliation from Samsung Electronics, one of the most successful subsidiaries of one of the largest and most powerful chaebols in the country, yet they refused to give up their fight, which escalated to a three-year tent encampment between 2015 and 2018.

Like in the case of a breakdown in union bargaining negotiations, the *nongsŏng* began when Banolim activists, which included victims and their families, felt that "their conversations [with company officials] were not going well." By that point, approximately fifty workers had died, and many more had chronic illnesses, and Samsung refused to take any legal or public accountability for the deaths. They started an action in front of the Samsung building entrance, which was organized as a "cultural festival" that lasted until approximately 1:00 a.m. each night. Ten days after their negotiations began, on the morning of October 7, 2015, they set up a protest camp and declared that they would "engage in twenty-four-hour, round-the-clock negotiations." According to the lead organizer, "Samsung had no idea we were starting a *nongsŏng*." Their ability to elude the company's attention was in part because they changed the location of their protest camp. One of the lead encampment organizers explained: "Others had held a *nongsŏng* site outside the number 8 exit, but we wanted a place that everyday people could see easily, not just a path to Samsung. So, we spread out the mat [돗자리를 펴고] and made a place to sit [자리를 만들고]. The guards did not seem particularly attentive to what we were doing since we were engaged in ongoing negotiations."

Their preparations for building the encampment were fairly straightforward. They set up a "waterproof cover and a strong pallet" as the foundation of the camp at 7:00 a.m., and their bedding and sleeping mats arrived at 8:00 a.m. They also made sure to register their protest rally on the day their protest camp began to "avoid the police letting Samsung know" their plans. Interestingly, in contrast to rank-and-file union activists, such as in the case of the Asahi union, the Banolim activists made sure to register their protest camp as a legally authorized event. As highly capable social-movement activists, they also planned many aspects of the *nongsŏng*, even though none of them had any direct experience participating in an encampment protest before. One organizer recalled, "Everyone was anxious, but it was also exciting. It was the first time I slept in the streets. I was worried about staying vigilant. We had space for about seven to eight people to sleep. I got choked up when I saw a picture of us sleeping in Kangnam covered in vinyl. We did everything at the highest level."

Her comment that they did "everything at the highest level" was reflected in the beautifully designed and maintained space of their encampment. We visited the Banolim *nongsŏng* several times throughout our fieldwork and were struck each time at the visually appealing displays of information outside the camp, including a placard that was changed each day to display the number of days of the encampment struggle. The care and thoughtfulness that went into creating a comfortable, homelike space inside the encampment also was a distinctive feature of Banolim's *nongsŏng*. The space was adorned with potted plants, a neatly organized bookshelf, colorful seat cushions, wall décor, and other items that enabled encampment protesters to keep the space tidy and pleasant. Given that many of the people who helped maintain the *nongsŏng* were medical students and other young people who were supportive of SHARPS, it is not surprising that the atmosphere of the *nongsŏng* site looked like the well-maintained office of Banolim, which was staffed predominantly by women activist-organizers. Yet because the *nongsŏng* was an outdoor occupation at an active protest site, not an office, its influence on people's experience and subject formation was heightened as a field of activity in which subjectivity is shaped through the enactment of interconnected forms of expertise, experience, and authority alongside real-world experience in waging and enduring such an arduous fight at a *hyŏnjang*. Banolim's fight concluded after 1,020 days defending their *nongsŏng* site and around the same time as the KTX workers' struggle, in July 2018.

It is important to note that there are countless street-level protest camps throughout Seoul and throughout the country, with tents large and small for protesters, such as residents fighting displacement or eviction due to military base expansion or development projects, student activists demanding changes in policy, and so on. Occupations in general are understood as proactive acts of political-claims making, a way for individuals who feel they have been treated unjustly to take up space to assert their "right to the city."[23] But occupations—especially when they persist for long-term periods, like in the *nongsŏng* we discuss throughout this book—must be understood as more than an effort to be included in the web of protections that are theoretically guaranteed in a liberal democracy. Throughout our research, we have found that *nongsŏng* participants emphasize an intrinsically defensive nature of their spatial fights. They were not asking for rights that they did not have; they were defending their rights and demanding the restoration of what they lost, such as their jobs and livelihoods. In many cases, what was taken away from them was also immaterial, such as a sense of dignity and respect.

VERTICALITY OF PROTEST: HIGH-ALTITUDE OCCUPATIONS, OR *KOGONG NONGSŎNG*

High-altitude occupations, or *kogong nongsŏng*, are a variation of protesters occupying corporate offices, factories, or other buildings to demand a meeting, apology, or reinstatement. Protesters—most commonly workers—climb structures, like construction cranes, suspension bridges, billboards, industrial smokestacks, and transmission towers, where they cannot be easily forced out. This is considered one of the most dangerous forms of protest especially when they last a long time because of the physical and psychological toll it takes. High-altitude protesters sometimes engage in hunger strikes at the same time, living in isolation usually without electricity or running water and fighting extreme weather conditions. In some ways, there is a pragmatic dimension to the simultaneity of a hunger strike and a high-altitude occupation because it is exceedingly difficult to prepare food or use the toilet when occupying, for instance, a construction crane or a high-voltage transmission tower. In most contemporary cases, protesters who wage a high-altitude occupation do prepare for a worst-case scenario in which they would not have access to food and other basic necessities for an indefinite period of time. Regardless of advance planning, however, high-altitude-occupation protesters recount that no amount of preparation could match the hardship of actual experience. One cannot imagine the terror of living on the edge of death—as the well-known labor leaders Kim Jin-suk and Lee Chang-kun from Ssangyong Motor have shared through their memoirs—or the incredible stress of the constant fear of taking one wrong step.

Waging occupations from "prisons in the sky" (하늘감옥) performs the life-and-death stakes of precarity through a refusal to succumb. The perils of performing *kogong nongsŏng* are often evoked by numbers as "numerical measures of endurance" for how long protesters can endure such death-defying conditions.[24] The most well-known case is the 2011 309-day-long occupation of a construction crane by beloved labor activist Kim Jin-suk—discussed in detail in the following chapter—which took place eight years after her coworker hanged himself after 130 days isolated atop the very same crane. The following year, two autoworkers from the Hyundai Motor Nonregular Workers' Union (현대자동차 비정규직 노동조합) occupied the top of a high-voltage transmission tower in Ulsan across from company headquarters. That same year, two women who worked as private educational workers for JEI and were fighting for job reinstatement lived for 202 days on the rooftop of a Catholic church bell tower, also located across the street from the JEI company headquarters. Cha Gwang-ho (차광호; Ch'a Kwang-ho), a dismissed worker from Star Chemical / FineTek spent a record-setting 408 days on a forty-five-meter high factory chimney, after which he was given a short health check and then taken into police custody on July 9, 2015. Five years later, two of his coworkers, Hong Ki-t'ak (홍기탁) and Pak Chun-ho (박준호), broke Cha Gwang-ho's record after enduring 426 days atop a seventy-five-meters tall factory chimney.

The extreme isolation of individual protesters at high altitudes indexes their vulnerability in a broader context. There is a politics of height in their vertical location. According to Joan Kee, in landscape painting, artists feature images that emphasize verticality and draw the "eye upwards," evoking questions about "whether there is even ground to begin with."[25] Thus, as she argues, "the emphasis on verticality" is "not an optic on progress but on vulnerability." For one activist, this vulnerability is directly related to the pervasive level of police repression on the ground and the ability to elude capture by occupying high-altitude structures. At least while suspended in the sky, so to speak, protesters can delay the consequences of engaging in disruptive protest actions, which almost always elicit legal and punitive consequences. Eventually, however, one must come down. Regardless of whether the occupation is supported on the ground or waged in relative invisibility, protesters usually face two options: police or hospital, but eventually the police.

Since the 1990s, occupations have taken on this dangerous form with the proliferation of *kogong nongsŏng* during the 1990s and 2000s.[26] As discussed in chapter 2, this tactic has roots in the internal conflicts between militant rank-and-file members and more conservative union leaders during historic struggles waged by the predominantly male workforce in heavy industries during the late 1980s, but they have since spread quickly to become a standard part of the protest repertoire. "Kogong'yŏjido" (고공여지도) is a remarkable graphic map designed by Park Eunsun (박은선; Pak Ŭn-sŏn) of the urban artist-activist collective Listen to the City. The original map was published in tabloid-newspaper size, accompanied by a long list of the start dates and locations of 116 labor protests that took place between 1990 and 2015 on a diverse array of high-rise structures with accompanying data on the how tall the structures were in meters and the total number of days spent at perilous heights (see figure 2.1).

As the tactic has become more widespread and frequent, clearer boundaries are sought in considering the ideal role of movement supporters vis-à-vis *tangsaja* protesters, the workers themselves who are

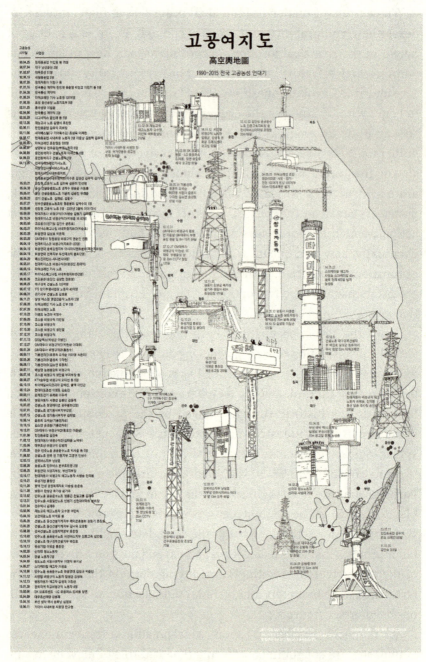

FIGURE 2.1. "Kogong'yŏjido," a map of high-altitude-occupation protests in Korea, 1990–2015. Reprinted with permission from Park Eunsun, Listen to the City.

directly affected. These discussions continue in both public venues and behind closed doors. The topic was the subject of a long interchange during our interview with Kim Hyejin. She expressed deep concern about the strategic value of high-altitude occupations, especially when such high-risk acts do not attract public attention or motivate internal movement support. She stated, "On some occasions, high-altitude occupations allow for diffusion and expansion of [workers' struggles] in society, but there are also a lot of occasions [of which workers] just come down after experiencing intense loneliness. Although we would do a lot of work in supporting high-altitude occupations, there are plenty of people who never even know that high-altitude occupations took place." The following case further illustrates an example of a high-altitude occupation that exacerbated the sense of isolation and abandonment that many workers experience. Kim Hyejin explained,

> A representative case involves two Pulmuone workers [of the Cargo Truckers' Solidarity Division of the Korean Public Service and Transport Workers' Union] who engaged in an occupation in Yŏido. The area in front of the National Assembly is a place where union suppression is particularly severe. Even though they went up, there was not much support there, and it did not generate much social awareness. Of course, a few people did come out to support, playing the *buk* [북] drums in front [of the building] and organizing marches. But these were pretty short and limited, with fleeting support and not a stable structure on the ground to support [workers above]. It was not easy for workers on top to bear their isolation. Their only option was to give up and come down since it was just too difficult to keep going.

Once workers come down, they face the consequences of engaging in an unauthorized occupation. The result can be utterly deflating and demoralizing. In one instance, workers ended a high-altitude occupation and took the bus to go home. In the 2016 case of the Pulmuone workers Kim Hyejin mentioned above, the protesters climbed down from a thirty-meter-high billboard tower in front of the National Assembly building they occupied for sixty-eight days, and one was taken into police custody, and another was taken to the hospital for urgent medical care. They were demanding increased rates for truckers' compensation (which had been frozen for twenty years), safer working conditions, including reduced work hours, and union recognition for truck drivers who were misclassified as "self-employed" because of their status as owner-operators.

Whether high-altitude occupations receive support or yield results, the risks that protesters take and the demands on protesters on the ground can leave everyone involved with enduring feelings of trauma and loss. Kim Hyejin poignantly discussed her own participation in one of the earliest long-term struggles in which KT nonregular contract workers staged a particularly hazardous high-altitude occupation that made her feel like she "wanted to die": "I was on the frontlines starting from dawn. . . . [F]rom the rooftop, . . . I saw the violence. I really wanted to die, and this isn't just an expression. From the high place where I was, I could have jumped to my death. I really could not bear it. After that, I suffered from severe trauma for about one or two years. That struggle continued for 517 days, but the shock from that day was very severe."

The KT contract workers' struggle she was referring to took place in 2001, when nearly two hundred workers occupied the Mokdong Chŏnhwaguk, now known as KT Mokdong Data Center. The occupation began predawn and ended in a mere five hours. It was depicted as an illegal and violent protest, and all the protesters who participated were arrested, even including a hospitalized worker, who was taken into police custody directly from an emergency room. The Kim Dae-jung administration's show of force in the exceedingly violent crackdown involving five units of special police ("riot police"), a ladder car, and even a helicopter unmistakably signaled a shift in the state's response to organized labor.

After sharing her traumatic experience, Kim Hyejin reflected on the implications of continuing to support *kogong nongsŏng*, especially for people like herself and the Korean Solidarity against Precarious Work. When support wavers due to various ongoing challenges, protest participants struggle to keep moving forward, to find ways to strengthen their collective power, and to stay resolved and not fall apart. Kim Hyejin has struggled to find more sustainable ways to continue her movement participation and shared the need to establish a clearer division between *tangsaja* and allies: "Establishing distance is very important. This doesn't exactly mean that we divide the roles, but in order to support *tangsaja* who are struggling to fight longer and more grueling fights to achieve a desired outcome, people around them should not become too emotionally invested because they might waver in their support. I have thought about this a lot—how important this is. So I put in a lot of effort into boundaries, but then it all went crumbling down for us during the *Sewol*-ferry protests."

As one of the cochairs of the *Sewol* Movement Committee, Kim Hyejin has played an integral role in supporting the struggles of bereaved parents and the pursuit to investigate the truth and justice for what happened in the tragic deaths of their children in April 2014. Bereaved *Sewol* parents did not wage a high-altitude occupation, but they staged numerous other protest forms and faced tremendous police repression and shocking public backlash—such as the infamous counterprotest event in which right-wing protesters mocked the *Sewol* protests by organizing a pizza party in front of *Sewol* parents who were on a hunger strike. Kim Hyejin did experience some relief during the mobilization of the Hanjin Hope Bus movement, in which she also played a central role, though this mobilization likewise faced intense police repression, including the violent use of police water cannons against *Sewol* protesters. As the named action chair, Kim Hyejin was held personally responsible for the legal and financial consequences of the protest actions, facing prison time and steep financial penalties for her role in both the *Sewol* and Hope Bus protest events. One important difference, however, was the relative spontaneous and festive nature of the Hope Bus movements, which we elaborate on in the following chapter.

HUNGER STRIKES

Hunger strikes are one of the most well-recognized and widely used protest forms, not only by labor- and social-movement activists in South Korea but in the global history of protest. While their historical origins can be traced to hunger-striking prisoners in Russia in the 1870s and 1880s, it is a form that has been replicated by different people in different contexts for different purposes over a century of struggle.[27] Hunger strikes consist of extraordinary acts of sacrifice and suffering by some of the most revered men in history—most famously Mahatma Gandhi, Nelson Mandela, Martin Luther King Jr., and Cesar Chavez. Not as well known is the history of radical women suffragists—as well as the anticolonial revolutionaries and exploited factory workers across Britain, Ireland, India, South Africa, and the United States—who turned to the "strategic power of fasting" to condemn policy brutality and state violence at the height of the British Empire.[28] In Korea, hunger strikes also represent a historical method of struggle by women against colonial domination, which dates back to the period of Japanese rule in Korea (1910–45) and the debilitating poverty and intolerable working and living conditions that women workers experienced in the context of colonial labor exploitation. Labor historian Hwasook Nam explains that "as early as 1923 female rubber workers in Seoul pioneered an *asa tongmaeng* (starving-to-death alliance)," and the news media's portrayal of explosive strikes in Pyŏngyang's rubber factories in the early 1930s reported a baffling "fixation" on "hunger strikes by women workers."[29]

In the contemporary period, hunger strikes represent a relatively predictable weapon of moral and political outrage for a range of aggrieved political actors, including striking workers whose collective labor rights have been undermined by their employment in informal and precarious jobs, as discussed in chapter 2. Typically considered a method of "last resort," striking workers turn to hunger strikes when other means have failed, escalating a localized labor dispute against unjust labor practices and retaliatory firings into a life-or-death drama. By refusing to eat, hunger strikers highlight the simultaneous frailty and resilience of the human body, yoking their willingness to fight for their beliefs to their capacity to endure a mortal crisis, continually pushing the limits of what the body and mind are capable of. "A protest like no other," as Nayan Shah puts it, the power of the hunger strike to move is both singular and plural.[30] The decision to start—and stop—a hunger strike rests solely with an individual protester, as do the damaging consequences of depriving oneself of basic sustenance for days, weeks, and even years afterward. Yet because the specter of death is the lever, rather than the goal, hunger strikes are inherently social. They create a microworld filled with different actors, who become pulled into the protest event as witnesses, supporters, bystanders, and antagonists. Thus, rather than function narrowly as a public-escalation strategy—with the penultimate aim of stoking moral outrage—hunger strikes might be more aptly understood as performative world-making practices. They assemble a cast of characters in a scenario that is "centered on the process of executing a particular action or task," which is the essence of the art of performance, to borrow from Joan Kee. In the case of the hunger strike, the task at hand is to keep the suffering body alive until the demand is met or until the conditions become untenable. Thus, to again borrow from Kee, it is "the image of the single, physical body as the crucible for thinking about the possibilities of action" that reconfigures the terrain of struggle.[31]

The ability of a hunger strike to induce a temporal crisis establishes the dramatic backdrop of a hunger strike as a performative world-making practice. Hunger strikes are commonly enacted to "restore faltering solidarity" amidst declining participation. Subjecting oneself to bodily harm and corporeal suffering elevates a political cause to a similar plane as religious conviction, indexing political will with spiritual devotion and unwavering commitment. Faith leaders with ties to progressive movements commonly heed the call for solidarity on moral and humanitarian grounds. In Korea, one can regularly see Buddhist monks and nuns, Protestant pastors and churchgoers, and Catholic priests, nuns, and lay members at sites where hunger strikes are taking place, reinforcing the worthiness of the struggle through visual presence, which sometimes include physically joining the hunger strike.

Yet Tilly reminds us that the power of a repertoire to forge collective solidarity is less about "who you are but what you do." In other words, religious actors may be more likely to join a hunger strike because of their identities and beliefs, but it is the enactment of the protest form itself that forges the basis of a shared connection in a broader repertoire of struggle as the enactment of "clusters of performances."[32]

While hunger strikes have often tipped the scales in a losing battle, the utility of the form is certainly not static. In Korean social movements, hunger strikes—as well as other protest forms that rely on the optic of the suffering body—are losing their power to persuade partly because its usage has become more routine. The prolonged refusal to eat has become so ubiquitous among some aggrieved actors that one leading civic activist characterized hunger strikes as "something anyone seems to be able to do these days." A labor activist echoed this sentiment, explaining to us in an interview that "a month-long hunger strike is pretty much the minimum standard these days." While both sentiments may seem exaggerated, activists are referring to the fact that extraordinarily long hunger strikes have become part of the "new normal." For example, Jiyul Sŭnim (지율 스님), a Buddhist nun of the Chogye Order, waged a ninety-nine-day-long hunger strike in 2005, relying on nothing but water and salt, to express an opposition to a tunnel construction project through Mount Ch'ŏnsŏng as part of the government's high-speed KTX rail-line construction.[33] She is credited as the most important figure in raising public consciousness about the damaging effects of large-scale capitalist infrastructure-development projects on environmental ecosystems, inspiring multiple solidarity actions around the country, including candlelight vigils and a fifty-kilometer Buddhist prostration procession to "Save Jiyul Sŭnim!" However, a few years later, when Kim So-yeon (김소연; Kim Soyŏn), a prominent leader of Kiryung Electronics Workers' Union, survived what turned out to be a ninety-four-day-long hunger strike in protest of repeated bad-faith negotiations there was hardly any public awareness. A key informant we spoke with at length remarked that neither the media nor the public "seemed to take notice, let alone offer encouraging words of support." While he was not directly involved in supporting the Kiryung unionists' fight, he had supported numerous hunger strikes in different contexts, including the forty-six-day hunger strike in 2014 by Kim Young-oh (김영오; Kim Yŏng-o), a bereaved father who lost his daughter Yu-min (유민) on the *Sewol* ferry. He was concerned that long-term hunger strikes have become "nothing special." He explained, "with so many hunger strikes extending beyond seventy or eighty days, we are confronted with an inflation-like situation, where we end up seeking longer and longer, more sensationalized durations."

The use of prolonged refusal to eat as a political weapon raises alarming questions for movement actors who witness the consequences of enduring this brutalizing protest form. Even though Jiyul Sŭnim could be considered a specialist in religious ascetism and one of the most revered environmental and Buddhist ecofeminist activists, for instance, activists were greatly concerned for the quality of her life after her hunger strike. The fact that she has survived multiple hunger strikes for a cumulative total of nearly 350 days over the course of the past fifteen years "must take a tremendous toll on her health," commented one activist we spoke with. "She is alive, but what is the state of her health?" he asked with concern. Hunger strikers indeed lead to long-term consequences. An activist we interviewed asked us if we had seen a mutual acquaintance, who had engaged in a long-term hunger strike many years ago: "Did you happen to see her there? With a broken finger and her arm in a plaster cast? Did you see her? She is always there at active protest sites. . . . Her finger won't heal. Nothing is ok or normal after something like that. Her body—it's constantly breaking and everything takes months to heal. How could it not? [Hunger strikes] literally eat away at one's own flesh and bones. It is a kind of fight we really should not do."

While most hospitals are not particularly adept at treating hunger strikers who are rushed for medical care, places such as the Green Hospital in Seoul have developed specific and specialized guidelines for nurses and doctors on how to safely treat patients for dehydration to prevent more permanent liver and kidney damage. The Green Hospital has a long history of treating workers, particularly people who were injured in workplace industrial accidents, and continues to be staffed by doctors and nurses who are familiar and supportive of progressive labor- and social-movement struggles. They are also known among activists for providing more affordable forms of routine health care, making the hospital facility a more welcoming place for movement activists. In a rather dramatic turn of events, Green Hospital now stands at the exact location where YH company offices used to be—the same YH that had laid off its women workers back in 1979, catapulting a historic labor struggle. It is no coincidence that Green Hospital provides specialized medical treatments and care for long-term protesters, especially for hunger strikers. One labor activist we interviewed explained, "The Green Hospital has guidelines for how long-term hunger strikers should start to eat and regain their health and what needs to be done to stabilize them and care for them. But regular hospitals have no idea, and, for example, they would prevent visitors. But the fact is, people who just endured isolation—they need to see people. They need to talk to people who support them, people who care about them. It is necessary. What places like the Green Hospital does is offer a space with all this understanding about the need for rest, comfort, and relationships."

As the power of hunger strikes to persuade the public and pressure the authorities diminishes, there can be a rift in opinion about the utility of the form. Supporting a protester's ability to survive extraordinary periods of starvation on the streets is different from hunger strikes that take place in institutional settings, such as prisons, where the matter of intervening could involve decisions made among medical staff and prison administrators to employ the violent use of force-feeding.[34] For movement supporters, their primary concern is that they cannot stop a hunger strike underway. For example, bereaved parents who lost their children in the *Sewol*-ferry tragedy initially planned a ten-day hunger strike in 2014, just months after the tragedy. But once they started, "it just kept on going and there was no way for us to stop them," an activist with the People's Committee for the *Sewol*-Ferry Tragedy explained. The collective hunger strike continued with only Yu-min's father, Kim Young-oh, remaining among the families, but there were politicians—including Moon Jae-in, who would become the president—artists, and ordinary citizens who participated in what is known as a solidarity hunger strike (*tongjo tansik*; 동조단식). When Kim Young-oh was rushed to the hospital after a total of forty-six days on hunger strike, hundreds of individuals and groups began to arrive in Kwanghwamun in a moving gesture of solidarity to keep the hunger strike going. At one point, over 250 participants joined the relay hunger strike per day, spending time with one another in the *Sewol*-ferry tents in Kwanghwamun.[35] It would be revealed over two years later, during the Candlelight Protests, that the president's office was very concerned about these hunger strikes. A memo leaked to the media showed that Kim Ki-ch'un (김기춘), who was then Park Geun-hye's chief of staff, described relay hunger strikes as a crime of aiding and abetting in suicide and a life-endangering act and that hunger strikes ought to be discouraged.[36] The Park Geun-hye administration would attempt to use this message framing to persuade media to turn the public opinion against hunger strikes and the swell of empathy for *Sewol*-ferry victims and survivors.

The arduous nature of engaging in long-term hunger strikes and the painstaking work entailed in supporting them have generated internal debates among movement activists as well. A longtime labor activist we spoke with raised these concerns: "Should we keep intentionally hurting ourselves to do this work? There are questions about this. As for me, I do not ever recommend hunger strikes. If the point in the first place is not to die, then we should not do hunger strikes. Why starve when you are trying to live?"

Another activist also shared her personal apprehensions with hunger strikes as a routinized protest form. She explained, "Hunger strikes negatively impact people a lot more than you might expect. Long-term hunger strikes, especially. There are a lot of people I know who still suffer from the trauma and side effects." Hunger strikes take a toll on the people who support hunger strikers as well. As someone who has supported almost every long-term hunger strike waged by precarious workers, including that of Kiryung Electronics Workers' Union leader Kim So-yeon, Kim Hyejin explained, "When a hunger strike passes ninety days, at that point, we have no idea what is going to happen to the person. But at the same time, from a human rights perspective, you cannot force them to stop. It's such a difficult situation. We can't really force anyone to stop, so the people on the ground—we feel the blood running dry in our own bodies as each day passes. We are filled with worry that something awful might happen."

Kim Hyejin's use of the expression about the "blood running dry" aptly captures the physicality of sentiments and emotions experienced by supporters, who also feel pushed to their breaking point as each passing day of a hunger strike means potential for a medical emergency or death. But like others, she is resigned in her ambivalence; "I just tell myself that we just need to figure out what we can do to support them and just do what we can," she said.

In contrast to high-altitude occupations, which are almost always enacted by *tangsaja*, or individuals raising their grievances as the directly affected party, hunger strikes often recruit participation from supporters and so-called external allies, though often for much shorter periods. There are even relay hunger strikes, or a chain of coordinated one-day hunger strikes in solidarity. While the activists we interviewed have supported and even participated in a number of hunger strikes, they emphasized that the driving force would always be the *tangsaja*, who would determine when and how a hunger strike would start and end.

BODIES IN SLOW MOTION: *SAMBOILBAE* AND *OCH'ET'UJI*

Buddhist prostration protests reflect dramatic and highly ritualized aspects of Korean workers' contemporary protest repertoire. Like hunger strikes, protest forms such as *samboilbae* and *och'et'uji*, which are adapted from Tibetan Buddhist traditions, subject one's body and mind to grueling conditions. *Samboilbae*, which literally means "three steps and one bow," turns an ordinary march into a slow-moving and physically strenuous procession. When performing *samboilbae*, protesters kneel to the ground face down with their forearms and forehead also touching the ground before rising and taking three large steps forward. This process is repeated over and over as protesters make their way across space, whether this takes place on congested urban streets or along the side of a roadway in the rural countryside. Even more grueling than *samboilbae* is *och'et'uji*, in which individual participants "throw" five points of their body onto the ground, including both knees, both elbows, and their forehead in a full horizontal spread, before getting up again and repeating the slow-moving procession. Both *samboilbae* and *och'et'uji* participants typically wear matching *minbok* (민복), traditional Korean peasant's clothing in all white, which progressively turns brown and black with dirt and grime while crawling on the streets over the course of hours and days. By engaging in such painstaking, slow, and grueling motion, protesters create religiously inflected spectacles of discipline and devotion.

Unlike hunger strikes, the use of Buddhist ritual practices as a form of protest has a recent history with an origin in Tibetan Buddhism. It was in 1992 that the Tibetan Buddhist ritual of *samboilbae* was first introduced to Korean Buddhists and subsequently adapted in 2001 as a nonviolent protest practice by Sukyŏng Sŭnim (수경스님), Sŏn (Zen) master at Silsangsa Temple in Namwon. A leader in the eco-Buddhist movement, Sukyŏng Sŭnim first performed *samboilbae* in the fight against ecologically destructive large-scale development projects around the country. The form became widely popularized in the spring of 2003 after he and three other interfaith leaders embarked on an epic three-hundred-kilometer, sixty-five-day-long procession across the country to protest the proposed Saemangŭm Restoration Project (새만금 간척 사업) and the associated destruction of the Saemangŭm wetlands.[37] In 2005, Korean farmers used *samboilbae* to make an impactful impression in Hong Kong by showing that Korean anti–World Trade Organization delegates were not violent, unlawful protesters as they had been depicted by the mainstream media. Protesting workers began adapting the practice as a regular part of their protest repertoire in the early 2000s and then took it one step further by engaging in *och'et'uji*, the full-body-prostration ritual performed by the most devout Tibetan Buddhist monks on their way to honor the Dalai Lama.

As performance, *samboilbae* and *och'et'uji* stretch our sense of time and space, collapsing the distinctions between past and present and focusing attention on the body and the ground as spaces of vulnerability and exposure. They juxtapose the slow time of ritual with the accelerated pace of economic development and urban transformation. One of the best known *och'et'uji* was waged by Kiryung Electronics workers in 2014, which we discuss in further detail in chapter 4, and led by the predominantly female Kiryung Electronics Workers' Union to mark the end of their twelve-year-long struggle. It was the second time they had engaged in this grueling protest performance. In February 2012, Kiryung Electronics Workers' Union leaders had participated in a sixty-seven-kilometer *och'et'uji* with fifty other unionists that lasted thirteen days to show solidarity for protesting workers from the Ssangyong Motor struggle.[38]

In 2016, protesting workers from the Yoosung Union (유성기업 노동조합) referenced the solidaristic nature of their ritualized protest procession when explaining why they chose to embark on a five-day-long *och'et'uji* in their long and dramatic Facebook post on November 10, 2016:

> In December 2014, Kiryung workers, who had been fighting for ten years, took to the streets again. . . . They wore white *minbok* and engaged in *och'et'uji*, marching with their bare bodies as snow fell on them. . . . On the fifth day, the police brutally blocked their crawling and stopped their cries in front of the statue of Admiral Yi Sun-sin [이순신 장군] in Kwanghwamun Square. It was indeed a cruel day. . . . Following the Kiryung workers were the workers of Ssangyong Motor. . . . fired and pushed to the streets by employers who cited an "impending crisis" and "financial difficulties for the company" . . . workers who climbed to the rooftop and donned white *minbok* to crawl on the ground. It was both gratifying and bittersweet for them to have to aim high to the rooftop and low to the ground in order to get people to pay attention. . . . That January night, which was said to be the worst cold snap in history, they endured ten degrees below zero in just their *minbok* and lap blankets. They had to spend a night lying on the ground, which was colder than ice, covered in cigarette butts and gum. . . . And now, it is the Yoosung workers.[39]

By explicitly referencing a litany of previous struggles and the protesters' corporeal vulnerability to both the elements and state violence, Yoosung workers emphasized how shared memories of embodied suffering and resilience forged cultures of solidarity.

Importantly, in departure from the labor-activist performances of *samboilbae* and *och'et'uji*, which demonstrate solidarity and discipline in coordinated movement, disability-justice activists have on occasion used protest forms to demonstrate the impossibility and inaccessibility of mobility. Solidarity for the Right to Mobility (이동권 연대), for example, has become notorious for engaging in protest strategies such as blocking roadways and occupying subway stations. Their disruption tactics are simple yet controversial: wheelchair users and other mobility-impaired activists engage in direct actions to draw attention to just how dangerous and difficult it is for nonnormative bodies to access public transit. In January 2001, a newly installed wheelchair lift at the Oido Station near Seoul failed catastrophically while carrying an elderly couple in their seventies. The couple plummeted twenty-three feet to the ground below, killing the wife and seriously injuring her husband. This tragic inci-

FIGURE 2.2. Yoosung unionists perform *och'et'uji*, November 2016. Photo by Jennifer Jihye Chun.

dent compelled disability-justice activists to launch a dramatic course of action. Activist Park Kyoung-seok (박경석; Pak Kyŏng-sŏk), a longtime leader of the group Solidarity against Disability Discrimination (전국장애인차별철폐연대) and a familiar face in the social-movement landscape, recounted in an interview that he was inspired by photos of protest strategies deployed in the 1980s by US disability rights activists who crawled under Greyhound buses to denounce the lack of accessibility and accommodation for the mobility impaired. Park decided to climb down from a subway platform to occupy the train tracks in what became the first of countless such protests. Joined by a growing number of disabled individuals and advocates, he has continued to protest and enlist public support by occupying buses and subways, building enduring tent encampments, and waging long-term hunger strikes.[40]

In 2004, seventy-six disability rights activists were arrested after occupying the subway tracks near Seoul City Hall, some even draping heavyweight metal chains around their bodies to resist removal. Two years later, in 2006, forty-nine activists with severe disabilities participated in a collective head-shaving ritual and crawled across the Hangang Bridge in what was intended as a *samboilbae*, blocking traffic for several hours to demand increased government support for disability assistance and support services. As recently as early 2022, disability rights activists have confronted conservative lawmakers by halting or slowing subway operation, sometimes drawing the ire of unsympathetic passengers. Protests like these have yielded some results, however limited; it may even be said that no policy would have changed on its own without pressure from activists. Yet state budgets are still woefully inadequate, and promises for elevators and accessible buses remain largely unfulfilled. Nonetheless, the disability-justice movement has secured its place at the center of a broad coalition of minoritarian and human rights advocates, refusing to normalize discrimination and inaccessibility. As activist-scholar Kim To-hyŏn (김도현) writes, "[Those] who hold power in society today are individuals presumed to have so-called 'normal' bodies, and the world is planned, constructed, and run with these 'norms.'"[41] Disability justice activism, at its core, challenges the violence of such normativity in public policy, in the built environment, and in protest forms.

Labor activists, like Kim Hyejin, acknowledge that the purpose of engaging in these ritualistic performances is to foster solidarity and underscore the importance of supporting workers to continue fighting, even when their bodies take a heavy toll. After joking that the main reason she participates is because of peer pressure, Kim took a more serious tone as she explained, "Beyond the issue of its religiosity, these protest forms show the urgency of *pijŏnggyujik* workers' struggles. Honestly, the majority of the time we do *samboilbae*, it's because *pijŏnggyujik* workers come up with it and ask us to join. Their bodies are already so damaged from doing long-term occupation protests, so of course we ask, Must they do this too? But still, it does demonstrate how urgent the situation is. They are trying to do absolutely everything they can, so it's not up to us to assess what's good or bad." Perhaps because of their undeniably religious inflections, *samboilbae* and *och'et'uji* seem to elicit especially thoughtful and nuanced reflections from faith-based participants. This is true for not only Buddhist participants but also the significant number of Catholic progressives who collaborate with Buddhist social-justice activists. Catholic activist nuns, such as our key informant Sister Maria (a pseudonym)—who is central in subsequent chapters of this book—became frequent participants in interfaith *samboilbae* since they started taking place frequently in the early to mid-2000s. Sister Maria described the experience as follows: "For me, the feeling I get while doing [*samboilbae*] is that it makes me humble. It's about lowering yourself on the ground, you know? It's about aspirations too. Each and every time you take a bow and get low to the ground—every one of those bows are an act of prayer. You yearn and long for those prayers to be realized." Her discussion echoed what Father Moon Gyu-hyeon (문규현 신부; Mun Kyu-hyŏn)—one of the most recognizable Catholic activist-priests today—wrote about *samboilbae* as an act of prayer. Reflecting on the *samboilbae* he had carried out in 2003 alongside the aforementioned Buddhist activist Sukyŏng Sŭnim against the destruction of the Saemangŭm wetlands, Father Moon wrote, "I walked and bowed to

108   CHAPTER 2

wash away the greed and foolishness and anger inside me. I repented for my part in the destruction of the natural environment. And I prayed for peace for all lives in Saemangŭm and all the world. Ardently and fervently."[42]

By lowering oneself while completely outstretched on the ground, Tibetan Buddhists reportedly combine aerobic exercise, which is beneficial for both the physical body and the mind, and spiritual practice.[43] Humility is part of the purpose as practitioners prepare themselves to take refuge in the enlightened body and mind of a religious leader such as the Buddha. Sara E. Lewis explains that Tibetan Buddhists also engage in this ritual-prostration practice as a temporal practice. By engaging in this meditational practice, practitioners cultivate a kind of spaciousness that enables them to "resist the chronicity" of a single cycle story of trauma, suffering, and "negative emotions such as fear, anger, and resentment."[44]

Sister Maria also emphasized the ways in which *samboilbae* produces strong and "sticky bonds" (끈끈한 유대) among protest participants by creating the conditions for a broader collective to share the burden of protesting. The physicality of enduring a grueling experience together, rather than leaving a couple people to bear it on their own, becomes a strong source of strength. She explained, "It is really difficult. Your legs hurt so much that you can barely stand up. But sometimes, I still went back to work right afterward or to another protest site. But it's not about feeling good about yourself. It's about sharing the burden, . . . so that the burden isn't shouldered by just a couple of people. Someone has to keep sharing the burden, even to just add one more pair of hands or one more set of shoulders." The religious symbolism of *samboilbae* and *och'et'uji* gets intensified by the participation of religious clergy, whether they are dressed as Buddhist monks or Catholic nuns or priests or Protestant ministers. Some Catholic nuns choose not to do the full bow to the ground because it is difficult with the floor-length tunics that are part of their habits. Nonetheless, their adaptation of the ritual adds to the symbolic power of the scene. As nuns stand and bow their heads in silence, the impact of reverence is not diminished. The power of the ritual action is further enhanced by the relative silence. Unlike mass rallies and strikes, which tend to be filled with loud sounds of chanting and amplified speeches and music, *samboilbae* and *och'et'uji* performances are largely quiet, marked only by periods of intermittent drumbeats. These somber scenes contrast the assumption that protests are inherently raucous, chaotic, or dangerous such that one might expect a violent clash with riot police. The ritual itself and the kinds of reflection and contemplation that it fosters do not end with the conclusion of the protest. Memories of how the strength of a larger group helped manage the pain and suffering of the protest itself continue to remind protesters, such as Sister Maria, of the power of solidarity—a power that is cultivated through action rather than words alone.

PUBLIC RELIGION: PRAYERS ON THE SIDEWALK

Repertoire innovation occurs in part by adapting a form from one space to another, modifying a form used for one purpose to serve a different purpose on another occasion. Ritual practices with strong religious inflections, such as prayer prostration and fasting, have been adapted in a variety of ways to help counter fading levels of commitment or public interest. Prayer services at active sites of protest are one such example—an effective ritual for religious leaders to impart a greater sense of urgency and moral worthiness. This can be especially important to protest sites weakened by fatigue, dwindling numbers of participants, or fractured unity. Performing liturgical services on the streets, rather than inside church walls, also helps amplify the morally charged displays of public solidarity through contemplative and ritual practices, creating spaces for protest participants to take stock of their protest experience and take a moment to reflect.

Like the prostration rituals *samboilbae* and *och'et'uji*, the Christian prayer service has taken on a modular and flexible quality. Protesters have adapted the ritual form to their needs, schedules, and goals. In the Korean Christian tradition, the prayer service provides an occasion for the faithful to assemble as a community. Typically, Protestant prayer services are held on Sundays at church, but Wednesday-evening services and daily predawn services are also common practices in Korea. Predawn prayer services are especially interesting in part because they combine devotional practices with early-morning physical activity, reinforcing certain cultural sensibilities, such as the value of revitalizing the body and spirit by taking early-morning hikes in the mountains.[45] They also draw from the long-standing practice of the Buddhist predawn prayer ceremony of *yebul* (예불), in which practitioners perform 108 bows (백팔배), repeatedly standing and kneeling to bow in place.

Prayer services have been used heavily by progressive and social-justice-oriented religious actors in South Korea, though there is also a history of conservative and right-wing political protests that draw on the power of public prayer. The Myŏngdong Cathedral of Seoul was the central site of vibrant solidarity actions by leaders of the JOC (Jeunesse ouvrière chrétienne, or Young Christian Workers) Korea (한국가톨릭노동청년회) as early as 1958, when the religious organization held a "'fighter' (*t'usa* [투사]) declaration ritual of nine female nurses at a Mass."[46] Throughout the 1960s and 1970s, JOC Korea as well as other progressive Christian organizations, including the Christian Academy (한국크리스찬아카데미) and the Urban Industrial Mission (UIM; 도시산업선교), were actively involved in supporting a workforce of predominantly young women recruited to work in the country's rapidly expanding yet hyperexploitative export-oriented industrial factories.[47] Kim Hyejin, whose own start in activism, after attending college, was in small and medium factories, described the UIM mission in the urban industrial neighborhood of Yŏngdŭngp'o as the "cradle of the labor movement in Korean society in the 1970s and 1980s." She shared an amusing joke: "Called Urban Industrial Mission, or TOSAN (도산) for short in Korean, the [UIM] was a group that quite literally birthed the labor movement. We used to say that when companies meet TOSAN, they are going to become *tosan* (도산)."[48]

Progressive religious organizations supported the growth of democratic unions through a variety of strategies, including operating night schools for workers and fostering political circles to promote radical consciousness raising, which are well documented by Hwasook Nam in her history of labor struggles among female factory workers in the twentieth century.[49] Organizations such as JOC Korea, UIM, and the Christian Academy not only strengthen the formation of a radical multisectoral movement sphere that explicitly criticizes the dehumanizing and polarizing forces of industrial capitalist development but also contribute to the development of a vibrant protest repertoire that infuses religious ritual with moral and political critique. For example, after holding explicitly political prayer services, Catholic priests might lead ritualized marches out of the cathedral and into the streets. They also frequently visit sit-ins of striking workers and issue public-solidarity statements to condemn labor exploitation, police repression, sexual assault, gender inequality, and authoritarian-state violence.

While progressive religious organizations continue to be actively involved in supporting issues related to economic and social injustice, their attention to unionized workers underwent a notable shift in the early to mid-1990s. As the organized labor movement grew in both numbers and formal authority, groups like the UIM shifted their focus to the burgeoning migrant-workers' movements, given the extreme exploitation they faced as "industrial trainees" during the 1990s. Kim Hyejin also attributes the distance between the church and the labor movement to the latter's numerical and organizational growth, explaining, "At one point in the past, the church did play a really huge role and had such close relationships [with workers]. But the labor movement began to set some distance between them and religion after labor unions started organizing and growing with the emergence of KCTU."

One area of the labor movement that church and other Protestant groups remain actively involved in concerns precariously employed and laid-off workers. The use of protest repertoires—such as hunger strikes, Buddhist prostration rituals, and high-altitude occupations—draws and secures the attention of movement-oriented religious leaders, who view these protest forms as a sign of broader struggles against social injustice and oppression.

One of the most important struggles that religious organizations have actively supported involved laid-off workers from Ssangyong Motor, who reached out to CPAJ for support in maintaining their long-term struggle against unjust layoffs and union repression. As discussed earlier, twenty-four workers associated with the Ssangyong Motor Union had died by the summer of 2013—a number that would grow to surpass thirty by the time a final agreement was reached between the Ssangyong Motor Union and management in September 2018. The protesting workers first sought CPAJ's help in identifying an alternate location for their long-term protest camp. Since their seventy-seven-day factory occupation was violently dispersed in 2009, laid-off workers who continued their fight had maintained a long-term protest camp, which began to include a mourning altar and twenty-four-hour vigil burning incense in commemoration of their fallen comrades. They had been chased out of various protest locations, including their own factory gates, not only by employer-hired thugs and police but also by some of their own union comrades in what had become one of the most bitterly fought and violent internal conflicts within the labor movement. Laid-off Ssangyong Motor workers who continued to protest often had "no choice but to send many requests" to movement allies, including religious leaders, to urge them to come and join their protests. Desperate to find a location where they could avoid constant harassment, they settled on the area in front of Taehanmun, the front gate of Tŏksu Palace, located across from the city hall building in central Seoul. This is where, as we discussed earlier in this chapter, laid-off Ssangyong Motor workers' encampment would be replaced by semipermanent concrete planters.

Under the nation's Assembly and Demonstration Act (ADA; 집회 및 시위에 관한 법률), religious public assemblies are not subject to the same onerous registration requirements placed on other public assemblies, especially when it comes to protesting workers. When discussing the unique circumstances of the Taehanmun encampment, one labor activist explained,

> The only reason we could even access Taehanmun to begin with was because it was a religious event [*laughs*]. We couldn't have set up a *nongsŏng* or held a rally if it wasn't a religious event. You can't register as a rally either in front of Taehanmun. On top of that, you know what companies do? They register for a rally in front of their own company for days on

end so that no one else can use the space. And in that case, there is no way for workers to protest in front of the company anymore. But there is an exception to these public assembly laws—religious event. So we gather as a religious event. You might say that we use religion as a cover.

On the one hand, the laid-off Ssangyong Motor workers could not safely and lawfully access the space in front of the company, but on the other hand, moving the protest site to Seoul and choosing the palace gates certainly offered additional meaning and significance. As Jisoo M. Kim discusses, commoners during the Chosŏn period (1392–1910) approached the palace to express grievances and make emotional appeals by beating a petition drum on palace grounds, a "legal channel to approach the king [that] was quickly adopted as a public stage by subjects of a broad population."[50] The organizers were certainly aware of this tradition and meaningful location as they set up their protest encampment there, though the palace is no longer a site of petitioning the king.

CONCLUSION: HISTORY AND MEMORY

This chapter has examined the development of a dramatic repertoire by labor- and social-movement actors in South Korea by focusing on the embodied, interactional, and ritual aspects of performing protest. The cultural and symbolic resources used to strengthen displays' moral worthiness and political commitment are fundamentally shaped by the reproduction of collective memory about past histories of popular struggle. However, when recognizing the "imprint" that past histories have on contemporary protest practices, we also have emphasized how certain historical traditions have persisted in the context of structural change. We see historically recurring struggles not because the conditions of inequality and oppression remain entirely unchanged but because the rhetoric of militant struggles stresses the persistent continuity of unequal and unjust conditions. It is also not because protesters remain stuck in the past when it comes to protest practices. Protest repertoires *have* changed—the range, style, and content of protest performances have dramatically diversified over time as a result of the democratization of public space and the expansion of the freedom of assembly under liberal political administration. Digitized media platforms and online communities help disseminate information about culturally diverse protest practices around the world, which have further enriched the protest repertoires of labor- and social-movement actors. Examples of new forms are plenty, such as the use of Post-it Notes to express an outburst of public sentiments; occupation of public space through non-confrontational and nonviolent actions, such as knitting circles or silent book-reading actions; or the use of popular music and popular culture in acts of political defiance. Yet there are still unmistakable legacies of protest that harken back to earlier periods of authoritarian violence and capitalist injustice in South Korea.

As we have pointed out in discussions of specific protest forms and tactics, memories of the past routinely surface when protesters and movement supporters brainstorm for ways to amplify their protest actions, especially in the face of prolonged neglect and intensified backlash. Often, references are drawn from repressive decades of authoritarian rule under Park Chung Hee (박정희; Pak Chŏng-hŭi) (1961–79) and the rich aesthetic and cultural practices that developed in conjunction with the *minjung* movement in the spheres of poetry, literature, popular theater, visual art, and performance art, as we highlighted earlier.[51] Performance art itself first emerged as an art-making practice at a time in South Korea when the "viability of outright protest or critique" seemed impossible.[52] By juxtaposing the slow time of ritual with the fast pace of frenzied capitalism, performance artists connect the regime's extreme restrictions on people's daily lives with their relentless pursuit of economic growth and industrialization, regardless of the costs to human life. Present-day protest performances of hunger strikes, Buddhist prostration processions, and street prayer protests echo these earlier protests.

Collective memory also reaches farther back, to the period of annexation and formal colonization during Japanese imperial rule (1910–45), which was a time in which the "cultural left" grew in size and significance, according to Sunyoung Park.[53] Writers, artists, poets, and performers all contributed to the formation of a collective political subject that fundamentally critiqued the dehumanization and exploitation of the poor and socially weak under highly unequal capitalist systems and repressive structures of colonial governance. Intense legal repression under Japan's brutal colonial police state kept left political movements from building active political parties and organized labor movements. Artists and writers instead focused on the realm of cultural production and the formation of an idea of the "people" as a collective political subject. As such, images of physical pain and corporeal suffering figured prominently in the representation of figures that embodied the "legitimate subject" of revolutionary history. Sunyoung Park explains that "a damaged body in leftist literary works was not emblematic of a laborer's mental disability or benightedness but rather symbolized the material conditions of him and his social class. By putting on display the abject bodies of laborers, leftist narratives dramatically portrayed the human cost of the capitalist exploitation and abuse resulting from the accelerated modernization of Korean society."[54]

The practice of traveling to the dynastic capital and seeking higher ground dates as far back as the Chosŏn period (1392–1910). As we discussed in the previous section, Jisoo M. Kim explains that commoners who felt wronged by the discretionary power and corruption of their local magistrates would travel to the capital to make their case "through a display of emotions" in front of the sovereign in a practice known as *sanggyŏng* (상경), a form of which continues to this day. Although there was no formal appeals process in the courts, commoners could directly petition the king. The process involved striking a large drum at the gates of the royal palace and then occupying the space in hopes of garnering a response. Petitioners innovated this practice during high-profile public events, such as royal processions through the streets of Seoul. In order to attract the attention of the sovereign, petitioners would find high ground, in the form of a building rooftop or the top of a hill, and then loudly proclaim their grievances as the king's procession passed by. Interestingly, Jisoo Kim explains that women petitioners were more likely to engage in these practices. Grievances often involved issues of inheritance denied or compensation owed after the death of one's husband or father because the system of Confucian patriarchy involves rigid gender hierarchies, and women who lost an economic provider encountered more extreme difficulties in their basic livelihood.[55] Violations around death rites also inflamed grievances, since children of the deceased were responsible for the well-being of their deceased parents in the afterlife. We see compelling evidence of continuity in contemporary protest performances in pursuit of justice and in defense of one's livelihood and dignity.

We highlight these examples of past historical struggles not to assume a direct lineage of the past to the present or to assert ideas about the cultural uniqueness of Korean protest traditions. Rather, taking cues from Michael Rothberg, we have examined how protest performances and rituals produce "multidirectional memory" as part of the rich and complex interior life of protest repertoires not as "already-established groups" but "through continual reconstruction."[56] We have analyzed how the enactment of ritualized protest performances generates "powerful social, political and psychic forces that articulate themselves in every act of remembrance," facilitating "dynamic transfers" across divergent spaces, times, and people.[57] Time, place, and scale have fostered the development of a shared vocabulary that links protesters and movement supporters to each other and with the past, shaping the cultivation of protest forms through the repeated enactment of morally charged protest performances and rituals.

3 CONJURING SOLIDARITY

> To be frank, how big of a media splash can a prayer protest
> or a religious rally create? What difference can it make
> toward winning? It's not just about that. It's about feeling,
> "Ah, there are people who stand by our side, continuously
> and persistently." That is what gives us so much strength.
>
> —Kim Seungha, KTX branch union leader

> Conjuring is a particular form of calling up and calling out the
> forces that make things what they are in order to fix and transform
> a troubling situation. As a mode of apprehension, conjuring merges
> the analytical, the procedural, the imaginative and the effervescent.
>
> —Avery Gordon, *Ghostly Matters*

AS WE DISCUSSED in the previous chapter, South Korean workers have turned to a dramatic and ritualized protest repertoire to bring attention to the extent to which they have been made disposable by the death-dealing forces of neoliberal labor precarity and to demonstrate their refusal and resistance against such treatment. In this chapter, we examine three ethnographic cases of women workers fighting precarity to illuminate how protest repertoires cultivate embodied spaces of solidarity, eliciting extraordinary acts of support, such as mobilizing emergency-response networks and providing critical lifesaving care as well as simply *being present*—whether physically or virtually—to make sure someone is not alone in their fight. As Kim Seungha noted in the epigraph, an important source of strength during their struggle was the support from allies who "continuously and persistently" stood by their side, reassuring them that they were not alone in their fight, especially as the years dragged on and on. She was particularly grateful to the multifaith group of religious leaders who became one of their most important allies during the last few years of their protracted struggle.

We theorize solidarity in this book as a political affect and an ethical orientation, not simply a tactic to increase leverage or media attention or demonstrate like-mindedness. We argue that protest repertoires *conjure solidarity*, in Avery Gordon's sense of "conjuring" as "calling up and calling out the forces that make things what they are." The idea of conjuring here refers not to an invocation of a spell or an apparition but rather a recitation of a shared but flexible script that "merges the analytical, the procedural, the imaginative and the effervescent." The women workers' protest repertoires conjure solidarity in order "to fix and transform a troubling situation," as Gordon puts it, building spaces of survival and social change.[1] Affect is central to conjuring solidarity in ways that are both extraordinary and ordinary. The production of "ordinary affects" reminds protest participants that they are part of evolving and ongoing struggles despite experiencing continual setbacks and repeated failures.[2] They also reveal the uneven gendered terrain of conjuring solidarity in the context of masculinist protest repertoires, revealing the ways in which solidarity as a political affect operates between and across, rather than in spite of, difference. By foregrounding the significance of political affect and gendered embodiment, this chapter shows how feminist political praxis redefines notions of collective solidarity beyond unitary notions of likeness and relatability to encapsulate the lived experience of difference and minoritization as the basis for transformative social change.

Through a focus on the way political affects circulate and gain traction across diverse bodies, causes, and sites, this chapter illuminates how solidarity works as a catalytic force through and beyond the space-times of individual protest events. We build on the relational concept of space advanced by feminist geographer Doreen Massey to understand how space operates as a "product of interrelations" that are "always in process" and "under construction," rather than a "container for always already constituted identities," be they about class, gender, race, or other differences that matter.[3] A spatial praxis of relational power recognizes the political possibilities of "connections yet to be made" and interactions "yet to flower," even when overdetermined by historically sedimented relations of power, inequality, and domination. This approach allows us to appreciate the ways in which social practices can exceed intention, fostering new ways of being and becoming that are rooted not merely in legal criteria and institutional recognition but in the social interactions and mutual interdependencies that sustain everyday life. The protest repertoires we examine may appear to be extraordinary and spectacular—and they often are—but close attention to the felt and embodied practices that produce and sustain them also highlight the transformative power of "ordinary space" in reconstructing the social.[4]

To understand how solidarity is conjured as a political affect rather than simply a strategic posture of unity, this chapter focuses on Kim Jinsuk's 309-day high-altitude occupation against Hanjin Heavy Industries and Construction (한진중공업; Hanjin hereafter) in 2011–12, the Kiryung Electronics Workers' Union and their nine-year fight in 2005–14, and the KTX train attendants' twelve-year struggle against the Korea Railroad Corporation in 2006–18. These cases vary in terms of the women workers' age, educational background, prior experience with unions and political activism, and tenure as labor-movement leaders. The gendered politics of their protests may not always be apparent in explicit terms of self-identity as women workers, but they are evident in the sustained expressions of mutuality, resiliency, and collective care. We draw on interviews conducted with key union leaders and a rich archive of published firsthand accounts and news reports to show how shared protest repertoires build relationalities among workers and supporters and enable them to survive against prolonged union retaliation. Two overarching questions guide our discussion in this chapter: How do protesters conjure solidarity as a political affect, and in the process, what kinds of affinities and relationalities are forged between disparate individuals and events across time and space?

CONJURING SOLIDARITY, KIM JIN-SUK, 2011–12

Many stories about extraordinary acts of protest waged by South Korean workers begin with Kim Jin-suk.[5] On January 6, 2011, Kim climbed thirty-five meters (115 feet) and occupied the small control box perched atop Crane 85 at the Yŏngdo Shipyard in Pusan. She was fifty years old at the time, having been fired at the age of twenty-six for union activity and working since then as a union activist. For ten consecutive months on the crane, Kim Jin-suk lived without running water and endured extreme weather conditions in protest of mass layoffs by Hanjin, a shipbuilding and logistics conglomerate. Support teams soon gathered on the ground as part of a nationwide Hope Bus solidarity mobilization, but alone up on the crane, Kim Jin-suk lived dangerously close to the edge of death, unable to forget that the "difference between life and death is only a centimeter," in her own words.[6]

A typical trait of high-altitude occupations is that workers choose sites that are near the target of their struggles, such as an industrial smokestack on company grounds. In Kim Jin-suk's case, Crane 85 held an especially poignant significance, as it was the site where her friend and fellow Hanjin union leader Kim Ju-ik (김주익; Kim Chu-ik) had ended his life eight years prior. From the outset, Kim Jin-suk conjured a connection between Kim Ju-ik's life and hers, seeking to render "visible, what [was] already there: the ghosts, the images, the stereotypes."[7]

Let us briefly contextualize what took place on Crane 85 eight years prior, in 2003. Hanjin union leader Kim Ju-ik occupied the crane to protest against a round of workforce-reduction policies at Hanjin, a shipbuilding and logistics conglomerate, which had been relocating parts of its production process overseas since the early 2000s. Hanjin had become well known in the 1970s for providing logistics for the US military and its war efforts in Vietnam and for winning lucrative contracts in Saudi Arabia and Kuwait in the so-called Middle East boom.[8] Throughout the 1980s and "following what has become known as the Great Workers' Struggle of 1987," labor historian Hwasook Nam writes, "shipbuilding workers came to occupy a central place in the newly empowered autonomous union movement," of which the Hanjin union was a leading force.[9] But this came at a great cost. For his work as a union leader, Kim Ju-ik faced exorbitant punitive financial penalties and was charged with the criminal act of "obstruction of business." The increasingly common practice of employers bringing civil lawsuits against individual union leaders led to devastating consequences, including the seizure of Kim Ju-ik's private property and the suspension of his union benefits.[10]

Kim Ju-ik initially occupied Crane 85 to boost union morale and force a breakthrough in negotiations with the management, but when the 2,500 unionists rallying with him below the crane started to dwindle to barely a hundred, he became despondent. On the 129th day on the crane, Kim Ju-ik hanged himself with the same rope that was used to lift food provisions up to him. He left behind a note that contained these sobering lines: "Comrades, regardless of what form my death may take, Crane 85 will be where my corpse lies. Until we win this fight, the crane will be my grave."[11] He was forty years old, having worked at Hanjin since he was just nineteen. Two weeks after Kim Ju-ik's death, his close friend and union comrade Kwak Chae-kyu (곽재규) also died by political suicide, jumping into the water off the dock by Crane 85 and joining the growing list of political martyrs (열사) associated with worker struggles at Hanjin.

A well-attended public funeral commemorated the deaths of these two union leaders. In a dramatic ceremony, one coffin was lowered from the top of the crane to symbolize Kim Ju-ik's death, and another coffin was raised from the dock to symbolize Kwak Chae-kyu's death. Both coffins were wrapped in the flags of the KCTU. The emotional, funereal pageantry was intended to remind the living that they had an obligation to continue the fight, no matter how arduous the challenges or perilous the consequences. In what Eunjung Kim calls "necro-activism," the presence of these coffins enacted "interdependent relations to continue resistance," with the "protest sites becom[ing] the sites of a wake that does not end."[12]

As part of the Hanjin union leadership, Kim Jin-suk personally knew both men and was herself already a well-known activist, with a track record of delivering heart-wrenching political speeches. She took the stage before three thousand grief-stricken workers and union activists at this political funeral to deliver an epic eulogy and a rousing call for solidarity. "Across centuries, across geography, across occupations and industries and across generations, capital has certainly proven the strength of its alliances. What about us? How strong is our solidarity?" she implored. "We cannot win against capital if we turn away from precarious workers, the disabled, farmers, and women. . . . [Capital does not] win because they are right. We break because we are not in solidarity."[13]

Eight years later, in 2011, Kim Jin-suk would again emphasize the urgency of solidarity as a transhistorical force, and the possibility that her fallen comrade's suffering and sacrifice might be forgotten created an important pressure point for her. After she embarked on her own high-altitude occupation, she wrote a letter from the top of Crane 85 and said, "I am sitting where Ju-ik had sat, sleeping where he had slept, and seeing the world that he saw while he was alive."[14] In another dispatch, she wrote, "Like a caged animal, [Ju-ik] had paced back and forth on top of this crane, worried about how many comrades would show up that day."[15] For Kim Jin-suk, the decision to reenact Kim Ju-ik's occupation tapped into the power of the protest site—the particular geographical location and physical environment as well as the bodily deprivation and emotional isolation involved in long-term occupation. Some Hanjin unionists opposed what they regarded as sensationalistic and overly antagonistic protest action and opted instead to accept the terms of concessions offered by Hanjin. But Kim Jin-suk was adamant that Kim Ju-ik's example compelled her to keep fighting as a way to remember his legacy and foster new connections. Feminist labor scholar Jiwoon Yulee describes this dynamic as haunted by a kind of necromancy, with Kim Jin-suk "mourning her dead comrades but filled with an aspiration for a restored life."[16] In this aspirational and life-affirming vision, Kim Jin-suk emphasized the need to demonstrate solidarity with the precariously employed—that is, *pijŏnggyujik* workers—who were leading some of the most militant struggles at the time yet experienced profound abandonment and betrayal, especially by other unionized workers.

We trace these stories of relationality and interdependency partly because high-altitude occupations are sometimes discussed as solitary endeavors, staged by one or two workers who respond to a major setback through escalation. Such extraordinary acts, however, cannot be sustained without the essential support of others on the ground (see chapter 1). In fact, without a solidarity team in place to keep vigil and keep the protest in the public eye, even the most dramatic protests can fade from view. The affective politics of solidarity are just as much about pragmatics as they are about visibility. To support Kim Jin-suk's high-altitude-occupation protest, her close friend and labor activist with KCTU Hwang Yira (황이라; Hwang I-ra) famously provided essential care without missing a day. According to several news reports, Hwang Yira took charge of the rope-and-pulley system used to lift up hot food, warm clothing, and charged batteries to Kim Jin-suk and took care of bringing down buckets containing waste as well. It was reportedly Hwang Yira who initially set up a Twitter account on a mobile phone and sent it up for Kim Jin-suk to figure out how to use it, and for all this, Kim Jin-suk used a remarkable phrase to describe Hwang Yira's life-sustaining support from the ground—as a kind of an "umbilical cord."[17]

Twitter turned out to be a crucial lifeline for Kim Jin-suk. Already known to be a charismatic figure within movement circles, Kim Jin-suk proved to be a savvy and influential social media user. Her frequent and witty tweets—from her handle @JINSUK_85, as in "Crane 85"—gained a sizable following and became an essential hub of activist connectivity during those early days of Twitter use in South Korea.[18] In an interview with a news reporter, Kim Jin-suk explained, "I was on Twitter all day long. After breakfast, I was on Twitter. After lunch, I was on Twitter. And after short exercise, I would wave my hands at the guests below on the ground and talk to them on the phone, and then I would be on Twitter again. Every night at 7:30 p.m., I would watch the solidarity festival across the street from the crane, and then I would be on Twitter until I fell asleep. I would not have survived the long occupation without Twitter."[19] Later, in other interviews and speeches, Kim Jin-suk commented that if Twitter—and the interactive web of online and offline solidarity it cultivated—had existed in 2003, her comrade Kim Ju-ik and Kwak Chae-kyu might not have fallen into despair and possibly could have lived.[20]

The stream of replies, retweets, and messages posted on Twitter and other digital platforms, such as group texts and online chat rooms, mapped new circuits of solidarity in support of Kim Jin-suk's high-altitude occupation. Support swelled in person as well. Within weeks of each other during June and July 2011, tens of thousands of individuals—artists, unionists, students, feminists, LGBTQ+ activists, human rights advocates, journalists, lawyers, teachers, and progressive politicians—traveled on caravans to the base of Crane 85, galvanizing a nationwide movement known as the Hope Bus movement.[21] Early rounds of these caravans, which were voluntarily organized and largely self-financed, are remembered by many as remarkably joyful spaces filled with spirited dancing, stimulating performances, and uplifting speeches—all of which were rather uncharacteristic for a labor protest under such somber circumstances. Later rounds of Hope Bus caravans, however, did encounter escalating violence at the hands of private security, or "thugs for hire," and riot police, who used water cannons laced with tear gas in their attempt to stop and disperse solidarity protesters from reaching their destination. Yet the Hope Bus caravan participants refused to be deterred, and when they managed to force their way to reach the base of Crane 85, they proceeded to stage solidarity performances that have since become emblematic of new protest affects—not somber and heavy but joyful and defiant protests in the form of "cultural festivals."[22] Kim Jin-suk herself has recognized the energizing force of these solidarity actions and has directly credited Hope Bus caravans for keeping her alive on the crane.

In 2012, Kim Jin-suk eventually ended her high-altitude-occupation protest on the 309th day, after the union won a new contract that promised to reinstate laid-off workers. This was considered a landmark win and a rare happy ending during a time when most protests seemed unwinnable and mass layoffs unavoidable. But beyond the specific outcome of Kim Jin-suk's protest act, we note the significance of the protest's transformation from grief-stricken and death-inflected solidarity that pulsed throughout the struggle to new affective politics of hope and interdependency that amplified a field of intensities that continue to this day. Subsequent Hope Bus caravans to Pusan—five in total—

were dispatched not only to Crane 85 but to an array of other ongoing protest sites in danger of abandonment: workers engaged in protracted fights atop industrial smokestacks, transmission towers, and high-rise billboards. Among them was a Star Chemical / FineTek worker, Cha Gwang-ho, who in 2014–15 would establish a new record by surviving 408 days on top of a forty-five-meter tall factory smokestack.

While no other high-altitude-occupation protest since Kim Jin-suk's catalyzed a similar scale of caravan mobilization, the form of the solidarity caravan has become legible as an affective and intrinsically spatial praxis. It enables a mobile assembly to guard against abandonment by capital and society and against abandonment by comrades and community and fuels the fight for a more livable life. Through Kim Jin-suk, high-altitude-occupation protest became known not only for its extreme isolation and precarity on the verge of death but also for the life-sustaining solidarity it fostered, an affective demonstration of collectivities in struggle.

SOLIDARITY IN RESILIENCE, KIRYUNG WORKERS, 2005–14

Protest affects connect, reverberate, and linger among bodies, objects, places, and memories in ways that produce what Massey characterizes as the "the contemporaneous existence of a plurality of trajectories; a simultaneity of stories-so-far."[23] They conjure solidarities forged elsewhere and redirect their power to draw new connections and affinities. Shortly before the third Hope Bus caravan set out to visit Kim Jin-suk in 2011, a group of more than two hundred individuals who shared an unusual firsthand experience signed a public letter of support. Each had previously taken part in a high-altitude-occupation protest, and the remarkable letter foregrounded empathy as an ethical imperative. This is a short excerpt from the letter:

Dear beloved Kim Jin-suk of Crane 85,
We know . . . that a small body so frail, hanging [up there] in the sky, undergoes a level of pain that is difficult to bear not only for two hundred days but also even just for a minute or a second. [We know] that even if

one can endure the physical pain, it is difficult up there to overcome the
loneliness that befalls day after day. . . . You must come back alive. . . . We
who have defied the shadow of death and survived urge you . . . please stay
alive.[24]

Signatories of this letter included a shipbuilding worker who had
spent eighty-eight days on a high-voltage transmission tower, a former
union leader who helped occupy a massive eighty-four-meter-tall Go-
liath crane twenty-one years prior, a steelworker who rallied for 132
days on a factory chimney, an evictee who fought against extreme police
violence from the rooftop of a condemned building, an environmental
activist who had climbed a bridge in protest, and so on. The compassion
that this group of workers displayed for Kim Jin-suk extended beyond
universal ideas about justice. Their firsthand experience of the protest
form itself, particularly the grueling and agonizing aspects, forged com-
passionate alignments and powerful attachments among the protesters and supporters. Kim Jin-suk's supporters emphasized their shared
experience of physical pain and emotional loneliness. They also made
explicit connections between their shared status as survivors of protests
that defy "the shadow of death."

A key organizer behind this joint letter of support and a subsequent
Hope Bus caravan was none other than forty-one-year-old trade union
activist Kim So-yeon from the Kiryung Electronics Workers' Union,
well known for waging one of the longest-running labor campaigns in
defense of precarious workers. On three separate occasions in 2008,
Kim So-yeon led Kiryung workers in dramatic *kogong nongsŏng* actions—
first perching on a light tower and then on a closed-circuit television
tower, followed by a longer-term high-altitude occupation that was also
simultaneously a hunger strike on top of the front-entrance structure
of Kiryung Electronics.

As leaders of the Kiryung Electronics Workers' Union, Kim So-yeon
and Yu Heung-hee organized these protest actions to pressure the management to reinstate terminated workers and secure regular and permanent positions for precarious workers. When the two women began
their indefinite hunger strike, they subsisted on water and salt until

both were taken to the hospital for emergency medical care. Due to serious health concerns, Yu Heung-hee was forced to end her hunger strike on the sixty-seventh day, while Kim So-yeon returned from the hospital to the protest encampment and continued her hunger strike for an astounding total of ninety-four days. Hundreds of workers, activists, and even politicians joined them in a *tongjo tansik*, or "solidarity hunger strike," taking turns to fast along with them for a short duration—like a day or even just a meal. From July 2005 to December 2014, when Kiryung workers officially declared the end of their fight for reinstatement, they symbolized both the persistence of precarious workers' resistance and the elusiveness of a just resolution.

What originally transpired in 2005 was that Kiryung Electronics, a subcontracting company that assembled parts for the US-based Sirius Satellite Radio, terminated the employment contracts of approximately 250 workers who formed a union, the majority of whom were married women and mothers of school-age children. Kiryung workers had al-

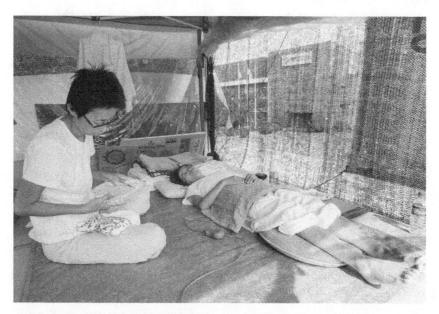

FIGURE 3.1. Kiryung workers Kim So-yeon and Yu Heung-hee on day sixty-five of their hunger strike, August 2008. Photo by Chung Taekyong.

128   CHAPTER 3

ready experienced blatant gender discrimination based on marital status when it came to job tenure. The company issued three-month contracts for newly married women, six-month contracts for unmarried women, and one-year contracts for women married for a longer time—a pattern that favored women with older children. Newly married women were deemed likely to take maternity leave or quit upon pregnancy, and unmarried women were deemed high-risk hires because of the assumption that marriage would upend the women's employment. In contrast, middle-aged married women faced patriarchal and often-incorrect assumptions that their wages would merely supplement the earnings of their husbands, who were presumed to be the primary breadwinners. Kiryung workers were treated with as much disrespect upon firing as they were in hiring. In response to the demands of their union, all that the Kiryung workers received was a text message over the weekend from the management that read, "Starting tomorrow, do not come to work."

There are indeed laws in South Korea that protect workers from losing their jobs overnight like this, but these protections rarely apply to workers on short-term-employment contracts. There are also laws that prohibit companies from retaliating against workers who form a union, but there are workarounds that enable the management to do so anyway. Just one month after the Kiryung workers were fired in 2005, the Ministry of Labor ruled that the company had broken the law to begin with because it hired the workers as "dispatch workers" through predatory broker agencies. "We thought we had [already] won" with this Ministry of Labor ruling, Kim So-yeon said in an interview in 2006, "and [back then] I thought we would win [the fight] in three days. But that turned into fifty-five days, and then we were forcibly dragged out by the police, and now it has been over a year."[25] It would continue for eight more years.

This state of legal liminality persisted over the course of ten years, producing intense feelings of betrayal and disillusionment each time the management refused to abide by court-mandated rulings that sided with the protesting workers. One of the most crushing moments took place in November 2011. After 1,895 consecutive days of protest, Kiryung workers secured a historic agreement with the management, which included a clause for direct employment, the first of its kind for dispatch workers. With this announcement, Kim So-yeon came down from the hydraulic excavator she had been occupying for over two weeks, and two other unionists ceased their hunger strike on the twentieth day. They were finally going to return to work. But when the reinstated workers showed up to work, they were simply ignored and given no work assignments and no pay until, one morning, they went to work to find an empty office—the company had vanished. Unbeknownst to them, the management had packed and moved to another location without informing the union members. When Yu Heung-hee later found the CEO's home address and rang his doorbell to demand an explanation, she was arrested for trespassing and fined approximately $1,500 for the crime. Refusing to pay the fine, she chose instead to serve fourteen days in prison.[26]

The seeming impossibility of resolving their dispute through existing channels, both legal and extralegal, led to a collective decision in 2014 by the seven remaining Kiryung workers to formally end their struggle for reinstatement. In December 2014, they performed a five-day-long, fifteen-kilometer *och'et'uji*, a full-prostration procession across the snow-covered streets of Seoul, as discussed in chapter 3. The Kiryung-protest contingent was ultimately unable to reach their intended destination, the president's residence, known as the Blue House, because of restrictions against public assembly near the location. Yet even when blocked at the nearby Kwanghwamun Square, the Kiryung workers refused to quit. For over six hours in the dead of winter in December, they laid face down at a standstill, lying prone on the frozen ground shivering, blocked by a line of police shields.

The stirring scenes produced by *och'et'uji* protests remind bystanders and passersby that confronting powerful opponents entails sacrifices and suffering. Yu Heung-hee herself acknowledged that witnesses can become overwhelmed by feelings of despair and helplessness when they encounter such pitiful protest scenes. But she also offered us another way to understand why aggrieved workers choose to perform such a protest act. She stressed the work of *och'et'uji* in fostering self-reflection and subject formation and as not simply for making appeals to public sympathy. She recounted, "Once I was face down on the ground, I realized that there is a mindfulness, a sense of devotion that comes with *och'et'uji*. . . . Someone strikes the *ching* [징], we take five or six steps, then we go down for a few seconds, and when another *ching* strike sounds, we pick ourselves up. Another *ching* strike, we start walking again."[27] For Yu Heung-hee, the repetition involved in performing *och'et'uji* created conditions for reflecting on time, embodiment, and movement. Indeed, *och'et'uji* is intended to cultivate what Tibetan Buddhists call a "spacious, flexible mind," which produces a different temporal orientation to the future rather than one simply dwelling in the space of negativity associated with being perpetually wronged as if that is the "one true and fixed story about what happened."[28] Yu Heung-hee powerfully captured this intention when she said, "You don't do *och'et'uji* to keep falling on the ground. You do *och'et'uji* to keep getting up."

For Yu Heung-hee, the ability to emerge from the injustices and trauma of the past with a renewed sense of "inner stability and strength" has had far-reaching personal and political consequences. With fellow union leader Kim So-yeon, she has brought her principles and commitments to guide new directions for the precarious workers' movement. Their vision, compassion, and skillful organizing led to the establishment of Cool Jam (Kkuljam; 꿀잠) in June 2017, the first worker-run shelter dedicated entirely to supporting workers who are engaged in long-term fights, especially in tent encampments. Located in Seoul's working-class industrial Kuro District, Cool Jam offers protesters a place to come bathe and wash their clothes, eat a hot meal, and, importantly, get quality sleep before returning to the streets.[29] In fact, the shelter's name in Korean, Kkuljam, means "[honey-like] sweet sleep." The shelter is especially crucial for workers who come from other provinces in the country to protest in the capital, for they have even more limited resources and housing options and typically resort to sleeping on the floor of union offices, which is "not that different from sleeping on the streets," as Yu Heung-hee remarked in our interview, "because all you have is a floor mat and a blanket."

Whereas the Hope Bus mobilization in support of Kim Jin-suk illustrates how solidarity serves as a lifeline for protesters during isolating conditions, such as in high-altitude occupations, the Kiryung Electronics Workers' Union's decade-long fight shows how resilience is not simply a matter of refusing to give up a fight; it is also about refusing to abandon the workers who continue to fight and building an alternative space in which protesters can rest and recharge in a safe and comforting place in the care of other workers.

SOLIDARITY AS RADICAL DEPENDENCY, KTX WORKERS, 2006–18

For KTX Crew Workers' Union leader Kim Seungha, the path to leading one of South Korea's longest labor struggles waged by precarious workers was neither expected nor planned. The valiant fight led by the KTX union nonetheless revealed the power of solidarity as a vital practice of mutual support in the context of repeated disavowals and prolonged abandonment. Like the case of Kiryung workers discussed in the previous section, KTX workers did not anticipate that their struggle would last for well over a decade when they first made the decision to strike. "Being young and inexperienced, we thought the strike would be over in a few days," one KTX union leader said. "If we knew it would continue for thirteen years, who could have started it?"[30] This was a sentiment that was commonly expressed by workers during their first experience waging a strike, yet it also was repeated by more seasoned union activists, such as Kwon Okja, whom we discussed in chapter 1, as she remarked on the exceptionally long duration of union fights waged by precariously employed women. After her fight with hospital aides who worked at the Ch'ŏngju City Geriatric Hospital lasted for 860 days, Kwon said that she now knows that "if a strike goes past three months, it is likely to last at least three years."

Some key differences between the women workers at Kiryung and KTX should be noted to give a sense of the diverse background of women who were disproportionately employed in precarious jobs. Unlike the factory workers at Kiryung, KTX train attendants were college-educated women, nearly all in their early to mid-twenties, who were selected through a highly competitive application process for a job that was marketed as a so-called flight attendant on the ground.[31] The women were led to believe that although they were initially hired under short-term contracts via a third-party company, they would become direct employees of KORAIL after one year, only to encounter repeated postponement. In the meantime, blatant sexism and abuse pervaded their working conditions, with women constituting the majority of outsourced positions, while men were directly employed by KORAIL as "team leaders."

As discussed in the introduction, the KTX Crew Workers' Union started their fight in 2006, a year after Kiryung workers began their own epic fight. On many occasions, the KTX workers used their femininity to add a stylistic flair to the public drama. When nearly four hundred women in their twenties—in a profession associated with a well-coifed and polished appearance—started camping out in makeshift tents at Seoul Central Station in 2008, the scene struck observers and even seasoned activists as highly unconventional. Kim Jin-suk, the famous labor figure whose high-altitude-occupation protest we discussed at the start of this chapter, took notice of KTX workers as well. Her site visits to workplace occupations or protest encampments, as well as her witty and inspirational speeches that connected local disputes to longer histories of working-class resistance, were known to provide a morale boost for the protesting workers. Kim Jin-suk recalled, "To someone like me who can roll around at a protest encampment for a month and not know where the mirror is, it was an unusual sight. Even in such uncomfortable settings, [KTX union members] found time to go the restroom to fix their makeup and straighten their clothes, tying and untying their hair throughout the day and using their phones as mirrors."[32]

This excerpt reveals that some protesting bodies deviated from the assumed universal masculinist subject of labor militancy. Even though Kim Jin-suk was one of the few women welders and female union leaders active during the fight against authoritarian labor repression in the 1980s, the issue of gender identity was never one she thought much about. Her short hair, makeup-free face, and androgenous clothing made her fairly indistinguishable from her male counterparts in the union and reinforced her image and reputation as a celebrated longtime labor activist. Yet as Leslie Salzinger notes, it is "precisely the absence of explicit naming that enables masculinity's historically accrued capacity to stand in for the general," even when indexing the particular experiences of men.[33] In the eyes of many unionists, like Kim Jin-suk, KTX workers' performance of femininity initially created a "legibility problem," but the protracted conditions of their struggle soon began to circulate recognizable protest affects, such as determination and resilience, that emphasized the KTX workers' commonalities with other unionists and shared experiences across gender, class, occupation, and collective-action practices. It was this convergence of the familiar and unfamiliar that intensified affectively charged scenes of resistance and solidarity by KTX workers.

Like many other workers in long-term fights, KTX workers started to become demoralized when facing dwindling participation rates. By April 2008, their ranks shrank to less than a quarter of their original numbers. After shifting to a legal strategy, KTX workers began to experience the profound unreliability of democratic law and jurisprudence when it came to enforcing labor rights. In 2010, a court decision ruled in favor of workers and ordered KORAIL to directly rehire the thirty-four dismissed train attendants, pay their back wages, and cover litigation costs. KORAIL appealed. Another ruling in 2011 again favored the union, but KORAIL appealed again. Then, during the conservative Park Geun-hye presidency, a Supreme Court decision dealt a blow by reversing the previous decisions and ruled in favor of KORAIL, requiring KTX unionists to return the court-ordered wages, plus interest, that were paid to them after the 2010 ruling. The financial ramifications of this third and final ruling in 2015—derided as the year's worst legal decision by the group Lawyers for a Democratic Society (민주사회를 위한 변호사 모임)—meant that each KTX Crew Workers' Union member now owed 86.4 million Korean won (approximately $72,000) to KORAIL. Under the crushing weight of this news, one KTX union leader took her life at thirty-six years of age, leaving behind a three-year-old daughter and a note that read, "I am sorry, baby. All I can leave for you is debt."[34]

Ordering dismissed KTX workers to return their wages and pay back litigation costs was like issuing a "death sentence," explained Kim Seungha.[35] To prevent KTX's legal quagmire from turning more lethal, Father Zacchaeus, a social-justice activist and Anglican clergyman, formed an interfaith special-task force in May 2017 that linked the KTX workers' struggle to widespread business corruption under the Park Geun-hye government, as we discussed in chapter 1. The timing was critical as the nation had been consumed by the six-month-long Candlelight Protests, a mass uprising that was sparked by grief and public outrage at the depths of government negligence, corruption, and abuse of power. In fact, pulsing throughout the mass-scale public marches and assemblies was not only the necro-activism of labor-related deaths but also the collective trauma of witnessing the botched rescue and subsequent capsizing of the *Sewol* ferry in 2014.[36]

Throughout the month of July 2017, a series of religious services were organized at the Seoul Central Station in solidarity with KTX workers, as we noted in the introduction. A different service was organized on each day—Catholic Mass on Monday, Protestant service on Tuesday, Anglican service on Wednesday, and Buddhist service on Thursday—transforming the secular space of the train station into a sacred space of solidarity. Attending relatively subdued religious services in a bustling train station certainly seemed out of place as announcements of departing and arriving trains interrupted sermons, liturgical prayer, and ritual chanting. Scenes of KTX workers who practiced particular faith traditions, such as wearing lace veils in Catholic church, and temporary altars set up next to high-speed rail platforms disrupted expectations of what a militant unionist or a militant protest looked like. Yet it was precisely these types of juxtapositions and contradictions that heightened the political affects generated by publicly sharing feelings of grief, mourning, indignation, and determination through spiritual communion.

A few months later, as one of their final protest actions together, KTX workers, including Kim Seungha, embarked on their first *och'et'uji* accompanied by representatives from the four major religious solidarity groups. During our interview, which took place months before the actual procession, they worried about how physically demanding *och'et'uji* would be and whether they would be able to complete the procession. Just the thought of having to endure such physically grueling acts generated a thought-provoking conversation about the purpose of these types of protests. But when they made the decision, Kim Seungha recognized that this was at least in part to acknowledge that this fight was larger than their own. Part of waging a long-term struggle that was supported by a dedicated group of allies, such as faith leaders, was to learn how to become recipients of solidarity. In July 2018, the KTX union finally reached an agreement with KORAIL to drop the financial liability and return to work, though not as train attendants but in administrative capacities (figure 3.2).

FIGURE 3.2. "We want to return to work!" poster for KTX workers, with art by Yi Yunyop, 2017. Reprinted with permission from Lee Yunyop.

WHERE PROTESTERS SLEEP

Chung Taekyong's (정택용; Chŏng T'aek-yong) seventh major collection of photojournalism was published in 2016 with the title *Oebak* (외박; Sleeping elsewhere). A well-known activist photographer, Chung Taekyong is well known for capturing iconic and dramatic scenes of protest. To be sure, Chung's photography offers captivating glimpses into the extraordinary repertoires that we discuss in this book, but also remarkable are the repeated juxtapositions of the ordinary and the extraordinary, the spotlight on the mundane arrangements of everyday-life spaces in which bodies are at rest or sleeping, even amidst protest. In one image, taken on April 13, 2014, we see a scene of a laid-off Ssangyong Motor worker sleeping in broad daylight while his comrades hold vigil in front of a makeshift altar placed in front of palace gates in central Seoul, mourning the lives of twenty-two fallen comrades (figure 3.3). As of 2023, the death count was at thirty. The banner over the altar urges a

FIGURE 3.3. Ssangyong Motor unionists' protest altar in Seoul, April 2014. Photo by Chung Taekyong.

stop to the tears and death of autoworkers. The man in the foreground is only temporarily at rest, with a hat covering his eyes while he tries to take a nap.

In the next image (figure 3.4), Chung presents an aerial view of striking train attendants from the nation's flagship KTX bullet train, taken on June 6, 2006, just two months after 350 workers were fired via text for forming a union and initiating a strike against the Korea Railroad Corporation. Gathered in a cordoned-off section of a busy terminal inside the Seoul train station, the young female KTX unionists alongside fellow unionists from the Korean Railroad Workers' Union (KRWU; 전국철도노동조합) are scattered across seat cushions and floor mats enclosed by union banners and protest signs. They are talking, eating, and a few are on the floor in sleeping positions.

These images provide a glimpse into the unexpected and often-hazardous places where striking workers in South Korea can find places to sleep. Chung's photographs show the unlikely and discomforting

FIGURE 3.4. KTX workers' encampment inside Seoul Central Station, June 2006. Photo by Chung Taekyong.

places of where protesters sleep in ways that protest conditions parallel the precariousness of life itself. The challenges of protesting and sleeping in public space make indispensable the questions of collective care and social reproduction. The intimate spaces of caring for oneself and each other while engaged in long-term fights shed light on the transformative praxis of everyday-life spaces and the collective political practice of life and living in solidarity. The diverse range of activities that keep life going for protesters in long-term public occupations is not simply a matter of addressing basic needs. The specific needs, sensibilities, and desires of protesters highlight the gendered and power-laden dynamics and subject formations that in turn shape the everyday spaces of protesting and sleeping in public.

Dwelling for months in makeshift shelters or indefinitely occupying public places requires creative and resourceful negotiations with the environments in which protesters find themselves. This includes figuring out how, when, and where to eat, wash, access toilets, rest, play, and sleep under conditions of uncertainty, shortage, duress, and conflict. It also involves reorganizing spaces and facilities in ways that support the basic needs of communal living, even when not designed to do so. Protesters involved in long-term encampments often establish guidelines and procedures for sharing limited bathrooms and cramped sleeping quarters. They rely heavily on disposable and easily transportable objects for cooking and cleaning. They designate separate spaces for rest and medical care. The support of neighbors, adjacent businesses, and allies who act as "emergency responders" through social media and group-text platforms also play a crucial role in helping protesters defend themselves against the constant threat of removal and the destruction of their belongings by police and privately hired security guards in addition to routine intimidation and harassment.

GENDERED SPACES OF SOCIAL REPRODUCTION

In the spring and summer of 2017 when we met with the key KTX Crew Workers' Union leaders in Seoul, they laughed looking back at their protest-encampment experiences that continued on and off for nearly three years. KTX workers had escalated their strike, which first began in March 2006 with 350 train attendants and turned into a full-fledged workplace occupation in 2008 with makeshift tents set up inside the Seoul train station for nearly two hundred workers. They basically lived there for nearly three years. Maintaining long-term protest camps like this might have become somewhat routine for precariously employed unionists, but for women, like the KTX workers, who were young and mostly unmarried or older and working-class, as was the case for most Kiryung Electronics workers, maintaining a long-term protest occupation seemed unthinkable at the time.

Living together and protesting together in close quarters during occupation protests, many became close friends. "It was the first time that so many women went on strike and did a long occupation protest like that, so nobody knew what to do with us," said Kim Seungha, who was serving as the president of the KTX Crew Workers' Union. "But we were fine. We figured out how to make do with very little. But sharing restrooms was very hard to do with hundreds of women. Every time there was running hot water, everyone would try to stick their head under the faucet to wash their hair." Another interviewee jumped in: "And using the hand dryer to dry our hair! I have a photo of this somewhere." And she started looking through her phone to find an old photo. "Here. I'm the one who's washing [my] hair. . . . I can tell from the stripes on my pants because I distinctly remember those pants." Through the intense experience of communal living in exceptional conditions, they built relations and structures, rules and even curfews to follow, yet they also recalled instances of sneaking out to neighboring clubs to "blow off steam" and get a momentary reprieve from the monotony of protesting day in and day out. In many ways, figuring out how to adapt to the rigidities of inherited protest practices was part of the affective sensibilities generated by engaging in specific protest forms, such as strike encampments. Learning how to creatively endure a long-term protest camp when it is such an extreme departure from one's everyday life is part of the endurance of the protest form itself in the broader repertoire.

It was clear during the course of our interview that their three-year protest encampment kindled particularly fond memories for KTX union

CHAPTER 3

leaders. Kim Seungha proudly recalled how skilled she and other KTX workers became in the art of tactical disruption:

> You know how men always talk about their military service? We always talk about the encampment [*nongsŏng*] experience. Three years. It really was almost like military service. We say that we went to the military, and not only that, we even pulled off special ops. We learned to form teams and disperse to avoid the police, and we knew how to enter enemy territory in threes and fours and gather somewhere at a certain time, ditching the plainclothes cops who followed us everywhere. We were able to assemble in a flash and pull off an occupation in minutes.

Their ability to disrupt business as usual through sudden and unexpected movements was possible when workers shared a base camp like the strike-encampment zone in the Seoul Central Station. While their heavily photographed actions attracted much media attention, it was their ability to do so while sharpening their capacity to disrupt everyday life that increased the affective charge of their collective actions.

Although KTX workers demonstrated high levels of commitment, tenacity, and suffering, their motivations and character were often called into question or treated with suspicion. Their protests generated high-profile media attention because their appearance defied expectations of labor militancy. Kim Seungha remarked that they "got a lot of crap" for displaying concern about their physical appearances and clothing. She explained, "Because we are train attendants, we pay a lot of attention to how we look." For example, some KTX union leaders altered the design and fit of their fairly androgenous-looking T-shirts with shorter sleeve lengths, enhanced their appearance with jewelry and colorful accessories, and routinely wore makeup while protesting. Such public displays of their femininity consistently drew the ire and disapproval of their male comrades in the Korean Railroad Workers' Union and the KCTU who protested alongside them. "They would say things like, 'Are you sure your situation is really dire?'" Kim Seungha recounted. But for KTX workers, their attention to their physical appearance was less about their investment in upholding a feminine ideal. They never once stated that their concerns were about looking feminine, though we are not discounting that this was the case. Rather, they said they did so simply because they were train attendants, accustomed to the ways they wore their makeup and dressed up.

The following vignette illuminates how this clash of gendered sensibilities resulted in a particularly comical scene. One evening, KTX workers were asked to gather on the second floor of the Seoul train station for an emergency group meeting with one of the male union leaders of KRWU. "It was nighttime, so each one of us was wearing a facial sheet mask"; we all immediately burst into laughter as she mimicked the horrified look on his face when he saw them. "It was because we were all living together [at the protest camp]. After spending many hours outside in the sun, we regularly did face masks. So everyone just gathered looking like white-faced ghosts staring at each other," she explained. At this point, her comrade joined in, roaring with laughter, stating "I'm sure it was a scene that he absolutely had never seen before [at a protest camp]." She continued, "But however much we have to protest, we have to take care of our precious and valuable skin." While she made this comment partly in jest, she made sure to underscore the links between their concerns about skin care and their work ethic. She said matter-of-factly, "The reason why we bothered [to do face masks] was because we thought we could be reinstated at any moment. We wanted to be ready to start work again, which meant we had to maintain our appearances."

BUILDING SPACES OF COLLECTIVE CARE AND RADICAL DEPENDENCY

On August 21, 2017, we met the KTX workers once again on the rooftop of Cool Jam, which is in a densely populated working-class neighborhood filled with multiunit residential buildings and winding alleys. It is telling that we met at the opening ceremony of the Cool Jam shelter, where they were joined by not only the Kiryung workers but dozens of other workers who contributed money and construction skills to build Cool Jam as a space of mutual aid. Cool Jam is a place created by and for workers, where people fighting on the streets in makeshift tent encampments can take a hot shower, wash their clothes, relax without interruption, and sleep peacefully, even if for just one night.

Cool Jam was celebrating its official opening, after two years of planning, fundraising, and building renovation, led by two leaders from the Kiryung Electronics Workers' Union, Kim So-yeon and Yu Heung-hee. The Kiryung unionists who led the process emphasized how their sense of compassion and empathy with fellow workers motivated them to spearhead such an ambitious project. In particular, the hardships of workers who lived outside of Seoul were forefront in their minds, explained Yu Heung-hee during our interview. KTX workers enthusiastically told us during our interview that they were part of this tremendous effort, volunteering "their manual labor in solidarity" during the last stages of construction. "Because we got so much help for our struggles in the past, we thought it would be great to have an opportunity to give back," Kim Seungha explained. Once they saw the nearly finished space with their own eyes, they immediately recognized its value and significance, especially for workers who did not have the support of a large and well-resourced union, such as KRWU. "We've seen other people have a really hard time because there wasn't anything like this [Cool Jam], so it's so great that people now have something they can depend on."

The fact that the process of building a communal shelter was led by two middle-aged working-class women leaders is not surprising to those who recognize the disproportionate labor of women in providing everyday forms of care. Feminist scholars have long critiqued the tendency to view care as freely and naturally given, flowing from the love and talent of women and mothers, as opposed to a set of learned activities and situational expertise, even if care itself and the people who provide it are devalued as part of a sexualized and racialized division of labor. Yet it is crucial to recognize that care can operate as a site of transformative praxis.

The Kiryung workers, who designed every aspect of the interior space, engaged in a specific type of care that prioritized taking care of others in ways that are reflexive and nurturing, combining caring about others at a cognitive level (as an index of solidarity) and the direct work of caregiving as consisting of both paid and unpaid labor.[37] The distinction between the mental and manual aspects of caring for others typically reflects the uneven power differentials that exist across race, class, and gender, such as between affluent white women and the predominantly immigrant and women of color workforce that is employed to clean, cook, and provide paid child- and elder-care in private households in places like the United States. In contrast, the kinds of caring activities that Kiryung workers performed and the boundaries they set around them revealed their investment in fostering more egalitarian practices of collective care.

The process of purchasing, designing, constructing, and running a worker-run shelter was not without its delays and conflicts, but the Kiryung workers who led every step of the process emphasized that their many experiences resolving conflicts and overcoming hardship throughout their 1,895-day-long struggle gave them the skills and expertise needed to embark on such an ambitious project. The ground floor was designed as a multifunction space that contained a full kitchen and multiple seating areas, which could serve as a self-serve café rather than a place where workers could expect women to cook and serve them. A large laundry room was located behind the kitchen, where workers could wash their clothes, which was a perennial problem for workers who lived on the streets. The ground floor also contained facilities for disabled workers, which Yu Heung-hee said was a top priority given the lack of an elevator in the four-story building with a rooftop and basement. Ensuring accessible spaces was particularly important for acknowledging the strong solidarity between the precarious workers' movement and the disability-rights movements, which had engaged in some of the most disruptive and militant forms of direct action.

The building's interior design also reflected Cool Jam's emphasis on solidarity, political education, and mutual aid, which Kiryung workers came to value throughout their 1,895-day-long struggle. The basement served as a multifunction event space, with sound insulation and the capacity to host performances, film screenings, political-education lectures, and art exhibitions as well as to gather in large numbers to discuss and vote on resolutions. At the time of the opening, photos of the Kiryung workers' decade-long struggle were prominently displayed on the walls, reminding visitors and residents of the tremendous resilience and fighting spirit of Cool Jam leaders like Kim So-yeon and

Yu Heung-hee, who survived ninety-four-day-long and sixty-seven-day-long hunger strikes, respectively. Cool Jam had already planned a number of events when they opened their doors aimed at solidarity building, political education, and mutual aid, including a class on "body care," a rice-sharing program, and a volunteer-run dental-care clinic every other Saturday for laid-off and precariously employed workers. None of Cool Jam's activities are funded by the government. Instead, they rely primarily on the monthly membership contributions of some eight hundred individuals.

Strengthening the relations and infrastructure of solidarity between and among workers and the broader public was essential for building the kind of world that the Cool Jam founders aspired to live in when a state of abandonment was the norm, rather than the exception, for many workers. This vision was articulated in the poem displayed on a welcoming plaque in front of the building:

> The modern world of nonregular workers without slavery,
> A world where no one is alienated from this precious and
>   dignified life, from themselves.
> A world where no one, no one suffers from unjust
>   discrimination and violence for any reason.
> A world without armies and wars. A world where no one is in
>   power over anyone, a world where all of life's utterances,
>   solidarity, and coexistence are beautiful enough.
> A house of solidarity that moves toward such a world.
> Let's build a new house of solidarity, a new house of love.

CONCLUSION

Our discussion shows how the affects produced by shared protest repertoires generate outcomes that take on a life of their own, connecting the plights of workers across geography, industry, and history. Aggrieved workers perform hunger strikes, high-altitude occupations, and ritualized Buddhist prostrations to amplify the stakes of their individual labor disputes, but these protests often exceed their intended goals. Dismissed workers from Kiryung and KTX persisted against all odds, for instance, showing what it means to refuse to accept neoliberal precarity as a fait accompli. Their embodied acts of resilience became conduits for revealing the consequences—and limits—of capitalist abandonment. Their fights may not always result in a win in a narrow sense of job reinstatement or restored rights, but they do nonetheless took on new meaning and purpose as "shape-shifting performance constellations," to borrow from Marcela Fuentes. By combining embodied acts of ritual and spectacle with multiple and repeated demonstrations of solidarity, their protests reflected an "assemblage of cross-platform, multisited gestures" that vividly exposed the dehumanizing processes of neoliberal subjectification and disembodied capital accumulation.[38] These performance constellations also helped fortify the "infrastructure of dissent" that sustains radical communities in the face of intensified opposition.[39] The very creation of Cool Jam as a collectively purchased, designed, and constructed worker shelter is the material manifestation of translating protest repertoires into a relational politics of solidarity.

The significance of affect, performance, and ritual in the cultural politics of protesting precarity highlights the need to reassess the conceptual divides that have long distinguished unruly forms of popular politics from deliberative modes of civic participation. Like in Argentina, where Fuentes conducted her research, protesters in South Korea have cultivated a rich repertoire of symbols, sounds, tactics, narratives, and images to defend workers' livelihoods and dignity against decades of growth-driven economic development, whether under military dictatorship or liberal democratic leadership. The proliferation of vibrant public protest in places as divergent as Egypt, Hong Kong, Iran, Mexico, Spain, and Thailand also highlight striking similarities in the ways in which disadvantaged and excluded communities are challenging the vast inequalities exacerbated by neoliberal global capitalism, including divisions organized by ethnicity, race, gender, sexuality, religion, caste, region, and generation. The embrace of the theatrical and the confrontational should not be misunderstood as a facile rejection of the formal political sphere or a deep chasm between new and old social movements. As Sonia E. Alvarez and her colleagues researching Latin

America's new wave of protest mobilizations point out, "Even the most defiant and confrontational among contemporary movements" has directly engaged the state, legal political institutions, and civil-society agendas, while the "most NGO-ized actors and sectors" have openly and defiantly taken to the streets.[40]

The growing trend toward conceptualizing political dissent as a willful politics of refusal underscores the profound dilemmas of realizing justice for subjugated groups under liberal democratic capitalist regimes.[41] The lived experience of neoliberal precarity is more than a denial of liberal democratic rights; it is the abnegation of the basic conditions that enable people to survive and live a dignified life. The intentional embrace of indignities and precarities involved in the protest repertoires we have discussed in this chapter shows how precarious women workers in South Korea conjure solidarity to fix and transform the conditions of subjugation and injustice, forging an affective politics rooted in mutual recognition and radical dependency. Kim Seungha's emphasis on consistency and persistence, showing up and being present over and over again alongside workers in the midst of struggle, resonates with the discussion of solidarity as "radical dependency" in the documentary *Geographies of Racial Capitalism with Ruth Wilson Gilmore*.[42] In this short film, Gilmore asserts that the work of solidarity making is often uneventful, especially as spectacular acts of protest fade from view, but that this uneventful work reveals the important ways in which "we come absolutely to depend on each other" when confronting the life-depriving structures of state violence and capitalist abandonment. Solidarity was for the protesting workers in South Korea not just about strategy or instrumentality; it was about building and affirming relationalities in ways that made survival meaningful and possible at all. In the next chapter, we turn to the behind-the-scenes work involved in creating caring infrastructures.

4 CARING INFRASTRUCTURE

Infrastructure is not identical to system or structure, as we
currently see them, because infrastructure is defined by
the movement or patterning of social form. It is the living
mediation of what organizes life: the lifeworld of structure.

—Lauren Berlant, "The Commons"

How can we think (and rethink and rethink) care
laterally, in the register of the intramural, in a different
relation than that of the violence of the state?

—Christina Sharpe, *In the Wake: On Blackness and Being*

SOLIDARITY IS PARADOXICAL. The power of solidarity must be visible to
move publics, yet the work involved in creating solidaristic collectivities is often most effective when unseen and unnoticed as part of the
infrastructure of social-movement praxis. Sister Maria highlighted this
paradox when talking about her crucial yet unnoticed work in organizing well-known struggles such as the fight in Miryang against the
Korea Electric Power Corporation (KEPCO; 한국전력공사), the country's
largest public company, which lasted over a decade starting in 2005. As
she says with a laugh, "I try not to be noticed as much as possible. Even
in Miryang, nobody knew that I was the one organizing things. I didn't
talk about it."

The fight in Miryang had officially started on Monday, December 5,
2005, when residents of Sangdongmyŏn Yŏsumaŭl, a district in Miryang, played traditional drums and rallied in front of the local KEPCO
office.[1] KEPCO planned to construct fifty-two transmission towers for
756-kilovolt ultra-high-voltage power lines transecting through the

farming communities in the mountainous southeastern region of the country. Not only would there be significant land dispossession and displacement of residents and natural habitats, but the power lines would carry high-voltage electricity from nuclear power plants on the coast to power-hungry urban centers. The steel transmission towers would stand as tall as forty-story buildings. The power lines would destroy trees and vegetation and annihilate farms and communities in their path, spilling so much electricity along the way that the ambient electromagnetic fields would be powerful enough to light fluorescent tubes held up in the air. By December 2014, a total of sixty-nine ultra-high-voltage transmission towers would be constructed in five districts of Miryang.

In the opening article of a remarkable 2015 book of documentary photography reflecting on the decade-long fight against this massive energy-infrastructure project, the leaders of the Miryang fight declare that they have actually won despite their inability to stop the construction.[2] They claim victory because they created documentary evidence of standing valiantly on the side of truth and justice, they exposed the greed of capital and the violence of the state colluding in megadevelopment projects, and they raised public awareness concerning the grave environmental impact of nuclear power and energy infrastructure. The subject of extensive attention by artists, filmmakers, photographers, writers, journalists, bloggers, vloggers, and social media producers on digital platforms, such as Twitter, Facebook, and YouTube, the Miryang fight is remarkable for the rich archive of protest that it has produced.

Most of the directly impacted residents were elderly farmers in their seventies and eighties with multigenerational ties and ancestral claims to the land. Commonly referred to as "Miryang grandmothers," the elderly-women protesters in particular put their physical bodies on the line, such as by climbing the steep and muddy mountainside before dawn to build tent encampments, occupying areas cleared for KEPCO construction, or crawling under heavy construction equipment, but to no avail. Both tough and frail, Miryang grandmothers emerged as powerful icons of direct action and grassroots-community resistance, the "visual embodiment of resistance culture under the neo-developmental

FIGURE 4.1. Protesters chain their bodies to a makeshift tent to halt construction in Miryang, 2014. Photo by Chung Taekyong.

state."[3] As scenes of their intense physical clashes with construction companies and riot police circulated widely on news and social media, they received widespread support and solidarity from environmental, antinuclear, and religious activists from across the country, with Sister Maria among them.[4]

Activist Catholic nuns wasted no time arriving on the scene. Alongside Miryang grandmothers, Catholic nuns blockaded mountain roads and chained themselves to bulldozers and tent encampments next to the growing pit in the ground that Miryang grandmothers referred to as "their grave."[5] Sister Maria and her colleagues, dressed in gray veils and plain tunics, also performed a broad range of organizing activities that were vital to sustaining the Miryang protesters' long-term struggle behind the scenes. They shared daily chores and completed essential tasks required to maintain the twenty-four-hour-long protest camp. They quietly helped coordinate the flow of solidarity caravans in and out of protest sites and took care of beleaguered and battered protesters. They responded to urgent publicity and fundraising needs, helping to maintain a steady flow of resources and information between protesters and supporters. They assisted in the preparation of solidarity meals, musical performances, short skits and plays, and candlelight vigils. Activist nuns also stood courageously alongside elderly women protesters in confronting police by asserting their presence in a show of religious solidarity, dignity, and perseverance. In important ways, the nuns' steadfast solidarity provided a kind of "protective accompaniment," which "puts bodies that are less at risk next to bodies that are under threat."[6] As the logic of accompaniment goes, the police might not hesitate to push aside a poor, uneducated, and elderly farmer without social standing, but they might pause before using force against a Catholic nun. The nuns were both visible and invisible, a mainstay in communities of resistance and solidarity rooted in cultural traditions of collective defense, survival, and uplift.

SOCIAL-MOVEMENT INFRASTRUCTURE

In this chapter, we delve into the optics of visibility and invisibility that undergird the social-movement infrastructures of care and solidarity that sustain high-risk protests. Behind many long-term struggles against energy- and transportation-infrastructure development, military-base construction, urban gentrification, and market-driven company restructuring and worker layoffs are individuals like Sister Maria who organize the front lines of fights. However, they are rarely, if ever, identified as leading figures of protest movements. Like so many social activists, Sister Maria's social movement know-how encompasses a broad range of activities involved in moving bodies, gathering resources, distributing supplies, and disseminating information across place and time as part of what Alan Sears calls an "infrastructure of dissent."[7] Albert Melucci describes these infrastructural activities as the "hidden structure" and "latent networks" that exists in the substratum of everyday life, which only "surface" during "transient periods of collective mobilization."[8] However, we contend that the assumption that infrastructure's social force comes from its invisibility overlooks a more complex reality. "Invisibility is certainly one aspect of infrastructure," as Brian Larkin asserts, "but it is only one and at the extreme edge of a range of visibilities that move from unseen to grand spectacles and everything in between."[9] Between visibility and invisibility are in-between processes of *becoming* visible and *becoming* invisible— the relational processes that Sister Maria and other activist-organizers constantly negotiate to ensure that *tangsaja* protest actors remain front and center as the protagonists of a fight and external allies remain part of the "quiet organizing going on in the shadows."[10]

As we argue in this chapter, social-movement infrastructure wields the power to move publics precisely because it operates in the relational spaces of everyday life. It addresses the gaps and fissures that keep people who experience systemic harm and oppression isolated and vulnerable. As activists who engage in public fights for a more just and sustainable world and organizers who strengthen the capacity of ordinary people to challenge unequal power dynamics in institutions and broader society, the activist-organizers that we profile in this chapter create critical forms of infrastructural support for protesters whose decision to wage life-or-death protests exposes them to intense levels of conflict, hardship, pain, deprivation, sacrifice, ambivalence, disappointment, and so on, especially during the course of protracted struggles. This includes the relational work that activist-organizers engage in to connect relatively vulnerable groups of protesters to the skills, resources, and capacities of external allies, networks, and organizations and the relationships of trust, accountability, and reciprocity that they nurture and cultivate among themselves and *tangsaja,* the most directly impacted persons in struggle. Social-movement infrastructure thus functions as much more than conduits of mobilization, as social-movement practices are not narrowly restricted to mobilization goals. Social-movement infrastructure is more aptly understood through the lens of what AbdouMaliq Simone calls "people as infrastructure" or what Lauren Berlant describes as the "lifeworld of structure," as "that which binds us to the world in movement and keeps the world practically bound to itself."[11] Structure in this sense is not static but elastic, and infrastructure is the glue that binds individual lives to the world in movement. The relationships, alliances, networks, and organizations that activists build create the kind of "critical social form" that "alter[s] the harder, softer, and looser infrastructures of sociality itself."[12]

We use the term "caring infrastructures" to describe the multivalent, system-level processes involved in caring about and caring for one another in times of threat, harm, suppression, and elimination. Two principles guide the creation of caring infrastructure: care as relational and care as reflexive. Care as relational "extends a vision of care as an ethically and politically charged practice" for people and things that have been written off. As Maria Puig de la Bellacasa puts it, "the point is not only to expose or reveal invisible labors of care" but "to generate care."[13] In the case of social movements, care is not simply about supporting people's basic needs during life-depriving protests, though tending to one's physical survival and emotional well-being is certainly an indispensable part of creating caring infrastructures. In a broader sense, care entails the "work of building social relations, community, and modes of relationality" in ways that help to sustain the momentum of oppositional politics.[14] Recognizing the relational dimensions of care extends foundational theorizing about the feminist ethics of care as both practical activity and cognitive reflection.[15] As Joan C. Tronto writes, caring "is neither simple nor banal; it requires know-how and judgement, and to make such judgements as well as possible becomes the moral task of engaging in care."[16] Care as reflexive is especially germane in the context of neoliberal capitalist systems that valorize competition, individualization, and privatization. As neoliberal logics would have it, "one must care for oneself by acting rationally, competitively and responsibly, and by procuring increasingly commodified market solutions to meet their care needs."[17] Families, not the state, are assumed to be responsible for providing care when individual efforts and market solutions fail. But what happens to people who experience profound abandonment at multiple levels—by the state, the labor market, their employers and coworkers, and even their families? What about individuals whose vulnerabilities are located across multiple vectors of gender, racial, and class inequalities? Where would these individuals find the care that they need and from whom?

Engaging in reflexive thinking about care ensures that people who might otherwise lack essential support systems receive the care they need yet do so in ways that recognize the dilemmas of power, vulnerability, and exclusion. Providing direct forms of support to *tangsaja* protesters who experience accumulated hardship and trauma over the duration of a bitterly contested fight can be a fraught enterprise. On the one hand, attracting external solidarity is vital to exposing the repression and violence that is often deployed to suppress marginalized groups of protesters. External solidarity also provides crucial forms of mutual aid and support to fights that can become quickly drained of human and financial resources. On the other hand, social-movement actors and organizations come with their own power dynamics and political agendas, which can thwart the broader goals and outcomes of a fight. To understand how "thinking needs care," as Christina Sharpe puts it, we ask how efforts to provide care necessarily entail addressing questions of positionality and intersectionality, which especially Black feminist scholars have identified as indispensable to reflexive analysis.[18] How do social activists grapple with the practical and ethical difficulties of providing time-consuming and labor-intensive care for people in need? How do they build and cultivate caring infrastructures in ways that avoid reifying existing inequalities and hierarchies while also protecting their own need for care and empathy? How do they, as Sharpe puts it, "think (and rethink and rethink) care laterally" and build lifeworlds that are "in a different relation . . . to the violence of the state"?[19]

To understand how infrastructures become "caring" through social-movement praxis, we anchor our analysis on the practices of relational care and movement reflexivity discussed by two key interlocutors who have devoted their lives to social activism in different movement spheres: Catholic nun Sister Maria, whom we introduced at the beginning of this chapter, and Ryu Eunsook (류은숙; Ryu Ŭn-suk), a veteran human rights activist and a founding member of the influential Sarangbang Group for Human Rights (인권운동 사랑방), which was established in 1992. Sister Maria and Ryu Eunsook may not be considered leading or historic figures in the fight against precarity, nor are they recognized as representative voices in the world of South Korean labor and social movements. We choose to focus on these interlocutors because they nonetheless illustrate two distinct examples of how individuals from different social backgrounds and political orientations become leading activist-organizers in building caring infrastructure at the level of the repertoire. They are part of a vibrant constellation of activist-organizers, the vast majority of whom are women, who perform the largely unseen and unsung work of movement building in the country's extraordinary social-movement sphere. Through an in-depth analysis of their ideas and reflections on protest experiences, we show how their divergent personal trajectories into social activism as progressive religious and human rights activists influence the ways in which they think about and provide care for protesters that move beyond fixed conceptions of challengers and opponents. Central to the cultivation of their caring practices are the meanings about protest and politics, which have been shaped by their own movements across place and history. We learn how their attention to reflexivity and positionality infuses every aspect of their movement-building work, mediated by their understanding of intersecting power dynamics along gender, class, social-status, and institutional-authority lines. Ultimately, we aim to account for the indispensable gendered labor of providing collective care and mutual support at the level of the entire repertoire that pervades every protest movement aimed at challenging the status quo of power relations in the landscape of twenty-first-century social movements in South Korea.

SISTER MARIA

We rely on Sister Maria as a key interlocuter, a principled practitioner of navigating the optics of visibility and invisibility that have produced social-movement infrastructures of care and solidarity that support high-risk forms of protest. There has indeed been a significant stream of religious support since the 1960s and 1970s, when progressive Catholic activism flourished in South Korea as part of the global liberation-theology movement. During the movements for democracy and human rights in the 1980s but also since then, activist Catholic nuns have quietly contributed to dramatic scenes of solidarity for countless long-

FIGURE 4.2. Catholic Mass in solidarity with *Sewol*-ferry victims, survivors, and families, Seoul, June 12, 2017. Photo by Ju Hui Judy Han.

term protest sites, with recent examples including the fight against ultra-high-voltage power lines in Miryang, on behalf of the residents displaced by military-base-construction projects in P'yŏngt'aek and Kangjŏng, alongside the bereaved parents of the *Sewol* disaster, and in support of laid-off and striking workers, most notably from Ssangyong Motor. The nuns have been steadfast in their presence at many of these protest sites, their simple white-and-gray head veils and habits creating a striking visual impact, though their presence should not be misconstrued as unwavering or homogenous. In fact, Sister Maria, in our interview, described a "bit of a gap" between her own activist trajectory and that of other veteran activist nuns. Though close in age, Sister Maria considered herself to be a bit different from the generation of more ideologically driven activist Catholics that fought against the violence of military dictatorship. Instead, the way she recounts it, her trajectory had

156   CHAPTER 4

more ordinary beginnings, shaped less by her political convictions than by her corporeal movements across time and space.

When Sister Maria first began apostolic life in the early 1990s, the convent that she entered was in Inchŏn, located east of Seoul. Inchŏn is the third most populous city in the country, but many parts of the city felt rural to her, including the neighborhood surrounding the convent. Going to Seoul always felt like going into the city from the country. In her early days as a Catholic nun, Sister Maria explained, she had little interest in social issues, and she did not have any knowledge or substantive understanding of what social movements set out to do. This began to shift after she started spending a significant amount of time in transit, traveling from the convent in Inchŏn to Seoul, sometimes on official convent business and other times to enjoy her days off. High-speed subway service was not available then for the nearly twenty-mile trek into the capital city, which meant that her roundtrip journeys took well over two hours each day.[20] "Interesting things kept catching my attention," she recalled during her time-consuming journeys that nonetheless provided time for observation and reflection. She often maximized her time in Seoul by staying until the very last train of the day departed.

One place that she began to spend more and more time was the front steps of Myŏngdong Cathedral. As the symbolic headquarters of the Korean Catholic Church, Myŏngdong Cathedral is one of the most historic and well-known sites of religious architecture in the country. Erected in 1898, Myŏngdong Cathedral was built in the Gothic style of European cathedrals that had open squares where people in the city could gather publicly in a sacred space.[21] While Sister Maria certainly chose to spend some of her time inside the church building to pray and attend Mass, she soon became enthralled by protest activities happening outside the church walls and in the surrounding vicinity.

Myŏngdong Cathedral was the epicenter of public protests and social-movement activism then, especially in the evenings when all public assembly after dark was prohibited by the state with the exception of religious and cultural activities. Social activists knew Myŏngdong Cathedral as a place that provided sanctuary to political dissidents throughout the 1980s and frequently congregated outside Myŏngdong Cathedral for major mass rallies and demonstrations throughout the 1990s. The practice continued after democratization as well. For example, in 1995, Nepalese migrant workers recruited to work under the highly exploitative migrant industrial-trainee system waged a historic occupation and hunger strike at Myŏngdong Cathedral, leaning on its symbolism of universality, sympathy, and solidarity and urging the Korean public, especially labor and social-justice activists, to take notice of the exploitative conditions of migrant labor in South Korea. They took their cue from South Korean trade unionists, who were part of the rapidly growing KCTU-led labor movement and regularly assembled on the steps of Myŏngdong Cathedral in the mid-1990s before marching en masse through the streets of central Seoul. KCTU unionists gathered in other public parks and squares around the city as well, yet many of these locations would become increasingly isolated from everyday public life, as we discuss in the next chapter. In contrast, Myŏngdong Cathedral was located at the top of a hill in Myŏngdong, one of the city's most centrally located commercial-retail districts, known for youth fashion, often creating a striking incongruity between protesters and the public. Trade unionists clad in matching union vests and wearing headbands with somber political slogans coexisted in proximity with shoppers and tourists interested in mass consumption.

Witnessing firsthand these vibrant and sometimes violent scenes of protest demonstrations stirred Sister Maria. "When I first started going [to Myŏngdong Cathedral], I did not know what things like a 'demo' were," she explained. Her initial perception of protesters had been largely influenced by the negative portrayal in authoritarian and anti-Communist education and media as well as by her conservative superiors in the convent, who would scold her for returning to the convent late at night, especially after attending public protests. Interestingly, even though she has had nearly thirty years of experience attending protests, Sister Maria lowered her voice to a whisper when she first mentioned the word "demo," as though the word should always be uttered in a hushed voice. Was it because our interview took place at a bustling café in Kwanghwamun? Did she feel self-conscious talking about this given the stereotypes and stigma that still remain attached to protest demonstrations?

Sister Maria recounted feeling unsure when she would first encounter other nuns at protest sites. To "break the awkwardness" with nuns she did not already know, Sister Maria "often made the first move" by extending a greeting of recognition. In ordinary circumstances, greetings are perfunctory and routine, consisting of habitual gestures that guide social behavior according to implicit norms and rules of conduct. However, since the nuns who attended protests were ostensibly engaging in activities that might result in disapproval or even reprimand or rebuke, Sister Maria recalled that their greetings carried something heavier—a sense of caution or mutual respect, a recognition of the risks involved in being there. As she and other activist nuns became better acquainted with each other over time, their interactions shifted from being tense and charged to more mundane and predictable. Pretty soon, a small circle of nuns became her "street friends" (거리친구).

These small changes in which the nuns greeted each other at protests may seem trivial, but we found this discussion to be illuminating. How does a new relational context for social interaction become established at protest sites? How do relationalities change over time? Sister Maria explained how these interactions affected norms and hierarchies:

> You know how when you go to demonstrations, you don't just stay in one place but sometimes go out into the street too? I would run into other nuns, and we would be happy to see each other. And so we would do high fives [*laughs*]. So just like that, we started to transcend age and seniority ranks in the convent. Convents used to have a lot more boundaries before. It's much better these days, and I feel like a lot of these boundaries started coming down when like-minded nuns from different convents started running into each other and meeting with each other at demonstrations and other [protest] events.

Breaking down the barriers of conservatism and hierarchy that pervaded everyday life at convents and monasteries created a different felt sense of sociality among activist nuns. By transgressing the usual hierarchies of age and rank as well as separation by convent membership, the nuns began connecting "more with each other" than with "nuns from their own convent." Sister Maria sometimes felt alienated in the insularity of her own convent, drifting away from the sisters in her own convent and becoming disconnected from the Catholic Church orthodoxy. "This gap can become big, and it can be difficult to relate to other nuns," she explained. However, rather than languish in the margins in her own community, Sister Maria continued to build bridges with sisters in other convents, directing her effort toward changing the organizational priorities from within.

Beginning in the late 1990s, Sister Maria took more proactive leadership in organizing fellow nuns to support specific social-justice causes. She and others first created a small group (모임) and then established a larger division (사회사목분) within the official structure of the Roman Catholic Church. In 2010, they changed the name of their division to the Life and Peace Division (생명평화분). The organizational structure of their formal suborganization within the Catholic Church (수도연 합회), which was established in 1965, allowed activist nuns to utilize the resources, communication systems, and leadership structure of a well-established transnational religious organization in order to support highly localized protest movements. Both the small group and the social-activist division were officially affiliated to the parent subgroup (수도연합), which had an organizational presence similar to other efforts such as the early-childhood-education department and the missionary department.

Ironically, the fact that nuns are women in subordinate positions in the male-dominated structure of the church enabled them to pursue their social activism with a greater degree of autonomy and flexibility than the male clergy. Their gender-specific organizing was also aided by the increasing participation levels of women entering apostolic life in the Catholic Church throughout the 1990s and 2000s, which contributed to an unprecedented period of growth and dynamism in the Korean Catholic Church.[22] Thus, even though priests and male religious leaders were perhaps more visibly present as leaders both in formal church settings and in social-movement spaces, the scale of nun-led women's

160   CHAPTER 4

social-justice organizing was numerically much larger than spaces organized by men.

There is perhaps nothing unique about fostering change and progressive reform within a large and bureaucratic organization like the Catholic Church. Efforts to create alternative priorities, relationships, and practices require motivation, commitment, and creativity, especially concerning issues that might clash with the way formal leaders define an organization's primary purpose. Bringing about internal change can require the kind of ethical labor that makes "matters of fact" like redirecting organizational resources more akin to "matters of care," as Puig de la Bellacasa puts it. "Thinking of matters of fact as matters of care does not require translation into a fixed or explanatory vision or a normative stance (moral or epistemological), it can be a speculative commitment to think about how things would be different if they generated care. This is a commitment, because it is indeed attached to situated and positioned visions of what a livable and caring world could be; but it remains speculative as it won't let a situation or a position—nor even the acute awareness of pervasive dominations—define in advance what *is* or *could* be."[23]

By challenging "specific assemblages," such ethical labor "leaves open the detection of specific needs for caring in each situation, instead of presupposing there is only one way of caring."[24] Making space for speculation is thus essential. It enables social actors to be steadfast in their collective commitment to care for the lives of others but in ways that do not prescribe ideological solutions to context-specific issues or elevate their own interests over those they purportedly care about.

Ethical labor also requires developing the capacity to pivot to make use of the difference between acting as an individual and as a member of a collective. Sister Maria explained, "How would I describe transgressing the boundaries of the convent as a nun? Taking action as an individual is different from being told by the convent to go and engage in actions with a name tag and affiliation card. For example, in an organization (like the convent), we would have discussions during regular meetings and decide together in advance on what to do. But when I participate on my own without affiliation, I can freely decide when to go and when to come back." By retaining flexibility and reflexivity in their activism, the nuns were able to create organizational structures that maximized their mobilities and the church's resources, especially in response to changing environmental conditions and unexpected events.

One significant period of such mobilization occurred in the immediate aftermath of the so-called IMF crisis in the late 1990s, explained Sister Maria. As South Korea became embroiled in the debilitating financial crisis, activist nuns quickly pivoted to the social provision of emergency relief and care. They used their organizational networks to collect donations, which they distributed to people with immediate needs. They visited the homeless encampments at Seoul and Yŏngdŭngp'o train stations. They went to impacted neighborhoods and communities that received little to no government support or media attention, supporting women who worked in red-light districts and military-camp towns. They traveled to urban and rural areas where poor people were facing imminent eviction, including on remote islands, due to the intensification of residential- and commercial-redevelopment projects. The nuns and other Catholic activist efforts throughout the 1990s and early 2000s responded to the needs of vulnerable communities and laid the basis for more sustained participation in key social-movement struggles in the mid to late 2000s as neoliberal reforms continued to transform diverse sectors of everyday life, including the labor market, trade, environment, and public safety.

SOLIDARITY ACTIVISM

While the 1990s were defined by service-oriented social activism, the early 2000s took on the distinct character of "solidarity activism," according to Sister Maria. Solidarity activism recognizes the political character of injustice and suffering and seeks to form alliances among the most directly impacted *tangsaja* and their supporters, advocates, and other solidarity groups in order to alleviate the harm and seek recourse. Sister Maria was emphatic when she named specific political forces as creating the conditions for her increasing participation in solidarity activism: "Lee Myung-bak and Park Geun-hye made nuns take to the streets," she declared. Lee Myung-bak (이명박; Yi Myŏng-bak) was previously the CEO of Hyundai Engineering and Construction and then mayor of Seoul before becoming South Korea's tenth president (2008–13). His election signaled a conservative political turn after a decade under liberal democratic presidents Roh Moo-hyun (2003–8) and Kim Dae-jung (1998–2003). To be fair, though, liberal presidents had hardly pacified movements for social change. In fact, it was during Roh's liberal administration that large-scale political mobilizations against war and fierce protests took place against the expansion of Camp Humphreys, a key US-military-base installation in South Korea, as part of relocating Yongsan Garrison from central Seoul. The project involved forceful land dispossession and displacement of residents from Taech'uri Village in P'yŏngt'aek, followed by a violent suppression of dissent in the aftermath.[25] Nearly all the activists we spoke with for this project had a story about Taech'uri, and some had even received prison sentences for their protest activities. But for Sister Maria, it was Lee Myung-bak's conservative politics and policies during his term as the "construction president" that unleashed the most controversial and environmentally destructive megainfrastructure projects that compelled her and other nuns to take to the streets.

Lee's presidency did spark an unprecedented rise in contentious religious politics. While many Protestant Christian conservatives mobilized in Lee's corner, dissenting Catholic priests and nuns joined multifaith coalitions with Sŏn Buddhists, Won Buddhists, progressive Protestants, and others to oppose state-led infrastructure projects and protect ecological habitats.[26] Lee's presidency is indeed associated with large-scale, fiercely fought labor protests, such as the Hanjin Hope Bus in 2011 (see chapter 3) as well as an event known as the Yongsan Ch'amsa (용산참사), which led to the death of five evictee protesters and a police officer in 2009 during violent police action and the escalation of the fight in Miryang against KEPCO in 2013, as we discussed earlier in this chapter. Lee was succeeded by Park Geun-hye (2013–17), another conservative president who was later impeached and removed from office on corruption charges after spectacular mass protests known as the Candlelight Protests of 2016–17.

Many of the protest forms that are now a mainstay started to take hold through these various solidarity-protest movements since the early 2000s. All required extraordinary work from not only the participants in the protest events but also the organizers and coordinators, who pored over plans and details from behind the scenes. "If we got started at ten in the morning," Sister Maria said about the *samboilbae*, "we would need to call it a day at around six in the evening. That meant we would also need to plan for rest times and car rides to the headquarters for people who were unable to walk anymore." The organizers needed to be attentive to individual physical abilities and care for those in emotional distress. "Definitely, it is not an easy thing to do. Under the scorching heat of the sun, to do it all day long from morning to night?" She shuddered at the memory.

The Catholic nuns' solidarity work to support Miryang grandmothers was also extremely grueling. Because Miryang grandmothers organized a daily protest every morning at the protest camp for several years, activist nuns, like Sister Maria, would have to leave their convents long before sunrise, sometimes as early as three o'clock in the morning even before the trains and buses start running, in order to start their journey to the mountaintops in time for the morning protest. Key organizers, like Sister Maria, were certainly resourceful, convincing priests to allow nuns to use church vans for local transport, for instance. But what Sister Maria remembered most vividly was the power of *corporeal* copresence, walking with other nuns in their habits toward the protest encampment, quietly and together, with determination.

When asked how she made choices regarding which protests to support, considering how many protests take place at any given moment in South Korea, Sister Maria explained that in most cases, the nuns had a policy of not physically attending a protest—or providing behind-the-scenes support—unless their support was explicitly requested by the *tangsaja* in an ongoing struggle. Unlike trade unionists or radical student activists, who may be more ideologically driven, she said, nuns go where they are *needed*, not where they want to go in order to advance their own goals. For example, when discussing the struggles around the *Sewol*-ferry disaster, Sister Maria spoke about the many groups that

FIGURE 4.3. Catholic Mass in solidarity with Ssangyong Motor unionists, facing the riot police at Taehanmun, Seoul, 2014. Photo by Ju Hui Judy Han.

swarmed the bereaved parents in opportunistic ways. The nuns were actively involved too, but Sister Maria was careful to emphasize that they tried not to get overly involved. This meant that they kept their participation to the level of essential caregiving and visible presence without taking part in internal-leadership structure or organizational decision-making.

Playing a supportive role sometimes created awkward situations. An example of this is the *chujŏm* (주점), a pop-up fundraising event where snacks and drinks are sold to supporters to generate financial and moral support. Allies and supporters share the responsibility for organizing *chujŏm* events at a restaurant, community space, or even in public on the sidewalk, and they must manage all aspects involved in event planning, including cooking and ticket sales. For Catholic nuns, we wondered if organizing a drinking-oriented event might be challenging. After all, does anyone—but especially Catholic nuns—feel uncomfortable about selling alcohol and serving *anju* (안주), or "drinking food," even for purposes of solidarity activism?

> Han. Somehow it seems odd to picture a nun organizing or going to a *chujŏm*.
>
> Sister Maria. I know! . . . Nuns do feel burdened by the selling of alcohol, so we don't fully participate. We would go early and help with preparations, and then we leave. . . . When someone approaches us for help with their fundraiser, we ask, "How many people, [and] from when to when?" And then we figure out who has experience and who can go. Even if it's just two to three of us, we are really good at doing things, getting work done. We participate.

Sister Maria's pragmatic approach shows that she was deeply invested in the concrete and material support that she and other nuns were able to provide through their work. In other words, it is not just spiritual guidance or religious solidarity in the abstract that Catholic nuns like Sister Maria contributed. They went above and beyond to contribute a steadfast presence at protest sites because they recognized the value of the care work they knew how to provide.

POLITICS OF COPRESENCE

Interestingly, in addition to the value of care work that can appear trivial and mundane, Sister Maria was also emphatic about something else: the value of persistent presence. Showing up time and time again and maintaining a presence is indeed a deep practice of solidarity. While Sister Maria and other activist nuns know that collective action is crucial to effect change, they also recognize that even a single individual can offer comfort and hopefulness to reassure protesters that they are not alone in their struggle. This evokes for us the practice of "radical socialist humanism," which works to oppose "authoritarian capitalism's and neoliberalism's anti-humanism."[27] It is also reminiscent of what David Harvey discusses as "revolutionary humanism" against alienation.

There is, I believe, a crying need to articulate a secular *revolutionary* humanism that can ally with those religious-based humanisms (most clearly articulated in both Protestant and Catholic versions of the theology of liberation as well as in cognate movements within Hindu, Islamic, Jewish and indigenous religious cultures) to counter alienation in its many forms and to radically change the world from its capitalist ways. There is a strong and powerful—albeit problematic—tradition of secular revolutionary humanism both with respect to both theory and political practice.... It is very different from bourgeois liberal humanism. It refuses the idea that there is an unchanging or pre-given "essence" of what it means to be human and forces us to think hard about how to become a new kind of human.[28]

Rather than delineate a rigid distinction between religious and secular revolutionary humanism, we are fascinated by the nuns' revolutionary attentiveness to individuals in need of care and especially their willingness and capacity to provide what is undoubtedly *gendered* labor of social reproduction as well. As women, the nuns typically work alongside other women, whose social locations as mothers, wives, and daughters put them in close proximity to gendered reproductive labor. What Sister Maria articulated in our interview was that her and other Catholic nuns' solidarity work must be understood on multiple registers. They are part of a broader network of religious solidarity, but they participate in struggles against alienation and abandonment by performing reproductive labor and essential care work.

Indeed, as researchers who have been following labor and other political protests since the late 1990s, we were struck by the frequent and persistent presence of Catholic nuns in the sites we visited. In 2013, when Han (coauthor) participated in a study tour organized by the Alliance of Scholars Concerned about Korea, a small group of Catholic nuns were part of the itinerary in Kangjŏng in Jeju. It was here that Han first met Sister Maria as they performed together the Buddhist ritual of 108 bows to protest against the construction of a massive new military base.

Sometimes, though not always, the nuns organize assemblies in ways that accentuate their religious affiliation. In a striking visual display of solidarity, for instance, activist nuns and priests were often found in front of the well-known Taehanmun gate of Tŏksu Palace in downtown Seoul, where they held daily masses at 6:30 p.m. for laid-off workers from Ssangyong Motor for a total of 225 days between April 8, 2013, and November 18, 2013. To underscore the significance of this mobilization, let us briefly explain the changing political landscapes that raised the need for religious solidarity. There is certainly a long history of religious solidarity with political movements in South Korea, especially for democracy and labor movements since the 1970s. The growth of independent unions across the country in the late 1980s and their subsequent legalization in the 1990s meant, however, that the democratic labor-union movement operated more as an independent social force. In other words, the labor movement needed to rely less on the moral legitimacy of religious leaders, like Catholic clergy. What emerged in the mid-2000s was a new dynamic, as more striking workers began to persist in their fight despite losing the support of their own unions. Primarily precarious workers in contract or temporary positions or laid-off workers with no legal recourse, the protesting workers would endure on their own, often rejected and abandoned by unions that prioritized salaried, or so-called regular, workers. They would fight against all odds, facing repeated and violent efforts by the state and the employer to destroy their base camp and forcibly bring the protest to an end. Catholic solidarity became more urgently needed in these contexts, Sister Maria explained, as the situations became more dire, more life-or-death. Such was the case of the Taehanmun daily Mass, which began on April 8, 2013, when the Seoul city police raided and forcibly dismantled the altar for deceased Ssangyong Motor workers outside Taehanmun. When more and more laid-off unionists on strike began dying prematurely, either by suicide or as a result of complications from traumatic injuries sustained during police action, the CPAJ sprang to action to hold a Mass to pray for the workers and to pray for democracy.

In the summer of 2013, as Ssangyong Motor workers kept vigil to protect the newly rebuilt altar and continue their fight, Taehanmun became a site for a series of multifaith gatherings involving not only Catholic but also Protestant prayer rallies. The nuns joined the clergy, taking turns to show up every day for the Catholic prayers. As a lead coordinator of

168   CHAPTER 4

this effort, Sister Maria vigilantly organized a steady flow of participants by contacting people ahead of time to encourage their attendance. As she explained, an organizer must create hospitable conditions to make participation possible and worthwhile. Every day at the prayer, she would make sure a *tangsaja* representative from Ssangyong Motor Union would share a firsthand personal story of struggle, and guest speakers would be invited to draw connections between the Ssangyong Motor situation and other pressing social issues taking place across the country. There were countless other sites of pain and suffering throughout South Korea, a priest read from a statement on April 14, 2013, but the Catholic leadership recognized that the Taehanmun daily Mass had to take place until the situation stabilized. It was an extremely challenging task, he acknowledged, but it was also an educational opportunity that "taught the clergy that their main task was to accompany those who are suffering, a clear signpost on the narrow road for clergy."[29]

Presence was the foundation upon which other solidaristic relations and practices were staged. Presence, in many ways, is the opposite of ideology. Sister Maria emphasized that she was careful when interacting with *tangsaja* individuals during religious-solidarity events to avoid any misperception that the nuns had "ulterior motives." She was exceedingly careful to never use solidarity-prayer events as opportunities to proselytize. Instead, Sister Maria recognized the transformational potential of a simple greeting when the nuns were invited to be present in solidarity. She recalled, "I never even once asked them [Ssangyong Motor workers in mourning] about their personal lives or families. When first arriving [at the protest site], I would greet them by asking, "Have you been well? How are you doing today? Have you eaten today?" I never asked about anything else. I also did not tell them who I was."

Keeping their social interactions to perfunctory greetings—at least initially—enabled Sister Maria to offer support without expectations of reciprocity. This would not be a transaction of give-and-take. Her only goal would be to give unconditionally, to support those who were suffering and in need. Through her sensitive and intentional approach, she would be able to build trust and rapport, deepening affinity over time: "Later, as time passed, [Ssangyong Motor workers] would begin sharing their stories. I felt a change. I went out there every single day, and over time, how shall I put it—camaraderie? Kinship? I felt it."

Consistent, predictable interactions between nuns and aggrieved workers also created the social basis upon which grieving workers could begin exploring their own feelings of betrayal and disappointment. The daily liturgy in front of the altar created the mise en place for the participants to be immersed in the ambient sounds and scenes of embodied rituals of faith. Although most of the Ssangyong Motor protesters were not actually "people of faith," according to Sister Maria, some of them began to find solace nonetheless in the Catholic liturgy, taking the opportunity to join hands, pray, and sing in collectivity. For Sister Maria, this was not about proselytization but building connections to help heal on individual and collective scales.

But there would be another group of participants in these gatherings—the police, sometimes in full riot gear with shields and batons. It became important for the protest organizers to greet the police officers at protest sites in order to try to soften the hostile atmosphere. Typically, Sister Maria said she and other activist nuns did everything they could to avoid police attention. But given the long duration of their solidarity action with laid-off Ssangyong Motor workers and the fact that police were a constant daily presence—though hostile and repressive—Sister Maria found herself learning to interact with the police in a different way.

> How do you react when you see the police? At first I had no idea how to respond to them. But as we continued [to show up every day], we learned to take a punch, so to speak. [And then we realized,] "Ahh, the police should not do this to us." So we would tell them to change how they are acting. [We would say to them,] "Why are you blocking me?" The police don't always know the law. So we constantly pushed. We never fight with the lower-level police officers. We ask for their superiors. And then, for example, we ask that the policemen be replaced with women because it can get scary with male police officers.

After they were successful in getting the police to dispatch policewomen instead, however, the nuns learned that women police officers could be equally as harsh in their daily dealings with activist nuns, pushing and shoving and even pinching and twisting the nuns during physical altercations. But over time, as the protests continued day after day, the organizers would begin to recognize familiar faces even among the police, able to discern the less hostile officers.

> You see these people [the police] every single day, and you start to be able to tell if someone has a slightly different attitude toward us. There are police officers who do not thoughtlessly engage in violence. We start to identify who we can approach. And [if] the moment feels right, we can say to them, "You work so hard because of us. You barely have time to rest." [*Laughs*.] And at the end of each protest, I say to them, "Great work! See you again tomorrow!" When the police hear this unexpected greeting, sometimes they can't help but laugh. And the next day, they soften.

Sister Maria elaborated on this tactic of softening police interactions.

> You know the saying "One cannot spit on a smiling face"? I try not to lose a sense of who I am, and I stay true to myself when I tell the police about the injustices that they are perpetuating against us. I say to them, "Society may tell you that you are doing the right thing, but in our eyes, you are the ones transgressing the law. In your eyes, I might be the one transgressing, but in reality, you are just a puppet. You need to understand the bigger purpose and learn how to say no to what is not right. That is how you become a proper citizen." I sometimes say things like that to the police, which I probably should not. They usually say, "What nonsense!" But then sometimes, there are officers who listen.

Even though activist nuns developed "softer" interpersonal relations with some of the police officers, Sister Maria was keenly aware that the police would not likely become a force of solidarity. At any moment, the police could turn on the protesters, as she had experienced on countless occasions. One ingenious tactic the Catholic nuns used was to hide in plain sight, using their veil and habits to become indistinguishable from one another and even interchangeable in the eyes of the police. "We have a few rules, like never give them your real name. Just tell the police your name is Maria. [*Laughs*.] There are so many people from our convent and order, and we all wear the same habits. The police can't tell who is who. They think we are all the same."

This moment during the interview elicited even more laughter among us, and we joked about renaming their organization "We Are All Marias." In fact, Sister Maria is a pseudonym she chose as a nod to this tactic. Importantly, this practice emphasizes the significance of presence not as soliciting individual recognition but as contributing consistent and reliable copresence. As such, copresence was in itself an act of solidarity and expression of relational care.

The momentum generated from relational care is rooted in the kind of group-based, horizontal leadership that Ella Baker deems essential to the effectiveness and sustainability of grassroots organizing.[30] Group-based leadership prioritizes the leadership of the most impacted in projects for social change, yet it acknowledges that this requires the cultivation of an alternative form of leadership. Rather than build movement organizations around the charisma of a single public spokesperson, group-based leadership prioritizes organizational, capacity-building, and communal forms of care and reciprocity. Inherent in Baker's critique of public spokespersons is the vulnerability of charismatic leaders to institutional co-option by the ruling elite, as well as of the masculinist logics that devalue the worth of the labor of social reproduction that is so vital to sustaining oppositional movements across time and place.

Throughout our conversations with Sister Maria, her commitment to reflexivity guided the decisions that she and other activist nuns made about who they chose to support in solidarity and how they did so in ways that prioritized the ethical labor of relational care. Central to this commitment was the explicit recognition of their positionality in broader institutional hierarchies and social structures of inequality and domination. Once she recognized the specific contributions that nuns could make to support political struggles against disposability and abandonment, she pushed to challenge and reorganize the internal structures of the church to make possible new priorities and enabled others within the church to more actively support struggles taking place around the country. Their solidarity activism always made striking visual impact, eliciting more public attention. But more importantly, their solidarity underscored the need for consistent and reliable presence, the ability and willingness to show up when needed, and to remain as long as they were needed. The care, reflexivity, and pragmatism that activist nuns, such as Sister Maria, bring to the work of solidarity create a social-movement infrastructure that essentially enables protesters to sustain their struggles. This infrastructure helps produce the distinct sense that one is not "stuck in place" in the extractive and degrading political economies that undermine the survival of people and communities, who nonetheless refuse to submit.[31]

MOVEMENT REFLEXIVITY

Similar to the ways in which activist Catholic nuns paid careful attention to group-based vulnerabilities and challenged existing internal hierarchies in the Catholic Church, feminist human rights activists we spoke with also revealed a commitment to fostering reflective processes to care for and strengthen their movement praxis as well as effect meaningful change in social relations. As we discuss in the sections that follow, their attention to reflexivity reflects more than a general rethinking of existing ideas and practices; it involves a great deal of care. It involves vigilant attention to the production and reproduction of social inequalities that can create harm, and it involves striving to cultivate more purposive methods to care for oneself and others. This labor of sustaining caring infrastructures, we argue, is an often overlooked yet incredibly powerful and intrinsic part of social and political transformation.

In the 1990s and 2000s, a growing number of national-democratization-movement practitioners who were closely aligned with the political values of fighting capitalist and state violence began challenging the movement status quo and a variety of dominant beliefs and practices. Widespread sexism and misogyny were certainly key feminist concerns, as were sexual harassment and violence within progressive and left political spaces. Also on the rise were new critiques of the culture of social hierarchy based on age, gender, and education. Take, for instance, the normative practices surrounding the *sŏnbae/hubae* culture—one of the most common and enduring hierarchies in everyday life, including social-movement life. Student activism relies heavily on this social hierarchy, placing on top the older students, or *sŏnbae* (seniors), and below them the younger students, or *hubae* (juniors). As *sŏnbae*, older student activists were invested with the authority and obligation to mentor younger students on what to do and how to do it. While these relations often generated feelings of affection, influence, and intimacy, they also normalized problematic patterns of behavior, including bullying, devaluing, and abuse. Younger people, because of their location in the age hierarchy, were often disregarded and exploited.

Gender was crucial in demarcating differentiated roles, responsibilities, and value systems in social movements. Activist scholar Tari Young-Jung Na identifies the family, the legal-identification system, and the military as three interlocking modalities of the South Korean binary gender system.[32] Stories abound, especially among LGBTQ+ and female student activists in the 1980s, about the sharply and normatively gendered landscape of movement participation that elevated the value of cisgender men's participation while discounting or erasing women's contributions. For instance, cisgender male student activists would be consistently celebrated for fighting on the front lines of militant protests, bearing the primary risk of clashing with the police and risking injury, arrest, and imprisonment. In contrast, cisgender women were expected to stand behind these men and play a secondary, more behind-the-scenes role. A feminist activist we interviewed laughed as she remembered that as a student activist, she often had to fall back in protests with other women, who were tasked with smashing and hammering cement blocks to break off smaller pieces for the male students to throw. She prided herself in being athletic and a good thrower, so she remembered being irritated by these gender roles. Women would have to assemble Molotov cocktails—again, for the men to throw—or even more blatantly play a supporting role to care for the needs of others, including cooking, cleaning, earning money, doing homework assignments for men so they could maintain student status, raising children, and so on.

Not surprisingly, as in many other radical left movements around the world, a challenge to these heteropatriarchal gender norms in everyday movement practice would be accused of weakening morale and ideological unity. A former student activist we interviewed explained that many activists certainly recognized the problems and issues around the male-dominated culture of activism and the subordination of women but that they were rarely even mentioned, let alone challenged. It was because an overwhelming sense of emergency pervaded their everyday lives, and one just seemed more important. "How could women bring up gender discrimination," she told us, "when so many male activists were being beaten or in prison or on the run from the law?"

By most accounts, it appears that as the ideologies and institutions of authoritarian rule were replaced by the principles and procedures of formal democratic equality, normative social relations did experience a tide of change. Former student activists who continued to work in the field of social change were becoming part of the burgeoning civil society and political parties, which began to flourish in a more liberal climate for public assembly and political dissent. The state's ongoing investment in public-infrastructure development, such as roads, subways, and train systems, as well as its commitment to improving the quality of life through neighborhood-based welfare services and the construction of public parks and facilities also created more opportunities for citizens to become involved in a wider variety of emerging social issues, such as environmental justice, migrant rights, and what came to be known as *inkwŏn undong* (인권운동), a distinct area of human rights activism.

Ryu Eunsook, our key interlocuter for the second half of this chapter, was one of the first to actively identify as an *inkwŏn* (인권; human rights) activist in South Korea. As one of the founding members of Sarangbang Group for Human Rights, or just Sarangbang for short, Ryu Eunsook became an influential voice against the state's appropriation of popular politics as part of the burgeoning civil society sphere. Recognizing the dangers of succumbing to the hegemonic logics of state incorporation, she focused on developing new ways for student and *minjung*-movement activists to remain intentional in their antisystemic work by engaging in reflexivity and adapting to changing institutional and political conditions.[33]

Ryu traces the origins of the term *hwaldongga* (활동가)—meaning "activist" or "organizer"—to her early days at Sarangbang. Today, the term denotes a self-identity or even a line of work for those working in social movements and broader fields of social-change making. Before, *hwaldongga* was *kansa* (간사), or "(organizational) staff," but that term did not adequately capture what they do. Individuals who identify as *hwaldongga* do not simply schedule meetings and coordinate events, taking minutes or managing records and documents; they lead efforts to set the agenda and organize like-minded individuals to implement visions for social change. Some are paid staff positions in well-established organizations, but the term refers more to a role rather than a title.

> The term *hwaldongga* is something that Sarangbang first started using. We said we were not just *kansa*, or "administrative staff." We actively do *hwaldong* [활동] and take leadership in setting movement agendas. Our role is not just to assist experts [전문가]. So let's call ourselves *hwaldongga*, we said. When we change the names we call ourselves, our roles and responsibilities change too. After twenty years of popularizing this term, *hwaldongga*, I think now there is a culture in which experts and activists work together and equally, side by side as colleagues.

She described an emerging sense of community in which each member had something to contribute and everyone could count on being supported in a more egalitarian and horizontal way. South Korean social-movement organizations typically have a hierarchical structure with chairs and presidents on top and directors and managers below them, but the term *hwaldongga* could apply to all of them the same. Though difficult and rarely well paid, to be a *hwaldongga* is to choose social change as a line of work, a way of life, and a field of expertise.

This meant changes in language too, including the way movement participants referred to each other in everyday conversation. Since names and titles are often unavoidable when speaking in Korean with its fundamentally hierarchical structure, conversations between any individuals typically begin with the customary understanding that one may only use first names when speaking to someone who is unmistakably younger or equal, but with individuals who are older or unfamiliar or in formal contexts, one must use honorific suffixes such as *ssi* (씨) or *nim* (님).

We were unsure what title we should use when addressing Ryu Eunsook when we first met her. She is a longtime human rights activist but also a widely published writer, so Han tentatively addressed Ryu Eunsook as *chakka-nim* (작가님), an honorific form for "author." Ryu immediately responded that she dislikes being referred to as an author just because she has written books. "Just call me 'activist' or 'colleague' or whatever," she said, "even 'older sister' if you like. Anything but 'author.'" It is a common dilemma, one which usually leads to a bit of negotiation. We had a good laugh about the awkwardness and agreed to refer to each other with the simple and very common yet respectful title *sŏnsaeng-nim* (선생님), or "teacher." Included in this negotiation was the agreement that she would not call us *kyosu-nim* (교수님), or "professor," as we would not call her Chairperson Ryu or Executive Director Ryu in reference to her formal position in the Ch'ang Human Rights Research Center (인권연구소 창). These negotiations over names and titles may seem trivial, but in our case, the interview began with this subtle but clear recognition that established a common ground—we did not take the hierarchical customs for granted, and we were all seeking more horizontal relations. We were not alone; these are increasingly common practices in movement communities in South Korea, where activists also use nicknames or movement-activist names (활동명) without any age- or status-based honorifics. These pseudonyms are used for privacy protection but also to create more egalitarian ways of relating to one another.

We consider these small but meaningful challenges to everyday hierarchies and social relations to be an important part of cultivating caring infrastructures. Ch'ang Human Rights Research Center was established in 2006 as a project within the Sarangbang Group for Human Rights. Formal organizational documents may identify Ryu as the head of the organization, but she describes this as a superficial label, one that is simply required to manage everyday operations, such as signing the rental agreement for an office space. The group is wary of grand titles or fame and runs on *hwaldongga* members who work part-time jobs to cover their expenses. Ryu referred to her role as a research activist (연구활동가), the same as other members, once again emphasizing egalitarian relations among the members. She said,

There are about ten or so members in the Ch'ang Human Rights Research Center. But not a single person is a paid activist, including me. Everyone has their own day job, and we meet on occasion to decide on the research project we want to take on and share our thoughts. Everyone has their own human rights field [인권현장], for instance as a human rights attorney or as a labor activist against Samsung, but here we gather as research activists. It's an unusual title that we came up with, actually, because we wanted to refer to the combination of studying and researching as well as activism. There are activists who really study issues, you know? There are lots of people like that, and they're starting to say "research activism" to describe what they do.

In 2006, Ch'ang Human Rights Research Center became independent from Sarangbang Group for Human Rights, establishing itself as an independent entity and reflecting Sarangbang's intentional strategy to avoid becoming too large or complacent. Similar offshoots of Sarangbang—each an independent entity—include the Seoul Human Rights Film Festival (서울인권영화제; est. 1996) and Deul Human Rights Education Center (인권교육센터 들; est. 2008). The name Ch'ang, meaning "window," was chosen after discussing what it meant for them to operate as a voluntary activist-research collective, said Ryu. For over a decade, Ch'ang members have met regularly, sometimes as often as three times per week, holding group-based study seminars to identify and discuss issues pertinent to human rights and social and political change. As research activists, many members have wide-ranging skills and experience in research and writing, producing an extensive archive of critical-research support for human rights issues, including labor activism and adjacent social movements.

THE WORK OF SUSTAINING ACTIVISM

Regular study-group meetings are a hallmark of South Korean social movements. Left social activists, including student and human rights activists, have a history of creating these spaces for collective learning and social interaction. South Korea is reportedly the most overworked nation in Asia, with workers logging an average of 1,915 hours a year in

2021, which is nearly two hundred hours more than the average among members of the Organization for Economic Cooperation (OECD) and about 33 percent more than in Germany. Activists work long hours too, and Ryu Eunsook often noticed activists not eating healthy or even skipping meals altogether because they were busy working. She started cooking and serving food and drinks for participants of study groups at Ch'ang Human Rights Research Center, and eventually, she said, "people started calling this space *sulbang* [술방; drinking room], as a play on the word *kongbubang* [공부방; study room]." She wanted to help build sociality and camaraderie one might find with friends in a pub, and that became part of her role in a caring infrastructure in human rights activism.

The *sulbang* is, in a way, an innovation of the Korean practice of *twip'uri* (뒤풀이), which refers to the informal gathering after the end of a meeting or event. One could expect to find meaningful conversations in a more casual *twip'uri* setting than perhaps at the meeting or event itself, allowing people to interact more intimately. Though it is typical for *twip'uri* to take place at a restaurant or bar, Ryu Eunsook felt that this often proved to be financially burdensome for activists with a limited income and needlessly stressful when it came time to split the bill. It just so happens that Ryu herself had worked for many years as a part-time restaurant cook to sustain her full-time activist career, and soon, what she recognized as the significance of food and drinking in these spaces of activist gathering became the impetus to host her own *sulbang*.

Above all, Ryu said, she wanted to make sure that Ch'ang Human Rights Research Center nourished, rather than drained or depleted, hardworking social activists and began to curate her *sulbang* as a gathering place for human rights activists working in a variety of fields. She thought of her role at Ch'ang as a discerning curator of conversations, much like in the style of hosting a salon. "I'm a pretty picky person," she smiled, "and I can tell after one or two times having a drink with someone whether or not I will invite them back." She also took pride in creating the *sulbang* as a kind of safe space for activists in leadership positions to grapple with difficult dilemmas or complex political issues, engaging in spur-of-the-moment and off-the-record discussions in depth without having to worry about public perception or a hostile audience. A simple idea in many ways, the *sulbang* that Ryu curated over the years served an indispensable purpose for building critically engaged, caring communities.

When we were invited to attend a *sulbang* in the summer of 2017, we were struck by the tremendous amount of work involved in hosting. It is no minor task to feed a dozen people. As soon as we arrived at Ch'ang, we could smell the hot oil sizzling and spicy soup simmering in the kitchen. Heaping plates of stir-fried kimchi and vegetable pancakes and bowls of various sizes and shapes containing soup and side dishes (*panch'an*; 반찬) filled the tabletop, and of course—it was a *sulbang* after all—there were various bottles of soju, *makkŏli* (막걸리; Korean rice wine), red wine, and beer. Ryu Eunsook herself did much of the cooking, and even though many *sulbang* participants insisted on helping afterward with cleaning up and washing the dishes, she felt that it was often necessary to wash them again to meet her high standards. We asked if she ever thought cooking and cleaning reproduced normative gender roles and inequalities, and she paused before responding: "I do want to be hospitable, as the host. It's not because I am a woman that I play this role. I simply want to treat my guests well and wouldn't want guests to clean things up. I do think it's important for everyone to do this kind of [reproductive] work though, so they know how to do it and do it together and recognize the value of this labor. A lot of groups deal with issues around cleaning by just outsourcing the work and hiring cleaners, but I think we should do it ourselves."

She saw her care work as cultivating self-sufficiency and hospitality rather than reproducing the traditional gender roles. She was critical of the idea that doing reproductive labor took anything away from the "real work" that was more glorified and deemed more important. Whether reading and writing books or cooking and washing dishes after a seminar, she urged us to consider both as equally valuable forms of political labor.

These ideas were related to the frustration Ryu Eunsook felt about the normative gender roles during her days of student activism in the 1980s. She was not able to adequately voice these concerns, as issues of discrimination or equity were widely considered secondary or even trivial. She did regret not challenging them more, though. "We did fight," she laughed, "but now when I look back, I don't think we fought enough. So we have to keep fighting." One consequence of not fighting enough for gender equity back then, she said, was that now many of these former student activists have become political leaders with little appreciation of gender equality or equity. "People who later entered national politics are all former student activists, you know? I just don't think they have any gender analysis at all because ever since the student days, they were taken care of by women students. For sure, their wives would have earned the money, and their wives would have raised the children, and these activists would have thought they were doing more important work outside the home. I don't think these individuals would know a thing about gender equality. I think we taught them bad habits from back then. We should have fought more."

The everyday space of protest is another arena where the felt politics of gender discrimination and inequity can jeopardize movement solidarity. Ryu Eunsook articulated this sentiment lucidly when discussing the types of protest camps that strengthen a sense of affinity and connection between protesters and supporters and highlighted two examples: the *nongsŏng* at Taehanmun by laid-off Ssangyong Motor workers and the *nongsŏng* at Kangnam subway station by Banolim activists. She explained that there are plenty of protest sites where one feels uncomfortable, as opposed to others, like these two exemplary *nongsŏng* sites, that exude feelings of warmth and hospitality toward visitors, regardless of gender, age, or movement affiliation. Part of being a *hwaldongga* is making the time to physically visit these sites of long-term struggles to learn and to facilitate a sense of community.

At the core of Ryu Eunsook's movement praxis was the recognition of activists as living, breathing, feeling, and evolving human beings who work long hours in high-risk, conflict-ridden settings, often to the detriment of their mental and physical well-being. By creating an intentional place where care work was not devalued but centered as an important part of movement work, she drew attention to the value of caring infrastructure. Political work was not just about going toe-to-toe against the hegemony of neoliberal capitalism or writing and publishing trenchant critiques but also about finding ways to deepen the quality of people's connections with one another. Creating alternative ways of eating, drinking, and talking together constitutes an important movement praxis to not only support each other but also find new ways to hold each other accountable in a shared project of social and political transformation on multiple scales.

CONCLUSION

An emphasis on process and relationality, rather than simply on goals and outcomes, is crucial for understanding how reflexive social movements contend with the dominance of neoliberal logics and practices in state-led development in the postauthoritarian era. "Care labor is everyone's labor," writes Abigail H. Neely and Patricia J. Lopez. "It is what not only sustains each individual through physical and emotional support, it is also the work of building social relations, community, and modes of relationality."[34] Both Sister Maria and Ryu Eunsook demonstrated the importance of a variety of multiscalar care work involved in activism not only to reinforce and reproduce but also to reimagine and revise movement practices.

Our in-depth analysis of the insights and reflections of Sister Maria and Ryu Eunsook reveals how relational and reflexive practices of care strengthen the capacity of social-movement allies to *care about* the issues and lives of *tangsaja* protesters as well as *take care of tangsaja* protesters themselves who persist in fighting even the battles that seem unlikely to succeed. In addition to intimate forms of care on an interpersonal level, caring encompasses the meso- and macrolevel politics of caring for communities and worlds involving power relations and in the context of inequality, injustice, violence, and destruction. Neely and Lopez argue that "care ethics is a politics of relationality and as such it is necessarily multi-scalar, moving beyond neoliberal capitalism's insistence on the atomized individual and family and a vision of care-as-protection."[35] Neoliberal logics "position care as a private practice and responsibility and prioritise paid work as the foundation of social inclusion and citizenship," writes Emma R. Power et al. in a 2022 article about what they call "shadow care infrastructures."[36] For both Sister Maria and Ryu Eunsook, sustaining the ability of protest-movement actors and activists involves positioning care similarly as "alternate infrastructure."[37]

Conceptualizing care as infrastructure certainly builds on the "infrastructural turn," especially in human geography and cultural anthropology. In capitalist systems predicated on colonial violence and dispossession, infrastructure often refers to the sturdy physical foundation of extractive-capital-accumulation projects that facilitate the movement of resources, goods, people, and money across vast distances. Rather than define "infrastructure" simply as the "material stuff" of cities, however, a growing body of scholarship on infrastructure foregrounds the social, relational, and affective dimensions of infrastructure.[38] Importantly, Winona LaDuke and Deborah Cowen further assert that infrastructure can also be "alimentary"—that is, "life-giving in its design, finance, and effects."[39] Cultivating alternative ways of managing, distributing, and sharing resources as well as reinventing traditions of collective survival and resilience struggle that are passed on through performative and ritual practices can build alimentary caring infrastructures that produce an experience of motion and change that is different from abstract notions of linear progress and material prosperity. It points to AbdouMaliq Simone's influential formation of "the radical openness of people as infrastructure."[40]

Optics of visibility and invisibility are crucial to understanding infrastructure's power to shape and influence people's everyday lives. After all, "all visibility is situated and what is background for one person is a daily object of concern for another. The point is not to assert one or another status as an inherent condition of infrastructure but to examine how (in)visibility is mobilized and why."[41] For Sister Maria, for example, the visibility of activist nuns at protest sites was used as a resource, but she and other nuns also worked hard to be part of caring infrastructures that were strategically invisible. For Ryu Eunsook, making visible the work of curating social spaces and cooking for activist gatherings, for example, was part of a radical politics that worked to counter the ongoing devaluation of women's reproductive labor in the political work of social transformation. For activists committed to building caring infrastructure, effecting social change means doing so not only *out there* but also *within* movement spaces, among movement actors. Creating spaces like *sulbang* ensures that participation builds affinities and a sense of belonging far beyond the specific site of protest.

5 PROTEST AS PLACE MAKING

> You can think of the history of the *kwangjang* [광장; public square] as proceeding from the margins to the center of the city.
>
> —Lee Taeho (이태호; Yi T'ae-ho), policy chairperson of PSPD and cochair of the Emergency Action for Park Geun-hye's Resignation

> A geographical imperative lies at the heart of every struggle for social justice; if justice is embodied, it is then therefore always spatial, which is to say, part of a process of making a place.
>
> —Ruth Wilson Gilmore, "Fatal Couplings of Power and Difference"

THE CROWD ERUPTED IN EXUBERANCE as the verdict was announced. The decision to impeach Park Geun-hye as the president of South Korea was approved by the Constitutional Court on March 10, 2017, a memorably sunny and chilly morning. We had joined a public gathering outside near Kwanghwamun Square and anxiously awaited the news, which was shown live on a large LED screen in real time. "We announce the decision as the unanimous opinion of all judges. We dismiss the defendant President Park," the chief justice declared, marking the first time in Korean history that a democratically elected president was removed from office.[1] All around us, people began crying, shouting, hugging, dancing, and shaking their fists in sheer joy, and soon, we started walking. We marched past Kwanghwamun Square toward the presidential Blue House—a route we knew like the back of our hands after several months of protesting in the streets of central Seoul. It was a victory march, but it still felt like a call to action because there was unfinished work. Most obviously, despite Park Geun-hye's ousting, there still had not been a reckoning for the bereaved parents and other families of the *Sewol*-ferry disaster three years prior. Wearing their iconic yellow color and carrying a large banner with portraits of the children who perished on April 16, 2014, the bereaved *Sewol* parents vowed never to give up as they sang the *Sewol*-movement anthem, "The Truth Never Sinks." Marchers affirmed this steadfast sense of resolve as they chanted in unison, "This is just the beginning"—a slogan we would hear over and over in the coming weeks as the candlelight protesters prepared for the special election to replace Park Geun-hye.

Later, we would learn that this was also a bloody day, a rare occurrence during what was mostly a peaceful period of protest events. A Facebook friend posted that he accidentally came out of the wrong exit at Anguk subway station and stepped into the heart of an angry pro–Park Geun-hye rally that was turning violent. When the crowd spotted a yellow ribbon for *Sewol* on his bag, a telltale sign of someone who did not belong in their midst, an angry mob shoved and started to beat him while shouting that he was a spy. He was thankfully able to escape without much harm. News reports would later reveal several other similar incidents of violence instigated by protesters who were incensed by the verdict against Park. Known generally as participants of the T'aegŭkki Rally, the Park loyalists tended to be well in their sixties and seventies and associated with a mishmash of nationalist, anti-Communist, anti–North Korea, and generally conservative and right-wing political ideas. They acquired this moniker for the South Korean national flag they waved in opposition to the Candlelight Protests they considered traitorous, but the T'aegŭkki Rallies were often identifiable also by the US, United Nations, or Israeli flags waved to emphasize the geopolitical alliances the participants held dear, as well as military fatigues and veteran association caps many men wore. Sometimes, even flags with giant red crosses would be seen among the T'aegŭkki flags to suggest a kind of Christian-nationalist political orientation. The T'aegŭkki Rally participants were a perplexing and heterogenous bunch, neither consistent nor coherent in ideology or organization, but one thing that united them was their devotion to Park Geun-hye and her father. In the hours following the impeachment verdict, they lashed out and physically as-

186   CHAPTER 5

saulted the police and members of the press, dispersing only after the police began spraying capsaicin-laced water cannons on the crowd. Dozens of injuries and a total of four deaths were reported that day, all involving T'aegŭkki Rally participants in violent confrontation against the police, including one elderly man in his seventies, who was fatally injured during the chaotic scuffle by a giant loudspeaker that fell on him, and others, who died from cardiac or respiratory failure.

The Candlelight Protests of 2016–17 and the T'aegŭkki Rallies took place along the same timeline and in proximity to one another, competing with each other to mobilize more participants at the center of Seoul. The proliferation of mass public assemblies on opposing ends of the political spectrum raises questions about the purpose and use of mass mobilization as a tool of popular democracy. Protesters on the right and left use similar tactics of grassroots organizing and social media mobilization as well as mass rallies and staged events to strengthen their popular base of power and influence, even though the content of their political discourse is radically divergent. An editor at the centrist daily newspaper the *Korea Times* quipped in an opinion column that neither the conservative T'aegŭkki Rallies nor the progressive Candlelight Protests represented the mainstream of South Koreans. "We want to show foreign visitors that Korea is more than the scene of chaos they see on Saturday in central Seoul and that Korea is a mature society," he writes. "For years now, downtown Seoul has turned into what resembles a war zone only with canons replaced by blaring loudspeakers spitting out political venom from protesters who advocate a variety of causes."[2] He suggests that these polarized voices do not represent the public interest or the silent majority of the country.

In this chapter, we enter the conversation about the persistence of protests from a different vantage point. Rather than see the explosive popularity of mass protests as constituting a dilemma for deliberative democracy or the future of contentious politics, and certainly without interest in sanitizing the image of South Korea for the sake of foreign visitors, we examine the escalation of protest spectacles as a critical part of place making in the global city. As Ruth Wilson Gilmore astutely theorizes, "If justice is embodied, it is then therefore always spatial, which is to say, part of a process of making a place."[3] Public protests and contestations over space illustrate such a geographical imperative, and movements on the left and right assert their political voice through repeated acts of spatial strategies, including assembling in and occupying key locations of the city.

Henri Lefebvre puts it simply when he states, "It is by means of the body that space is perceived, lived and produced."[4] When people engage in defiant acts of public assembly, they learn that space is neither an abstract concept nor an empty container. They *experience* space as political and ideological, navigating space as a terrain of struggle. Cities have certainly become lucrative sites of financial investment and profit making, so making claims on public space not only disrupts everyday flows of capital accumulation but also threatens the ideological function of what Lefebvre calls "abstract space"—that is, the representation, organization, and commodification of everyday life as a capitalist utopia.[5] This line of thinking stands in contradiction to imagining cities as a "space made safe for capitalism," one that is trouble free and filled with leisure, playfulness, and the promise of unfettered consumer freedom.[6] In effect, mass protests in public areas impede the use of urban space as exclusive zones of capital accumulation and national mythmaking and expose the disconnect between hegemonic metanarratives of consumer freedom and capitalist prosperity. After all, why should the space of downtown Seoul be used exclusively for capitalist consumption?

Protest actors make a place for themselves and their movements in the city. Making a place through protest is more than demanding the "right to the city" as part of a liberal politics of inclusion, though such demands are also important.[7] The work of place making involves disruption of commercial and public life and entails the creative transformation of urban space to expose the growing centrality of infrastructure and the built environment in the simultaneous precaritization and securitization of everyday capitalist life. Doreen Massey asserts that "place as an ever-shifting constellation of trajectories poses the question of our throwntogetherness."[8] Put differently, once the idea of place is unpacked as a constellation of many trajectories, we can recognize place as a state of coexistence that may very well be heterogenous and contingent, fleeting and ephemeral, even cacophonous and chaotic.[9] Massey's evocative idea of "throwntogetherness" suggests that cities are sites that hold immense "multiplicity, antagonisms, and contrasting temporalities," presenting opportunities for social groups, including those entrenched in unequal power relations, to assert their vision of "how the terms of space might be coded" and "how connectivity might be negotiated."[10]

We argue that social-movement actors and organizations engage in practices of making and remaking urban space in challenging the exclusion of poor and working people and the precarious conditions in which they live. Protesters relate to the urban space as a dynamic resource in ways that are both purposive and planned as well as contingent and improvisational. They mobilize their skills, expertise, and knowledge to make use of public space and the built environment as well as the collective memories and social relations embedded in space. While activists in the legal arena work to contest restrictions and expand the right of the freedom of assembly, organizers take advantage of strategic opportunities to amplify their message and expand their presence in public space, especially at the center of the city, which symbolizes political progress and economic prosperity. As longtime activist Lee Taeho emphasizes in the epigraph of this chapter, "You can think of the history of the *kwangjang* as proceeding from the margins to the center of the city." Asserting their right to assemble in key locations in Seoul, protesters claim their role as the architects of the future they want to build.

CANDLELIGHT PROTESTERS AND THE RIGHT TO THE GLOBAL CITY

Candlelight protesters in 2016–17 were diverse in age, gender, class, occupation, political beliefs, and the extent of previous protest experience, but they were united in the goal to oust Park Geun-hye. For those who assembled, chanted, and marched in unison, the catalytic force was not limited to their ability to mobilize as a singular voice of change. As we participated in the space of the Candlelight Protests during our research, we found remarkable ways that the protest participants demonstrated an ethical comportment—they often walked, spoke, and related to each other in fundamentally different ways, inhabiting the everyday spaces of the city with a newfound political awakening and a sharpened sense of purpose and community. Senior adults who professed to have witnessed many protests before but did not imagine themselves to take an active part in politics found themselves on the streets this time, holding picket signs, chanting, shouting, singing, dancing, and taking delight in doing the iconic "candlelight wave." Mothers and youth—as young as middle school students—took turns at the open-mic time on stage to speak in front of hundreds of people about how they could no longer sit back and do nothing. The familiar protest landscape of organizational flags by unions and nongovernmental organizations was replaced by more festive and less ideological scenes of public assembly, filled with food and beverage vendors and visually captivating public art. When we did see flags, they were not for organizations; there were creative and irreverent flags, like that of the Union of Cat Lovers, or tongue-in-cheek parodies, like that of the Association of Unaffiliated Individuals. Some came to the protests on their own, and others came with friends and family members, classmates and coworkers, often with a backpack filled with essential protest supplies, including battery-powered LED candles, a portable seat cushion—the kind one would bring to a bathhouse or an outdoor picnic—bottled water, and snacks. And if you did not have time to prepare in advance, you could always stop by one of the many convenience stores that are open twenty-four hours to pick up whatever you might need.

Every Saturday evening was the main-stage event during the Candlelight Protests, which began with an elaborate program filled with live speeches and performances interspersed with short video clips spotlighting critical news events and satirizing political events. The high-tech audiovisual equipment created a dramatic contrast against the premodern palace walls and roofs in the backdrop. The program was live casted from the large stage set up on the northern end of the square, not far front of the gates of Kyŏngbok Palace, with multiple superjumbo LED screens with sound amplified through giant loudspeakers the size of small buildings that were suspended from construction cranes. Skillful emcees—many of them former student activists and democracy-

190   CHAPTER 5

movement leaders—facilitated the program and led the weekly ritual of performing the "candlelight wave," choreographing the countdown so the wave of candlelight would start from one end and "flow" to the other end of a crowd in the tens of thousands while everyone was watching this unfold in real time on the screens in front of them. After the end of the program on stage, candlelight protesters would march toward the Blue House. Since access restrictions prohibited the Candlelight Protests actually reaching the president's residence, event organizers would announce alternative routes. Sometimes, we would march to the east of Kyŏngbok Palace, walking down the relatively wide and open streets of Hyoja-dong, passing the exits for line 3 subway station as well as popular markets, restaurants, cafés, bakeries, and other stores along the way. Other times, we would meander through lesser known routes in Samch'ŏng-dong, passing art galleries and national museums before heading toward narrower alleys lined with smaller shops, restaurants, and traditional Korean *hanok* (한옥) houses. It was a political march to be sure, as there were plenty of slogans and placards, but it also felt like we were imprinting the streets with our footsteps.[11]

At times, the streets became so crowded and movement so slow that we could barely move a hundred feet in ten minutes, like at an over-crowded outdoor concert. But at other times, the streets in the city center felt open and extraordinarily spacious and reserved all for pedestrian traffic without any cars or buses. We could take leisurely walks to take stock of the mixture of the new and old, slowly observing the visual markers of the city's history over several centuries. Weeks into the Candlelight Protests, one could also enjoy the flourishing public art, from the Post-its and stickers plastered on the walls of police buses and the mini-laser-light shows projected onto palace walls to the spontaneous musical and drumming performances that filled the streets with stimulating sounds, rhythms, and visuals beyond anything that was officially planned by the central organizing committee. Remarkably, one could easily find and access a public restroom on the ground floors of downtown commercial buildings as they were, apparently, required by law to keep restrooms open and accessible to the public. Of course, one could shop, eat, and drink in one of the hundreds of establishments

FIGURE 5.1. Candlelight Protest, facing north, with yellow-ribbon public art installation commemorating the *Sewol* ferry in the foreground, Seoul, January 2017. Photo by authors.

in the Kwanghwamun area or nearby. But perhaps most remarkably, one could also leave the area easily by heading to the subway station or walking a bit more to reach a bus line in operation. One late night after the Candlelight Protest march ended, we started walking uphill in the snow because the streets were still closed for bus traffic. A small police van pulled up next to us and offered us a ride up the hill, which we hesitantly accepted with some trepidation. After all, it felt strange to accept a ride from the police on the way home from attending what was arguably an antigovernment protest. There was no one else in the streets at that hour except the occasional police officer and candlelight protesters heading home. We would return week after week in awe to see the city become transformed again and again into a space of public protest and something else afterward.[12]

FIGURE 5.2. A map of public restrooms near the Seoul City Hall and Kwanghwamun area, courtesy of the City of Seoul, Seoul, November 2016. Photo by authors.

For seasoned activists who had previously spent countless hours protesting in these streets, the Candlelight Protest experience sparked memories of the past, under very different circumstances. We spoke with Mi-kyŏng (미경; pseudonym), a veteran student, feminist, and anticapitalist activist since the late 1980s who felt joy and exhilaration for being able to simply walk and protest openly in the Kwanghwamun area—in front of the US embassy, the Government Complex Buildings, and in front of Kyŏngbok Palace—without police harassment or surveillance. Just the year before, she was harassed at police checkpoints along the main Kwanghwamun corridor at the November 2015 People's Rally (민주총궐기). She recalled the high-velocity water cannons the police used on the protesters that year, hitting Baek Nam-ki at close range and causing a traumatic cerebral hemorrhage that eventually led to his death, and she remembered when the grief-stricken parents of the *Sewol*-ferry-disaster victims gathered in the same space in Kwanghwamun to commemorate the first anniversary of their children's deaths in April 2015. She was there in 2008 when hundreds of riot-police buses surrounded the protests and barricaded the streets during the "anti-US-beef" candlelight protests. She even remembered marching in the streets during the mass protests in the immediate aftermath of the IMF financial crisis in 1997–98 as well as the year before in December 1996 and January 1997 when a massive, nationwide general strike took place in South Korea for the first time in fifty years. Mi-kyŏng could hardly believe her eyes in January 2017 when the so-called riot-police buses were out of sight at the Candlelight Protests. She beamed as she exclaimed, "This is the first time I feel like a citizen who owns these streets."

The idea that ordinary people ought to be able to enjoy full citizenship rights and act as the rightful owners or subjects (*chuin*; 주인) of the city pulsed throughout the Candlelight Protests. That "the people" have been deprived of the ability to live and prosper is tied to the formation of political subjectivity that Namhee Lee characterizes as a distinctly "postcolonial phenomenon." Denied the right to rebuild society with autonomy and sovereignty after Korea's liberation from Japanese colonialism, intellectuals and political dissidents contended with decades of geopolitical dominance under US imperialism and militarism. Fashioned as a crisis of subjectivity over its failure to take the reins of its own history after Korea's liberation from Japanese colonial rule, intellectuals crafted a collective political ideology that "reconstituted the people . . . as serious protagonists of a political and cultural project that was posited as opposed to and resisting the metanarrative of state-led development." By emphasizing the importance of interrelationality and community, movement practitioners in the 1980s sought to create "a community of the people in which various contradictions of capitalism, such as dehumanization, individualization, and fragmentation, and alienation are overcome, and wealth, equality, and a restored community would be enjoyed by all."[13] The project of rebuilding democracy

194   CHAPTER 5

in the aftermath of authoritarian rule, which took place after the transition to parliamentary democracy in 1987, formalized certain elements of *undongkwŏn* (운동권) as a counterpublic realm in the rapidly expanding sphere of civil society organizations, including the People's Solidarity for Participatory Democracy (PSPD).[14] In their founding mission, PSPD emphasizes that in order to be the real *chuin* of the country, civil society organizations committed to ongoing democratization must "closely supervise the activities of state power on a daily basis."[15] Commentators and observers with personal and organizational ties to the 1980s prodemocracy movements were careful to point out that it would be unreasonable to suggest that even a large, well-resourced organization like PSPD could have singlehandedly organized the Candlelight Protests—an unprecedented scale of mass mobilization in which an estimated 14 percent of the country's entire population participated in at one point over its six-month duration.[16] We likewise turn our attention to the role of activist leadership and social-movement organizations in transforming the urban space into a space of protest without implying that they are primarily responsible in a centralized or top-down manner. By strengthening their organizational capacity and know-how as strategic urban actors, key social-movement actors played an influential role in determining where, when, and how public space and resources were used in service of expanding people's democratic right of the freedom of assembly.

THE *KWANGJANG*: FROM THE URBAN PERIPHERY TO THE CENTER

At the peak of the Candlelight Protests, Kwanghwamun Square and its surrounding areas convened nearly two million people, who arrived by bus, subway, and train. The Kwanghwamun Station on Seoul subway line 5 has a total of nine entrance/exits that are connected by an elaborate underground system of passageways that lead directly to museums, performance centers, and, perhaps most famously, the massive Kyobo Book Store. A major hub of multiple rapid-transit bus and subway lines that connect the suburbs to the government and commercial buildings in the city center, the Kwanghwamun Square represents a mix of historic buildings and modern skyscrapers, surrounded by major headquarters and government office buildings. On the eastside is the Sejong Cultural Center for the Performing Arts, next door to the Government Complex on the northwest corner. To the north of the Kwanghwamun Square is Kyŏngbok Palace, the largest of the five royal palaces in the City of Seoul, and to the west of the square is the National Museum of Korean Contemporary History, just a few doors down from the US embassy. Until 1996, one would have also seen, on the grounds of the Kyŏngbok Palace, the massive Japanese colonial-era Government-General Building, which was demolished in a controversial decision to obliterate this symbol of Japanese colonial rule and decolonize the city's architectural history.

During the years of rapid industrialization, authoritarian state regimes in South Korea focused on big infrastructure projects, such as highways, irrigation systems, and electrical systems, to spark the "take-off'" so widely touted by US proponents of modernization and development theory, cultivating capital-intensive manufacturing industries that could contribute to higher levels of national economic growth. These values began to shift, however, in the context of rising consumption levels and the growth of urban service economies, and during the 1990s, plans to redesign the Kwanghwamun area were underway. This included significant state investment in the transformation of the urban built environment. Subsequent major projects over the next decade included the complete redesign of Seoul City Hall, which involved the construction of a modern counterpart to the historic building and the creation of an open green space with an outdoor stage that projected amplified sound for large gatherings and concerts. Nearby, Seoul train station also received a major upgrade to make way for the high-speed KTX rail lines, which can carry a ticketed passenger from Seoul to Pusan in less than three hours. The Seoul city government under Mayor Lee Myung-bak spearheaded the restoration of the Chŏnggyech'ŏn, which had been covered with cement since the Park Chung Hee era, to make way for paved city streets. Chŏnggyech'ŏn area is now a popular urban park and recreation area, though antipoverty and antigentrification activists would remember Chŏnggyech'ŏn area as a place where shop owners and street vendors resisted vigorously and often militantly against the destruction of local traditional markets, displacement of lower-income neighborhoods, and ongoing gentrification. Behind these urban redesign and redevelopment projects was the idea that Seoul would shed its "Third World past" and embrace its new prominence as a global destination for discerning visitors and tourists.

The transformation of Kwanghwamun Square and surrounding areas into a vibrant center of public life in the city should not be misunderstood as a top-down process of urban revitalization led by city planners and business and political leaders. Social-movement actors that had led the democratization movement in the 1980s and its organizational legacies played a major role in ensuring that public use and access were inextricably linked to projects involving urban planning and redesign. We can see the way this process unfolded in the shifting locations of mass protest events from campus universities and the urban periphery to the geosymbolic center of the *kwangjang* in Seoul's historic city center. Our extensive engagement with Lee Taeho as both a longtime activist and a paid social-movement worker in an NGO that identifies itself as a driving organizational force of participatory democracy provides deeper insight into the diverse ways in which protest transformed the urban landscape of Seoul.

OPEN THE KWANGJANG

When talking about his days as a former student activist, Lee Taeho, who served as the secretary general of the Student General Assembly at Seoul National University, paused and then laughed heartily in response to our question about the first time that he participated in a tent encampment or went on a hunger strike. He recalled his first *changgi t'ujaeng* (장기투쟁; long-term struggle) while a university student when he and his comrades pretty much occupied the student union building for two years straight, rarely going home or going to class. He also remarked that their lives as student activists prepared them for doing hunger strikes, even though they were involuntary, since they routinely had to figure out how to go without food while barricaded on campus. At the height of dictatorship, there were no places in the city center for protesters to gather safely and outside the purview of police repression. For the most part, student protesters were restricted to university campuses as the site of public protest during the 1980s. They routinely clashed with police at the central gates of campuses, such as Yonsei University and Seoul National University, the epicenters of the student movement, and found ways to navigate the complicated mountainous terrain of their back alleys to elude police capture. At the height of their activism in the mid to late 1980s, students became experts in waging protracted occupations on and around campus.

One of the first key locations of the city outside universities that they attempted to pry open was city hall, which has been a historic site of popular uprising since the days of the March First independence movement. At the time, however, it was a difficult area for protesters to navigate. Lee Taeho said, "As you know, city hall is now a large grassy area, but in the past, there was a fountain surrounded by a road with cars racing by, so it was not a space that people could gather." Regardless of these physical impediments, student activists continued to push their way into these central sites of protest, clashing frequently and often with the riot police who blocked their entry. Student protests escalated after the death of the twenty-one-year-old student Park Jong-chul (박종철; Pak Chong-ch'ŏl), who died in police custody after being interrogated and tortured in January 1987. Mass mobilization reached a historic peak the following July after another young student, the twenty-one-year-old Yonsei University student Lee Han-yeol, died less than one month after sustaining fatal injuries to the head after riot police shot him with a tear gas cannister. Over one million people poured into the streets in protest in a funeral procession that traveled to city hall via multiple routes, including from the gates of Yonsei University, in what is now known as the June Uprising. Not surprisingly, given the historic parallels that were frequently drawn between the revolutionary uprisings of 1987 and 2016–17, the official, government-sponsored commemoration of the June Uprising in June 2017 included dramatic reenactments of defiant protesters on the routes into the city center to symbolize the decisive role that protesters across history have played in changing the meaning and significance of urban space.

FIGURE 5.3. Marchers commemorate the thirtieth anniversary of Lee Han-yeol's death, Seoul, June 2017. Photo by authors.

Although the student protesters were successful in creating the conditions that led to the end of decades of military dictatorship, they continued to be blocked from holding events like the memorial ceremony for Lee Han-yeol at city hall throughout the 1990s. During the years after the transition to parliamentary democracy in the early 1990s, most of the gatherings that took place in downtown Seoul were still considered "illegal" occupations. Protesters who waged public protests would basically assemble for "thirty minutes with Molotov cocktails before quickly dispersing," explained Lee Taeho. When a large public space was needed for a mass gathering, protesters convened on the outskirts of downtown Seoul at places like Yŏido Park, which was "pretty much a huge open space with mostly cement that could accommodate gatherings of over one hundred thousand people." Another site of large-scale protest on the outskirts of the city was Poramae Park, "which used to be a big grassy area in the South but is now full of apartments," Lee Taeho added. These venues represented the creation of public spaces that accompanied urban residential-development projects during the 1980s as part of the ongoing apartment-complex boom. We attended several large-scale gatherings at Yŏido Park and were always struck by how deserted and empty the location was, especially when the large rallies took place on a Sunday when few other passersby were using the space. Thousands of workers assembled according to their specific union and organizational flags, marking their identities by wearing their workplace uniforms, union vests, and other aesthetic indicators. Smaller social-movement organizations, student organizations, and women's organizations lined up behind organized labor and their respective flags and banners. In our fieldnotes during this time, one question that was circled and highlighted was, "Who were these incredibly elaborate symbolic processions for since the streets were so empty?"

As KCTU grew in size and scope, they amassed greater leverage and associational power to convene mass assemblies in downtown Seoul. Approximately fifty thousand workers converged in the capital on November 21, 1996, after the National Assembly tried to railroad the passage of revisions that would weaken the nation's labor laws. KCTU then launched the first successful nationwide general strike since 1962 the following December, which, at its height, included over six hundred thousand workers. KCTU union leaders camped out inside Myŏngdong Cathedral, where thousands of workers, as well as students and other supporters, clashed with riot police in the surrounding Myŏngdong shopping district. KCTU ended its mass mobilization by the end of February 1997 when it was able to stop the National Assembly from moving forward labor-law revisions, but the subsequent collapse of South Korea's financial markets and the terms of austerity under the IMF loan agreement resulted in another round of mass protests. The election of Kim Dae-jung in March 1998 shifted the political climate of direct state violence and repression, enabling protesters to march through the streets of downtown Seoul within designated police lines. Although there were still and continues to be physically violent clashes between unionized workers and police, these developments resulted in the transformation of the landscape of protest in the city center. One significant shift was the rebranding and reorganization of the police to convey a sense of "lightness" about policing protests, as Jong Bum Kwon remarks.[17] For example, new ranks of female police officers wearing civilian uniforms on protest sites, rather than full riot gear with steel shields and batons, were dispatched as riot police for the first time under the new leadership of the National Police Agency.

During the late 1990s and early 2000s, civic groups held rallies at places like Seoul train station, outside Jongno 3-ga subway station, inside T'apgol Park, and in the Taehangno District near the historic campus of Seoul National University, where the size of public assemblies ranged from a few hundred people to a peak of several thousand protesters. More important than size, however, were the new spaces of protest created across the city by a broader set of actors who directly challenged the social disasters created by profit-driven, rather than human-centered, capitalist growth. By this time, Lee Taeho had shifted from student activism to civic activism, becoming part of the small group of approximately ten staff members who worked at PSPD in its early years. One of the first major protest actions that Lee Taeho organized in his new staff position was the one-year-commemoration event of the Sampoong Department Store (삼풍 백화점) tragedy, which resulted in the deaths of 502 people and the injury of 937 more people on a single day: June 29, 1995. The five-story luxury department store, which was located in the wealthy Kangnam neighborhood of Seocho, collapsed in a matter of twenty seconds despite engineering reports that had previously warned the company of the building's vulnerabilities.[18]

During the mid-1990s, PSPD was involved in fighting various corruption campaigns tied to the election of political candidates.[19] There was not much awareness of "things like victims' rights [피해자 인권]," explains Lee Taeho. On the legal side, the protection of victims' identities in the media was grossly mishandled, and division and infighting among victims' families plagued negotiations around compensation for wrongful deaths and demands for investigating the truth of what happened. Much of the Sampoong Department Store's wealthy customer base was made up of "judges, lawyers, and sons and daughters in ministries" who "collaborated with the government to try and cover up the issue," explained Lee Taeho, "and poor workers [who commuted to work from other neighborhoods] did not receive proper compensation." In addition, at least twenty families were unable to identify the remains of their loved ones because their "bodies were crushed beyond recognition." Their efforts became more public facing after PSPD began to support their efforts, including by staging a funeral procession in the streets. To expose the ways in which the pursuit of capitalist development jeopardized people's lives and well-being, PSPD worked with *tangsaja* protesters to create affectively charged scenes of public grief and mourning, which have now become routine practices. They planned a route that was exactly one kilometer. They wore yellow. They also prepared a long piece of yellow cloth that extended the length of the funeral procession in a public display that has become closely associated with the *Sewol*-ferry disaster, which Lee Taeho has also been actively involved in through his work at PSPD and as an individual activist. Interestingly, PSPD connected the deaths from the department store tragedy to the sudden collapse of the Sŏngsu Bridge in 1994—another shocking example of the kind of reckless construction under the relentless drive for rapid industrial growth that resulted in unnecessary human death and injury.

The beginning of the new millennium also brought changes to the affective and visual landscape of public protest, which coincided with the changing face of Seoul as a global city. Public protests organized by civil society organizations expanded the use of downtown streets and spaces in the historic city centers as Seoul mayors Lee Myung-bak and Oh Se-hoon (오세훈; O Se-hun) began redesigning the downtown area to remove car traffic and create pedestrian-friendly spaces of urban leisure and public enjoyment. The redesign of Kwanghwamun after the June 10 World Cup games in 2002, which South Korea jointly hosted with Japan, created the conditions for the popular gathering of Red Devil sports fans, known for wearing conspicuous red T-shirts while gathered in public venues to watch the games.[20] As is well documented in the literature about the first candlelight protest that broke out in 2002 in the months immediately following the end of the 2002 World Cup, many of the same Red Devil youth poured into the streets to mourn the deaths of two middle school girls, Hyo-sun (효순) and Mi-sun (미선), who were killed by an armed US military vehicle near the US military base in Paju, and demand an end to the highly unequal terms of the US-ROK Status of Forces Agreement, which allowed such deaths to go unpunished.[21]

After the redesign of city hall in 2004, organizations like PSPD took a much more active role in demanding that the "people" had access to public space for protest. Even if organized labor and social movements were not the driving forces of mass public assembly in phenomena like the Red Devils, movement organizers were able to take advantage of these developments to expand their "right to the city" as protesters. One important area of development was the role of organizations like PSPD in expanding the freedom of assembly itself. Lee Taeho explained, "We at PSPD raised the issue of opening the square and changing the ordinance [for public assembly] through our Open the Kwangjang campaign. We needed to get signatures from 1 percent of Seoul residents, which was around 130,000 people, which was difficult. But we took advantage of the creation of a local initiative system in Seoul, and for the first time, we obtained signatures from 1 percent. We then petitioned, leading to the revised ordinance on the Uses and Management of the Seoul Square." Ironically, PSPD and other social-movement groups created the language and the policy mechanisms that were later used by conservative politicians, like Lee Myung-bak and Oh Se-hoon, to campaign on platforms that promised citizens that they would "beautify" the city through investment in urban revitalization and infrastructure-development projects.

EXPANDING PUBLIC ASSEMBLY

Achieving the "right to the city"—that is, the right to use, benefit, and resignify the meaning of urban space for political dissent—represents a material and political accomplishment of movement organizers and organizations such as PSPD, yet it cannot be understood without contextualizing their efforts as part of a broader process of "opening the *kwangjang*" that was initiated by people largely outside conventional social-movement networks and organizations associated with the previous decade of democracy struggles led by students and workers.

One of the most influential movements that helped expand the public space of protest in areas that were previously restricted to protesters occurred outside the Japanese embassy just four hundred meters away from Kwanghwamun Square. Since January 8, 1992, weekly protests have been held at noon every Wednesday in front of the Japanese embassy led by former "comfort women" and activists demanding that the Japanese government issue a formal apology and acknowledge the truth of its wartime atrocities against them during the Pacific War. Former comfort women, known simply as grandmothers (위안부 할머니), and their advocates have sustained this Wednesday protest rally (수요집회) in what constitutes the world's longest-running peace protest.[22] Their fight was also against the clock; as of May 2023, only nine former comfort women who are registered with the Korean government, all of whom are well in their nineties, remain alive out of the estimated fifty thousand to two hundred thousand, the vast majority of whom were poor young women from Korea, conscripted into a system that has been characterized as militarized sexual slavery.

Though there has been a significant amount of scholarship on the history and politics of comfort women in recent years—even an award-winning graphic narrative and a book of poetry as well as several documentary and feature films—we are most interested in adding our analysis of the place-based nature of the protest.[23] The celebration of milestone anniversaries of the weekly Wednesday demonstrations often brings out record numbers of supporters, such as the thirtieth anniversary on January 6, 2022, which marked the 1,525th weekly protest. We have attended a number of these commemorations over the course of nearly thirty years, varying in the size of the turnout. What was striking about the scene of Wednesday demonstrations was the normalization of city space as a site that was flooded with the sights, sounds, feelings, and interactions of vibrant protest activity while also being heavily sur-

FIGURE 5.4. Visitors wrap the "comfort woman" statue in a warm blanket for the winter and leave snacks and beverages, Seoul, January 2017. Photo by authors.

veilled and regulated by police, who maintained a constant presence outside the area with a designated police line and officers on duty.

The addition of the bronze *Statue of Peace*, created by artists Seo-kyung Kim and Eun-sung Kim in 2011, which depicts the image of a young Korean girl sitting next to an empty chair measuring 1.5 meters high, further amplified the affective charge of the area as a central gathering place beyond the regular day and time of the Wednesday demonstrations. Day or night, individuals can visit the *Statue of Peace* to take photos, post messages of support and solidarity, and leave gifts and mementos.

Oftentimes, when we visited during the winter months, a warm scarf and hat adorned the statue, and flowers had been placed at her feet, as another indication that people related to the place of protest with a sense of human connection and empathy. The site has also become a place for special protest rallies and commemorative events not only in Seoul but also in Chŏnju, Pusan, and seventy other sites around the world where replicas of the *Statue of Peace* now reside as a symbol of resistance and solidarity, many of which have attracted strong opponents from local community members and the Japanese government. One such place that had long been the target of opposition by the Japanese government was the original location outside its embassy in Kwanghwamun. Recognizing the symbolic power of the public art, the Japanese government made the removal of the *Statue of Peace*, which they viewed as a source of constant irritation, a condition of its negotiations with the South Korean government on the matter of comfort women, much to the discontent of former comfort women, who were the main *tangsaja* actors in the struggle but were not consulted at any point during the bilateral negotiations.

During the weekly Saturday candlelight protests, visitors routinely took a short walk to the area, where they could witness another struggle taking place at a tent encampment in the vicinity of the square. After Park Geun-hye's government officially signed the Agreement of Comfort Women with the Japanese government on December 28, 2015, the site of the weekly Wednesday demonstrations became a dedicated place where people could gather and express solidarity with an active social movement in the heart of the historic center of Seoul. Although the Japanese embassy had relocated to a nearby building, protesters had created strong associations with the original location and the comfort-women-redress movement. During our interview with one of the encampment organizers, we learned that there have been three different protest leaders since the encampment was first erected, although there is also no official relationship with the longtime organizers of the Wednesday rally.[24] Given the ebb and flow of participation since the encampment began, it has been difficult to maintain a large presence of people. However, the construction of the makeshift tent encampment allowed the *nongsŏng* to maintain a visible presence.

206　CHAPTER 5

Interestingly, despite the unauthorized nature of protesting within one hundred meters of a foreign government embassy, tent-encampment protesters received broad support from many other people, who assisted them in maintaining their fight. One organizer explained, "In the beginning, we did not know anything. The vinyl plastic [used to cover our heads] touched my nose, and during the winter, I wore three pairs of pants and two padded jackets. But as word got out, we received twenty sleeping bags, puffy coats, socks, and other items. People showed us how to construct a pallet and told us how to deal with bugs that came out at night." Even when a nearby construction site was completed and protesters no longer had a source of electricity to draw upon, one of the workers from the construction site dropped by and showed them how to draw power from a nearby streetlight. They even started receiving donations from nearby businesses and their regular customers, including a shop selling vinyl and a nearby gas station. The fact that the *Statue of Peace*, the Wednesday demonstrations, and the long-term tent encampment were positioned in a cramped but well-trafficked back alley of Kwanghwamun, adjacent to the US embassy, which was also the site of active antiwar protests during the 2000s, contributed to the centrality of Kwanghwamun as a microcosm of diverse protest struggles.

Many of the participants were young women and men who became politicized about the issue from their high school teachers, many of whom were members of the Korean Teachers and Education Workers Union (전국교직원노동조합). The fact that they received help from the broader public was a significant source of support and encouragement, which they recognized was a departure from the kind of neglect and isolation that other tent-encampment protesters, such as tenants opposing eviction and workers opposing layoffs, experienced. Although some of the key leaders tried to avoid publicizing their participation, especially to their own families, once they were "outed" by protest cameras that surveilled and live casted the encampment protest, they began to embrace their public roles as activists and educators. Given the many idle hours spent defending the tent encampment, they began to spend much of their time reading and studying related issues. The young activist that we interviewed explained that the study groups that they formed help them educate visitors to the site about why they should support the fight for justice and reparations for comfort women, especially from Japan. Although she still felt discouraged at the time by the relative lack of public interest, the ability to gather in a single place and share feelings of disappointment, joy, and solidarity in a physical space with other like-minded activists gave her the strength to keep defending the encampment, even after devoting two full years to the struggle at the time of our interview.

PROTESTS AT THE BLUE HOUSE

Another key area of the central city where protesters have expanded their public presence is outside the Blue House, which had maintained strict prohibitions on the proximity of public assembly. The Blue House became a popular destination site to express political dissent during Lee Myung-bak's presidency (2008–13), which pursued multiple state-led projects around large-scale infrastructure projects under the aggressive promotion of neoliberal capitalist development. One of the first and most defining clashes between protesters and police took place during the 2008 "anti-beef protests," which was shorthand for the candlelight protests that erupted in opposition to the passage of the US-ROK Free Trade Agreement. This was a period of unprecedented mass assembly in the streets of central Seoul, but it was also a time of intensified police repression, as Sister Maria discussed in the previous chapter. Police barricades had become so common that people were not able to move more than two hundred meters without confronting another blockage. Activists we spoke with often mentioned the "Myung-bak *sansŏng*" (명박 산성), an expression that combines Lee Myung-bak's name and the word for "mountain fortress," referring to the rows of shipping containers that were used as barricades against protesters. Many confrontations with the police during this period were "like a game of *ttang tta mŏkki* [땅 따먹기]]," recalled Lee Taeho, which is similar to hopscotch, in which a player makes gains against a competitor by expanding his/her ability to move two hundred meters into the other's "territory." PSPD filed suit against the Lee Myung-bak administration for violations of freedom of assembly and secured pivotal decisions in which the Constitutional Court declared car barricades to be unconstitutional and amended the law on the use of public spaces like Kwanghwamun Square.

Lee Myung-bak's administration also became infamous for the use of extraordinary military force against civilian protesters, both in Seoul and around the country. This included the deadly confrontation with evicted tenants who occupied the rooftop of a five-story building in Yongsan in January 2009, which resulted in the deaths of five protesters and one police officer. Later that year, in August 2009, thousands of riot police carried out a violent crackdown on striking Ssangyong Motor workers during their factory occupation in P'yŏngt'aek, located sixty-five kilometers south of Seoul. Protesters and police also routinely clashed at many sites of long-term protests around the country that Sister Maria was integrally involved in, including Miryang, Kangjŏng Village in Jeju, and others. The refusal to provide a permit to allow people to publicly mourn the death of former president Roh Moo-hyun also enflamed anger on the part of progressive social-movement activists over the excessive restriction of their bodily movements.

In this climate, one area of protest innovation that took place involved the tactic of one-person protests, which were aimed to deter constant police retaliation and repression. Lee Taeho recalls carrying out the first one-person protest in front of the Blue House in opposition to the lack of recordkeeping and transparency about meetings that took place. After being denied his repeated requests to make proceedings public, Lee Taeho decided to take action by "bringing humor" into their protest performance by dressing up as a Chosŏn dynasty official and emphasizing that their practice of keeping "veritable records" is even commemorated as part of UNESCO's (United Nations Educational, Scientific, and Cultural Organization) Memory of the World Register. He elaborated,

> During the Chosŏn period, the records officer documented the king's affairs and even whether he ate or not, writing down in great detail what he liked and did not like to eat. But now in the twenty-first century, does it make sense that the nation's president does not leave minutes of

their meetings? If you think about the Chosŏn's proud archival culture [*laughs*], is this something that even remotely makes sense? This is how we satirized it. So we borrowed attire of the recordkeeping officer of the president in the past from MBC's costume department and dressed up as a recording officer from this period, carrying a calligraphy brush and a picket sign.

Efforts by protesters to reach the Blue House became extremely intense during the *Sewol* movement when bereaved parents were determined to demand the truth of what happened during the botched rescue of their children directly from Park Geun-hye, whose unaccounted absence over a seven-hour period was considered part of the mysterious circumstances resulting in the tragic sinking. As one of the cochairs of the 416 Coalition (416 연대) of the *Sewol* movement, Lee Taeho recalled his anger at being denied access, stating,

> The president is in the palace of the Blue House, and it is a long way back from the main gate, but we can't do anything even within one hundred meters of the front of the Blue House. They claimed that the Assembly and Demonstration Act [집시법] and the Presidential Security Act [대통령 경호법] are different. That's what they are like [*laughs*]. Anyway, we are an organization advocating for political participatory democracy. . . . We fought a lot because of the *Sewol* protests. Even people trying to visit our office would be stopped by the police by the Kyŏngbokgung Station if they were wearing [yellow] ribbons, and the police would question them about where they are going. If they answer with, "What's it to you?" then well, they don't get through.

Constant skirmishes with police added to the sense of political indignation over restrictions on people's mobility and the right to assembly. *Sewol* parents and the activists who supported them faced everyday harassment, especially when marked with the movement's iconic yellow ribbons.

Restricting certain types of bodily movement in the city has become a key site of policing space. Liberal democratic governments that support neoliberal economic policies were especially adroit at restricting forms of protest that disrupt everyday life in valorized locations in the city without revoking the right to the freedom of assembly itself.[25] For example, the Kim Dae-jung government (1998–2003) "introduced the 'police-line'" to manage the flow of car and bus traffic in busy city centers when protesters occupied the roads. The Roh Moo-hyun government (2003–8) imposed legal constraints on acceptable levels of noise disturbance, spurring the increased use of surveillance technologies such as noise meters and cameras to gather evidence of unlawful activity at active sites of protest.[26] By seeking to criminalize protesters that impede smooth flows of pedestrian and motor traffic and disturb the comfort and privacy of urban residents in their own homes, South Korea's protest laws have become entangled with the image of global cities as "safe and trouble-free zones, filled with leisure, playfulness, and the promise of unfettered consumer freedom."[27] But as Hagar Kotef notes, "spaces themselves become political" through the bodily movements that the state "allows and prevents, and the relations that are formed and prevented via these im/mobilities."[28]

This work has come at a cost. The Assembly and Demonstrations Act (ADA) was passed in 2007 by the Lee Myung-bak government for the stated purpose of imposing harsher punishment against "organizers" as a class of persons. The term "organizer," according to the ADA, "means a person or organization holding an assembly or staging a demonstration in that person or organization's name and with his/ her or its own responsibility." Given the ADA's emphasis on protecting the "public peace," any person deemed an "organizer" could be "subject to criminal sanctions or administrative sanctions resulting in fines or imprisonment" if they were charged with violations that threatened "public peace" while "holding an assembly or staging a demonstration" in "public places available for the free movement of the general public, such as roads, plazas, parks, etc. with the aim of exerting influence on the opinions of a large number of unspecified persons or overwhelming them."[29] Such violations include procedural infractions, such as failing to comply with notice requirements, and threats to "public peace," like disruptions to the "smooth flow of traffic" (under article 12 of the ADA).

The steep fines that organizers face reflect the tremendous cost of resistance. Park Rae-gun (박래군; Pak Rae-kun), a longtime human rights activist and a key figure in the 416 Coalition for the families and supporters of the *Sewol*-ferry-disaster victims, was "indicted on charges of organizing an unlawful protest, destruction of public goods, general obstruction of traffic, (and) defamation among other charges," Amnesty International reports, and "the Seoul Central District Court on 22 January 2016 sentenced Mr. Park to three-years imprisonment with four-years probation and 160 hours of community service."[30] Many, if not most, of our interlocuters and organizers of solidarity, including Lee Taeho of PSPD, Kim Hyejin, and others have faced extraordinarily punitive fines for their roles in organizing protest events.

MASS PROTESTS AS MEGAEVENTS

The Candlelight Protests of 2016–17 are often heralded for the unprecedented participation of "ordinary citizens" in public protest. However, this emphasis belies a more complex organizational picture. The Emergency Action for Park Geun-hye's Resignation, also known as the Action Committee for Presidential Resignation (퇴진행동), was made up of over 2,300 civic groups in seventy cities across the country and was the major organizational force behind the six-month-protest wave. According to one member, the Action Committee for Presidential Resignation could be described like a "control tower" or "situation room," managing changing conditions as they presented themselves. The on-the-ground work of organizing was carried out by different teams, which took responsibility for the protest rallies (집회), publicity (홍보), protest supplies (물품), and everything else that "attracts public attention and visibility." The protest rally team planned and coordinated each weekly mass gathering, including deciding who would take on the role as the event emcee, who would be asked to speak during the rally program, and what would be the main concept guiding the weekly event. In addition to ensuring that protest spaces were filled with moving, entertaining, and worthwhile speeches and performances, they also took responsibility for ensuring people's safety during crowded protest events. They created practical maps that outlined different options for marching routes to the Blue House, as well as indicated where protesters could find public toilets and designated areas for medical attention or lost children.

Filmmakers, video editors, cinematographers, and other media producers with deep relationships and ties to various social movements played important roles in ensuring that each week's main event contained compelling short video clips and was also well documented for public consumption long afterward. For example, the acclaimed activist documentary filmmaker Kim Il-rhan (김일란; Kim Il-lan)—whose work with the queer-feminist film collective Pinks (연분홍치마) resulted in gripping stories about the Yongsan Ch'amsa, *The Remnants* (공동정범; 2018) and *Two Doors* (두 개의 문; 2011)—produced a moving five-minute video for the official organizing committee of the Candlelight Protests of 2016–17 that was played on the final day in March, after the impeachment of Park Geun-hye was upheld by the Constitutional Court. The video clip

FIGURE 5.5. Portrait of Baek Nam-ki on a truck as part of the public funeral procession, Seoul, November 2016. Photo by Jennifer Jihye Chun.

begins by capturing the feelings of grief and anger that pervaded the six-month period, drawing upon the "people's funeral" for sixty-seven-year-old farmer and former democracy activist Baek Nam-ki and the tragic capsizing of the *Sewol* ferry. Then, the video captures spectacular scenes of a city transformed that draws on remarkably competent and highly experience social-movement personnel who know how to set up and take down the huge stages each week, equipped with sophisticated audiovisual equipment.

MOBILIZING DEATH AND PUBLIC MOURNING

For months, many of the same organizations and representatives from those organizations were part of coalitional efforts to demand accountability for Baek Nam-ki. Because he was such a beloved longtime activist with close ties to farmers, religious organizations, and civil society organizations, there were over one hundred organizations that participated in the coalition. After he passed away, there were internal discussions about how to proceed, and they had initially decided to cancel their notice of intent to hold a rally in Kwanghwamun Square. Yet they decided to simply repurpose their plans and organize a small protest. At the time, organizers thought, at most, perhaps five thousand people would turn out. Unexpectedly, nearly fifty thousand attended the first protest. According to Kwak EKyeong, the KCTU external solidarity coordinator and one of the key organizers at the time, they knew that "there was something different in the air." Even before they began promoting the rally, the media had already publicized that a rally was taking place calling for the removal of Park Geun-hye. Kwak EKyeong explained, "We usually share promotional posts online and distribute press releases as part of our promotion process, but the article published in the media declared, 'Social-movement organizations decide to hold their first rally demanding resignation of Park Geun-hye in Chŏnggye Plaza on October 29 at this time in the afternoon.' As this was happening, I felt how fast the media was reporting and what an enormous effect it could have."

The planning around the November People's Rally changed in light of Baek Nam-ki's death. Because of the severe police repression in 2015

214   CHAPTER 5

and the heavy harassment and legal actions taken against everyone involved, the organizers had been "heavily beat down." They represented the historic triad of the *minjung* movement—unions, farmers, and the urban poor and plus, a broader constellation of labor- and social-movement organizations worked together to present a united front throughout the Candlelight Protests.

When considering the events leading up to the explosion of the mass Candlelight Protests of 2016–17, the fact that death served as a historic catalyst is consistent with the fact that many of the most significance mass public gatherings featured funeral processions and mourning rituals. Since Baek Nam-ki's funeral procession occurred in the midst of the Candlelight Protests in mid-November, it filled the streets with a felt sense of death and public mourning Baek Nam-ki's funeral procession was an epic elegy, which began at Myŏngdong Cathedral and proceeded down the street to Kwanghwamun Square. At the front of the procession was a truck carrying a large painted funeral portrait, as well as a large decorated casket that was transported by foot. Also accompanying the procession was another contingent with rows of large vertical banners that are often used in rural funeral processions to mourn the dead. The procession was also accompanied by two *p'ansori* (판소리) singers and one hundred drummers, all wearing black T-shirts, who formed a massive contingent behind the surviving members of Baek Nam-ki's family, as well as well-known social-movement leaders in progressive Catholic circles.

The entrance of the funeral procession into Kwanghwamun Square was just one of many different processions and gatherings streaming into the area. On the steps of the Sejong Cultural Center was a lively contingent of middle school students, all wearing their school uniforms and taking turns holding a low-tech bullhorn. This gathering was a refreshing change from the very solemn rally that took place after the funeral procession arrived at Kwanghwamun. Also relatively unnoticed was the *och'et'uji* staged by Yoosung workers, who had organized their ritual march also to commemorate their comrades who had passed away during the course of their grueling fight. The *Sewol*-ferry tragedy's constant presence at the center of Kwanghwamun was rendered more visible through the proliferation of public art installations, including a visually striking scene of 306 life vests, each symbolizing one of the deceased victims, at the bottom of the steps of the square leading to one of the underground subway entrances. We mention these various happenings to emphasize that the Candlelight Protests cannot be framed as an either/or event—one that either embraced longtime social movements or eschewed them. The Candlelight Protests were a site of the unfolding of many different simultaneous movements, some of which aligned and others which conflicted.

SOCIAL-MOVEMENT KNOW-HOW

Movement organizers drew on their extensive relationships with vendors and small businesses, who provided stage and sound equipment for the outdoor gatherings. "As you can imagine, what single company would be able to supply all the equipment needed to put on mass rallies in the scale of the millions? One company was not sufficient for fulfilling all our sound and staging needs," explains one of the members of the coordinating committee. Interestingly, the sound- and staging-equipment companies that large organizations like PSPD and KCTU worked with also brought their own social-movement know-how as former activists themselves. They knew what kind of sound equipment to bring, what size stage was needed, and how many screens to set up to accommodate large-scale gatherings. Contracted companies also took care of all the work required to set up and take down the huge stages each week, taking the burden directly off of event organizers. The ability to rely on external equipment companies, even when the organizers did not have the funds up front, was also crucial to their success. When asked whether or not they were ever refused because of lack of funds, one organizer laughed and said, "KCTU is a very big customer, so they know it's important to maintain good relationships with us."

KCTU's relationship with bus companies and their broader exper-

216   CHAPTER 5

tise around navigating transportation networks helped sustain the Candlelight Protest's momentum, especially in the early weeks as participant numbers skyrocketed. On November 11, which was the day of the annual People's Rally, KCTU external solidarity coordinator Kwak EKyeong explained that they experienced a crisis in how to bring their members from outside Seoul. Activists referred to this type of travel as *sanggyŏng t'ujaeng* (상경투쟁) to reflect the recognized activity of "going to the capital" to wage a protest. She elaborated in detail,

> Even [trying to] get [people] to Seoul all at once was an epic task. To do this, we managed every aspect of logistics, including coordinating the routes, arrival points, number of buses, and other information to make sure that our planning and mobilization were not the cause of a traffic jam. For example, let's say there are some who are coming up from South Chŏlla Province. They would take the Sŏyang Interchange, right? Then, this team would be in charge . . . to ask them to transfer to subways or other transit methods, but there's an exception: farmers. Farmers do not know Seoul. So farmers have to make it to the destination in one go—because they are all elderly too. Their bodies ache [with long travel], and [they] often suffer from related health issues. As you can tell with this example, we plan with real attention to the details, depending on who they are.

The ability to coordinate and plan with the highest level of attention to detail was a major factor in the success of the prolonged mass mobilization. On November 25, another dramatic *sanggyŏng t'ujaeng* took place but, this time, led by the striking scene of thousands of farming tractors attempting to drive all the way to Kwanghwamun from around the country. The Korean Peasants League (KPL; 전국농민회총연맹) organized an epic procession that was led by slow-moving tractors accompanied by a truck brigade, which it named after Chŏn Pong-jun (전봉준), the leader of the Tonghak Peasant Revolution in the late nineteenth century. The Chŏn Pong-jun T'ujaengdan (전봉준투쟁단) traveled by two different routes, one from the western region leaving on November 15 and one from the eastern region leaving on November 16, each of which included drivers who spent eight-plus long hours on the roads driving an average speed of just fifteen to twenty kilometers an hour.

The journey itself was physically grueling. Lee Hyo-sin (이효신), the vice president of the KPL, who led the western group, described the journey as follows: "Holding the steering wheel all day long makes my shoulders hurt so bad. Tractors aren't like cars because they don't absorb the shock. The fact is, tractors are a farming vehicle so ordinarily you would never drive it this fast. This is probably the first and only time a tractor will travel such a long distance."[31] The activist farmers decided to organize the "tractor battle group" after the death of Baek Nam-ki despite the ill timing during the busy harvest season. The Seoul Administrative Court granted the nation's largest farmers' group the right to attend the rally that weekend, but they rejected their request to allow even just two tractors to travel in close proximity of the Blue House.[32] Police blocked the tractors' entry at various points, including the city of P'yŏngt'aek, located seventy kilometers south of Seoul, and the Ansŏng interchange in Kyŏnggi Province. News of their impending arrival was live cast on rally screens on a day that coincided with a full day of rallies and marches by diverse movement groups, including the 416 Coalition; the National Emergency Committee of University Students, a coalition against the censorship of Korean history textbooks; and a citizens' council—all of which were gathering at different locations in the area.

The scale and scope of participation presented tremendous challenges for the organizing committee, and managing internal conflict was a key part of this process. Although the committee worked very closely together to pull off each weekly gathering, they contended with serious differences of opinion throughout the weeks. For example, one organizer explained that there was a "lot of internal conflict around whether to demand impeachment because there was no faith in the National Assembly." When the National Assembly made the decision to go forward with the articles of impeachment, the Central Coordinating Committee could then take advantage of the political momentum from this "win." In essence, by seeing that the National Assembly was actually capable of doing something, "people began to trust that the National

Assembly would then proceed," and they adapted their weekly slogans accordingly.

The fact that organizations were able to form a national coalition and work in such close communication with each other throughout the Candlelight Protests speaks to the development of strong internal networks within the labor- and social-movement sphere. Although the Action Committee for Presidential Resignation organizers were responsible for managing every aspect of event planning and logistics, and they leveraged the many relationships that movement organizations had to do so, movement leaders were careful not to overstate the role of major progressive movement organizations and longtime left movement activists. More than anything, organizers commonly emphasized the role of the Action Committee for Presidential Resignation as simply creating the *madang* (마당), or "outdoor courtyard," as a place for people to gather, assemble, and create community. By invoking the term *madang* as a spatial metaphor, organizers drew on its open-ended and multivalent associations in fostering collective political transformation, such as "*madang* as a space of 'being in the moment' or *hyŏnjang*."[33] This type of spatial work was not about playing a vanguard role in leading the masses or mobilizing a certain ideological class, such as left or progressive activists. It was about laying the groundwork for people to come together and express their political will through affectively and emotionally charged communal experiences.

The ability of the Action Committee for Presidential Resignation to create the *madang* was also a result of the close working relationships that they had developed with each other. To organize any large public gathering in the city, organizations need to register their intent with the City of Seoul and the Korean National Police Agency through the submission of an application and the payment of a rental fee. The shift to a notification system, rather than a permission request system, was also due to the pressure campaigns of civic organizations, such as PSPD, which was able to win this change when Park Won-soon (박원순; Pak Wŏn-sun) became mayor of Seoul. Submitted notice of intent did not mean that access to public space was free, however. Although the fee was not considered onerous, "the plaza is not free," explained one event organizer.

"We have to pay a certain amount per square meter of use to contribute to the costs of maintaining and cleaning the space," they added. The notification of intent must also include detailed information about how many people that event organizers estimate will attend, what kind of supplies and equipment will be used during the event, and what kinds of activities will occur in the space. Coordination between organizations is crucial to ensure that there are not competing demands on the use of public space. Organizers of the annual Seoul Queer Culture Festival shared that as the conservative Christian-led opposition to their event grew, they faced greater obstacles around planning. In some cases, event organizers began camping out a full week before they were eligible to submit their notice of a public gathering to prevent their opponents from submitting an application ahead of time. For the Candlelight Protests, the fee was paid by the Action Committee for Presidential Resignation, yet they also benefitted from a fortuitous convergence of events.

Throughout the Candlelight Protests, time, duration, and numbers were also repeatedly emphasized as an indication of the mass mobilization's historical significance. "There was the risk that the numbers of protest participants would decrease once the National Assembly's decision was made public," explains one of the committee organizers. "So we worked hard to make sure the numbers did not fade." This included keeping up the momentum by emphasizing the kinds of growth and dynamism that they were building, rather than actual numbers. Ironically, one factor that organizers believed helped the Candlelight Protests maintain their momentum was the growing visibility of counterprotesters, particularly in the weeks leading up to the Constitutional Court's confirmation of impeachment. While the emphasis on size was an easy indicator during the early months of the candlelight mobilization, the growing force of the conservative opposition—which also took to the streets in greater numbers after the confirmation of Park Geun-hye's impeachment in mid-March—began to threaten the persuasiveness of numbers as a legitimating frame. More important than numbers became the creation of the kind of space that was open-ended and generative of new connections and imaginations, rather than uniform and closed in orientation and outlook.

The emphasis on distinguishing form from feeling is relevant when talking about the impact of the Candlelight Protests on the horizons of progressive politics in democratic life. In many ways, the political goals of the Candlelight Protests were frustrating to many longtime activists, who bemoaned the fact that there was little space to expand the terrain of public discourse to broader issues, such as gender discrimination or opposition to military projects, like the construction of the Terminal High Altitude Area Defense system by the United States—an issue that was the subject of protest mobilization before, during, and after the Candlelight Protests. But the experience of participating in a communal effort to try and change society through collective solidarity has left people with an indelible experience of the "taste of liberation." As Ryu Eunsook shared,

> After the Candlelight Protests ended, what continues is that taste of liberation. . . . One of my favorite phrases from Rebecca Solnit's book is the saying "You can't put the genie back in the bottle." Some people in power might think that the square is now closed, but we have released the genie, and the genie will not return no matter what people say. A good example of this is the issue of gender discrimination. I don't think we'll ever go back. It's continuing to come out, these issues, so the political task is how we create these into significant tasks for the future. There are tendencies to be exclusionist in the square, and we have to continue to be open and be more capacious.

In many ways, the lasting impact of the Candlelight Protests was not the material outcome of having successfully removed Park Geun-hye from the presidency; it was the fact that diverse groups of people created a space in the city where everyone could experience a sense of solidarity that was rooted in mutual recognition and affirmation. Producing spaces of possibility and creating experiences of collective solidarity and social transformation that are grounded in the felt and embodied relations of place making are thus crucial to the ongoing power of South Korean progressive protest politics in expanding the horizons of political transformation toward collective visions of mutual support and caring.

CONCLUSION

The Candlelight Protests of 2016–17 reveal the tremendous capacity of South Korean movement organizers and organizations to produce mass protests as recurring multimedia megaevents in Seoul's historic city center. They also demonstrate the difference that high-capacity movement actors make in interweaving distinct yet interrelated political crises into a watershed moment of eventful history. Yet more importantly, as we have argued in this chapter, the enactment of protests as place making has transformed the everyday social relations of the city itself as a space of dense connection and opportunity. As a city that has been transformed by intense financial speculation and the agglomeration of wealth and power through property ownership, Seoul has been the site of increasing social inequality and polarization, reflected most viscerally in the geographic concentration of extreme privilege and entitlement in Kangnam, the wealthy commercial and residential area south of the Han River.[34] Yet protest actors across a wide variety of issues, from mass mobilization against political corruption and corporate greed to national and global movements for gender justice and human rights, have changed the way people use and move around urban space through the enactment of protest itself. As we have examined in the narratives of key interlocutors, such as Lee Taeho and Kwak EKyeong, among other social activists, protesters have demanded access to the central sites of the city itself, be they historic sites of mobilization, such as city hall, or a new *kwangjang* at Kwanghwamun Square. The idea of making a place through protest reveals how spatial politics is a tool for expressing social and political belonging in a political economy that has excluded the poor and the marginalized from benefitting in the collective resources and opportunities of a global city.

The spatial transformation of the historic centers of Seoul as vibrant sites of protest highlights the success of protest movements in building critical communities of resistance and solidarity across a broad range of issues and actors. This depth and diversity were perhaps most evident during the epic Candlelight Protest rallies, which transformed the central city into an open space to freely express one's political anger and frustration as well as the individual and collective hopes that people hold for a more just and equitable world. Yet, as we discussed throughout the chapter, the candlelight mobilizations alone were not the source of dynamism beforehand, nor are they a continuing source, of the collective work of place making that has transformed the city into a place of political aspirations for a different future. Certainly, there are conflicts and disagreements that continue to constrain the possibilities for forging broad-based solidaristic movements that value social difference and otherness regarding gender, sexuality, age, generation, and political ideology, among others. And, in fact, the potential of space to both hold and catalyze these very differences is what makes protest as place making a driving force of political transformation. Working together to expand spaces of the city for free expression and public assembly highlights the practical and imaginative work that undergirds place making as a source of ongoing change and possibility. As Massey asserts, "For the future to be open, space must be open too."[35]

CONCLUSION
HOPE AND FAILURE

> For me, hope is not a metaphor; it's a lived practice. It isn't a thing I possess. Rather, I have to remake it daily. I don't have hope, I do hope. It's an active process that I have to regularly commit to—hope not as an emotion but as a discipline. Hope for me is grounded in the reality that wondrous things happen alongside and parallel to the terrible. Every single day.
>
> —Mariame Kaba, *Let This Radicalize You*

IN MANY WAYS, *AGAINST ABANDONMENT* is a book about failure and the specter of failure that looms over so many protests. Throughout each chapter, we have chronicled the extraordinary stories of workers and other aggrieved actors whose fights remain unresolved or ended in defeat. The struggles of women in precarious jobs, the principal subject of our ethnographic research, have involved protest tent encampments that have lasted months and even years, hunger strikes that have ended only when lifesaving medical intervention is deemed necessary, high-altitude occupations at dizzying heights, miserable conditions of deprivation, painstakingly slow and physically strenuous street processions, and so on. Though these protest repertoires have sometimes brought forth remarkable wins, they have also yielded legal victories that are difficult to enforce or mired in an unending series of appeals and reversals. Even when long-overdue victory is proclaimed, as in the case of the KTX workers we introduced at the start of the book, the sum total of hardship dampens the air of celebration.

In fact, this weighs heavily on our minds as we recognize that there is no shortage of bitter and devastating experiences across South Korea's vibrant and diverse social movements. Activists have not been able to stop the destruction of people's homes and the destruction of environments at the hands of megaconstruction projects in the energy, transportation, and military sectors. Coalitions of disenfranchised minority groups, including disabled and LGBTQ+ communities, have been unable to secure basic antidiscrimination protections into law. It has now been over ten years since the families and survivors began to seek full investigation and accountability for the government agencies' deadly negligence in the sinking of the *Sewol* ferry. Even though the outrage against Park Geun-hye over her mishandling of the *Sewol*-ferry disaster—as well as corruption charges—led to the Candlelight Protests of 2016–17, her impeachment and imprisonment, and, ultimately, the election of Moon Jae-in, who claimed to be the "Candlelight President," the political pendulum would swing again to the right with the conservative Yoon Suk Yeol (윤석열; Yun Sŏk-yŏl) being elected president in 2022.

Protests are so commonplace that journalist Sang-Hun Choe remarks, "Distrustful of their government, South Koreans have a penchant for taking all manner of grievances to the streets, so much so that it has turned demonstrating into a kind of national pastime."[1] Similar misgivings about the utility of protest abound in discussions of popular democracy around the world. Intensifying inequality and Fascism, even after decades of populist insurgency and leaderless protest movements, have raised concerns about whether political protests can ever yield meaningful and lasting change.[2] These concerns, however, are glib at best, even unfair. As labor-studies scholars writing for *Jacobin* point out, "A year after Occupy Wall Street was sparked, the mainstream media reached their consensus on the movement: it failed to create change. . . . In a nation with a notoriously short attention span, it's not surprising that the lack of immediate success gave rise to lamentations about its failure."[3] Taking a longer view, we believe that issues highlighted by the Occupy Wall Street movements continue to have deep relevance. The world's superrich 1 percent continue to amass obscene levels of wealth and resources in comparison to 99 percent of the world's population, even after the devastating COVID-19 global pandemic, revealing the dire state of affairs.[4] In the shadows of antiausterity protests that once energized town squares across Greece, Spain, England, Ireland, Portugal, and Turkey throughout the 2010s, there has been an upsurge of neo-Fascist unrest.[5] In the wake of the Arab Spring uprisings in North Africa and the Middle East, protesters face extreme risks when taking to the streets in defiance against repressive authoritarian regimes. Although the actual figure is unknown, human rights groups estimate that in 2022, as many as sixty-five thousand political prisoners, many without formal charges or awaiting trial indefinitely, are languishing in Egypt's prisons since President Abdel Fattah el-Sisi came to power in 2013.[6] Hong Kong's umbrella movement in 2014 galvanized a new generation of prodemocracy activists, becoming "the largest and most enduring civil disobedience campaign in the history of the city."[7] However, the movement was subsequently met with what Amnesty International called "the full weight of a relentless government assault," followed by the passage of a new National Security Law in 2020 that criminalized protestors and dissidents.[8] In the United States, outrage against anti-Black racism and police violence evolved into large-scale Black Lives Matter mobilizations throughout the country in the summer of 2020, but less than six months later, the resurgence of far-right extremism and white nationalism reached a feverish pitch in the form of the violent insurrection on the US Capitol on January 6, 2021.[9] It would be difficult, if not impossible, to point to an instance of political protest that resulted in permanent, durable change.

Failure is an "unpopular subject among social movement scholars," remarks Kim Voss in her assessment of the dearth of analysis about the topic.[10] The empirical study of social movements not only focuses disproportionately on the conditions that foment mass insurgency, whether during a precipitous moment of eventful history or a longer protest wave, but also tends to highlight winning strategies and successful outcomes at the expense of reflecting on the significance of failures. In *Against Abandonment*, we are in agreement with David S. Meyer's suggestion that rather than pursue "rigor and parsimony [that] leads us

226 CONCLUSION

to frame the objects of each study as narrowly as possible," it would be worthwhile to analyze how "social movement outcomes extend over time in unpredictable ways."[11] One crucial aspect of this challenge for us in writing this book has been to recognize failure itself as a significant outcome. Failure shapes how protesters regroup, rebuild, and sustain the will to keep fighting in the face of heartbreak, disappointment, and exhaustion. Given the unequal power relations that pervade almost every social-movement sphere, understanding how protesters grapple with failure is indispensable to understanding protest as an enduring weapon of the weak.

SOLIDARITY MATTERS

To move beyond failure on the horizon of protest politics, *Against Abandonment* has examined the paradoxical nature of protest as simultaneously life-threatening and life-sustaining. Protests that appear "extreme" or "desperate" are not merely militant or futile; they cannot be measured solely by their usefulness in winning demands or their effectiveness in achieving policy change. In fact, we have argued that the reverberating effects of protests can exceed intention. This is precisely what happens when protesters put their bodies and lives on the line, imploring others to "not to look away," as Diana Taylor puts it. She writes, "Bearing witness is a live process, a doing, an event that takes place in real time, in the presence of a listener who comes to be a participant and a co-owner of the traumatic event."[12] As such, the performance of a protest act calls on others to show solidarity as part of a "community of witnesses," which then generates ethical dilemmas for the observers, bystanders, and participants alike. This resonates with what we have seen. Protests catalyze enduring bonds of solidarity among a variety of protest participants and between protesters and those who witness them. As we elaborated on in chapter 2, protesters who grapple with repeated setbacks and internal contradictions turn to the embodied pedagogies of performance and ritual to renew relational ties and recharge a shared sense of purpose. Specific protest acts may express and articulate campaign demands and movement goals, but they also energize and invigorate the grounds of solidarity.

We have shown that protest repertoires of women workers put precarity at the front and center. Their protest repertoires conjure solidarity as an antidote to isolation, harm, and death, which are endemic features of neoliberal precarity. As chapter 3 elucidates, when Kim Jinsuk risked her life by engaging in her epic high-altitude occupation for 309 days or when KTX and Kiryung workers performed the grueling *och'et'uji* performances on the frigid streets of Seoul, their protest acts enacted heart-wrenching sacrifice and suffering for the public to bear witness. But it would be disingenuous to describe these protest acts as mere publicity stunts. It is true that as protests get drawn out, their ability to create a spectacle or capture news headlines become weaker over time. Because prolonged campaigns have diminishing returns over time, there is a growing sense of urgency. As many of our interlocuters emphasized, protest repertoires become all the more essential as lifelines against being forgotten, against being isolated and abandoned. They compel life-sustaining ties of solidarity and support not because they seek the limelight but because they urgently need solidarity for survival, and protest repertoires make it possible to elicit the presence of those who are able to provide solidarity as part of an ethics of care and community. Solidarity, in this sense, is about a simple fact of *being there*, to bear witness, and to stand alongside one another. But to be in solidarity also entails a willingness to comfort and console because they care.[13]

Theorizing solidarity as a relational force of copresence thus illuminates the affective power of protest that extends beyond simply bringing people together. As we discuss the struggles of precarious women workers in this book, we draw inspiration from Silvia Federici, who writes, "In many parts of the world, women have historically been seen as the weavers of memory—those who keep alive the voices of the past and the histories of the communities, who transmit them to the future generations and, in so doing, create a collective identity and profound sense of cohesion."[14] The activists we discuss in this book are likewise "weavers of memory," we argue, using rituals and repertoires to animate images and produce sounds, conjuring sentiments, hauntings, and reverbera-tions that draw together a variety of collectivities in struggle. As protest repertoires circulate, gain traction, and bring together bodies, causes, and sites, they produce what Doreen Massey calls the "throwntogeth-erness" of place, the "contemporaneous existence of a plurality of tra-jectories; a simultaneity of stories-so-far."[15] Protests are undoubtedly messy, complicated, and full of contradictions, and solidarity as we see it in this book does not insist on rigidly defined like-mindedness or unity for unity's sake. Rather, solidarity is a generative and catalytic force, as we argue in chapter 3, not simply the outcome. Solidarity is a relational space where connections are made and remade and sometimes even unmade or transformed as part of a collective political praxis.

Conceptualizing the space of solidarity as a relational and transfor-mative opening, not as a closure, is essential to understanding the out-comes of protest repertoires. Massey conceptualizes space as a site of political struggle that is neither fixed nor closed, even when there are forces that attempt to portray it as such, and writes, "For the future to be open, space must be open too."[16] One crucial way in which we see this is the creation of caring infrastructures. As we discussed in chapter 4, an essential part of a long-term struggle is the constant and multifaceted activity of mutual support and collective care, which sustains the life of the protest and protesters themselves. The labor of providing soli-darity is profoundly gendered and indispensable to the reproduction of social movements. Caring infrastructures sustain protests especially when participation declines and attention wanes. Time and time again during the course of our research, we were struck by the tremendous effort and steadfast labor required to mobilize and sustain protracted struggles. Core protest actors would not be able to survive without allies and supporters who organized constant solidarity rallies, marches, and press conferences while also taking care of the protesters' daily survival needs by securing access to water, food, and medicine. Supporters act as capable event planners and savvy fundraisers, coordinating program schedules and audiovisual-equipment setup while also making sure no one goes hungry or thirsty and that there are chairs or cushions and so forth. If things took a turn for the worse and someone required urgent medical care, someone would be in charge of rushing to their bedside at the hospital or alerting their family members. Someone would know how to plan vigils and arrange funerals. Yet much of the extensive work of activist-organizers involved in supporting *tangsaja*-led protests was nested in a broader dynamic of negotiating both visibility and invisibility in the infrastructural practices of social movements.

We saw countless examples of the capacity of South Korean social movements to carry out complex mobilizations of caring infrastructures with remarkable swiftness and foresight. One such example was the mobilization surrounding longtime activist Baek Nam-ki and his death. Places of protest, like the Kwanghwamun Square or even the road in front of the Seoul National University Hospital, where the activists fought against the police to protect Baek Nam-ki's body, have been theorized by urban and political geographers as sites of counterhegemonic resistance against the capitalist logics of predatory extraction and social devaluation.[17] By occupying the streets, public parks, city squares, subway and train stations, government and school buildings, and other strategic locations, social groups in resistance assert their right to reclaim and remake the city. Sometimes, though not always, these place-making claims are breathtaking and spectacular. The Candlelight Protests of 2016–17 transformed the streets of Seoul into spaces of recurring protest week after week—a space where thousands of participants basked in the optimism that another world was possible. Candlelight protesters repeatedly pointed to earlier iterations of mass mobilization in 2002 and 2008, when ordinary citizens poured into the city center to express their outrage against the US military and government for their blatant disregard of the health and safety of Korean citizens. Both past and present sites and memories converged in these spaces, producing concurrent and overlapping assemblies. After all, in the middle of the Candlelight Protests were the *Sewol* tents, clearly identified by yellow ribbons and flags alongside a memorial altar, and just a few blocks away was the site of the Wednesday protest (수요시위) at the Japanese embassy, where survivors and advocates for so-called comfort women have rallied on every Wednesday at noon since January 1992 in what is known as the longest-running peace protest in the world.

Through place-making practices that transcend the boundaries of a single protest or an individual protester, protest repertoires create ripple effects that change the way people feel about themselves as an agent of social change and the everyday spaces in which they live, work, eat, play, and build communities. During mass assemblies in Kwanghwamun Square and city hall, for example, the spaces of the city center brimmed with exchanges among people who greeted each other not as strangers but as fellow participants, as collaborators. During these moments of eventful history, protest participants looked out for each other, shared snacks and supplies, and comforted and laughed with each other in ways that are not commonplace in public. We do not wish to romanticize these spaces. Plenty of participants felt marginalized and alienated even in these spaces of collectivity and raised criticisms of the sexism, agism, and other bigotries, prejudices, and inequalities that persist even in left and progressive protest spaces. But we nonetheless note the significance of the efforts that were made to create these alternative worlds, the attempt that was made to foster a way of being that diverges from the hyperindividualized and competitive spaces of neoliberal capitalist life.

Transforming the felt and embodied relations in space is indeed a significant part of exercising the right to the city. As David Harvey asserts, demanding access to public space is "not merely a right of access to what already exists"; it is about the "the right to remake ourselves by creating a qualitatively different type of urban sociality."[18] While the euphoria of a large protest assembly can be fleeting and swiftly appropriated by opportunists and opponents alike, the labor of fostering alternative forms of sociality though emancipatory processes of place making can leave an enduring imprint. It is the labor, the collective pursuit in protest, that instills the hope that another world is possible, even after the protest is over and even if the protest fails to achieve its aims. What the activist Mariame Kaba says—as we quoted in the epigraph of this chapter—deeply resonates with us: "Hope is not a metaphor; it's a lived practice. . . . It's an active process that I have to regularly commit to—hope not as an emotion but as a discipline. Hope for me is grounded in the reality that wondrous things happen alongside and parallel to the terrible. Every single day."[19] We are reminded of the procession of protesters performing *och'et'uji*, a repetition of falling to the ground and getting back up, both terrible and wondrous to behold.

THE WILLFUL POLITICS OF REFUSAL

Protests have become so popular and commonplace that even mainstream film and TV plotlines now routinely include portrayals of idealistic college students and political dissidents as well as ordinary housewives and blue-collar factory workers pumping their fists in unison and shouting slogans in organized protest actions against an injustice. Most of these portrayals are stereotypical—troublemakers wearing matching headbands and union vests, waving handwritten placards and banners, and so on—but even the more unusual tactics, such as high-altitude protests and tent occupations, sometimes appear in popular culture as well. In the Netflix K-drama *Queenmaker* (퀸메이커), which aired on the global streaming platform in April 2023, viewers are introduced to a character named Oh Kyung-sook just fifteen minutes into the first episode. We find out that the outspoken labor and human rights lawyer Oh Kyung-sook, played by the critically acclaimed actress Moon So-ri (문소리; Mun So-ri), has been occupying the rooftop of the fictional Eunsung Department Store for seventy-eight consecutive days on behalf of five hundred women workers who were fired from their part-time jobs in the food court. After the CEO and daughter of the chaebol family that owns the luxury department store is captured on video hitting her subordinates with an expensive high-heeled shoe, Oh Kyung-sook takes advantage of the timing of the scandal by linking the public outcry and calls for the CEO's resignation to the aims of her own clients—the resolution of the union's demands through *kogong nongsŏng*, the high-altitude-occupation protest. The rest of the episodes in the series move on to a revenge plot and Oh's unsuccessful bid to become the next mayor of Seoul, featuring her underdog pursuit against corporate greed and political corruption as the main throughline, but more than anything, we could not help but notice with interest that protest repertoires, including *kogong nongsŏng*, have become such a familiar part of social life that they serve as a plot device for a Netflix series. A discerning viewer would have noted, however, that this plotline had a major flaw. As we have discussed in this book, *kogong nongsŏng* is part of an escalation strategy within a wide-ranging protest repertoire, undertaken nearly always by the *tangsaja*, or those most directly impacted by the grievance. It is unheard of that an attorney—even one played by a charismatic actor like Moon So-ri with great conviction and dramatic flair—would engage in a long-term high-altitude-occupation protest on behalf of someone else, such as her clients.

Setting aside our quibbles over a minor storyline on Netflix, we appreciate that even a fictional character can protest against the powerful economic and political elites and challenge the ways in which precarious workers are denied a dignified life. Oh Kyung-sook's character in *Queenmaker* refuses to accept the status quo and speaks truth to power. In the labor- and social-movement protests that we have followed, the willful refusal to give up the fight can seem irrational and futile, yet like in the fictional plot in *Queenmaker*, the very act of refusal generates ethical critiques and practical interventions that subsequently enable the survival of social actors engaged in lopsided battles against powerful opponents. We are reminded of Carole McGranahan's assertion that refusal not only "marks the point of a limit having been reached," but as a political strategy, refusal also "brings us back to transformation and generation, to the possibility of acting to spark change."[20] Challenging the terms and rules of engagement is crucial to refusal. Rather than giving consent to a situation in which the rules are unjustly and unfairly applied, as Audra Simpson writes, refusal is a "theory of the political" that is "pronounced over and over again." Put simply, one refuses "to let go, to roll over, to play [the] game," even if it means being willing to "withstand and accommodate pain and the structures of injustice." In this sense, refusal very much "operates as the revenge of consent."[21]

For Simpson, refusal as a theory of the political is inextricably linked to the long and ongoing history of settler colonialism and extractive capitalism. Whether in defiance of federal treaties that are routinely violated or citizenship rights that are always conditional, we see the willful politics of refusal at work in contemporary protest movements against the dispossession of Indigenous communities of their land, resources, and cultural traditions. For the Standing Rock Sioux and their embattled opposition to the Dakota Access Pipeline, or the #NoDAPL movement, protesting corporate resource-extraction projects that violate federal land treaties, disregard protected and sacred land, and threaten the basis of sustainable human and ecological life have resulted in the subjection of Indigenous peoples and their supporters to intense police repression and state violence as well as debilitating legal fines and court sanctions. Despite these costly risks, antipipeline protesters persist in large part because they refuse to accept the "logic of elimination" that drives a wide range of institutional policies and practices aimed at destroying Indigenous knowledge and governance systems.[22] Simpson elaborates, "Settler colonialism is not eventful; it is enduring, it has its own structure and logic and refusal as well, operating like a grammar and posture that sits through time. It is a politics deeply cognizant of its own production, of the never-ending nature of inequity and the need to stay the course."[23] Staying the course may include getting arrested, deportation, and even death, but the refusal to recognize the legitimacy of the state-sanctioned theft of land and resources ensures that settler colonialism does not become complete as a finished political project.[24]

Simpson's brilliant thesis on refusal illuminates the unjust structures of power and domination that enable ruling elites to continue amassing the world's wealth and resources without the consent of the subordinated classes and populations. It also points to how colonialism is a structure, not an event.[25] We would add that failure—failure to comply and failure to give consent—is also a structure, not a single event. Alain Badiou highlights the urgency of paying close attention to how and under what conditions protest can alter the calculus of political power between the rulers and the ruled in ways that endure over time and place. Whether protest is expressed as a localized riot or spreads around the world, Badiou cautions us not to assume that the "popular democratic practices of the movement (or any historical riot, no matter when and where it occurs) form a kind of paradigm for the state to come."[26] When the oppressed masses repeatedly take to the streets in defiance and expose the illegitimacy and brutality of the people and systems in power, the change they effect is not necessarily political in the formal sense, even if they are able to create change in the electoral and legislative arenas. What they change, asserts Badiou, is the social fact of their existence.[27] Rather than allow the powerful to treat them as if they "count for nothing," protesters make themselves visible as a social force that is capable of rising up, again and again, regardless of the actual capacity to win. In doing so, protesters reinvent a sense of time and place by turning themselves into the "guardian[s] of all temporal forms of oppression."[28] It is this capacity to reimagine and reinvent history through the embodied and place-based politics of protest that makes refusal an enduring force of social change.

We see the power of protest to reimagine history in the repertoires of solidarity in South Korean protest. Namhee Lee points to the "politics of time" as working to "make certain experiences of the past illegible or concealed in the present," but in our discussion, protesters refuse the terms of such time.[29] In contrast, they respond to the abject conditions of everyday life under neoliberal precarity precisely by connecting their contemporary fights to a long history of popular struggle against colonial oppression and capitalist injustice. This is a history from below that is associated with the emancipatory project of the *minjung* movement against national capitalism—an influential movement that peaked in the 1980s as part of a broad constellation of popular and intellectual forces against the dehumanizing conditions of authoritarian industrialization under dictatorial rule; though, the *minjung* movement has been discredited by its own ideological founders as a bygone of a past era, as Lee details in her book. Yet as we have elaborated throughout the book, protest movements have imagined and reimagined history in a variety of ways. Not limited to referencing the dark days of dictatorship during the 1970s and 1980s, contemporary cultural politics of protest against precarity reach even further back to the early decades of the twentieth century and the colonial subjugation of Korea by the Japanese empire (1910–45). One specific example is the story of Kang Chu-ryong, whose 1931 protest on the rooftop of a rubber factory in Pyŏngyang is invoked with increasing frequency in protest discourse as the first woman worker in history to engage in *kogong nongsŏng*. When protesters wear plain white *minbok* clothing associated with ordinary peasant life during their *och'et'uji*, they conjure connections to past generations that have fought the brutality of land dispossession and labor exploitation under colonial and feudal rule. Although such historical imaginaries may suggest that protesters are drawing a linear trajectory between the past and present, we think otherwise: their ability to invoke multiple historical temporalities in a single place reveals the multifaceted nature of social memory. By recuperating images, sounds, cultural sensibilities, and aesthetic practices considered to be part of the nation's past, protesters evoke what has been called "multidirectional memory"—that is, a "way of conceptualizing what happens when different histories of extreme violence confront each other in the public sphere."[30]

The afterlives of colonialism and empire are vivid and palpable in the myriad ways that contemporary protesters forge connections with past histories of struggle.[31] Let us share another recent example, this time in literary fiction. *Mater 2-10*, an International Booker Prize–nominated novel by renowned author Sok-yong Hwang (황석영; Hwang Sŏk-yŏng), illustrates the vibrant cultural imaginations that connect workers' contemporary struggles against precarity and neoliberalism to the century-long history of resistance waged by multiple generations of aggrieved workers. *Mater 2-10* begins with the plight of Yi Jino, a fifty-year-old factory worker and staunch unionist, who climbs forty-five meters to the top of an industrial chimney stack and proceeds to stage a high-altitude sit-in. We learn about Jino's bodily discomfort and the extreme difficulties of basic survival in cramped, isolated, and poorly ventilated conditions. We also learn about his "support team" on the ground, who supply him with food, water, and other basic provisions, including sending up and down disposable food containers that he can convert into a makeshift toilet. As we read more about why Jino would go to such lengths to protest his unjust layoff after devoting twenty-five years to the job, following in the footsteps of other comrades who have waged similarly grueling high-altitude protests, we learn about his own family's history of labor resistance and union organizing, including his great-grandfather and grandfather, who worked on the colonial railways and helped lead risky strikes against Japanese supervisors and managers. One particularly moving storyline takes place at a textile factory, where Jino's grandmother Geumi worked as a young girl. When the mother of her coworker, Yeongsun, is beaten up by a factory supervisor, a middle-aged Japanese woman who refuses to allow Yeongsun to see her four-year-old son during the long workday, three hundred and fifty textile workers decide to wage a wildcat strike in solidarity. In the prepared statement about the incident read out loud at the morning of the strike, Yeongsun recounts the sentiment that fueled their defiant act: "We may be a people without a country, but does that mean we deserve to be treated like this?"[32]

CARING AS POLITICAL PRAXIS

The refusal of protesting workers to accept the legitimacy of a system that treats them as disposable and deprives them of their worth and dignity directs our attention to the creation of alternative modes of living and caring for one another beyond the capitalist value systems of accumulation and commodification. Further, protesters' repeated enactment of grueling protest acts reveals the cultivation of a solidaristic politics that is attuned to a feminist ethics of care. As Bernice Fisher and Joan C. Tronto explain in their classic article "Toward a Feminist Theory of Caring," caring encompasses "everything that we do to maintain, continue, and repair our 'world' so that we can live in it as well as possible."[33] This includes providing care to those in need on an intimate and interpersonal level and the cognitive and reflexive work of caring about others in a crisis-ridden world. Even when all supporters can do is sit by and witness the acts of tremendous resolve and self-harm, as in the case of the ninety-four-day hunger strike by Kiryung unionist Kim So-yeon, being there represents a commitment to care about and care for each and every life, refusing to abandon one another.

The principle of caring has appeared in many historic movements, from the Industrial Workers of the World slogan "Injury to one is an injury to all" to the oft-used adage "If they come for me in the morning, they will come for you in the night."[34] Yet the idea that oppositional movements must prioritize the physical and emotional well-being of participants, let alone invest time and resources toward building caring infrastructures that can sustain high-risk collective action, has consistently been sidelined and sometimes even derided. This is partially due to the gendered nature of care as unpaid and devalued reproductive labor. As we discussed in chapter 4, the activists that we interviewed recounted being dismissed by others or, in many cases, remember previously dismissing their own concerns about the dominance of masculinist values and practices, especially when facing authoritarian state violence in the 1980s and 1990s.[35]

There is perhaps even more urgent need to foreground caring as a political praxis today given the expanding geographies of human deprivation and ecological destruction as well as the relentless expropriation of life under the extractive conditions of global capitalism.[36] Neferti X. M. Tadiar asserts, "At no other time in history have more and more people been pushed to the very edge, if not completely beyond the bounds of global humanity." Yet Tadiar emphasizes that people whose lives have been stripped of worth and value are not disposable, and rather, through the kind of organizing Tadiar calls "life-making," they create value as "remaindered life"—that is, the "tangential, fugitive, and recalcitrant creative capacities" that are oriented toward "forms of viable, enjoyable life."[37] Similarly, the groundbreaking theorizing of Black and Indigenous feminists, as well as of queer and trans scholars of color, call attention to the "vital but underappreciated strategies" of radical care and mutual aid that foster anticapitalist worlds.[38] Kelly Hayes and Mariame Kaba identify "caring as a form of cultural rebellion," which has the potential to "alter a community's sense of what's possible."[39] This type of organizing, which has long been performed in the United States by the unpaid and devalued labor of Black women and other racialized and minoritized groups, not only attends to basic aspects of survival and resilience but also cultivates the capacity of oppressed communities to care for themselves and one another in ways that reveal the life-giving work of organizing as an everyday practice of change.

We are reminded once again of the refusal to abandon hope despite years of experiencing disappointment and failure in the example of celebrated labor activist Kim Jin-suk, who became widely known for her

238 CONCLUSION

309-day *kogong nongsŏng* atop Crane 85, as we discussed in chapter 3. On December 30, 2020, Kim Jin-suk waged another epic protest, yet this time, it was not on behalf of other workers but to resolve her own life-long fight for job reinstatement. As she approached the retirement age of sixty, she decided to revive her own fight for reinstatement at Hanjin, a struggle that rarely, if ever, took center stage in her own long history of activism. Battling breast cancer and the many health problems she had developed over the thirty-six years of living life in the public eye as a radical labor activist, Kim Jin-suk traveled, almost entirely on foot, from the shipyard in Pusan, where she once worked and lost her job as a welder in 1986, to the Blue House in Seoul, the president's place of residence. It is a distance of more than three hundred kilometers, or nearly two hundred miles. The journey was filled with both quiet and joyful moments, surrounded by new and familiar supporters who showed up to walk with her and to make sure that Kim Jin-suk stayed well hydrated, took restful breaks, had nourishing meals, and slept as comfortably as possible. Providing support and care also meant continuing to publicize Kim Jin-suk's demands, organizing high-profile media events such as the mass welcome staged outside the Blue House by hundreds of people from the Remember the Hope Bus organizing committee, whose own hunger strike for Kim Jin-suk's reinstatement had reached its forty-eighth day. There were many unpublicized, unspectacular moments too, such as when people simply accompanied Kim Jin-suk as she walked, thankful for the tremendous support and care that her willful politics of refusal had cultivated. On February 7, 2021, Kim Jin-suk was able to celebrate the resolution of her thirty-seven-year-long fight, winning symbolic reinstatement with retirement, which would commence immediately.

Kim Jin-suk's fight illustrates the kind of hope that Mariame Kaba emphasizes must be made and remade as a "lived practice."[40] We are heartened to know that in a world full of gross injustice and genocidal violence, social movements are radically reimagining our collective futures through the hard work of enacting solidarity in disciplined, embodied ways. Through the protest repertoires that underscore refusal, activists fasten together the past and present in telling our stories repeatedly and recursively, insisting on a future beyond failure. We conclude with the humble realization that our account in the here and now is hardly complete or comprehensive. We end with a sense of hope in the ongoing history of resistance and perseverance and, perhaps most importantly, emboldened by what we have seen in the power of refusal to abandon one another.

GLOSSARY

List of Key Terms

changgi t'ujaeng (장기투쟁). Long-term struggle or fight.

ch'amsa (참사). Disaster or catastrophe.

chŏmgŏ nongsŏng (점거 농성). Occupation protest.

chŏnggyujik (정규직). Regular or standard employment.

ch'otbul chiphoe (촛불집회). Candlelight protest.

hwaldongga (활동가). Activist or organizer.

inkwŏn (인권). Human rights.

irinsiwi (일인시위). One-person protest.

kogong nongsŏng (고공농성). High-altitude protest.

kwangjang (광장). Public square.

nongsŏng (농성). Prolonged protest that typically involves occupying a particular site and can include sit-ins, encampments, and other activities.

och'et'uji (오체투지). Procession involving full prostration with five parts of the body touching the ground.

pijŏnggyujik (비정규직). Precarious, irregular, nonregular, or nonstandard employment.

yŏngu hwaldongga (연구 활동가). Research activist.

samboilbae (삼보일배). Procession involving three steps and a bow.

sanggyŏng t'ujaeng (상경투쟁). Protest struggle that entails heading to the capital.

tansik (단식). Hunger strike.

tangsaja (당사자). Directly impacted persons in a dispute or grievance.

T'aegŭkki Rally (태극기 집회). Protest rally featuring the T'aegŭkki (Korean national flag), typically associated with conservative progovernment politics.

tongjo tansik (동조단식). Solidarity hunger strike.

t'ujaeng (투쟁). Fight or struggle, as in labor struggle.

twip'uri (뒤풀이). Postactivity debrief, typically informal and social.

undongkwŏn (운동권). Shorthand for movement activists with student-government backgrounds.

yongyŏk kkangp'ae (용역 깡패). Employer-hired thugs.

List of Key Organizations

416 Coalition (416 연대)

Asahi Glass In-House Subcontracting Workers Union (아사히비정규직지회)

Banolim (반올림)

Catholic Priests' Association for Justice (CPAJ; 천주교정의구현전국사제단)

Ch'ang Human Rights Research Center (인권연구소 창)

Ch'ŏngju City Geriatric Hospital Workers' Union (청주시노인전문병원 노조)

Christian Academy (한국크리스찬아카데미)

Cool Jam (Kkuljam; 꿀잠)

Cort/Cor-Tek Guitar Workers' Union (콜트-콜텍 기타노동자 노조)

E-Land Union (이랜드노조)

Emergency Action for Park Geun-hye's Resignation, or Action Committee for Presidential Resignation (박근혜정권 퇴진 비상국민행동, or 퇴진행동)

Jaenung Educational Tutors' Union (재능교육교사노조)

Kiryung Electronics Workers' Union (기륭전자노조)

Korea Electric Power Corporation (KEPCO; 한국전력공사)

Korea Telecom Contract Workers' Union (한국통신계약직노조)

Korean Confederation of Trade Unions (KCTU; 전국민주노동조합총연맹)

Korean Council for the Women Drafted for Military Sexual Slavery by Japan (한국정신대문제대책협의회)

Korean Metal Workers' Union (전국금속노동조합)

Korean Railroad Workers' Union (KRWU; 전국철도노동조합)

Korean Solidarity against Precarious Work (전국불안전노동철폐연대)

Korean Teachers and Education Workers Union (전국교직원노동조합)

Korean Train Express (KTX; 한국고속철도 ㅇ)

Korean Women Workers Association (한국여성노동자회)

KTX Crew Workers' Union (KTX 승무원 노조)

Lawyers for a Democratic Society (민주사회를 위한 변호사모임)

People's Committee for the *Sewol*-Ferry Tragedy (세월호 참사 국민대책회의)

People's Solidarity for Participatory Democracy (PSPD; 참여연대)

Sarangbang Group for Human Rights (인권운동 사랑방)

Solidarity against Disability Discrimination (전국장애인차별철폐연대)

Solidarity for the Right to Mobility (이동권 연대)

Ssangyong Motor Union (쌍용자동차 노조)

NOTES

INTRODUCTION

1. Speech by Kim Seungha at press conference organized by laid-off Korean Train Express union workers announcing tentative agreement with the Korea Railroad Corporation on July 21, 2018. SBS News, "'Urinŭn t'ŭliji anatsŭmnida' . . . KTX haego sŭngmuwŏndŭl 'nunmul ŭi haedansik'" ["We were not in the wrong" . . . terminated KTX crew hold a "tearful end-of-struggle ceremony"], Naver TV, July 21, 2018, video, 8:11, https://tv.naver.com/v/3656367. All translations by authors unless otherwise noted.

2. We use the English terms "precarious" and "precarity" interchangeably with the Korean term *pijŏnggyujik*. Although the literal translation of *pijŏnggyujik* is "nonregular," "irregular," or "nonstandard employment," the use of non-regular/irregular employment tends to reify the notion that *pijŏnggyujik* is simply the opposite of *chŏnggyujik,* or "standard" or "regular employment." It also has the potential to distance the Korean case from global and transnational conversations concerning precarity. We recognize that these terms have their inconsistencies and limitations but wish to stress the key nuance in "precarity" and *pijŏnggyujik* alike, and that is the ideas of asymmetry and inequity, insecurity and vulnerability to harm. We use the term "irregular" or "nonregular" as direct translations of published articles and organizational names.

3. Yŏ Chŏng-min, "1 ŏk mulge toen KTX sŭngmuwŏn 'kajŏng wihae ihon komindo'" [KTX crew hit with a hundred-million-won fine, "even considering a divorce for the sake of the family"], *Pressian*, March 4, 2015, https://www.pressian.com/pages/articles/124383.

4. All uncited quotations are from interviews conducted by the authors.

5. On the concept of the moral economy, see Jaime Palomera and Theodora Vetta, "Moral Economy: Rethinking a Radical Concept," *Anthropological Theory* 16, no. 4 (December 2016): 413–32. All uncited quotations are from interviews conducted by the authors.

244 NOTES TO THE INTRODUCTION

6. Ruth Wilson Gilmore, "Fatal Couplings of Power and Difference: Notes on Racism and Geography," *Professional Geographer* 54, no. 1 (February 2002): 16. The phrase was originally used in Stuart Hall, "Race, Culture, and Communications: Looking Backward and Forward at Cultural Studies," *Rethinking Marxism* 5, no. 1 (1992): 17. Gilmore's idea that certain groups are rendered vulnerable to a premature death under the racial conditions of globalized neoliberal capitalism has been hugely influential across many disciplines and critical studies. See also Ruth Wilson Gilmore, *Abolition Geography: Essays towards Liberation* (London: Verso, 2022); Ruth Wilson Gilmore, *Golden Gulag: Prisons, Surplus, Crisis, and Opposition in Globalizing California* (Berkeley: University of California Press, 2007); Ruth Wilson Gilmore, "Organized Abandonment and Organized Violence: Devolution and the Police," Humanities Institute at the University of California, Santa Cruz, CA, November 9, 2015, Vimeo video, https://vimeo.com/146450686.

7. Raymond Williams, *Marxism and Literature* (Oxford: Oxford University Press, 1977), 132.

8. Williams, *Marxism and Literature*, 131.

9. Hannah Arendt, *The Origins of Totalitarianism* (New York: Harcourt Brace Jovanovich, 1973), 296.

10. Neferti X. M. Tadiar, *Remaindered Life* (Durham, NC: Duke University Press, 2022), 7, 16.

11. Ju Hui Judy Han, "High-Altitude Protests and Necropolitical Digits," in *Infrastructures of Citizenship: Digital Life in the Global City*, ed. Deborah Cowen et al. (Vancouver: University of British Columbia Press, 2020), 175–79.

12. Yoonkyung Lee, "Sky Protest: New Forms of Labour Resistance in Neoliberal Korea," *Journal of Contemporary Asia* 45, no. 3 (July 2015): 445, https://doi.org/10.1080/00472336.2015.1012647; Sun-Chul Kim, "The Trajectory of Protest Suicide in South Korea, 1970–2015," *Journal of Contemporary Asia* 51, no. 1 (July 2019): 38, https://doi.org/10.1080/00472336.2019.1607889.

13. Ching Kwan Lee, *Against the Law: Labor Protests in China's Rustbelt and Sunbelt* (Berkeley: University of California Press, 2007), 9.

14. Sydney Tarrow, *Power in Movement: Social Movements and Contentious Politics* (New York: Cambridge University Press, 1998), 3–4.

15. Tarrow, *Power in Movement*; Charles Tilly and Sydney Tarrow, *Contentious Politics* (Boulder: Paradigm, 2007).

16. Charles Tilly, *Contentious Performances* (Cambridge: Cambridge University Press, 2008).

17. Charles Tilly, *The Contentious French* (Cambridge, MA: Belknap, 1986).

18. Charles Tilly, *The Politics of Collective Violence* (Cambridge: Cambridge University Press, 2003); Charles Tilly, *Regimes and Repertoires* (Chicago: University of Chicago Press, 2006).

NOTES TO THE INTRODUCTION 245

19. Tilly, *Contentious Performances*.

20. Deborah B. Gould, *Moving Politics: Emotion and ACT UP's Fight against AIDS* (Chicago: University of Chicago Press, 2009); Erika Summers Effler, *Laughing Saints and Righteous Heroes: Emotional Rhythms in Social Movement Groups* (Chicago: University of Chicago Press, 2010); James M. Jasper, "Emotions and Social Movements: Twenty Years of Theory and Research," *Annual Review of Sociology* 37 (2011): 285–303, https://doi.org/10.1146/annurev-soc-081309-150015.

21. Gould, *Moving Politics*, 234.

22. Effler, *Laughing Saints*.

23. Diana Taylor, *The Archive and the Repertoire: Performing Cultural Memory in the Americas* (Durham, NC: Duke University Press, 2003).

24. Taylor, *Archive and the Repertoire*, 28–29.

25. Taylor, *Archive and the Repertoire*, 32.

26. Marcela Fuentes, *Performance Constellations: Networks of Protest and Activism in Latin America* (Ann Arbor: University of Michigan Press, 2020), 4–5.

27. Scholars across disciplinary and interdisciplinary fields—including feminist studies, political geography, and cultural sociology—have raised similar questions. Sara Ahmed, *Living a Feminist Life* (Durham, NC: Duke University Press, 2017); Iván Arenas, "The Mobile Politics of Emotions and Social Movement in Oaxaca, Mexico," *Antipode* 47, no. 5 (November 2015): 1121–40, https://doi.org/10.1111/anti.12158; Ron Eyerman, "How Social Movements Move: Emotions and Social Movements," in *Emotions and Social Movements*, ed. Helena Flam and Debra King (London: Routledge, 2005), 41–58.

28. Brian Massumi, *Parables for the Virtual: Movement, Affect, Sensation* (Durham, NC: Duke University Press, 2002).

29. The study of political affect and space is animating a growing literature in ethnographic studies in sociology, anthropology, and geography. Patricia Ticineto Clough, introduction to *The Affective Turn: Theorizing the Social*, ed. Patricia Ticineto Clough and Jean Halley (Durham, NC: Duke University Press, 2007), 1–33; Zeynep Kurtulus Korkman, "Feeling Labor: Commercial Divination and Commodified Intimacy in Turkey," *Gender and Society* 29, no. 2 (April 2015): 195–218, https://doi.org/10.1177/0891243214566269; Purnima Mankekar and Akhil Gupta, "Intimate Encounters: Affective Labor in Call Centers," *Positions: Asia Critique* 24, no. 1 (February 2016): 17–43, https://doi.org/10.1215/10679847 -3320029; Ben Anderson, "Neoliberal Affects," *Progress in Human Geography* 40, no. 6 (December 2016): 734–53, https://doi.org/10.1177/0309132515613167.

30. Sara Ahmed, "Affective Economies," *Social Text* 22, no. 2 (2004): 119.

31. Anderson, "Neoliberal Affects," 747.

32. Deborah Cowen, "Crisis in Motion," University of London Institute in Paris, Paris, France, January 29, 2021, Theory, Culture, and Society video, https://www.theoryculturesociety.org/blog/video-deborah-cowen-crisis-in-motion.

33. Donatella Della Porta, "Political Economy and Social Movement Studies: The Class Basis of Anti-austerity Protests," *Anthropological Theory* 17, no. 4 (2017): 453–73, https://doi.org/10.1177/1463499617735258. Della Porta makes this point in her critique of the absence of attention to the political economy in social-movement inquiry.

34. Nadia Y. Kim, *Refusing Death: Immigrant Women and the Fight for Environmental Justice in LA* (Stanford: Stanford University Press, 2021). Kim provides an excellent analysis of a social movement led by immigrant women of color in Southern California against environmental injustice as social death.

35. Audra Simpson, *Mohawk Interruptus: Political Life across the Borders of Settler States*, ill. ed. (Durham, NC: Duke University Press, 2014), 9.

36. Albert Melucci, *Challenging Codes: Collective Action in the Information Age* (Cambridge: Cambridge University Press, 1996).

37. Doreen Massey, *For Space* (London: SAGE, 2005), 12.

38. David Featherstone, *Solidarity: Hidden Histories and Geographies of Internationalism* (London: Zed Books, 2012), 7.

39. Ruth Wilson Gilmore, *"Geographies of Racial Capitalism with Ruth Wilson Gilmore*—An Antipode Foundation Film," dir. Kenton Card, Antipodeonline, June 1, 2020, YouTube video, https://www.youtube.com/watch?v=2CS627aKrJI.

40. Gilmore, *Abolition Geography*, 93.

41. Nancy Fraser, "Abnormal Injustice," *Critical Inquiry* 34, no. 3 (2008): 393–422.

42. Silvia Federici, *Revolution at Point Zero: Housework, Reproduction, and Feminist Struggle*, 2nd ed. (Oakland, CA: PM Press, 2020), 121.

43. Guy Standing, *The Precariat: The New Dangerous Class* (London: Bloomsbury Academic, 2011).

44. Judith Butler, *Notes toward a Performative Theory of Assembly* (Cambridge, MA: Harvard University Press, 2015), 16.

45. Ben Scully, "Precarity North and South: A Southern Critique of Guy Standing," *Global Labour Journal* 7, no. 2 (2016): 160–72, https://doi.org/10.15173/glj.v7i2.2521; Jan Breman and Marcel van der Linden, "Informalizing the Economy: The Return of the Social Question at a Global Level," *Development and Change* 45, no. 5 (2014): 920–40, https://doi.org/10.1111/dech.12115; Rina Agarwala, *Informal Labor, Formal Politics, and Dignified Discontent in India* (New York: Cambridge University Press, 2013).

46. Kathleen M. Millar, "Towards a Critical Politics of Precarity," *Sociology Compass* 11, no. 6 (2017): 6.

47. Williams, *Marxism and Literature*, 130.

48. Lauren Berlant, *Cruel Optimism* (Durham, NC: Duke University Press, 2011).

49. Franco Barchiesi, *Precarious Liberation: Workers, the State, and Contested*

Social Liberation in Post-apartheid South Africa (Albany: State University of New York Press, 2011).

50. Kwang-Yeong Shin and Ju Kong, "Why Does Inequality in South Korea Continue to Rise?," *Korean Journal of Sociology* 48, no. 6 (2014): 31–48; Hagen Koo, *Privilege and Anxiety: The Korean Middle Class in the Global Era* (Ithaca, NY: Cornell University Press, 2022).

51. OECD, *Society at a Glance 2024: OECD Social Indicators* (Paris: OECD, 2024), https://doi.org/10.1787/918d8db3-en. Koo provides an in-depth discussion of the stark transformation of income inequality trends between the 1960s and the mid-2010s. Koo, *Privilege and Anxiety*, 34–37.

52. Sehyun Hong et al., "Income Inequality in South Korea, 1933–2022: Evidence from Distributional National Accounts" (working paper, N. 2024/03, World Inequality Lab, January 13, 2024), 16, https://wid.world/news-article/income-inequality-in-south-korea-1933-2022/. See also Yi-Geun Ryu, "Income Inequality in S. Korea Is Widening at Second-Fastest Rate in OECD," *Hankyoreh*, Eng. ed., April 10, 2023, https://english.hani.co.kr/arti/english_edition/e_national/1087257.

53. Hyeongjung Hwang, Axel Purwin, and Jon Pareliussen, "Strengthening the Social Safety Net in Korea" (working paper, OECD Economics Department, OECD iLibrary, November 30, 2022), 6, https://doi.org/10.1787/45486525-en.

54. Kim Yoo Sun, "The Non-regular Work in South Korea," *Friedrich-Ebert-Stiftung Issue Paper Series, Labour and Society*, no. 1 (October 2021): 1, 4, https://library.fes.de/pdf-files/bueros/seoul/18415.pdf.

55. H. Hwang, Purwin, and Pareliussen, "Social Safety Net," 14.

56. Victoria Kim and Daisuke Wakabayashi, "What to Know about the Chaebol Families That Dominate South Korea's Economy," *New York Times*, December 18, 2023, https://www.nytimes.com/2023/12/18/business/chaebol-south-korea.html#:~:text=Chaebol%20families%20have%20controlled%20South,support%20to%20rebuild%20the%20economy.

57. Sook Jung Lee, "The Politics of Chaebol Reform in Korea: Social Cleavage and New Financial Rules," *Journal of Contemporary Asia* 38, no. 3 (2008): 439–52.

58. Jaeeun Lee, "S. Korea's Gender Pay Gap Worst in OECD," *Korea Herald*, May 23, 2024, https://www.koreaherald.com/view.php?ud=20240523050548.

59. Neil Bonneuil and Youngja Kim, "Precarious Employment among South Korean Women: Is Inequality Changing with Time?," *Economic and Labour Relations Review* 28, no. 1 (2017): 20–40, https://doi.org/doi:10.1177/1035304617690482.

60. Sophia Seung-Yoon Lee and Yuhwi Kim, "Female Outsiders in South Korea's Dual Labour Market: Challenges of Equal Pay for Work of Equal Value," *Journal of Industrial Relations* 62, no. 4 (2020): 651–78.

61. Koo, *Privilege and Anxiety*.

NOTES TO THE INTRODUCTION

62. Hae-joang Cho Han, "'You Are Entrapped in an Imaginary Well': The Formation of Subjectivity within Compressed Development," *Inter-Asia Cultural Studies* 1, no. 1 (2000): 52, https://doi.org/10.1080/146493700360999.

63. H.-j. C. Han, "You Are Entrapped," 53.

64. Hae-joang Cho Han, "National Subjects, Citizens and Refugees: Thoughts on the Politics of Survival, Violence and Mourning Following the *Sewol* Ferry Disaster in South Korea," in *New Worlds from Below: Informal Life Politics and Grassroots Action in Twenty-First-Century Northeast Asia*, ed. Tessa Morris-Suzuki and Eun Jeong Soh (Acton: Australian National University Press, 2017), 175.

65. Hyun Ok Park, *The Capitalist Unconscious: From Korean Unification to Transnational Korea* (New York: Columbia University Press, 2015), 23. See also Hyun Ok Park, "The Politics of Time: The *Sewol* Ferry Disaster and the Disaster of Democracy," *Journal of Asian Studies* 81, no. 1 (2022): 131.

66. H. O. Park, *Capitalist Unconscious*, 35–70.

67. Jamie Doucette and Susan Kang, "Legal Geographies of Labour and Post-democracy: Reinforcing Non-standard Work in South Korea," *Transactions of the Institute of British Geographers* 43, no. 2 (June 2018): 203, https://doi.org/10.1111/tran.12216.

68. Yoonkyung Lee, "Neo-liberal Methods of Labour Repression: Privatised Violence and Dispossessive Litigation in Korea," *Journal of Contemporary Asia* 51, no. 1 (2021): 20–37.

69. Grace Kyungwon Hong, *Death beyond Disavowal: The Impossible Politics of Difference* (Minneapolis: University of Minnesota Press, 2015), 17.

70. Jodi Melamed, "Racial Capitalism," *Critical Ethnic Studies* 1, no. 1 (2015): 77, https://doi.org/10.5749/jcritethnstud.1.1.0076.

71. Melamed, "Racial Capitalism," 79.

72. Hagen Koo, *Korean Workers: The Culture and Politics of Class Formation* (Ithaca, NY: Cornell University Press, 2001), 13. For a comparative account of the convergence of social-movement unionism in Brazil and South Africa under authoritarian state regimes that engaged in active labor repression, see Gay Seidman, *Manufacturing Militance: Workers' Movements in Brazil and South Africa, 1970–1985* (Berkeley: University of California Press, 1994).

73. Ken C. Kawashima, *The Proletarian Gamble: Korean Workers in Interwar Japan* (Durham, NC: Duke University Press, 2009), 11–12.

74. See, e.g., Hwasook Bergquist Nam, *Women in the Sky: Gender and Labor in the Making of Modern Korea* (Ithaca, NY: ILR Press, an imprint of Cornell University Press, 2021).

75. Koo, *Korean Workers*.

76. Nam, *Women in the Sky*, 12–23.

77. Nam, *Women in the Sky*, 15–18.

78. Taylor, *Archive and the Repertoire*, 27–28.

79. Fuentes, *Performance Constellations*.

80. Michael Burawoy, "The Extended Case Method," *Sociological Theory* 16, no. 1 (1998): 4–33, https://doi.org/10.1111/0735-2751.00040.

81. Chela Sandoval, *Methodology of the Oppressed* (Minneapolis: University of Minnesota Press, 2000), 68.

82. Françoise Lionnet and Shu-mei Shih, "Introduction: Thinking through the Minor, Transnationally," in *Minor Transnationalism*, ed. Françoise Lionnet and Shu-mei Shih (Durham, NC: Duke University Press, 2005), 1–21; Gillian Hart, "Relational Comparison Revisited: Marxist Postcolonial Geographies in Practice," *Progress in Human Geography* 42, no. 3 (2018): 371–94.

83. Macarena Gómez-Barris, *The Extractive Zone: Social Ecologies and Decolonial Perspectives* (Durham, NC: Duke University Press, 2017), xiv–xvii.

84. All formal interviews were conducted by one or both of the authors. The majority of interviews took place in Seoul, Korea, unless otherwise stated in the analysis. The interviews generally lasted between 90 to 180 minutes in duration, with some interviews taking place on multiple occasions.

Chapter 1

1. The six workers involved in the Kwanghwamun Billboard Occupation were Kim Kyŏng-rae (김경래), forty-nine years old, from the Tongyang Cement Union (동양시멘트지부) in Samch'ŏk, Kangwon Province; O Su-il (오수일), forty-five years old, from the Asahi Precarious Workers' Union (아사히비정규직지회) in Kumi, North Kyŏngsang Province; Chang Chae-yŏng (장재영), forty-two years old, from the Hyundai Ulsan Precarious Work Union (현대차울산 비정규직지회) in Ulsan, South Kyŏngsang Province; Ko Chin-su (고진수), forty-four years old, from the Sejong Hotel Union (세종호텔노조) in Seoul; Kim Hyejin (김혜진), forty-eight years old, from the Hitec RCD Korea Democratic Union Defense Protest Committee (하이텍알씨디코리아 민주노조 사수 투쟁위원회) in Chŏngwŏn, North Ch'ungch'ŏng Province; and Lee In-geun (이인근), fifty-one years old, from the Cort/Cor-Tek Guitar Workers' Union (콜트-콜텍 기타노동자 노조).

2. Kim Sŏn-sik, "Hanŭlgamok sugamjadŭri 3gi 'minju chŏngbu' e paranda" [The inmates of the prison in the sky have hopes for the third "democratic government"], *Hankyoreh*, May 15, 2017, http://h21.hani.co.kr/arti/special/special_general/43538.html.

3. Yun Chi-yŏn, "Kwanghwamun hanŭl 6-myŏng-ŭi nodongja, ijeya kŭdŭl-ŭi moksori-ga tŭllinda" [The six workers in the Kwanghwamun sky, we can finally hear their voices], *Cham sesang*, April 27, 2017, http://www.newscham.net/news/view.php?board=news&nid=102201.

4. Given his multiple experiences of engaging in hunger strikes and high-

altitude occupations as part of the thirteen-year struggle of the Cort/Cor-Tek Guitar Workers' Union, Lee In-geun had come down earlier than his comrades due to health issues.

5. G. K. Hong, *Death beyond Disavowal*, 8.

6. Namhee Lee, *The Making of Minjung: Democracy and the Politics of Representation in South Korea* (Ithaca, NY: Cornell University Press, 2007).

7. The 386 Generation refers to people who were in their thirties in the 1990s ("3"), attended university in the 1980s ("8"), and were born in the 1960s ("6"). More specifically, the term points to university-educated people born between 1960 and 1969. Decades later in 2024, this group has grown older and are now in their mid-fifties and early sixties, and thus they are sometimes referred to as the 586 Generation.

8. "No Taet'ongnyŏng 'punsin t'ujaeng sudan samnŭn sidae chinatta' parŏne taehae" [On President Roh's remark, "The time has passed for using the alter ego as a means of struggle"], KCTU, November 6, 2003, https://nodong.org/state ment/98371.

9. One clear exception was the case of the bereaved parents of the *Sewol* ferry disaster, who were immediately recognizable by their signature yellow jackets, umbrellas, and banners.

10. Jiyeon Kang, *Igniting the Internet: Youth and Activism in Postauthoritarian South Korea* (Honolulu: University of Hawai'i Press, 2016).

11. Jong Bum Kwon, "Forging a Modern Democratic Imaginary: Police Sovereignty, Neoliberalism, and the Boundaries of Neo-Korea," *Positions: Asia Critique* 22, no. 1 (February 2014): 71–101, https://doi.org/10.1215/10679847-2383858; Namhee Lee, *Memory Construction and the Politics of Time in Neoliberal Korea* (Durham, NC: Duke University Press, 2022).

12. G. K. Hong, *Death beyond Disavowal*, 25.

13. Gilmore, *Abolition Geography*, 15.

14. Hye-jeong Cho, "Cort Guitar Labor Struggle Ends after 13 Years," *Hankyoreh*, Eng. ed., April 23, 2019, https://english.hani.co.kr/arti/english_edition/e_ national/891184.html.

15. Byoung-Hoon Lee, "Worker Militancy at the Margins: Struggles of Nonregular Workers in South Korea," *Development and Society* 45, no. 1 (June 2016): 1–37, https://doi.org/10.21588/dns/2016.45.1.001.

16. As a government-invested enterprise, KT enjoyed a monopoly in the domestic telecommunications market until the 1990s, when it faced increasing pressure to open its domestic markets to international competition, spurred in large part by the World Trade Organization and later the International Monetary Fund and carried out by the Kim Dae-jung administration as part of a targeted privatization effort in public-sector industries in 1998.

17. Aelim Yun, *The ILO Recommendation on the Employment Relationship and*

Its Relevance in the Republic of Korea (Geneva: Global Union Research Network, International Labour Organization, 2007), 18, https://webapps.ilo.org/public/libdoc/ilo/2007/107B09_95_engl.pdf

18. JEI began as an educational company in the supplementary market that developed and then marketed a "self-learning method" to be taught by tutors who sold textbooks to students not as directly employed workers but as self-employed entrepreneurs. It currently brands itself as an international education company that operates in the United States, Korea, Canada, Australia, Japan, and New Zealand, among other countries around the world.

19. Yŏn Chŏng, "Nodongjohap i issŏssŭl ttae Jaenŭng Kyoyuk sŏnsaengnim-ŭro kajang haengbokhaessŭyo" [I was happiest as a Jaenung teacher when there was a labor union], *Chŏngse wa nodong* 84 (November 2012): 44–53. https://www.dbpia.co.kr/journal/articleDetail?nodeId=NODE02029373. See also Kim Chin-uk, "Jaenŭng Kyoyuk Nojo 'chongt'ap siwi' tugaji misŭt'ŏri" [Two mysteries of the 'bell tower protest' by the Jaenung Educational Union], *MoneyS*, May 30, 2013, https://www.moneys.co.kr/article/2013052320588030457.

20. Jeon Jong-hwi and Park Seung-heon, "Temp Tutors Win World's Longest Labor Struggle," *Hankyoreh*, Eng. ed., August 27, 2013, https://english.hani.co.kr/arti/english_edition/e_national/601054.html.

21. H.-j. Cho, "Cort Guitar Labor Struggle."

22. H.-j. Cho, "Cort Guitar Labor Struggle."

23. Quoted in H.-j. Cho, "Cort Guitar Labor Struggle."

24. Since 2009, when the public hospital was founded by the city of Ch'ŏngju, the management of the hospital has been mired in charges of corruption, negligent patient care, and exploitative labor practices. Hospital aides employed by multiple third-party contractors on an annual-contractual basis experienced repeated delayed wage payments, arbitrary wage and benefit reductions, and discriminatory working conditions.

25. Hospital management escalated their retaliation by repeatedly targeting union leaders for termination, ignoring rulings by the Ch'ungbuk [North Ch'un-gch'ŏng] Provincial Labor Relations Commission to reinstate union leaders who were unjustly terminated. They also tried to undermine union solidarity by offering incentives for workers to stop striking and return to work, resulting in dwindling numbers of strike participants over time.

26. Hwang Ye-rang, "Pijŏnggyujik, mipjiman miwŏhal su ŏpnŭn tanŏ" [Nonstandard, a word that is disliked but cannot be hated], *Hankyoreh*, March 21, 2015, https://h21.hani.co.kr/arti/society/society/39180.html.

27. No Ŭng-gŭn, "Kabŭl kwan'gye" [*Kap-ŭl* relationship], *Kyŏnghyang sinmun*, October 30, 2011, https://www.khan.co.kr/opinion/yeojeok/article/2011103021 06315.

28. No, "Kabŭl kwan'gye."

29. Hwang Ye-rang, "Pijŏnggyujik."

30. Quoted in Hwang Ye-rang, "Pijŏnggyujik."

31. Aelim Yun, "Building Collective Identity: Trade Union Representation of Precarious Workers in the South Korean Auto Companies," *Labour, Capital and Society / Travail, capital et société* 44, no. 1 (2011): 161.

32. Dae-Oup Chang, "Korean Labour Movement: The Birth, Rise and Transformation of the Democratic Union Movement," in *Routledge Handbook of Contemporary South Korea,* ed. Sojin Lim and Niki J. P. Alsford (London: Routledge, 2021), 168.

33. Kim Yoo Sun, "Non-regular Work," 6.

34. Kim Yoo Sun, "Non-regular Work," 6.

35. Min-kyung Kim, "Six Years after Layoffs, Ssangyong Workers Keep Passing Away," *Hankyoreh*, Eng. ed., May 4, 2015, https://english.hani.co.kr/arti/eng lish_edition/e_national/689678.

36. Lee Chang-kun, "*Squid Game*'s Strike Flashbacks Were Modeled on Our Real-Life Factory Occupation," trans. Kap Seol, *Jacobin,* November 1, 2021, https://jacobin.com/2021/11/squid-game-ssangyong-dragon-motor-strike-south -korea.

37. Lee Chang-kun, "*Squid Game*'s Strike Flashbacks."

38. Lee Chang-kun, "*Squid Game*'s Strike Flashbacks."

39. "3 Years after the Ssangyong Motors Clash and the Real Labor Environment," *Kyunghyang Sinmun,* Eng. ed., August 7, 2012, https://english.khan.co.kr /khan_art_view.html?artid=201208071356027.

40. For more in-depth discussion of queer left and labor solidarities, see Ju Hui Judy Han, *Queer Throughlines: Spaces of Queer Activism in South Korea and the Korean Diaspora* (Ann Arbor: University of Michigan Press, forthcoming).

41. Jennifer Jihye Chun, *Organizing at the Margins: The Symbolic Politics of Labor in South Korea and the United States* (Ithaca, NY: Cornell University Press, 2009).

42. Ju Hui Judy Han, "Out of Place in Time: Queer Discontents and *Sigisangjo,*" *Journal of Asian Studies* 81, no. 1 (February 2022): 122, https://doi.org/10.1017/S00 21911821001455.

43. The female equivalent is Kim-*yang*.

44. Mi-young Kim and Jae-uk Lee, "Young Worker's Death Spurs National Discussion on Irregular Work," *Hankyoreh*, Eng. ed., June 6, 2016, https://english .hani.co.kr/arti/english_edition/e_national/747007.

45. *Arbeit* is a German word that means "work," and it is commonly used in Korea to refer to part-time work. The Arbeit Workers Union, also known as Arba Nojo (Korean abbreviation), represents part-time workers.

46. Tae-hyeong Kim, "[Photo] Don't Be Hungry in Heaven," *Hankyoreh*, Eng. ed., June 7, 2016, https://english.hani.co.kr/arti/english_edition/e_national/747 152.

NOTES TO CHAPTERS 1 AND 2   253

47. Koo, *Korean Workers*, 89–90.

48. Min-na Park, *Birth of Resistance* (Seoul: Korea Democracy Foundation, 2005), 157.

49. M.-n. Park, *Birth of Resistance*, 161–62.

50. M.-n. Park, *Birth of Resistance*, 162.

51. M.-n. Park, *Birth of Resistance*, 15.

52. Lisa Marie Cacho, *Social Death: Racialized Rightlessness and the Criminalization of the Unprotected* (New York: New York University Press, 2012), 6–7.

53. Palomera and Vetta, "Moral Economy."

54. Palomera and Vetta, "Moral Economy," 424.

Chapter 2

1. Barrington Moore, *Injustice: The Social Bases of Obedience and Revolt* (London: Macmillan, 1978).

2. Diana Taylor, *Performance* (Durham, NC: Duke University Press, 2016), 15.

3. Saba Mahmood, *Politics of Piety: The Islamic Revival and the Feminist Subject* (Princeton, NJ: Princeton University Press, 2005).

4. Taylor, *Archive and the Repertoire*, 18.

5. Sunyoung Park, *The Proletarian Wave: Literature and Leftist Culture in Colonial Korea 1910–1945* (Cambridge, MA: Harvard University Press, 2015); Youngju Ryu, *Writers of the Winter Republic: Literature and Resistance in Park Chung Hee's Korea* (Honolulu: University of Hawai'i Press, 2016).

6. Eitan Y. Alimi, "Repertoires of Contention," in *The Oxford Handbook of Social Movements*, ed. Donatella Della Porta and Mario Diani (Oxford: Oxford University Press, 2015), 410–22.

7. Tilly, *Contentious Performances*, 143.

8. Tilly, *Contentious Performances*, 13.

9. Charles Tilly, "From Interactions to Outcomes in Social Movements," in *How Social Movements Matter*, ed. Marco Giugni, Doug McAdam, and Charles Tilly (Minneapolis: University of Minnesota Press, 1999), 255–56.

10. Tilly, *Contentious Performances*, 144.

11. Tilly, "From Interactions to Outcomes," 262.

12. Tilly, "From Interactions to Outcomes," 261.

13. Patrick McCurdy, Anna Feigenbaum, and Fabian Frenzel, "Protest Camps and Repertoires of Contention," *Social Movement Studies* 15, no. 1 (January 2016): 98, https://doi.org/10.1080/14742837.2015.1037263.

14. "Yogurŭl chujang ttae ssŭnŭn tanŏ 'nongsŏng' ŭi yurae nŭn?" [What is the origin of the word "*nongsŏng*" used to assert a demand?], *YTN nyusŭ*, January 8, 2018, https://news.v.daum.net/v/20180108033301977?s=print_news.

15. For a discussion on protest spectacles in China, see Guobin Yang, "Emotional Events and the Transformation of Collective Action," in *Emotions and*

Social Movements, ed. Helena Flam and Debra King (London: Routledge, 2005), 80.

16. For an excellent discussion of these practices of gift giving and hosting during the Miryang struggle, see Su Young Choi, "Recognition for Resistance: Gifting, Social Media, and the Politics of Reciprocity in South Korean Energy Activism," *Media, Culture and Society* 43, no. 7 (2021): 1247–62.

17. Ch'a Hŏn-ho has a long history of labor activism in the Kyŏngsang region, joining union organizing at Korean Synthetic Fiber at the age of twenty-three in 1995. He was elected to hold a union leadership position in 1996 and led a militant struggle against a plant closure, which lasted 565 days. In 2009, he began working at an in-house subcontracting company for Asahi Glass in Kumi Industrial Complex, a manufacturing region that is deeply integrated into transnational, multitiered contracting networks, exerting downward pressures on the wages and working conditions of manufacturing workforce nationwide. Ch'a Hŏn-ho experienced intense legal repression, including arrest and imprisonment. On July 11, 2024, the Supreme Court of Korea issued a ruling in the union's favor, marking a historic victory after 3,321 days. A total of twenty-two workers returned to work on August 1, 2024. Pak Chung-yŏp, "Nodongsa saero ssŭn Asahi Klasŭ t'ujaeng, 9 nyŏn'ganŭi ch'wijaegi" [Asahi Glass rewrites labor history, reporting over nine years], *SisaIN,* August 16, 2024, https://www.sisain .co.kr/news/articleView.html?idxno=53716.

18. Ki-weon Cho, "Asahi Glass Workers Stage Protest against Court's Ruling on Labor Unions," *Hankyoreh,* Eng. ed., March 8, 2018, https://english.hani.co .kr/arti/english_edition/e_international/835210.

19. Asahi Glass is the largest glass-manufacturing company in the world and one of the Mitsubishi conglomerate's core operations. Now called AGC Inc., the global company has transnational subsidiaries across Europe and the Americas as well as in Korea, India, the Philippines, and other countries around the world.

20. "Samsung leukemia" is the name given to a new industrial disease claimed to be caused by uncertain toxic chemicals. For an excellent account of SHARPS and its broader significance as a worker-centered case of labor-health activism, see Jongyoung Kim, Heeyun Kim, and Jawoon Lim, "The Politics of Science and Undone Protection in the 'Samsung Leukemia' Case," *East Asian Science, Technology and Society* 14, no. 4 (2020): 576.

21. Yumi began working at Samsung Semiconductor in 2003 with a cohort of ten other graduates from Sokcho Commercial High School. She worked on line three, which is now known as one of the most degraded wafer-processing lines at the Kihŭng factory, which began operations in 1984. According to one source, "Yumi started showing symptoms of nausea, fatigue, and dizziness around May 2005 and was diagnosed with acute myelocytic leukemia around June 10 of the same year. She underwent bone-marrow transplant surgery in December of

that year. However, after the leukemia recurred around November 2006, she died on March 6, 2007, while undergoing outpatient treatment."

22. The campaign attracted national and international attention and, like other high-profile cases, became the subject of intense interests by the broader community of activist bloggers, social media producers, journalists, artists, and filmmakers. A feature film was also made about the case, entitled *Another Promise* (2013), which was funded by private donations and crowd funding. It vividly documents the intense intimidation and retaliation of Samsung company officials on victims' families pursuing justice.

23. Don Mitchell, *The Right to the City: Social Justice and the Fight for Public Space* (New York: Guilford Press, 2003).

24. J. H. J. Han, "High-Altitude Protests," 175.

25. Joan Kee, "Why Performance in Authoritarian Korea?," in *Cultures of Yusin: South Korea in the 1970s*, ed. Youngju Ryu (Ann Arbor: University of Michigan Press, 2018), 245–78.

26. Y. Lee, "Sky Protest."

27. Nayan Shah, *Refusal to Eat: A Century of Prison Hunger Strikes* (Oakland: University of California Press, 2022).

28. Ralph Armbruster-Sandoval, *Hunger Strikes, Spectacular Speech, and the Struggle for Dignity* (Tucson: University of Arizona Press, 2017), 15–16.

29. Nam, *Women in the Sky*, 65–66.

30. Shah, *Refusal to Eat*, 1.

31. Kee, "Why Performance," 248.

32. Tilly, "From Interactions to Outcomes," 253, 256, 258–59.

33. *Sŭnim* is the honorific title for Korean Buddhist monks and nuns. Ronald S. Green and Changju Mun, "The Korean Buddhist Nun Chiyul (Jiyul) and Ecofeminism: Hunger Strikes, the Lawsuit for Salamanders, and Walking Protests" (working paper, California Coast University, Santa Ana, CA, 2013), https://digitalcommons.coastal.edu/philosophy-religious-studies/37/.

34. Shah, *Refusal to Eat*, 7.

35. Myeong-seon Jin, "Citizens Continuing Hunger Strike on Behalf of Kim Young-oh," *Hankyoreh*, Eng. ed., August 29, 2014, https://english.hani.co.kr/arti/english_edition/e_national/653393.

36. An Yŏng-ch'un, "Kim Ki-ch'un, *Sewŏlho* tongjo tansik e 'pinan kahaejidorok ŏllon chido'" [Kim Ki-ch'un, "directed media to criticize" the relay hunger strike for *Sewol*], *Hankyoreh*, December 6, 2016, https://www.hani.co.kr/arti/society/society_general/773542.html.

37. Young-Hae Yoon and Sherwin Jones, "Ecology, Dharma and Direct Action: A Brief Survey of Contemporary Eco-Buddhist Activism in Korea," *Buddhist Studies Review* 31, no. 2 (2015): 293–311, https://doi.org/10.1558/bsrv.v31i2.293.

38. "Kiryung Workers Make Revolutionary March before Returning to Work," IndustriALL, February 9, 2012, http://www.industriall-union.org/ar chive/imf/kiryung-workers-make-revolutionary-march-before-returning-to -work.

39. Yusŏng Kiŏp Nodongjadŭl kwa Hamkke, "Yusŏngbŏmdaewi esŏ hoso dŭrimnida" [National Response Committee for Yoosung appeals to you], Facebook, November 10, 2016, https://www.facebook.com/photo/?fbid=1132263820 184440.

40. Nick Marsh, "South Korea: 'Protesting for 20 Years and Still No Equal Rights,'" *BBC News*, January 27, 2023, https://www.bbc.com/news/world-us-can ada-64369810.

41. Kim To-hyŏn, *Changaehak ŭi Tojŏn* [The challenge of disability studies] (Paju: Owŏl ŭi bom, 2019), 57.

42. Moon Gyu-hyeon, "Saemangŭm samboilbae 3 chunyŏn: Saemangŭm Kaetbŏl ŭi puhwarŭl kidarimyŏ" [Third anniversary of the Saemangŭm samboilbae: Waiting for the revival of Saemangŭm Wetlands], *Green Korea* (blog), March 28, 2006, https://www.greenkorea.org/%EB%AF%B8%EB%B6%84%EB %A5%98/16121/.

43. Sara E. Lewis, *Spacious Minds: Trauma and Resilience in Tibetan Buddhism* (Ithaca: Cornell University Press, 2019), 89.

44. Lewis, *Spacious Minds*, 87.

45. Su Yon Pak et al., *Singing the Lord's Song in a New Land: Korean American Practices of Faith* (Louisville, KY: Westminster John Knox Press, 2005), 17–18, 21.

46. Nam, *Women in the Sky*, 131. According to labor historian Hwasook Nam, this *t'usa* ritual bestows laypersons with the fighting spirit of a "devoted apostle." Ibid.

47. Where the role of progressive religious organizations is well known, there is disagreement on the extent of religious organizations' influence, with Hagen Koo identifying their role as the "crucial factor" in the development of the labor movement during this period and Hwasook Nam qualifying the extent of their influence. See Koo, *Korean Workers*, 94–95; Nam, *Women in the Sky*, 231.

48. In case it is not clear, this is wordplay. The Korean word for "bankruptcy" is *tosan*, and the acronym for UIM in Korean is TOSAN. The joke suggests that organizing is powerful; when UIM strikes against a company, the company goes bust.

49. Nam, *Women in the Sky*, 132–50.

50. Jisoo M. Kim, *The Emotions of Justice: Gender, Status, and Legal Performance in Choson Korea* (Seattle: University of Washington Press, 2015).

51. Y. Ryu, *Writers*.

52. Kee, "Why Performance," 249.

53. S. Park, *Proletarian Wave*, 1–2.

54. S. Park, *Proletarian Wave*, 119–20.

55. J. M. Kim, *Emotions of Justice*, 43–44, 50.

56. Michael Rothberg, *Multidirectional Memory: Remembering the Holocaust in the Age of Decolonization* (Stanford: Stanford University Press, 2009), 5.

57. Rothberg, *Multidirectional Memory*, 11.

Chapter 3

1. Avery Gordon, *Ghostly Matters: Haunting and the Sociological Imagination* (Minneapolis: University of Minnesota Press, 1997), 22.

2. Kathleen Stewart, *Ordinary Affects* (Durham, NC: Duke University Press, 2007).

3. Massey, *For Space*, 9, 12.

4. Massey, *For Space*, 11, 13.

5. Kim Jin-suk's name is sometimes romanized as Kim Jin-sook, and her 2007 book *Sogŭm kkot namu* (소금 꽃 나무) is catalogued under Kim Chin-suk, which adheres to the McCune-Reischauer system. Like other personal names used in this book, we have decided to use the spelling she prefers to use, including on social media.

6. Kim Jin-suk shared these thoughts on camera during her interview in the 2015 documentary film *Factory Complex*. Im-Heung Soon, dir., *Factory Complex* (Brooklyn, NY: Torch Films, 2015).

7. Taylor, *Archive and the Repertoire*, 28.

8. Youngju Ryu, "Korea's Vietnam: Popular Culture, Patriarchy, Intertextuality," *Review of Korean Studies* 12, no. 3 (2009): 101–23; Jim Glassman and Young-Jin Choi, "The *Chaebol* and the US Military–Industrial Complex: Cold War Geopolitical Economy and South Korean Industrialization," *Environment and Planning A: Economy and Space* 46, no. 5 (May 2014): 1160–80, https://doi.org/10.1068/a130025p; Jinn-yuh Hsu, Dong-Wan Gimm, and Jim Glassman, "A Tale of Two Industrial Zones: A Geopolitical Economy of Differential Development in Ulsan, South Korea, and Kaohsiung, Taiwan," *Environment and Planning A: Economy and Space* 50, no. 2 (March 2018): 457–73, https://doi.org/10.1177/0308518X16680212.

9. Hwasook Bergquist Nam, *Building Ships, Building a Nation: Korea's Democratic Unionism under Park Chung Hee*, Korean Studies of the Henry M. Jackson School of International Studies (Seattle: University of Washington Press, 2009), 214.

10. Changgeun Lee, "Another Worker Driven to His Death in Korea," Base21, October 19, 2003, http://base21.jinbo.net/show/show.php?p_cd=o&p_dv=o&p_docnbr=29390.

11. These translations are based on Kim Ju-ik's two suicide notes, dated September 9, 2003, and October 4, 2003. "Kim Chu-ik ssi yusŏ chŏnmun" [Full text

of Kim Ju-ik's suicide notes], *Kyŏnghyang sinmun*, October 17, 2003, https://www
.khan.co.kr/national/national-general/article/200310171430581. A video recording of Kim Jin-suk's eulogy is archived online. MediaVOP, "Tasi ponŭn Kim
Chin-suk chidowiwŏn Kim Chu-ik yŏlsa ch'udosa (2003)" [Re-viewing Kim Jin-
suk's eulogy for Kim Ju-ik (2003)], January 22, 2021, YouTube, 16:53, https://
youtu.be/xbYstA3LGFU?si=nHcJFjaym8GMa2Gp.

12. Eunjung Kim, "Continuing Presence of Discarded Bodies: Occupational
Harm, Necro-activism, and Living Justice," *Catalyst: Feminism, Theory, Technoscience* 5, no. 1 (April 2019): 14, https://doi.org/10.28968/cftt.v5i1.29616.

13. Yun Sŏng-hyo, "'70 nyŏn Chŏn T'ae-il gwa 03 nyŏn Kim Chu-ik yusŏga
katdani" [For suicide notes by Chŏn T'ae-il in 1970 and by Kim Ju-ik in 2003 to
be the same], *OhMyNews*, October 22, 2003, http://www.ohmynews.com/nws_
web/view/at_pg.aspx?CNTN_CD=A0000149804.

14. Yun Sŏng-hyo, "'70 nyŏn."

15. Yun Sŏng-hyo, "'70 nyŏn."

16. Jiwoon Yulee, "Progress by Death: Labor Precaritization and the Financialization of Social Reproduction in South Korea," *Capital and Class*, May 13,
2022, 12, https://doi.org/10.1177/03098168221084113.

17. Hŏ Chae-hyŏn, "Kim Chin-suk 'Chasal saenggak'adŏn narŭl chinjŏngsik'in gŏn . . .'" [Kim Jin-suk "What calmed me down from thinking about suicide was . . ."], *Hankyoreh*, November 15, 2011, http://www.hani.co.kr/arti/
society/society_general/505520.html.

18. Twitter, a US-based company now known as X, was founded in 2006 and
officially launched in Korea in 2011.

19. Kim Kwang-su, "Chasal yuhok yŏrŏbŏn . . . T'wit'ŏro sesanggwa sot'onghamyŏ Hŭimang ŏdŏ'" [Several suicidal urges . . . hope gained through communicating with the world using Twitter], *Hankyoreh*, November 14, 2011, http://
www.hani.co.kr/arti/society/labor/505415.html.

20. "Kim Chin-suk, 'Maeil yusŏ ssŭnŭn simjŏng-ŭro pŏtinda'" [Kim Jin-suk,
"I hang on every day with the mindset that I'm writing a will"], *OhMyNews*, July
30, 2011, https://www.ohmynews.com/nws_web/view/at_pg.aspx?CNTN_CD=
A0001604029.

21. Jennifer Jihye Chun, "Protesting Precarity: South Korean Workers and
the Labor of Refusal," *Journal of Asian Studies* 81, no. 1 (February 2022): 107–18,
https://doi.org/10.1017/S0021911821001479; Yulee, "Progress by Death."

22. Minouk Lim, "The (Im)possible Art as Life : On-the-Crane #85 Performance by Kim Jin-Suk," in *Being Political Popular: South Korean Art at the Intersection of Popular Culture and Democracy, 1980–2010*, ed. Sohl Lee (Seoul: Hyunsil;
Seattle: University of Washington Press, 2012), 162.

23. Massey, *For Space*, 12.

24. "Sara naeryŏon uridŭri tangsinkke ponaenŭn p'yŏnji" [A letter from us

who have survived to you], *Redian*, July 28, 2011, http://www.redian.org/news/articleView.html?idxno=37597.

25. O To-yŏp, "Pijŏnggyunodongja kadŭk'an Kuro rŭl twijipnŭnda" [Overturning Kuro, full of precarious workers], *Ch'amsesang*, August 31, 2006, http://www.newscham.net/news/view.php?board=news&nid=35818.

26. Even her release from prison made the news. Mee-young Kim, "Why Do Some Inmates Get out Just after Midnight, Whiles [*sic*] Others Have to Stay till 5 am?," *Hankyoreh*, Eng. ed., May 13, 2016, https://english.hani.co.kr/arti/english_edition/e_national/743737.

27. A *ching* is a large brass gong-type percussion instrument used in traditional Korean music—and protest—performances that is struck with a soft, padded mallet for a loud, resonant sound.

28. Lewis, *Spacious Minds*, 87.

29. In addition to raising over 700 million won from two thousand sponsors between 2015 and 2017, Cool Jam organizers raised money through the sale of magazines, postcards, and artwork as well as story funding and exhibition fees.

30. Pak Mi-kyŏng, "Tasi pitnal urinŭn KTX sŭngmuwŏn ipnida" [We are KTX train attendants, and we will shine again], *Chŏngsewa nodong* 144 (July 2018): 49–54.

31. Pak Mi-kyŏng, "Urinŭn KTX sŭngmuwŏn."

32. Yun Sŏng-hyo, "KTX Yŏsŭngmuwŏne hanbŏnjjŭmŭn kwi kiurigo, nun majuch'yŏya" [We should at least once listen to and hear KTX women train attendants], *OhMyNews*, August 13, 2008, http://www.ohmynews.com/nws_web/view/at_pg.aspx?CNTN_CD=A0000962193.

33. Leslie Salzinger, "Revealing the Unmarked: Finding Masculinity in a Global Factory," *Ethnography* 5, no. 1 (2004): 13. http://www.jstor.org/stable/24047917.

34. Chu Chin-u, "Pitman namgigo ttonasŏ mianhada, aga" [I am sorry, baby: All I can leave for you is debt], *SisaIN*, July 14, 2015, https://www.sisain.co.kr/news/articleView.html?idxno=23777.

35. Kap Seol, "South Korea: After 12 Years of Protests, Women Workers Get 'Dream Jobs' Back," Labor Notes, August 2, 2018, https://labornotes.org/2018/08/south-korea-after-12-years-protests-women-workers-get-dream-jobs-back.

36. E. Kim, "Continuing Presence." See also Jinah Kim, "The Insurgency of Mourning: *Sewol* across the Transpacific," *Amerasia Journal* 46, no. 1 (June 2020): 84–100, https://doi.org/10.1080/00447471.2020.1772699.

37. In their classic article "Toward a Feminist Theory of Caring," Bernice Fisher and Joan C. Tronto distinguish different types of caring activities, including caring about, taking care of, caregiving, and care receiving, each of which produces their own set of hierarchies and contradictions. Bernice Fisher and Joan C. Tronto, "Toward a Feminist Theory of Caring," in *Circles of Care:*

Work and Identity in Women's Lives, ed. Emily K. Abel and Margaret K. Nelson (Albany: State University of New York Press, 1990), 36–54.

38. Fuentes, *Performance Constellations,* 16, 20.

39. Alan Sears, "Creating and Sustaining Communities of Struggle," *New Socialist* 52 (2007): 32–33.

40. Sonia E. Alvarez et al., "Introduction: Interrogating the Civil Society Agenda, Reassessing Uncivic Political Activism," in *Beyond Civil Society: Activism, Participation, and Protest in Latin America,* ed. Sonia E. Alvarez et al. (Durham, NC: Duke University Press, 2017), 17.

41. Audra Simpson, "Consent's Revenge," *Cultural Anthropology* 31, no. 3 (August 2016): 326–33, https://doi.org/10.14506/ca31.3.02.

42. Gilmore, "Geographies of Racial Capitalism."

Chapter 4

1. For an excellent ethnographic discussion of the Miryang struggle, see Su Young Choi, "Protesting Grandmothers as Spatial Resistance in the Neo-developmental Era," *Korean Studies* 43 (2019): 40–67; S. Y. Choi, "Recognition for Resistance."

2. Miryang 765kV songjŏnt'ap pandae taech'aekwi, ed., "Miryang ssaum 10 nyŏn, uri nŭn imi sŭngni hayŏtsŭpnida!" [10 years of Miryang fight, we have already prevailed!], in *Miryang, sipnyŏn ŭi pit* (Seoul: Listen to the City, 2015), 8–10.

3. S. Y. Choi, "Protesting Grandmothers," 45.

4. Solidarity bus caravans transported supporters to Miryang from far and wide to attend weekly candlelight vigils and support encampment protesters with offerings of food, gifts, music, art, performance, short videos, documentary-film productions, and other messages of solidarity. See S. Y. Choi, "Recognition for Resistance."

5. S. Y. Choi, "Protesting Grandmothers," 50.

6. Sara Koopman, "Alter-geopolitics: Other Securities Are Happening," *Geoforum* 42, no. 3 (2011): 278.

7. Sears, "Communities of Struggle," 32. Sears coined the term "infrastructure of dissent" to encompass the "means of analysis, communication, organization, and sustenance that nurture the capacity for collective action." Ibid.

8. Melucci, *Challenging Codes,* 115.

9. Brian Larkin, "The Politics and Poetics of Infrastructure," *Annual Review of Anthropology* 42 (2013): 336.

10. Rebecca Solnit, *Hope in the Dark: Untold Histories, Wild Possibilities* (Chicago: Haymarket Books, 2016), xv.

11. AbdouMaliq Simone, "People as Infrastructure: Intersecting Fragments in Johannesburg," *Public Culture* 16, no. 3 (October 2004): 407–29; Lauren Ber-

lant, "The Commons: Infrastructures for Troubling Times," *Environment and Planning D: Society and Space* 34, no. 3 (2016): 393.

12. Berlant, "Commons," 394.

13. Maria Puig de la Bellacasa, "Matters of Care in Technoscience: Assembling Neglected Things," *Social Studies of Science* 41, no. 1 (2011): 90, 94–95.

14. Abigail H. Neely and Patricia J. Lopez, "Toward Healthier Futures in Post-pandemic Times: Political Ecology, Racial Capitalism, and Black Feminist Approaches to Care," *Geography Compass* 16, no. 2 (2022): e12609, https://doi.org/10.1111/gec3.12609. Also see Deva Woodly et al., "The Politics of Care," *Contemporary Political Theory* 20, no. 4 (December 2021): 890–925, https://doi.org/10.1057/s41296-021-00515-8.

15. Fisher and Tronto, "Feminist Theory of Caring," 40. Fisher and Tronto first outlined their framework of a feminist ethic of care as follows: "On the most general level, we suggest that caring be viewed as *a species activity that includes everything that we do to maintain, continue, and repair our 'world' so that we can live in it as well as possible.* That world includes our bodies, our selves, and our environment, all of which we seek to interweave in a complex, life-sustaining web." Ibid. Emphasis original.

16. Joan C. Tronto, "An Ethic of Care," *Generations: Journal of the American Society on Aging* 22, no. 3 (1998): 17.

17. Ilan Wiesel, Wendy Steele, and Donna Houston, "Cities of Care: Introduction to a Special Issue," *Cities* 105 (2020): 2.

18. Christina Sharpe, *In the Wake: On Blackness and Being* (Durham, NC: Duke University Press, 2016), 5. See foundational works on intersectionality as an interlocking system of multiple oppressions, such as Deborah K. King, "Multiple Jeopardy, Multiple Consciousness: The Context of a Black Feminist Ideology," *Signs: Journal of Women in Culture and Society* 14, no. 1 (October 1988): 42–72, https://doi.org/10.1086/494491; Kimberle Crenshaw, "Mapping the Margins: Intersectionality, Identity Politics, and Violence against Women of Color," *Stanford Law Review* 43, no. 6 (July 1991): 1241–99, https://doi.org/10.2307/1229039; Patricia Hill Collins, *Black Feminist Thought: Knowledge, Consciousness, and the Politics of Empowerment*, Perspectives on Gender 2 (New York: Routledge, 1991). Also see Jennifer Jihye Chun, George Lipsitz, and Young Shin, "Intersectionality as a Social Movement Strategy: Asian Immigrant Women Advocates," *Signs: Journal of Women in Culture and Society* 38, no. 4 (June 2013): 917–40, https://doi.org/10.1086/669575.

19. Sharpe, *In the Wake*, 20.

20. Inchŏn Station, established in 1899, is the oldest train station in the Seoul Metropolitan Area, which includes the districts of Seoul Special City, Inchŏn Metropolitan City, and Kyŏnggi-do. After being destroyed during the Korean War, a new railway called the Kyŏng'in Line began running regular service in

1974 between various stops in Inchŏn to Kuro Station, located on Seoul's southwestern side. The railway's construction was part of the first five-year economic plan to promote national economic development, created after General Park Chung Hee waged a 1961 military coup that began his nearly two-decade dictatorial reign.

21. In-Hwan Hwang and Jin-Yong Jeon, "Spatiality of Two Urban Religious Spaces in Seoul: A Case Study of Myeong-Dong Cathedral and Bongeun Buddhist Temple Precincts," *Journal of Asian Architecture and Building Engineering* 14, no. 3 (2015): 626.

22. Don Baker, "The Transformation of the Catholic Church in Korea: From a Missionary Church to an Indigenous Church," *Journal of Korean Religions* 4, no. 1 (2013): 11–42.

23. Puig de la Bellacasa, "Matters of Care," 96. Emphasis original.

24. Puig de la Bellacasa, "Matters of Care," 96.

25. Simeon Man, A. Naomi Paik, and Melina Pappademos, "Violent Entanglements," *Radical History Review* 2019, no. 133 (January 2019): 1–10, https://doi.org/10.1215/01636545-7160029; Nam Chul Bu and Young-hae Chi, "The Christian and Buddhist Environmental Movements in Contemporary Korea: Common Efforts and Their Limitations," *Korea Journal* 54, no. 4 (December 2014): 52–79, https://doi.org/10.25024/KJ.2014.54.4.52; Andrew Yeo, "Local-National Dynamics and Framing in South Korean Anti-base Movements," *Kasarinlan: Philippine Journal of Third World Studies* 21, no. 2 (2006): 34–60.

26. Eun-su Cho, "From Ascetic to Activist: Jiyul Sunim's Korean Buddhist Eco-movement," in *Nature, Environment and Culture in East Asia: The Challenge of Climate Change,* ed. Carmen Meinert (Leiden: Brill, 2013), 259–81; Ju Hui Judy Han, "Urban Megachurches and Contentious Religious Politics in Seoul," in *Handbook of Religion and the Asian City: Aspiration and Urbanization in the Twenty-First Century,* ed. Peter van der Veer (Berkeley: University of California Press, 2015), 133–51.

27. Christian Fuchs, *Marxist Humanism and Communication Theory,* vol. 1, *Media, Communication and Society* (London: Routledge, 2021), 15. See also Christian Fuchs, *Digital Demagogue: Authoritarian Capitalism in the Age of Trump and Twitter* (London: Pluto Press, 2018).

28. David Harvey, "Seventeen Contradictions and the End of Capitalism," *White Review,* April 2014, https://www.thewhitereview.org/feature/seventeen-contradictions-and-the-end-of-capitalism/. Emphasis original.

29. MunYang Hyo-suk, "11 wŏl 18 il majimak Taehanmun misa ponghŏn" [Final Taehanmun Mass dedication on November 18], *K'at'olik nyusŭ chigŭm yŏgi,* November 15, 2013, http://www.catholicnews.co.kr/news/articleView.html?idxno=11126.

30. Charles Payne, "Ella Baker and Models of Change," *Signs: Journal of Women in Culture and Society* 14, no. 4 (Summer 1989): 892.

31. AbdouMaliq Simone, "Ritornello: 'People as Infrastructure,'" *Urban Geography* 42, no. 9 (October 2021): 1348, https://doi.org/10.1080/02723638.2021.1894397.

32. Tari Young-Jung Na, "The South Korean Gender System: LGBTI in the Contexts of Family, Legal Identity, and the Military," trans. Ju Hui Judy Han and Se-Woong Koo, *Journal of Korean Studies* 19, no. 2 (2014): 357–77, https://doi.org/10.1353/jks.2014.0018.

33. Giovanni Arrighi, Terence K. Hopkins, and Immanuel Maurice Wallerstein, *Antisystemic Movements* (London: Verso, 2011).

34. Neely and Lopez, "Toward Healthier Futures," 16.

35. Neely and Lopez, "Toward Healthier Futures," 7.

36. Emma R. Power et al., "Shadow Care Infrastructures: Sustaining Life in Post-welfare Cities," *Progress in Human Geography* 46, no. 5 (October 2022): 1166, https://doi.org/10.1177/03091325221109837.

37. Ashraful Alam and Donna Houston, "Rethinking Care as Alternate Infrastructure," *Cities* 100 (May 2020): 102662, https://doi.org/10.1016/j.cities.2020.102662.

38. Susan Leigh Star, "The Ethnography of Infrastructure," *American Behavioral Scientist* 43, no. 3 (November 1999): 377–91, https://doi.org/10.1177/00027649921955326; Simone, "People as Infrastructure"; Larkin, "Politics and Poetics"; Ash Amin, "Lively Infrastructure," *Theory, Culture and Society* 31, no. 7–8 (December 2014): 137–61, https://doi.org/10.1177/0263276414548490.

39. Winona LaDuke and Deborah Cowen, "Beyond Wiindigo Infrastructure," *South Atlantic Quarterly* 119, no. 2 (April 2020): 245, https://doi.org/10.1215/00382876-8177747.

40. Simone, "Ritornello," 1343.

41. Larkin, "Politics and Poetics," 336.

Chapter 5

1. Paula Hancocks and Euan McKirdy, "South Korea: Court Upholds President Park Geun-hye's Impeachment; Protests Erupt," *CNN*, March 10, 2017, https://www.cnn.com/2017/03/09/asia/south-korea-park-guen-hye-impeachment-upheld/index.html. For the full opinions of the Constitutional Court, see "Pak Kŭn-hye taet'ongnyŏng t'anhaek simp'an" [The Impeachment of the President Park Geun-hye], Case No. 2016Hun-Na1, March 10, 2017, https://ccourt.go.kr.

2. Young-jin Oh, "You Don't Represent Us," *Korea Times*, October 4, 2019, https://www.koreatimes.co.kr/www/opinion/2024/09/137_276627.html.

NOTES TO CHAPTER 5

3. Gilmore, "Fatal Couplings of Power," 16.

4. Henri Lefebvre, *The Production of Space* (Oxford: Blackwell, 1991), 162.

5. Henri Lefebvre, "Space: Social Product and Use Value (1979)," in *State, Space, World: Selected Essays*, ed. Neil Brenner and Stuart Elden (Minneapolis: University of Minnesota Press, 2009), 187. See also Eugene J. McCann, "Race, Protest, and Public Space: Contextualizing Lefebvre in the U.S. City," *Antipode* 31, no. 2 (1999): 163–84; Stefan Kipfer, "Urbanization, Everyday Life and the Survival of Capitalism: Lefebvre, Gramsci and the Problematic of Hegemony," *Capitalism Nature Socialism* 13, no. 2 (June 2002): 117–49, https://doi.org/10.1080/10455750208565482.

6. McCann, "Race," 170.

7. David Harvey, *Social Justice and the City* (London: Edward Arnold, 1973); Mitchell, *Right to the City.*

8. Massey, *For Space*, 151.

9. For a discussion of the implications of "throwntogetherness" for queer politics in more detail, see J. H. J. Han, *Queer Throughlines.*

10. Massey, *For Space*, 151–52.

11. Teresa P. R. Caldeira uses the word "imprinting" as a mode of intervention in the city of São Paulo, Brazil, referring to the graffiti and tagging found throughout the city. However, our description here is more closely related to the Korean folk drumming practice of *chisin balpgi* (지신밟기), which involves a group of *p'ungmul* (풍물) drummers walking to visit each house to bring good luck, or, literally, "stepping on the spirit of the earth." See Teresa P. R. Caldeira, "Imprinting and Moving Around: New Visibilities and Configurations of Public Space in São Paulo," *Public Culture* 24, no. 2 (May 2012): 385–419, https://doi.org/10.1215/08992363-1535543.

12. Even after the last official candlelight protest was held on March 11, the day after the Constitutional Court ruled to confirm the impeachment of Park Geun-hye, people continued to pour into the streets and squares of the historic city center. Presidential hopefuls campaigned actively throughout Kwanghwamun Square, with the base camp of frontrunner Moon Jae-in set up in the same spot as the main-event stage for the candlelight protests. JTBC News constructed an impressive glass-enclosed live studio in the middle of the square from which they aired live news during the special presidential election. Public celebrations and commemorative events in Kwanghwamun continued into the spring and summer months, including on May 23, 2017, when thousands gathered for the eighth-year commemoration of the death of the former president Roh Moo-hyun.

13. N. Lee, *Making of Minjung*, 2, 5, 10.

14. NGOs, such as PSPD as well as the Citizens' Coalition of Economic Justice (경제정의실천시민연합) and the Korea Federation for Environmental Movement

(환경운동연합), trace their beginnings to the late 1980s and early to mid-1990s as small organizations with a just a handful of volunteer and low-paid staff. Progressive and left-wing activists in the diverse social-movement sphere are generally skeptical of these large organizations, commonly viewed as part of the "NGOification" of democracy in service of neoliberal state agendas.

15. People's Solidarity for Participatory Democracy, *PSPD Annual Report* (Seoul: PSPD, 2020), 8, https://docs.google.com/document/d/124TN-HpcltZ5EPc V2YRlvlvfs_3Tz6ZwbsWnVFCUsJs/edit.

16. Young Ho Cho and Injeong Hwang, "Who Defends Democracy and Why? Explaining the Participation in the 2016–2017 Candlelight Protest in South Korea," *Democratization* 28, no. 3 (2021): 625–44.

17. J. B. Kwon, "Modern Democratic Imaginary," 81–82.

18. Investigations into the faulty construction of the Sampoong Department Store reveal that the original designs only contained engineering for four floors. However, a fifth-floor extension was added without government approval. The continual disregard of safety protocols and the corrupt dealings with city-government officials who agreed to "look the other way" regarding unauthorized building changes all contributed to the tragic and shocking collapse of the department store.

19. In his writing about PSPD, as well as other large democracy organizations, such as Citizens' Coalition for Economic Justice and Korean Federation for Environmental Movement, Dae-Yop Cho explains that in the mid-1990s, PSPD led a campaign for judicial reform "aimed at guaranteeing prosecutorial neutrality eliminating judicial corruption." It also led efforts to sanction "corrupt jurists," evaluate and monitor "lawmakers' legislative activities," expose "corrupt and incompetent politicians," "enact political reform laws" and pass an anticorruption act. Dae-Yop Cho, "Korean Citizens' Movement Organizations: Their Ideologies, Resources and Action Repertoires," *Korea Journal* 46, no. 2 (Summer 2006): 77.

20. Rachael Miyung Joo, *Transnational Sport: Gender, Media, and Global Korea* (Durham, NC: Duke University Press, 2012).

21. J. Kang, *Igniting the Internet.*

22. Jaeyeon Lee, "Melancholia Is (Geo)political! Postcolonial Geography in the Wednesday Demonstration in Seoul," *Cultural Geographies* 29, no. 1 (January 2022): 45–61, https://doi.org/10.1177/14744740211054147; Jaeyeon Lee, "The Ethno-nationalist Solidarity and (Dis)comfort in the Wednesday Demonstration in South Korea," *Gender, Place and Culture* 30, no. 4 (April 2023): 528–41, https://doi.org/10.1080/0966369X.2021.2016655; Laura Hyun Yi Kang, *Traffic in Asian Women* (Durham, NC: Duke University Press, 2020). Also see Chunghee Sarah Soh, "The Korean 'Comfort Women' Tragedy as Structural Violence," in *Rethinking Historical Injustice and Reconciliation in Northeast Asia: The Korean Experience,*

ed. Gi-Wook Shin, Soon-Won Park, and Daqing Yang (London: Routledge, 2007), 17–35.

23. Suk Gendry-Kim Keum, *Grass*, trans. Janet Hong (Montreal, QC: Drawn and Quarterly, 2019); Emily Jungmin Yoon, *A Cruelty Special to Our Species: Poems* (New York: Ecco, an imprint of HarperCollins, 2018). For our most highly recommended documentary film, see Emmanuel Moonchil Park, dir., *Podŭrapke* [Comfort] (n.p.: Citizens' Association for Comfort Women, 2020), https://www.kmdb.or.kr/db/kor/detail/movie/A/09832, which features Kim Soonak (1928–2010).

24. The Korean Council for the Women Drafted for Military Sexual Slavery by Japan (한국정신대문제대책협의회) is the official organization that started and has continued to organize the weekly Wednesday demonstrations, though there are other groups and individuals who participate.

25. Tilly, *Politics of Collective Violence*, 48–50.

26. Eun-sung Kim, "The Sensory Power of Cameras and Noise Meters for Protest Surveillance in South Korea," *Social Studies of Science* 46, no. 3 (June 2016): 403, https://doi.org/10.1177/0306312716648403.

27. McCann, "Race," 170.

28. Hagar Kotef, *Movement and the Ordering of Freedom: On Liberal Governances of Mobility* (Durham : Duke University Press, 2015), 15.

29. Republic of Korea Assembly and Demonstration Act of 2007, No. 8424 (2007), No. 8733 (2007), No. 13834 (2016), Korea Legislation Research Institute, Law Viewer, https://elaw.klri.re.kr/eng_mobile/viewer.do?hseq=37525&type=part&key=11.

30. Amnesty International, *Freedom of Peaceful Assembly in South Korea and International Human Rights Standards* (London: Amnesty International, November 8, 2016), 11, https://www.amnesty.org/en/documents/asa25/5099/2016/en/.

31. Ye-rin Choi, "Farmers' Tractors Rumbling on Long Journey to Seoul to 'Kick Out' Pres. Park," *Hankyoreh*, Eng. ed., November 25, 2016, https://english.hani.co.kr/arti/english_edition/e_national/771987.

32. "Court Bans Farmers from Mobilizing Tractors at Seoul Rallies," Yonhap News Agency, November 25, 2016, https://en.yna.co.kr/view/AEN20161125005352315.

33. Donna Lee Kwon, "'Becoming One': Embodying Korean *P'ungmul* Percussion Band Music and Dance through Site-Specific Intermodal Transmission," *Ethnomusicology* 59, no. 1 (Winter 2015): 39.

34. Myungji Yang, *From Miracle to Mirage: The Making and Unmaking of the Korean Middle Class, 1960–2015* (Ithaca, NY: Cornell University Press, 2018).

35. Massey, *For Space*, 11–12.

Conclusion

1. Sang-Hun Choe, "Why South Korea Has So Many Protests, and What That Means," *New York Times*, October 19, 2023, https://www.nytimes.com/2023/10/19/world/asia/south-korea-protests.html.

2. Yasmeen Serhan, "The Common Element Uniting Worldwide Protests," *The Atlantic*, November 19, 2019, https://www.theatlantic.com/international/archive/2019/11/leaderless-protests-around-world/602194/.

3. Ruth Milkman, Stephanie Luce, and Penny Lewis, "Occupy after Occupy," *Jacobin*, June 1, 2014. https://jacobin.com/2014/06/occupy-after-occupy/.

4. Martin-Brehm Christensen et al., "Survival of the Richest," Oxfam International, January 16, 2023, https://www.oxfam.org/en/research/survival-richest.

5. Cihan Tuğal, "Elusive Revolt: The Contradictory Rise of Middle-Class Politics," *Thesis Eleven* 130, no. 1 (2015): 74–95.

6. Vivian Yee, "'A Slow Death': Egypt's Political Prisoners Recount Horrific Conditions," *New York Times*, August 8, 2022, https://www.nytimes.com/2022/08/08/world/middleeast/egypts-prisons-conditions.html.

7. Francis L. F. Lee et al., "Hong Kong's Summer of Uprising," *China Review* 19, no. 4 (November 2019): 4. See also Francis Lee, "Solidarity in the Anti-extradition Bill Movement in Hong Kong," *Critical Asian Studies* 52, no. 1 (2020): 18–32, https://doi.org/10.1080/14672715.2020.1700629.

8. Joshua Rosenzweig, "Year of Repression: How Hong Kong's Leaders Twisted the Protest Narrative to Strangle a Movement," Amnesty International, June 9, 2020, https://www.amnesty.org/en/latest/news/2020/06/how-hong-kong-leaders-twisted-the-protest-narrative-to-strangle-a-movement/. See also Sonny Lo, "Hong Kong in 2020," *Asian Survey* 61, no. 1 (February 2021): 34–42, https://doi.org/10.1525/as.2021.61.1.34; Ying-Ho Kwong, "After State Repression: Movement Abeyance in Hong Kong under the Enforcement of the National Security Law," *Journal of Asian and African Studies* 58, no. 1 (February 2023): 68–85, https://doi.org/10.1177/00219096221124940.

9. Barbara Ransby, *Making All Black Lives Matter: Reimagining Freedom in the Twenty-First Century* (Oakland: University of California Press, 2018).

10. Kim Voss, "The Collapse of a Social Movement: The Interplay of Mobilizing Structures, Framing, and Political Opportunities in the Knights of Labor," in *Comparative Perspectives on Social Movements: Political Opportunities, Mobilizing Structures, and Cultural Framings*, ed. Doug McAdam, John D. McCarthy, and Mayer N. Zald (Cambridge: Cambridge University Press, 1996), 227.

11. David S. Meyer, "Movement Analysis on the Fly: The Limits and Promise of Social Science," *Mobilization: An International Quarterly* 26, no. 2 (2021): 145, https://doi.org/10.17813/1086-671X-26-2-137.

12. Taylor, *Archive and the Repertoire*, 211, 167.

13. Koopman makes a similar point about solidarity as "protective accompaniment" when describing the critical support provided to migrants and refugees who make perilous journeys across increasingly militarized borders. Koopman, "Alter-geopolitics," 278.

14. Silvia Federici, *Witches, Witch-Hunting, and Women* (Oakland, CA: PM Press, 2018), 41.

15. Massey, *For Space*, 12, 149.

16. Massey, *For Space*, 11–12.

17. Mitchell, *Right to the City*; McCann, "Race."

18. David Harvey, "The Right to the City," *International Journal of Urban and Regional Research* 27, no. 4 (2003): 939.

19. Mariame Kaba, "Conclusion: Beyond Doom, Toward Collective Action," in *Let This Radicalize You: Organizing and the Revolution of Reciprocal Care*, by Kelly Hayes and Mariame Kaba (Chicago: Haymarket Books, 2023), 232. It is also noteworthy that just before that passage, Kaba offers this quote by Henry Giroux about the notion of radical hope that echoes our discussion of space: "Hope expands the space of the possible and becomes a way of recognizing and naming the incomplete nature of the present." Henry A. Giroux, "Amid Apocalyptic Cynicism, Let's Embrace Radical Hope in the New Year," *Truthout*, January 5, 2022, https://truthout.org/articles/amid-apocalyptic-cynicism-lets-embrace-radical-hope-in-the-new-year/.

20. Carole McGranahan, "Theorizing Refusal: An Introduction," *Cultural Anthropology* 31, no. 3 (2016): 320, 323, https://doi.org/10.14506/ca31.3.01.

21. Simpson, "Consent's Revenge," 330–31.

22. Patrick Wolfe, "Settler Colonialism and the Elimination of the Native," *Journal of Genocide Research* 8, no. 4 (2006): 390.

23. Simpson, "Consent's Revenge," 329.

24. Simpson, "Consent's Revenge," 331.

25. Patrick Wolfe is commonly cited for defining "colonialism" as a structure, not an event. Wolfe, "Settler Colonialism," 390.

26. Alain Badiou, *The Rebirth of History: Times of Riots and Uprisings* (London: Verso, 2012), 44.

27. Badiou, *Rebirth of History*, 55–56.

28. Badiou, *Rebirth of History*, 70.

29. Namhee Lee, *Memory Construction and the Politics of Time in Neoliberal South Korea* (Durham, NC: Duke University Press, 2022), 6.

30. Michael Rothberg, "Multidirectional Memory," *Témoigner: Entre histoire et mémoire* 119 (2014): 176, https://doi.org/10.4000/temoigner.1494.

31. G. K. Hong, *Death beyond Disavowal*. Hong makes this incisive point when characterizing neoliberalism not as a totalizing "free market orthodoxy" but as the state's *selective* protection of minoritized life. By pronouncing that "racial

and gender violence are things of the past," neoliberal states utilize the logics of multicultural democracy to disavow historically subjugated racial groups that have long critiqued intersecting forms of social oppression and capitalist expropriation as part of emancipatory struggles for decolonization and Third World sovereignty. Ibid., 17.

32. For the full text of Yeongsun's moving statement, see Sok-yong Hwang, *Mater 2-10* (Melbourne: Scribe, 2020), 127.

33. Fisher and Tronto, "Feminist Theory of Caring," 40.

34. This sentiment is commonly attributed to the words of German pastor Martin Niemöller to indict the moral apathy and indifference of the genocide of Jews during the Holocaust by the Nazi regime. Black feminist activist-scholar Angela Y. Davis popularized the saying. See Angela Y. Davis, *If They Come in the Morning: Voices of Resistance* (New York: Third Press, 1971).

35. This is hardly unique to South Korea. Similar sentiments are expressed by activists who participated in a range of oppositional movements in North America during the 1960s and 1970s, such as the revolutionary Black Power and Third World Liberation Front struggles in the United States.

36. Oona Morrow and Brenda Parker, "Care, Commoning and Collectivity: From Grand Domestic Revolution to Urban Transformation," *Urban Geography* 41, no. 4 (2020): 608.

37. Tadiar, *Remaindered Life*, 5, 331–33.

38. Hi'ilei Julia Kawehipuaakahaopulani Hobart and Tamara Kneese, "Radical Care: Survival Strategies for Uncertain Times," *Social Text* 38, no. 1 (2020): 2. Also see Dean Spade, "Solidarity Not Charity: Mutual Aid for Mobilization and Survival," *Social Text* 38, no. 1 (2020): 131–51.

39. Hayes and Kaba, *Let This Radicalize You*, 80, 82.

40. Kaba, "Conclusion," 232.

BIBLIOGRAPHY

Agarwala, Rina. *Informal Labor, Formal Politics, and Dignified Discontent in India*. New York: Cambridge University Press, 2013.

Ahmed, Sara. "Affective Economies." *Social Text* 22, no. 2 (2004): 117–39.

———. *Living a Feminist Life*. Durham, NC: Duke University Press, 2017.

Alam, Ashraful, and Donna Houston. "Rethinking Care as Alternate Infrastructure." *Cities* 100 (May 2020): 102662. https://doi.org/10.1016/j.cities.2020.102662.

Alimi, Eitan Y. "Repertoires of Contention." In *The Oxford Handbook of Social Movements*, edited by Donatella Della Porta and Mario Diani, 410–22. Oxford: Oxford University Press, 2015.

Alvarez, Sonia E., Gianpaolo Baiocchi, Agustín Laó-Montes, Jeffrey W. Rubin, and Millie Thayer. "Introduction: Interrogating the Civil Society Agenda, Reassessing Uncivic Political Activism." In *Beyond Civil Society: Activism, Participation, and Protest in Latin America*, edited by Sonia E. Alvarez, Gianpaolo Baiocchi, Agustín Laó-Montes, Jeffrey W. Rubin, and Millie Thayer, 1–24. Durham, NC: Duke University Press, 2017.

Amin, Ash. "Lively Infrastructure." *Theory, Culture and Society* 31, no. 7–8 (December 2014): 137–61. https://doi.org/10.1177/0263276414548490.

Amnesty International. *Freedom of Peaceful Assembly in South Korea and International Human Rights Standards*. London: Amnesty International, November 8, 2016. https://www.amnesty.org/en/documents/asa25/5099/2016/en/.

An Yŏng-ch'un. "Kim Ki-ch'un, *Sewŏlho* tongjo tansik e 'pinan kahaejidorok ŏllon chido'" [Kim Ki-ch'un, "directed media to criticize" the relay hunger strike for *Sewol*]. *Hankyoreh*, December 6, 2016. https://www.hani.co.kr/arti/society/society_general/773542.html.

Anderson, Ben. "Neoliberal Affects." *Progress in Human Geography* 40, no. 6 (December 2016): 734–53. https://doi.org/10.1177/0309132515613167.

Arenas, Iván. "The Mobile Politics of Emotions and Social Movement in Oaxaca,

Mexico." *Antipode* 47, no. 5 (November 2015): 1121–40. https://doi.org/10.1111/anti.12158.

Arendt, Hannah. *The Origins of Totalitarianism*. New York: Harcourt Brace Jovanovich, 1973.

Armbruster-Sandoval, Ralph. *Hunger Strikes, Spectacular Speech, and the Struggle for Dignity*. Tucson: University of Arizona Press, 2017.

Arrighi, Giovanni, Terence K. Hopkins, and Immanuel Maurice Wallerstein. *Antisystemic Movements*. London: Verso, 2011.

Badiou, Alain. *The Rebirth of History: Times of Riots and Uprisings*. London: Verso, 2012.

Baker, Don. "The Transformation of the Catholic Church in Korea: From a Missionary Church to an Indigenous Church." *Journal of Korean Religions* 4, no. 1 (2013): 11–42.

Barchiesi, Franco. *Precarious Liberation: Workers, the State, and Contested Social Liberation in Post-apartheid South Africa*. Albany: State University of New York Press, 2011.

Berlant, Lauren. "The Commons: Infrastructures for Troubling Times." *Environment and Planning D: Society and Space* 34, no. 3 (2016): 393–419.

——. *Cruel Optimism*. Durham, NC: Duke University Press, 2011.

Bonneuil, Neil, and Youngja Kim. "Precarious Employment among South Korean Women: Is Inequality Changing with Time?" *Economic and Labour Relations Review* 28, no. 1 (2017): 20–40. https://doi.org/doi:10.1177/1035304617690482.

Breman, Jan, and Marcel van der Linden. "Informalizing the Economy: The Return of the Social Question at a Global Level." *Development and Change* 45, no. 5 (2014): 920–40. https://doi.org/10.1111/dech.12115.

Bu, Nam Chul, and Young-hae Chi. "The Christian and Buddhist Environmental Movements in Contemporary Korea: Common Efforts and Their Limitations." *Korea Journal* 54, no. 4 (December 2014): 52–79. https://doi.org/10.25024/KJ.2014.54.4.52.

Burawoy, Michael. "The Extended Case Method." *Sociological Theory* 16, no. 1 (1998): 4–33. https://doi.org/10.1111/0735-2751.00040.

Butler, Judith. *Notes toward a Performative Theory of Assembly*. Cambridge, MA: Harvard University Press, 2015.

Cacho, Lisa Marie. *Social Death: Racialized Rightlessness and the Criminalization of the Unprotected*. New York: New York University Press, 2012.

Caldeira, Teresa P. R. "Imprinting and Moving Around: New Visibilities and Configurations of Public Space in São Paulo." *Public Culture* 24, no. 2 (May 2012): 385–419. https://doi.org/10.1215/08992363-1535543.

Chang, Dae-Oup. "Korean Labour Movement: The Birth, Rise and Transformation of the Democratic Union Movement." In *Routledge Handbook of Contem-*

porary South Korea, edited by Sojin Lim and Niki J. P. Alsford, 159–74. London: Routledge, 2021.

Cho, Dae-Yop, "Korean Citizens' Movement Organizations: Their Ideologies, Resources and Action Repertoires." *Korea Journal* 46, no. 2 (Summer 2006): 68–98.

Cho, Eun-su. "From Ascetic to Activist: Jiyul Sunim's Korean Buddhist Eco-movement." In *Nature, Environment and Culture in East Asia: The Challenge of Climate Change*, edited by Carmen Meinert, 259–81. Leiden: Brill, 2013.

Cho, Hye-jeong. "Cort Guitar Labor Struggle Ends after 13 Years." *Hankyoreh*, Eng. ed., April 23, 2019. https://english.hani.co.kr/arti/english_edition/e_national/891184.html.

Cho, Ki-weon. "Asahi Glass Workers Stage Protest against Court's Ruling on Labor Unions." *Hankyoreh*, Eng. ed., March 8, 2018. https://english.hani.co.kr/arti/english_edition/e_international/835210.

Cho, Young Ho, and Injeong Hwang. "Who Defends Democracy and Why? Explaining the Participation in the 2016–2017 Candlelight Protest in South Korea." *Democratization* 28, no. 3 (2021): 625–44.

Choe, Sang-Hun. "Why South Korea Has So Many Protests, and What That Means." *New York Times*, October 19, 2023. https://www.nytimes.com/2023/10/19/world/asia/south-korea-protests.html.

Choi, Su Young. "Protesting Grandmothers as Spatial Resistance in the Neo-developmental Era." *Korean Studies* 43 (2019): 40–67.

———. "Recognition for Resistance: Gifting, Social Media, and the Politics of Reciprocity in South Korean Energy Activism." *Media, Culture and Society* 43, no. 7 (2021): 1247–62.

Choi, Ye-rin. "Farmers' Tractors Rumbling on Long Journey to Seoul to 'Kick Out' Pres. Park." *Hankyoreh*, Eng. ed., November 25, 2016. https://english.hani.co.kr/arti/english_edition/e_national/771987.

Christensen, Martin-Brehm, Christian Hallum, Alex Maitland, Quentin Parrinello, Chiara Putaturo, Dana Abed, Carlos Brown, Anthony Kamande, Max Lawson, and Susana Ruiz. "Survival of the Richest." Oxfam International, January 16, 2023. https://www.oxfam.org/en/research/survival-richest.

Chu Chin-u. "Pitman namgigo ttonasŏ mianhada, aga" [I am sorry, baby: All I can leave for you is debt]. *SisaIN*, July 14, 2015. https://www.sisain.co.kr/news/articleView.html?idxno=23777.

Chun, Jennifer Jihye. *Organizing at the Margins: The Symbolic Politics of Labor in South Korea and the United States*. Ithaca, NY: Cornell University Press, 2009.

———. "Protesting Precarity: South Korean Workers and the Labor of Refusal." *Journal of Asian Studies* 81, no. 1 (February 2022): 107–18. https://doi.org/10.1017/S0021911821001479.

Chun, Jennifer Jihye, George Lipsitz, and Young Shin. "Intersectionality as a

Social Movement Strategy: Asian Immigrant Women Advocates." *Signs: Journal of Women in Culture and Society* 38, no. 4 (June 2013): 917–40. https://doi.org/10.1086/669575.

Clough, Patricia Ticineto. Introduction to *The Affective Turn: Theorizing the Social*, edited by Patricia Ticineto Clough and Jean Halley, 1–33. Durham, NC: Duke University Press, 2007.

Collins, Patricia Hill. *Black Feminist Thought: Knowledge, Consciousness, and the Politics of Empowerment*. Perspectives on Gender 2. New York: Routledge, 1991.

"Court Bans Farmers from Mobilizing Tractors at Seoul Rallies." *Yonhap News Agency*, November 25, 2016. https://en.yna.co.kr/view/AEN20161125005352315.

Cowen, Deborah. "Crisis in Motion." University of London Institute in Paris, Paris, France, January 29, 2021. Theory, Culture, and Society video. https://www.theoryculturesociety.org/blog/video-deborah-cowen-crisis-in-motion.

Crenshaw, Kimberle. "Mapping the Margins: Intersectionality, Identity Politics, and Violence against Women of Color." *Stanford Law Review* 43, no. 6 (July 1991): 1241–99. https://doi.org/10.2307/1229039.

Davis, Angela Y. *If They Come in the Morning: Voices of Resistance*. New York: Third Press, 1971.

Della Porta, Donatella. "Political Economy and Social Movement Studies: The Class Basis of Anti-austerity Protests." *Anthropological Theory* 17, no. 4 (2017): 453–73. https://doi.org/10.1177/1463499617735258.

Doucette, Jamie, and Susan Kang. "Legal Geographies of Labour and Postdemocracy: Reinforcing Non-standard Work in South Korea." *Transactions of the Institute of British Geographers* 43, no. 2 (June 2018): 200–214. https://doi.org/10.1111/tran.12216.

Effler, Erika Summers. *Laughing Saints and Righteous Heroes: Emotional Rhythms in Social Movement Groups*. Chicago: University of Chicago Press, 2010.

Eyerman, Ron. "How Social Movements Move: Emotions and Social Movements." In *Emotions and Social Movements*, edited by Helena Flam and Debra King, 41–58. London: Routledge, 2005.

Featherstone, David. *Solidarity: Hidden Histories and Geographies of Internationalism*. London: Zed Books, 2012.

Federici, Silvia. *Revolution at Point Zero: Housework, Reproduction, and Feminist Struggle*. 2nd ed. Oakland, CA: PM Press, 2020.

——. *Witches, Witch-Hunting, and Women*. Oakland, CA: PM Press, 2018.

Fisher, Bernice, and Joan C. Tronto. "Toward a Feminist Theory of Caring." In *Circles of Care: Work and Identity in Women's Lives*, edited by Emily K. Abel and Margaret K. Nelson, 36–54. Albany: State University of New York Press, 1990.

Fraser, Nancy. "Abnormal Injustice." *Critical Inquiry* 34, no. 3 (2008): 393–422.

Fuchs, Christian. *Digital Demagogue: Authoritarian Capitalism in the Age of Trump and Twitter*. London: Pluto Press, 2018.

———. *Marxist Humanism and Communication Theory*. Vol. 1, *Media, Communication and Society*. London: Routledge, 2021.

Fuentes, Marcela. *Performance Constellations: Networks of Protest and Activism in Latin America*. Ann Arbor: University of Michigan Press, 2020.

Gilmore, Ruth Wilson. *Abolition Geography: Essays Towards Liberation*. London: Verso, 2022.

———. "Fatal Couplings of Power and Difference: Notes on Racism and Geography." *Professional Geographer* 54, no. 1 (February 2002): 15–24.

———. "*Geographies of Racial Capitalism with Ruth Wilson Gilmore*—An Antipode Foundation Film." Directed by Kenton Card. Antipodeonline, June 1, 2020. YouTube video. https://www.youtube.com/watch?v=2CS627aKrJI.

———. *Golden Gulag: Prisons, Surplus, Crisis, and Opposition in Globalizing California*. Berkeley: University of California Press, 2007.

———. "Organized Abandonment and Organized Violence: Devolution and the Police." Humanities Institute at the University of California, Santa Cruz, CA, November 9, 2015. Vimeo video. https://vimeo.com/146450686.

Giroux, Henry A. "Amid Apocalyptic Cynicism, Let's Embrace Radical Hope in the New Year." *Truthout*, January 5, 2022. https://truthout.org/articles/amid-apocalyptic-cynicism-lets-embrace-radical-hope-in-the-new-year/.

Glassman, Jim, and Young-Jin Choi. "The *Chaebol* and the US Military–Industrial Complex: Cold War Geopolitical Economy and South Korean Industrialization." *Environment and Planning A: Economy and Space* 46, no. 5 (May 2014): 1160–80. https://doi.org/10.1068/a130025p.

Gómez-Barris, Macarena. *The Extractive Zone: Social Ecologies and Decolonial Perspectives*. Durham, NC: Duke University Press, 2017.

Gordon, Avery. *Ghostly Matters: Haunting and the Sociological Imagination*. Minneapolis: University of Minnesota Press, 1997.

Gould, Deborah B. *Moving Politics: Emotion and ACT UP's Fight against AIDS*. Chicago: University of Chicago Press, 2009.

Green, Ronald S., and Changju Mun. "The Korean Buddhist Nun Chiyul (Jiyul) and Ecofeminism: Hunger Strikes, the Lawsuit for Salamanders, and Walking Protests." Working paper, California Coast University, Santa Ana, CA, 2013. https://digitalcommons.coastal.edu/philosophy-religious-studies/37/.

Hall, Stuart. "Race, Culture, and Communications: Looking Backward and Forward at Cultural Studies." *Rethinking Marxism* 5, no. 1 (1992): 10–18.

Han, Hae-joang Cho. "National Subjects, Citizens and Refugees: Thoughts on the Politics of Survival, Violence and Mourning Following the *Sewol* Ferry Disaster in South Korea." In *New Worlds from Below: Informal Life Politics and*

Grassroots Action in Twenty-First-Century Northeast Asia, edited by Tessa Morris-Suzuki and Eun Jeong Soh, 167–96. Acton: Australian National University Press, 2017.

———. "'You Are Entrapped in an Imaginary Well': The Formation of Subjectivity within Compressed Development." *Inter-Asia Cultural Studies* 1, no. 1 (2000): 49–69. https://doi.org/10.1080/146493700360999.

Han, Ju Hui Judy. "High-Altitude Protests and Necropolitical Digits." In *Infrastructures of Citizenship: Digital Life in the Global City,* edited by Deborah Cowen, Emily Paradis, Brett Story, and Alexis Mitchell, 175–79. Vancouver: University of British Columbia Press, 2020.

———. "Out of Place in Time: Queer Discontents and *Sigisangjo.*" *Journal of Asian Studies* 81, no. 1 (February 2022): 119–29. https://doi.org/10.1017/S0021911821001455.

———. *Queer Throughlines: Spaces of Queer Activism in South Korea and the Korean Diaspora.* Ann Arbor: University of Michigan Press, forthcoming.

———. "Urban Megachurches and Contentious Religious Politics in Seoul." In *Handbook of Religion and the Asian City: Aspiration and Urbanization in the Twenty-First Century,* edited by Peter van der Veer, 133–51. Berkeley: University of California Press, 2015.

Hancocks, Paula, and Euan McKirdy. "South Korea: Court Upholds President Park Geun-hye's Impeachment; Protests Erupt." *CNN,* March 10, 2017. https://www.cnn.com/2017/03/09/asia/south-korea-park-guen-hye-impeachment-upheld/index.html.

Hart, Gillian. "Relational Comparison Revisited: Marxist Postcolonial Geographies in Practice." *Progress in Human Geography* 42, no. 3 (2018): 371–94.

Harvey, David. "The Right to the City." *International Journal of Urban and Regional Research* 27, no. 4 (2003): 939–41.

———. "Seventeen Contradictions and the End of Capitalism." *White Review,* April 2014. https://www.thewhitereview.org/feature/seventeen-contradictions-and-the-end-of-capitalism/.

———. *Social Justice and the City.* London: Edward Arnold, 1973.

Hayes, Kelly, and Mariame Kaba. *Let This Radicalize You: Organizing and the Revolution of Reciprocal Care.* Chicago: Haymarket Books, 2023.

Hŏ Chae-hyŏn. "Kim Chin-suk 'Chasal saenggak'adŏn narŭl chinjŏngsik'in gŏn . . .'" [Kim Jin-suk "What calmed me down from thinking about suicide was . . ."]. *Hankyoreh,* November 15, 2011. http://www.hani.co.kr/arti/society/society_general/505520.html.

Hobart, Hi'ilei Julia Kawehipuaakahaopulani, and Tamara Kneese. "Radical Care: Survival Strategies for Uncertain Times." *Social Text* 38, no. 1 (2020): 1–16.

Hong, Grace Kyungwon. *Death beyond Disavowal: The Impossible Politics of Difference.* Minneapolis: University of Minnesota Press, 2015.

Hong, Sehyun, Nak Nyeon Kim, Zhexun Mo, and Li Yang. "Income Inequality in South Korea, 1933–2022: Evidence from Distributional National Accounts." Working paper, N. 2024/03, World Inequality Lab, January 13, 2024. https://wid.world/news-article/income-inequality-in-south-korea-1933-2022/.

Hsu, Jinn-yuh, Dong-Wan Gimm, and Jim Glassman. "A Tale of Two Industrial Zones: A Geopolitical Economy of Differential Development in Ulsan, South Korea, and Kaohsiung, Taiwan." *Environment and Planning A: Economy and Space* 50, no. 2 (March 2018): 457–73. https://doi.org/10.1177/0308518X16680212.

Hwang, Hyeongjung, Axel Purwin, and Jon Pareliussen. "Strengthening the Social Safety Net in Korea." OECD Economics Department Working Papers, OECD iLibrary, November 30, 2022. https://doi.org/10.1787/45486525-en.

Hwang, In-Hwan, and Jin-Yong Jeon. "Spatiality of Two Urban Religious Spaces in Seoul: A Case Study of Myeong-Dong Cathedral and Bongeun Buddhist Temple Precincts." *Journal of Asian Architecture and Building Engineering* 14, no. 3 (2015): 625–32.

Hwang, Sok-yong. *Mater 2-10*. Melbourne: Scribe, 2020.

Hwang Ye-rang. "Pijŏnggyujik, mipjiman miwŏhal su ŏpnŭn tanŏ" [Nonstandard, a word that is disliked but cannot be hated]. *Hankyoreh*, March 21, 2015. https://h21.hani.co.kr/arti/society/society/39180.html.

Jasper, James M. "Emotions and Social Movements: Twenty Years of Theory and Research." *Annual Review of Sociology* 37 (2011): 285–303. https://doi.org/10.1146/annurev-soc-081309-150015.

Jeon Jong-hwi and Park Seung-heon. "Temp Tutors Win World's Longest Labor Struggle." *Hankyoreh*, Eng. ed., August 27, 2013. https://english.hani.co.kr/arti/english_edition/e_national/601054.html.

Jin, Myeong-seon. "Citizens Continuing Hunger Strike on Behalf of Kim Young-oh." *Hankyoreh*, Eng. ed., August 29, 2014. https://english.hani.co.kr/arti/english_edition/e_national/653393.

Joo, Rachael Miyung. *Transnational Sport: Gender, Media, and Global Korea.* Durham, NC: Duke University Press, 2012.

Kaba, Mariame. "Conclusion: Beyond Doom, Toward Collective Action." In *Let This Radicalize You: Organizing and the Revolution of Reciprocal Care*, by Kelly Hayes and Mariame Kaba, 226–32. Chicago: Haymarket Books, 2023.

Kang, Jiyeon. *Igniting the Internet: Youth and Activism in Postauthoritarian South Korea*. Honolulu: University of Hawai'i Press, 2016.

Kang, Laura Hyun Yi. *Traffic in Asian Women*. Durham, NC: Duke University Press, 2020.

Kawashima, Ken C. *The Proletarian Gamble: Korean Workers in Interwar Japan*. Durham, NC: Duke University Press, 2009.

Kee, Joan. "Why Performance in Authoritarian Korea?" In *Cultures of Yusin:*

South Korea in the 1970s, edited by Youngju Ryu, 245–78. Ann Arbor: University of Michigan Press, 2018.

Keum, Suk Gendry-Kim. *Grass*. Translated by Janet Hong. Montreal, QC: Drawn and Quarterly, 2019.

"Kim Chin-suk, 'Maeil yusŏ ssŭnŭn simjŏng-ŭro pŏtinda'" [Kim Jin-suk, "I hang on every day with the mindset that I'm writing a will"]. *OhMyNews*, July 30, 2011. https://www.ohmynews.com/nws_web/view/at_pg.aspx?CNTN_CD=A0001604029.

"Kim Chu-ik ssi yusŏ chŏnmun" [Full text of Kim Ju-ik's suicide notes]. *Kyŏnghyang sinmun*, October 17, 2003. https://www.khan.co.kr/national/national-general/article/200310171430581.

Kim Chin-uk. "Jaenŭng Kyoyuk Nojo 'chongt'ap siwi' tugaji misŭt'ŏri" [Two mysteries of the 'bell tower protest' by the Jaenung Educational Union]. *MoneyS*, May 30, 2013. https://www.moneys.co.kr/article/2013052320588030457.

Kim, Eunjung. "Continuing Presence of Discarded Bodies: Occupational Harm, Necro-activism, and Living Justice." *Catalyst: Feminism, Theory, Technoscience* 5, no. 1 (April 2019): 1–29. https://doi.org/10.28968/cftt.v5i1.29616.

Kim, Eun-sung. "The Sensory Power of Cameras and Noise Meters for Protest Surveillance in South Korea." *Social Studies of Science* 46, no. 3 (June 2016): 396–416. https://doi.org/10.1177/0306312716648403.

Kim, Jinah. "The Insurgency of Mourning: *Sewol* across the Transpacific." *Amerasia Journal* 46, no. 1 (June 2020): 84–100. https://doi.org/10.1080/00447471.2020.1772699.

Kim, Jisoo M. *The Emotions of Justice: Gender, Status, and Legal Performance in Choson Korea*. Seattle: University of Washington Press, 2015.

Kim, Jongyoung, Heeyun Kim, and Jawoon Lim. "The Politics of Science and Undone Protection in the 'Samsung Leukemia' Case." *East Asian Science, Technology and Society* 14, no. 4 (2020): 573–601.

Kim Kwang-su. "Chasal yuhok yŏrŏbŏn . . . T'wit'ŏro sesanggwa sot'onghamyŏ Hŭimang ŏdŏ'" [Several suicidal urges . . . hope gained through communicating with the world using Twitter]. *Hankyoreh*, November 14, 2011. http://www.hani.co.kr/arti/society/labor/505415.html.

Kim, Mee-young. "Why Do Some Inmates Get out Just after Midnight, Whiles [sic] Others Have to Stay till 5 am?" *Hankyoreh*, Eng. ed., May 13, 2016. https://english.hani.co.kr/arti/english_edition/e_national/743737.

Kim, Min-kyung. "Six Years after Layoffs, Ssangyong Workers Keep Passing Away." *Hankyoreh*, Eng. ed., May 4, 2015. https://english.hani.co.kr/arti/english_edition/e_national/689678.

Kim, Mi-young, and Jae-uk Lee. "Young Worker's Death Spurs National Discussion on Irregular Work." *Hankyoreh*, Eng. ed., June 6, 2016. https://english.hani.co.kr/arti/english_edition/e_national/747007.

Kim, Nadia Y. *Refusing Death: Immigrant Women and the Fight for Environmental Justice in LA*. Stanford: Stanford University Press, 2021.

Kim Sŏn-sik. "Hanŭlgamok sugamjadŭri 3gi 'minju chŏngbu' e paranda" [The inmates of the prison in the sky have hopes for the third "Democratic Government"]. *Hankyoreh*, May 15, 2017. http://h21.hani.co.kr/arti/special/spe cial_general/43538.html.

Kim, Sun-Chul. "The Trajectory of Protest Suicide in South Korea, 1970–2015." *Journal of Contemporary Asia* 51, no. 1 (July 2019): 38–63. https://doi.org/10.10 80/00472336.2019.1607889.

Kim, Tae-hyeong. "[Photo] Don't Be Hungry in Heaven." *Hankyoreh*, Eng. ed., June 7, 2016. https://english.hani.co.kr/arti/english_edition/e_national/747152.

Kim To-hyŏn. *Changaehak ŭi tojŏn* [The challenge of disability studies]. Paju: Owŏl ŭi bom, 2019.

Kim, Victoria, and Daisuke Wakabayashi. "What to Know about the Chaebol Families That Dominate South Korea's Economy." *New York Times*, December 18, 2023. https://www.nytimes.com/2023/12/18/business/chaebol-south-ko rea.html#:~:text=Chaebol%20families%20have%20controlled%20South, support%20to%20rebuild%20the%20economy.

Kim Yoo Sun. "The Non-regular Work in South Korea." *Friedrich-Ebert-Stiftung Issue Paper Series, Labour and Society*, no. 1 (October 2021): 1–8. https://library .fes.de/pdf-files/bueros/seoul/18415.pdf.

King, Deborah K. "Multiple Jeopardy, Multiple Consciousness: The Context of a Black Feminist Ideology." *Signs: Journal of Women in Culture and Society* 14, no. 1 (October 1988): 42–72. https://doi.org/10.1086/494491.

Kipfer, Stefan. "Urbanization, Everyday Life and the Survival of Capitalism: Lefebvre, Gramsci and the Problematic of Hegemony." *Capitalism Nature Socialism* 13, no. 2 (June 2002): 117–49. https://doi.org/10.1080/10455750208565482.

"Kiryung Workers Make Revolutionary March before Returning to Work." IndustriALL, February 9, 2012. http://www.industriall-union.org/archive/imf /kiryung-workers-make-revolutionary-march-before-returning-to-work.

Koo, Hagen. *Korean Workers: The Culture and Politics of Class Formation*. Ithaca, NY: Cornell University Press, 2001.

———. *Privilege and Anxiety: The Korean Middle Class in the Global Era*. Ithaca, NY: Cornell University Press, 2022.

Koopman, Sara. "Alter-geopolitics: Other Securities Are Happening." *Geoforum* 42, no. 3 (2011): 274–84.

Korkman, Zeynep Kurtulus. "Feeling Labor: Commercial Divination and Commodified Intimacy in Turkey." *Gender and Society* 29, no. 2 (April 2015): 195–218. https://doi.org/10.1177/0891243214566269.

Kotef, Hagar. *Movement and the Ordering of Freedom: On Liberal Governances of Mobility*. Durham, NC: Duke University Press, 2015.

"Kwanghwamun 40m kogong nongsŏng hyŏnjang 'Chigŭm naŭi chujŏkŭn . . .'"
[From the Kwanghwamun 40m-high-altitude occupation site, "My main
enemy right now is . . ."]. *OhMyNews*, April 27, 2017. https://m.ohmynews.
com/NWS_Web/Mobile/at_pg.aspx?CNTN_CD=A0002320568#cb.

Kwon, Donna Lee. "'Becoming One': Embodying Korean *P'ungmul* Percussion
Band Music and Dance through Site-Specific Intermodal Transmission." *Ethnomusicology* 59, no. 1 (Winter 2015): 31–60.

Kwon, Jong Bum. "Forging a Modern Democratic Imaginary: Police Sovereignty, Neoliberalism, and the Boundaries of Neo-Korea." *Positions: Asia
Critique* 22, no. 1 (February 2014): 71–101. https://doi.org/10.1215/10679847
-2383858.

Kwong, Ying-Ho. "After State Repression: Movement Abeyance in Hong Kong
under the Enforcement of the National Security Law." *Journal of Asian and
African Studies* 58, no. 1 (February 2023): 68–85. https://doi.org/10.1177/0021
9096221124940.

LaDuke, Winona, and Deborah Cowen. "Beyond Wiindigo Infrastructure."
South Atlantic Quarterly 119, no. 2 (April 2020): 243–68. https://doi.org/10.1215
/00382876-8177747.

Larkin, Brian. "The Politics and Poetics of Infrastructure." *Annual Review of
Anthropology* 42 (2013): 327–43.

Lee, Byoung-Hoon. "Worker Militancy at the Margins: Struggles of Non-regular
Workers in South Korea." *Development and Society* 45, no. 1 (June 2016): 1–37.
https://doi.org/10.21588/dns/2016.45.1.001.

Lee, Changgeun. "Another Worker Driven to His Death in Korea." Base21, October 19, 2003. http://base21.jinbo.net/show/show.php?p_cd=0&p_dv=0&p_
docnbr=29390.

Lee Chang-kun. "Squid Game's Strike Flashbacks Were Modeled on Our Real-
Life Factory Occupation." Translated by Kap Seol. *Jacobin*, November 1, 2021.
https://jacobin.com/2021/11/squid-game-ssangyong-dragon-motor-strike
-south-korea.

Lee, Ching Kwan. *Against the Law: Labor Protests in China's Rustbelt and Sunbelt*.
Berkeley: University of California Press, 2007.

Lee, Francis. "Solidarity in the Anti-extradition Bill Movement in Hong Kong."
Critical Asian Studies 52, no. 1 (2020): 18–32. https://doi.org/10.1080/14672715
.2020.1700629.

Lee, Francis L. F., Samson Yuen, Gary Tang, and Edmund W. Cheng. "Hong
Kong's Summer of Uprising." *China Review* 19, no. 4 (November 2019): 1–32.

Lee, Jaeeun. "S. Korea's Gender Pay Gap Worst in OECD." *Korea Herald*, May 23,
2024. https://www.koreaherald.com/view.php?ud=20240523050548.

Lee, Jaeyeon. "The Ethno-nationalist Solidarity and (Dis)comfort in the Wednesday Demonstration in South Korea." *Gender, Place and Culture* 30, no. 4 (April 2023): 528–41. https://doi.org/10.1080/0966369X.2021.2016655.

———. "Melancholia Is (Geo)political! Postcolonial Geography in the Wednesday Demonstration in Seoul." *Cultural Geographies* 29, no. 1 (January 2022): 45–61. https://doi.org/10.1177/14744740211054147.

Lee, Namhee. *The Making of Minjung: Democracy and the Politics of Representation in South Korea*. Ithaca, NY: Cornell University Press, 2007.

———. *Memory Construction and the Politics of Time in Neoliberal South Korea*. Durham, NC: Duke University Press, 2022.

Lee, Sook Jung. "The Politics of Chaebol Reform in Korea: Social Cleavage and New Financial Rules." *Journal of Contemporary Asia* 38, no. 3 (2008): 439–52.

Lee, Sophia Seung-Yoon, and Yuhwi Kim. "Female Outsiders in South Korea's Dual Labour Market: Challenges of Equal Pay for Work of Equal Value." *Journal of Industrial Relations* 62, no. 4 (2020): 651–78.

Lee, Yoonkyung. "Neo-liberal Methods of Labour Repression: Privatised Violence and Dispossessive Litigation in Korea." *Journal of Contemporary Asia* 51, no. 1 (2021): 20–37.

———. "Sky Protest: New Forms of Labour Resistance in Neo-liberal Korea." *Journal of Contemporary Asia* 45, no. 3 (July 2015): 443–64. https://doi.org/10.1080/00472336.2015.1012647.

Lefebvre, Henri. *The Production of Space*. Oxford: Blackwell, 1991.

———. "Space: Social Product and Use Value (1979)." In *State, Space, World: Selected Essays*, edited by Neil Brenner and Stuart Elden, 185–95. Minneapolis: University of Minnesota Press, 2009.

Lewis, Sara E. *Spacious Minds: Trauma and Resilience in Tibetan Buddhism*. Ithaca: Cornell University Press, 2019.

Lim, Minouk. "The (Im)possible Art as Life : On-the-Crane #85 Performance by Kim Jin-Suk." In *Being Political Popular: South Korean Art at the Intersection of Popular Culture and Democracy, 1980–2010*, edited by Sohl Lee, 158–63. Seoul: Hyunsil; Seattle: University of Washington Press, 2012.

Lionnet, Françoise, and Shu-mei Shih. "Introduction: Thinking through the Minor, Transnationally." In *Minor Transnationalism*, edited by Françoise Lionnet and Shu-mei Shih, 1–21. Durham, NC: Duke University Press, 2005.

Lo, Sonny. "Hong Kong in 2020." *Asian Survey* 61, no. 1 (February 2021): 34–42. https://doi.org/10.1525/as.2021.61.1.34.

Mahmood, Saba. *Politics of Piety: The Islamic Revival and the Feminist Subject*. Princeton, NJ: Princeton University Press, 2005.

Man, Simeon, A. Naomi Paik, and Melina Pappademos. "Violent Entanglements." *Radical History Review* 2019, no. 133 (January 2019): 1–10. https://doi.org/10.1215/01636545-7160029.

Mankekar, Purnima, and Akhil Gupta. "Intimate Encounters: Affective Labor in Call Centers." *Positions: Asia Critique* 24, no. 1 (February 2016): 17–43. https://doi.org/10.1215/10679847-3320029.

Marsh, Nick. "South Korea: 'Protesting for 20 Years and Still No Equal Rights.'" *BBC News*, January 27, 2023. https://www.bbc.com/news/world-us-canada-64 369810.

Massey, Doreen. *For Space*. London: SAGE, 2005.

Massumi, Brian. *Parables for the Virtual: Movement, Affect, Sensation*. Durham, NC: Duke University Press, 2002.

McCann, Eugene J. "Race, Protest, and Public Space: Contextualizing Lefebvre in the U.S. City." *Antipode* 31, no. 2 (1999): 163–84.

McCurdy, Patrick, Anna Feigenbaum, and Fabian Frenzel. "Protest Camps and Repertoires of Contention." *Social Movement Studies* 15, no. 1 (January 2016): 97–104. https://doi.org/10.1080/14742837.2015.1037263.

McGranahan, Carole. "Theorizing Refusal: An Introduction." *Cultural Anthropology* 31, no. 3 (2016): 319–25. https://doi.org/10.14506/ca31.3.01.

MediaVOP. "Tasi ponŭn Kim Chin-suk chidowiwŏn Kim Chu-ik yŏlsa ch'udosa (2003)" [Re-viewing Kim Jin-suk's Eulogy for Kim Ju-ik (2003)]. January 22, 2021. YouTube, 16:53. https://youtu.be/xbYstA3LGFU?si=nHcJFjaym8GMa2Gp.

Melamed, Jodi. "Racial Capitalism." *Critical Ethnic Studies* 1, no. 1 (2015): 76–85. https://doi.org/10.5749/jcritethnstud.1.1.0076.

Melucci, Albert. *Challenging Codes: Collective Action in the Information Age*. Cambridge: Cambridge University Press, 1996.

Meyer, David S. "Movement Analysis on the Fly: The Limits and Promise of Social Science." *Mobilization: An International Quarterly* 26, no. 2 (2021): 137–56. https://doi.org/10.17813/1086-671X-26-2-137.

Milkman, Ruth, Stephanie Luce, and Penny Lewis. "Occupy after Occupy." *Jacobin*, June 1, 2014. https://jacobin.com/2014/06/occupy-after-occupy/.

Millar, Kathleen M. "Towards a Critical Politics of Precarity." *Sociology Compass* 11, no. 6 (2017): 1–11.

Miryang 765kV songjŏnt'ap pandae taech'aekwi, ed. "Miryang ssaum 10 nyŏn, uri nŭn imi sŭngni hayŏtsŭpnida!" [10 years of Miryang fight, we have already prevailed!]. In *Miryang, sipnyŏn ŭi pit*, 8–10. Seoul: Listen to the City, 2015.

Mitchell, Don. *The Right to the City: Social Justice and the Fight for Public Space*. New York: Guilford Press, 2003.

Moon Gyu-hyeon. "Saemangŭm samboilbae 3 chunyŏn: Saemangŭm Kaetbŏl ŭi puhwarŭl kidarimyŏ" [Third anniversary of the Saemangŭm samboilbae: Waiting for the revival of Saemangŭl Wetlands]. *Green Korea* (blog), March 28, 2006. https://www.greenkorea.org/%EB%AF%B8%EB%B6%84%EB%A5 %98/16121/.

Moore, Barrington. *Injustice: The Social Bases of Obedience and Revolt*. London: Macmillan, 1978.

Morrow, Oona, and Brenda Parker. "Care, Commoning and Collectivity: From Grand Domestic Revolution to Urban Transformation." *Urban Geography* 41, no. 4 (2020): 607–24.

MunYang Hyo-suk. "11 wŏl 18 il majimak Taehanmun misa ponghŏn" [Final Taehanmun Mass dedication on November 18]. *K'at'olik nyusŭ chigŭm yŏgi*, November 15, 2013. http://www.catholicnews.co.kr/news/articleView.html?idxno=11126.

Na, Tari Young-Jung. "The South Korean Gender System: LGBTI in the Contexts of Family, Legal Identity, and the Military." Translated by Ju Hui Judy Han and Se-Woong Koo. *Journal of Korean Studies* 19, no. 2 (2014): 357–77. https://doi.org/10.1353/jks.2014.0018.

Nam, Hwasook Bergquist. *Building Ships, Building a Nation: Korea's Democratic Unionism under Park Chung Hee*. Korean Studies of the Henry M. Jackson School of International Studies. Seattle: University of Washington Press, 2009.

———. *Women in the Sky: Gender and Labor in the Making of Modern Korea*. Ithaca, NY: ILR Press, an imprint of Cornell University Press, 2021.

Neely, Abigail H., and Patricia J. Lopez. "Toward Healthier Futures in Postpandemic Times: Political Ecology, Racial Capitalism, and Black Feminist Approaches to Care." *Geography Compass* 16, no. 2 (2022): e12609. https://doi.org/10.1111/gec3.12609.

"No Taet'ongnyŏng 'punsin t'ujaeng sudan samnŭn sidae chinatta' parŏne taehae" [On President Roh's remark, "The time has passed for using the alter ego as a means of struggle"]. KCTU, November 6, 2003. https://nodong.org/statement/98371.

No Ŭng-gŭn. "Kabŭl kwan'gye" [*Kap-ŭl* relationship]. *Kyŏnghyang sinmun*, October 30, 2011. https://www.khan.co.kr/opinion/yeojeok/article/201110302106315.

O To-yŏp. "Pijŏnggyunodongja kadŭk'an Kuro rŭl twijipnŭnda" [Overturning Kuro, full of precarious workers]. *Ch'amsesang*, August 31, 2006. http://www.newscham.net/news/view.php?board=news&nid=35818.

OECD. *Society at a Glance 2024: OECD Social Indicators*. Paris: OECD, 2024. https://doi.org/10.1787/918d8db3-en.

Oh, Young-jin. "You Don't Represent Us." *Korea Times*, October 4, 2019. https://www.koreatimes.co.kr/www/opinion/2024/09/137_276627.html.

Pak Chung-yŏp. "Nodongsa saero ssŭn Asahi Klasŭ t'ujaeng, 9 nyŏn'ganŭi ch'wijaegi" [Asahi Glass rewrites labor history, reporting over nine years]. *SisaIN*, August 16, 2024. https://www.sisain.co.kr/news/articleView.html?idxno=53716.

Pak Mi-kyŏng. "Tasi pitnal urinŭn KTX sŭngmuwŏn ipnida" [We are KTX train attendants, and we will shine again]. *Chŏngsewa nodong* 144 (July 2018): 49–54.

Pak, Su Yon, Unzu Lee, Jung Ha Kim, and Myung Ji Cho. *Singing the Lord's Song in a New Land: Korean American Practices of Faith*. Louisville, KY: Westminster John Knox Press, 2005.

Palomera, Jaime, and Theodora Vetta. "Moral Economy: Rethinking a Radical Concept." *Anthropological Theory* 16, no. 4 (December 2016): 413–32.

Park, Emmanuel Moonchil, dir. *Podŭrapke* [Comfort]. N.p.: Citizens' Association for Comfort Women, 2020. https://www.kmdb.or.kr/db/kor/detail/movie/A/09832.

Park, Hyun Ok. *The Capitalist Unconscious: From Korean Unification to Transnational Korea*. New York: Columbia University Press, 2015.

——. "The Politics of Time: The *Sewol* Ferry Disaster and the Disaster of Democracy." *Journal of Asian Studies* 81, no. 1 (2022): 131–44.

Park, Min-na. *Birth of Resistance*. Seoul: Korea Democracy Foundation, 2005.

Park, Sunyoung. *The Proletarian Wave: Literature and Leftist Culture in Colonial Korea 1910–1945*. Cambridge, MA: Harvard University Press, 2015.

Payne, Charles. "Ella Baker and Models of Change." *Signs: Journal of Women in Culture and Society* 14, no. 4 (Summer 1989): 885–99.

People's Solidarity for Participatory Democracy. *PSPD Annual Report*. Seoul: PSPD, 2020. https://docs.google.com/document/d/124TN-HpcltZ5EPcV2YRlvlvfs_3Tz6ZwbsWnVFCUsJs/edit.

Power, Emma R., Ilan Wiesel, Emma Mitchell, and Kathleen J. Mee. "Shadow Care Infrastructures: Sustaining Life in Post-welfare Cities." *Progress in Human Geography* 46, no. 5 (October 2022): 1165–84. https://doi.org/10.1177/03091325221109837.

Puig de la Bellacasa, Maria. "Matters of Care in Technoscience: Assembling Neglected Things." *Social Studies of Science* 41, no. 1 (2011): 85–106.

Ransby, Barbara. *Making All Black Lives Matter: Reimagining Freedom in the Twenty-First Century*. Oakland: University of California Press, 2018.

Rosenzweig, Joshua. "Year of Repression: How Hong Kong's Leaders Twisted the Protest Narrative to Strangle a Movement." Amnesty International, June 9, 2020. https://www.amnesty.org/en/latest/news/2020/06/how-hong-kong-leaders-twisted-the-protest-narrative-to-strangle-a-movement/.

Rothberg, Michael. "Multidirectional Memory." *Témoigner: Entre histoire et mémoire* 119 (2014): 176. https://doi.org/10.4000/temoigner.1494.

——. *Multidirectional Memory: Remembering the Holocaust in the Age of Decolonization*. Stanford: Stanford University Press, 2009.

Ryu, Yi-Geun. "Income Inequality in S. Korea Is Widening at Second-Fastest Rate in OECD." *Hankyoreh*, Eng. ed., April 10, 2023. https://english.hani.co.kr/arti/english_edition/e_national/1087257.

Ryu, Youngju. "Korea's Vietnam: Popular Culture, Patriarchy, Intertextuality." *Review of Korean Studies* 12, no. 3 (2009): 101–23.

——. *Writers of the Winter Republic: Literature and Resistance in Park Chung Hee's Korea*. Honolulu: University of Hawai'i Press, 2016.

Salzinger, Leslie. "Revealing the Unmarked: Finding Masculinity in a Global Factory." *Ethnography* 5, no. 1 (2004): 5–27. http://www.jstor.org/stable/24047917.

Sandoval, Chela. *Methodology of the Oppressed*. Minneapolis: University of Minnesota Press, 2000.

"Sara naeryŏon uridŭri tangsinkke ponaenŭn p'yŏnji" [A letter from us who have survived to you]. *Redian*, July 28, 2011. http://www.redian.org/news/articleView.html?idxno=37597.

SBS News. "'Urinŭn t'ŭliji anatsŭmnida' . . . KTX haego sŭngmuwŏndŭl 'nunmul ŭi haedansik'" ["We were not in the wrong" . . . terminated KTX crew hold a "tearful end-of-struggle ceremony"]. Naver TV, July 21, 2018. Video, 8:11. https://tv.naver.com/v/3656367.

Scully, Ben. "Precarity North and South: A Southern Critique of Guy Standing." *Global Labour Journal* 7, no. 2 (2016): 160–72. https://doi.org/10.15173/glj.v7i2.2521.

Sears, Alan. "Creating and Sustaining Communities of Struggle." *New Socialist* 52 (2007): 32–33.

Seidman, Gay. *Manufacturing Militance: Workers' Movements in Brazil and South Africa, 1970–1985*. Berkeley: University of California Press, 1994.

Seol, Kap. "South Korea: After 12 Years of Protests, Women Workers Get 'Dream Jobs' Back." Labor Notes, August 2, 2018. https://labornotes.org/2018/08/south-korea-after-12-years-protests-women-workers-get-dream-jobs-back.

Serhan, Yasmeen. "The Common Element Uniting Worldwide Protests." *The Atlantic*, November 19, 2019, https://www.theatlantic.com/international/archive/2019/11/leaderless-protests-around-world/602194/.

Shah, Nayan. *Refusal to Eat: A Century of Prison Hunger Strikes*. Oakland: University of California Press, 2022.

Sharpe, Christina. *In the Wake: On Blackness and Being*. Durham, NC: Duke University Press, 2016.

Shin, Kwang-Yeong, and Ju Kong. "Why Does Inequality in South Korea Continue to Rise?" *Korean Journal of Sociology* 48, no. 6 (2014): 31–48.

Simone, AbdouMaliq. "People as Infrastructure: Intersecting Fragments in Johannesburg." *Public Culture* 16, no. 3 (October 2004): 407–29.

——. "Ritornello: 'People as Infrastructure.'" *Urban Geography* 42, no. 9 (October 2021): 1341–48. https://doi.org/10.1080/02723638.2021.1894397.

Simpson, Audra. "Consent's Revenge." *Cultural Anthropology* 31, no. 3 (August 2016): 326–33. https://doi.org/10.14506/ca31.3.02.

——. *Mohawk Interruptus: Political Life across the Borders of Settler States.* Ill. ed. Durham, NC: Duke University Press, 2014.

Soh, Chunghee Sarah. "The Korean 'Comfort Women' Tragedy as Structural Violence." In *Rethinking Historical Injustice and Reconciliation in Northeast Asia: The Korean Experience,* edited by Gi-Wook Shin, Soon-Won Park, and Daqing Yang, 17–35. London: Routledge, 2007.

Solnit, Rebecca. *Hope in the Dark: Untold Histories, Wild Possibilities.* Chicago: Haymarket Books, 2016.

Soon, Im-Heung, dir. *Factory Complex.* Brooklyn, NY: Torch Films, 2015.

Spade, Dean. "Solidarity Not Charity: Mutual Aid for Mobilization and Survival." *Social Text* 38, no. 1 (2020): 131–51.

Standing, Guy. *The Precariat: The New Dangerous Class.* London: Bloomsbury Academic, 2011.

Star, Susan Leigh. "The Ethnography of Infrastructure." *American Behavioral Scientist* 43, no. 3 (November 1999): 377–91. https://doi.org/10.1177/00027649 921955326.

Stewart, Kathleen. *Ordinary Affects.* Durham, NC: Duke University Press, 2007.

Tadiar, Neferti X. M. *Remaindered Life.* Durham, NC: Duke University Press, 2022.

Tarrow, Sydney. *Power in Movement: Social Movements and Contentious Politics.* New York: Cambridge University Press, 1998.

Taylor, Diana. *The Archive and the Repertoire: Performing Cultural Memory in the Americas.* Durham, NC: Duke University Press, 2003.

——. *Performance.* Durham, NC: Duke University Press, 2016.

"3 Years after the Ssangyong Motors Clash and the Real Labor Environment." *Kyunghyang Sinmun,* Eng. ed., August 7, 2012. https://english.khan.co.kr/khan_art_view.html?artid=201208071356027.

Tilly, Charles. *The Contentious French.* Cambridge, MA: Belknap, 1986.

——. *Contentious Performances.* Cambridge: Cambridge University Press, 2008.

——. "From Interactions to Outcomes in Social Movements." In *How Social Movements Matter,* edited by Marco Giugni, Doug McAdam, and Charles Tilly, 253–70. Minneapolis: University of Minnesota Press, 1999.

——. *The Politics of Collective Violence.* Cambridge: Cambridge University Press, 2003.

——. *Regimes and Repertoires.* Chicago: University of Chicago Press, 2006.

Tilly, Charles, and Sydney Tarrow. *Contentious Politics.* Boulder: Paradigm, 2007.

Tronto, Joan C. "An Ethic of Care." *Generations: Journal of the American Society on Aging* 22, no. 3 (1998): 15–20.

Tuğal, Cihan. "Elusive Revolt: The Contradictory Rise of Middle-Class Politics." *Thesis Eleven* 130, no. 1 (2015): 74–95.

Voss, Kim. "The Collapse of a Social Movement: The Interplay of Mobilizing Structures, Framing, and Political Opportunities in the Knights of Labor." In *Comparative Perspectives on Social Movements: Political Opportunities, Mobilizing Structures, and Cultural Framings*, edited by Doug McAdam, John D. McCarthy, and Mayer N. Zald, 227–58. Cambridge: Cambridge University Press, 1996.

Wiesel, Ilan, Wendy Steele, and Donna Houston. "Cities of Care: Introduction to a Special Issue." *Cities* 105 (2020): 1–3.

Williams, Raymond. *Marxism and Literature*. Oxford: Oxford University Press, 1977.

Wolfe, Patrick. "Settler Colonialism and the Elimination of the Native." *Journal of Genocide Research* 8, no. 4 (2006): 387–409.

Woodly, Deva, Rachel H. Brown, Mara Marin, Shatema Threadcraft, Christopher Paul Harris, Jasmine Syedullah, and Miriam Ticktin. "The Politics of Care." *Contemporary Political Theory* 20, no. 4 (December 2021): 890–925. https://doi.org/10.1057/s41296-021-00515-8.

Yang, Guobin. "Emotional Events and the Transformation of Collective Action." In *Emotions and Social Movements*, edited by Helena Flam and Debra King, 79–98. London: Routledge, 2005.

Yang, Myungji. *From Miracle to Mirage: The Making and Unmaking of the Korean Middle Class, 1960–2015*. Ithaca, NY: Cornell University Press, 2018.

Yee, Vivian. "'A Slow Death': Egypt's Political Prisoners Recount Horrific Conditions." *New York Times*, August 8, 2022. https://www.nytimes.com/2022/08/08/world/middleeast/egypts-prisons-conditions.html.

Yeo, Andrew. "Local-National Dynamics and Framing in South Korean Antibase Movements." *Kasarinlan: Philippine Journal of Third World Studies* 21, no. 2 (2006): 34–60.

Yŏ Chŏng-min. "1 ŏk mulge toen KTX sŭngmuwŏn 'kajŏng wihae ihon komindo'" [KTX crew hit with a hundred-million-won fine, "even considering a divorce for the sake of the family"]. *Pressian*, March 4, 2015. https://www.pressian.com/pages/articles/124383.

"Yogurŭl chujang ttae ssŭnŭn tanŏ 'nongsŏng' ŭi yurae nŭn?" [What is the origin of the word *"nongsŏng"* used to assert a demand?]. *YTN nyusŭ*, January 8, 2018. https://news.v.daum.net/v/20180108033301977?s=print_news.

Yŏn Chŏng. "Nodongjohap i issŏssŭl ttae Jaenŭng kyoyuk sŏnsaengnim-ŭro kajang haengbokhaessŭyo" [I was happiest as a Jaenung teacher when there was a labor union]. *Chŏngse wa nodong* 84 (November 2012): 44–53. https://www.dbpia.co.kr/journal/articleDetail?nodeId=NODE02029373.

Yoon, Emily Jungmin. *A Cruelty Special to Our Species: Poems*. New York: Ecco, an imprint of HarperCollins, 2018.

Yoon, Young-Hae, and Sherwin Jones. "Ecology, Dharma and Direct Action: A

Brief Survey of Contemporary Eco-Buddhist Activism in Korea." *Buddhist Studies Review* 31, no. 2 (2015): 293–311. https://doi.org/10.1558/bsrv.v31i2.293.

Yulee, Jiwoon. "Progress by Death: Labor Precaritization and the Financialization of Social Reproduction in South Korea." *Capital and Class*, May 13, 2022. https://doi.org/10.1177/03098168221084113.

Yun, Aelim. "Building Collective Identity: Trade Union Representation of Precarious Workers in the South Korean Auto Companies." *Labour, Capital and Society / Travail, capital et société* 44, no. 1 (2011): 154–78.

——. *The ILO Recommendation on the Employment Relationship and Its Relevance in the Republic of Korea*. Geneva: Global Union Research Network, International Labour Organization, 2007. https://webapps.ilo.org/public/libdoc/ilo/2007/107B09_95_engl.pdf.

Yun Chi-yŏn. "Kwanghwamun hanŭl 6-myŏng-ŭi nodongja, ijeya kŭdŭl-ŭi moksori-ga tŭllinda" [The six workers in the Kwanghwamun sky, we can finally hear their voices]. *Cham sesang*, April 27, 2017. http://www.newscham.net/news/view.php?board=news&nid=102201.

Yun Sŏng-hyo. "KTX yŏsŭngmuwŏne hanbŏnjjŭmŭn kwi kiurigo, nun majuch'yŏya" [We should at least once listen to and hear KTX women train attendants]. *OhMyNews*, August 13, 2008. http://www.ohmynews.com/nws_web/view/at_pg.aspx?CNTN_CD=A0000962193.

——. " '70 nyŏn Chŏn T'ae-il gwa 03 nyŏn Kim Chu-ik yusŏga katdani" [For suicide notes by Chŏn T'ae-il in 1970 and by Kim Ju-ik in 2003 to be the same]. *OhMyNews*, October 22, 2003. http://www.ohmynews.com/nws_web/view/at_pg.aspx?CNTN_CD=A0000149804.

Yusŏng Kiŏp Nodongjadŭl kwa Hamkke. "Yusŏngbŏmdaewi esŏ hoso dŭrimnida" [National Response Committee for Yoosung appeals to you]. Facebook, November 10, 2016. https://www.facebook.com/photo/?fbid=1132263820184440.

INDEX

abandonment, in protesting, 39, 61, 70, 122, 125, 167

abstract space, defined, 187. *See also* space

Action Committee for Presidential Resignation (Emergency Action for Park Geun-hye's Resignation), 45–46, 211, 218, 219

activist or organizer *(hwaldongga)*: characteristics of, 180; in legal arena, 188, 206, 213; overview of, 174–77; as skeptical of organizations, 264–65n14; as storytellers, 238–39, 241; as weavers of memory, 227–28. *See also specific activists/organizers*

Act on Protections for Temporary Agency Workers (1998), 57

affect, 12–15; as embodied, 145; as ordinary affects, 118; in protest, 125, 133

Agreement of Comfort Women (2015), 205

Ahmed, Sara, 12

AIDS epidemic, 10

alcohol, 57, 164–65, 178–79, 183

Alliance of Scholars Concerned about Korea, 166

Alvarez, Sonia E., 145–46

American dream, 16–17

anger, in protesting, 10

Another Promise (2013 film), 254n22

antirelationality, 22

anti-US-beef rally (2008), 193, 207–8

Arbeit Workers Union, 67, 252n45

Asahi Glass, 83, 254n17, 254n19

Asahi Glass In-House Subcontracting Workers Union, 82–84, 85–86, 249n1

Asian financial crisis (1997), 8, 17

Assembly and Demonstration Act (ADA), 112–13, 210

autoworkers, 63. *See also* Ssangyong Motor workers

Badiou, Alain, 233

Baek, Nam-ki (Paek Nam-gi), 65–66, 193, 212–15, 229

Baker, Ella, 171

Bando, 69

bankruptcy *(tosan)*, 256n48

Banolim, 86–87, 88–89

bearing witness, as live process, 226
Berlant, Lauren, 147, 151
Black Lives Matter movement (United States), 225
blame, allocation of, 10, 68
Blue House, 4, 129, 190, 207–11
Buddhism, 78, 102–9
Burawoy, Michael, 25
Butler, Judith, 16

Cacho, Lisa Marie, 70
Caldeira, Teresa P. R., 264n11
Camp Humphreys, 162
candlelight protest (*ch'otbul chiphoe*), defined, 241
Candlelight Protests: actions following, 264n12; atmosphere of, 189; Baek Nam-ki's funeral procession and, 214; business response to, 190–91; candlelight wave in, 189, 190; Central Coordinating Committee, 217; conditions for, 77; diversity of protesters in, 188; ethical comportment of, 188–89; fee for, 219; flags of, 189; form and feeling in, 220; impacts of, 220–21, 222; Kwanghwamun Billboard Occupation as compared to, 44; lack of police presence at, 193; main-stage event of, 189–90; march routes of, 190–91; as megaevent, 211–12; *najunge* [later] incident and, 65; new generation in, 44; opposition to, 28, 185–86, 219; origin of, 66, 194; overview of, 2–3, 32, 43–44, 134, 229; photo of, 191; public art at, 40, 229; purpose of, 43–44; right to the global city and, 188–94; statistics regarding, 194; study of, 27–28; T'aegŭkki Rallies

in opposition of, 28, 185–86, 219; unity in, 188
capitalism: domination of, 4; free market, 21; gendering, 21–24; literature regarding, 23; *minjung* (the people) movement against, 234; precarity from, 13, 16; as racial capitalism, 22; space for, 187
care/caring: activities of, 259n37; actors in, 228–29; as alimentary, 182; alternative ways of, 182; becoming in, 151; building spaces for, 141–44; creation of, 228; as cultural rebellion, 237; defined, 147, 152; external solidarity in, 153; food in, 178; gendered nature of, 237; as indispensable, 138; infrastructures for, 32; invisibility in, 150–51, 182; mental and manual aspects of, 142–43; movement reflexivity of, 172–77; overview of, 31–32, 181–83; as political praxis, 236–39; politics of copresence in, 165–72; reflexive thinking regarding, 152–53; relational dimensions of, 152; social-movement infrastructure and, 150–54; solidarity activism and, 161–65, 228; supplies in, 228–29; thinking of matters of fact in, 160; value of, 180–81; visibility of, 182; work of sustaining activism in, 177–81
Cargo Truckers' Solidarity Division of the Korean Public Service and Transport Workers Union, 93
Catholicism/Catholic Church, 11, 107–9, 111, 154–55, 159–60, 164. *See also* nuns
Catholic Priests' Association for Justice (CPAJ), 63, 112

Cha, Gwang-ho (Ch'a Kwang-ho), 90, 125

Cha, Hŏn-ho, 83, 254n17

chaebols, control of, 18

ch'amsa (disaster or catastrophe), 241

changgi t'ujaeng (long-term struggle or fight), 196–97, 241

Ch'ang Human Rights Research Center, 176–77, 178

Chavez, Cesar, 96

China, protesting in, 8

chisin balpgi (folk drumming), 264n11

Choe, Sang-Hun, 224

Cho Han, Hae-joang (Cho Han Hye-jŏng), 20

Choi, Sŏng-yŏng, 84

chŏmgŏ nongsŏng (occupation protest), 241

Chŏn, Pong-jun, 216

Chŏn Pong-jun T'ujaengdan, 216–17

Chŏnggyech'ŏn area, 195–96

chŏnggyujik (regular or standard employment), 17–18, 37, 241. See also employment

Ch'ŏngju City Geriatric Hospital Workers' Union, 53–54, 70

Chŏngkae Clothing, 69

Christian Academy, 110

Christian prayer service, 4, 12, 63, 76, 78, 107, 109–13, 117, 134, 167–68

chujŏm, 164–65

Chun, Tae-il (Chŏn T'ae-il), 61

Chung, Taekyong (Chŏng T'aek-yong), 136–38

Citizens' Coalition of Economic Justice, 264–65n14

clothing, of protesters, 234–35

coffins, as necro-activism, 121

collective bargaining, 6, 60

collective-identity formation, processes of, 77

collectivities, forming of, 10

colonialism, 20, 23, 96, 114–15, 182, 193, 195, 232–36

comfort women, protesting by, 203–7

commitment, 77, 78

community, creation of, through protesting, 193–94

confrontation, sacrifice and suffering in, 129

conjuring, 118

Constitutional Court of Korea, 3, 184

Contentious Performances (Tilly), 10

contentious performances, in protesting, 10. *See also* performance/performance protesting

contracts: of precarious workers, 47; short-term duration, 128, 132; termination of, 56–57

Cool Jam (Kkuljam), 130, 141–42, 143–44, 145, 259n29

copresence, politics of, 165–72

Cort/Cor-Tek Guitar Workers' Union, 48, 50–52, 249n1

court decisions, process of, 50–51

Cowen, Deborah, 182, 245n32, 263n39

Crane 85, 120–21, 122, 124

Dakota Access Pipeline, 233

Davis, Angela Y., 269n34

death: as catalyst, 214; emotional reach of, 66–67; examples of, 66; gendering labor politics of, 68–70; memorial to, 67–68; mobilizing force of, 61–68, 213–15; necropolitics and, 121–22; *Sewol* disaster and, 66; significance of, 66

decolonial methodology, 27

democracy, 16, 193–94

Democratic Labor Party, 59

deprivation, 17, 54

desperation, 7–9, 13

Deul Human Rights Education Center, 177

devaluation, 17

direct employment, agreement regarding, 128–29

directly impacted persons in dispute or grievance *(tangsaja)*, 241

disability activism, 106–7

disaster or catastrophe *(ch'amsa)*, 241

disavowal, 21–22, 42–46

discrimination, 54

disposability: of precarious workers, 47; refusal of, 32; as social death, 70

documentaries, of protesting, 212–13

Dongil Textiles, 69

drinking room *(sulbang)*, 178–79, 183

duration, dwindling numbers and, 78

Effler, Erika Summers, 10–11

Egypt, 145, 225

E-Land/Homever workers, 81

E-Land Union, 48, 58–59

embodiment: performing protest and, 11; ritual and, 130; visual, 148

Emergency Action for Park Geun-hye's Resignation (Action Committee for Presidential Resignation), 45–46, 211

emergency care, actors for, 76. *See also* care/caring

emergency responders, role of, 138

emotions, 10–11, 12, 13, 70

employer-hired thugs *(yongyŏk kkangp'ae)*, 242; or as thugs for hire, 81, 124

employment: degrading quality of, 12–13; nonregular, precarious (*See* precarious, irregular, nonregular employment *(pijŏnggyujik)*); regular/standard, 17–18, 37, 241; self-, 18; statistics regarding, 17–18

ethical comportment, of Candlelight Protests, 188–89

ethical labor, requirements of, 160

ethnography, relational approach to, 25

external allies, interactional dynamics of, 31

failure, 223–24, 225, 226

family, 152, 173, 181, 189, 229

Federation of Korean Trade Unions, 83

Federici, Silvia, 227

feminist human rights activists, 172–77

fight or struggle *(t'ujaeng)*, 242

fight to the death, of militant unionism, 2

financialization, 16

firings, 34, 37, 49, 251n25

Fisher, Bernice, 236

flags, of Candlelight Protests, 189

fortresses, *nongsŏng* in, 79–80

416 Coalition, 217

France, popular contention in, 10

freedom of assembly, expansion of, 202

friendship, in protest camps, 139

Fuentes, Marcela, 145

funerals, 121; processions, 198, 201, 213–14

Gandhi, Mahatma, 96

gender: inequality, 18–19, 21–24, 128, 173–74; in social movements, 173; spaces of social reproduction and, 138–41

Geographies of Racial Capitalism with Ruth Wilson Gilmore (2020 documentary video), 146

Germany, labor statistics of, 178

Gilmore, Ruth Wilson, 1, 4, 15, 146
Giroux, Henry, 268n19
global financial collapse, 17
Gómez-Barris, Macarena, 27
Gordon, Avery, 117, 118
Gould, Deborah B., 10
government, leadership transitions in, 34–35
Government Complex (Seoul), State-of-the-Nation Sit-in Protest at, 37–38
Government-General Building (Seoul), 195
Great Workers' Struggle of 1987, 120–21
Green Hospital, 39, 99–100
grief: gendering labor politics of, 68–70; public displays of, 67, 201; of Sewol tragedy, 20, 40
ground-level protest camp, 38. *See also* protest camp
group-based leadership, 171
G-Voice, 64–65

Han, Sang-gyun, 62–63
Hangang Bridge, 106
Hanjin Heavy Industries and Construction, 120–25
Harvey, David, 165–66, 230
Hayes, Kelly, 237
head-shaving, 4, 54, 106
high-altitude protest (*kogong nongsŏng*): boundaries for, 93; dangers of, 35; defined, 241; desperation of, 8; as escalation strategy, 232; fictional portrayal of, 231–32; following the election, 35; ground-level protesting with, 37–38; at Hanjin Heavy Industries and Construction, 120–25; history of, 91, 115; hunger strikes and, 90;

isolation of, 89–90, 91, 93; of Jaenung Educational Tutors' Union, 49–50; of Kiryung Electronics Workers' Union, 126; map of, 92; overview of, 6, 89–95; perils of, 90; photo of, 24, 36; politics of height in, 91; preparation for, 90; press conference for, 39; risks regarding, 94; solidarity camp with, 37–38; as solitary endeavors, 123; at Star Chemical/FineTek, 125; support system for, 123; trauma from, 94; verticality emphasis of, 91; worst-case scenario regarding, 90. *See also* protesting; specific organizations
Hitec RCD Korea Democratic Union Defense Protest Committee, 249n1
home study tutors, women as, 49–50
Hong, Grace Kyungwon, 21, 34, 42, 44
Hong, Ki-t'ak, 90
Hong Kong, 145, 225
hope, 230–31, 238, 268n19
Hope Bus movement, 45, 95, 120, 124–25, 162
hopelessness, 13
hospitals, corruption and retaliation by, 251n24, 251n25
human rights (*inkwŏn*), 241
human rights, labor rights as, 22
human rights activism (*inkwŏn undong*), 174
humility, 108
hunger strike (*tansik*): apprehension regarding, 101–2; blood running dry in, 102; challenges of, 75; characters in, 97; decision for, 97; defined, 241; examples of, 51–52, 96; Green Hospital and, 99–100; high-altitude protest (*kogong nongsŏng*) and, 90; history of, 96;

INDEX

hunger strike (*tansik*) (*cont.*)
of Kiryung Electronics Workers'
Union, 126–27; long-term consequences of, 99–100; as "nothing
special," 99; overview of, 96–102;
photo of, 127; purpose of, 97; relay,
101; religious actors in, 97–98; as
social, 97; solidarity (*tongjo
tansik*), 97, 101, 127; standards for,
98; as temporal crisis, 97; utility
of, 100; worthiness in, 98
hwaldongga (activist or organizer),
174–75, 241
Hwang, Sang-ki, 87
Hwang, Sok-yong (Hwang Sŏk-yŏng),
235–36
Hwang, Yira (Hwang-I-ra), 123
Hwang, Yumi (Hwang Yu-mi), 86,
254n21
Hyehwa-dong Catholic Church, 49–50
hyŏnjang (core site), 80, 218
hypocrisy, 16
Hyundai Motors Nonregular Workers' Union, 90
Hyundai Ulsan Precarious Work
Union, 249n1

imprinting, 264n11
Inchŏn, South Korea, 156
Inchŏn Station, 261–62n20
income inequality, 17
indignation, in protesting, 10
Industrial Workers of the World, 236
informality, 16
infrastructural turn, 182
infrastructure: of care/caring, 32,
152, 182; in contrast to structure,
147; of dissent, 145, 150; people as,
151–52; social movement, 150–54
injustice, 73
inkwŏn (human rights), 241

inkwŏn undong (human rights
activism), 174
interlocuters, characteristics of, 26
International Monetary Fund (IMF)
crisis, 5, 8, 20, 161, 193, 250n16
intersectionality, 153, 245n18
invisibility, in caring infrastructure,
150–51, 182
Iran, 145
irinsiwi (one-person protest), 241
isolation, 39, 89–90, 91, 93

Jaenung Educational Industries (JEI),
49–50, 90, 251n18
Jaenung Educational Tutors' Union,
49–50
Japanese embassy, protesting at,
203–7
Jeunesse ouvrière chrétienne, or
Young Christian Workers (JOC)
Korea, 110
Jiyul sŭnim, 98, 99
Joint Struggle for Abolishing Mass
Layoffs and Precarious Employ-
ment, Defending Democratic
Unions, and Calling the Removal
of Park Geun-hye for Union
Repression and the Destruction of
People's Livelihoods, 35
Jongno 3-ga subway station, 200
June Uprising (1987), 197

Kaba, Mariame, 223, 230, 237
Kang, Chu-ryong, 23, 234
Kangnam (Seoul), 19, 220
kansa (organizational staff), 175
kap-ŭl discourse, 54–55
Kee, Joan, 91, 97
Kim, Dae-jung (Kim Tae-jung), 21, 94,
162, 199–200, 210, 250n16
Kim, Eunjung, 121

Kim, Gyeong-bong (Kim Kyŏng-bong), 51
Kim, Hyejin (Kim Hey-jin): on church and labor movement, 111; on collective bargaining, 60; on disability activism, 107; fines of, 211; on firings, 34, 37; on high-altitude protest (*kogong nongsŏng*), 93–95; at Hope Bus movement, 95; on hunger strikes, 101–2; interview with, 45; on KCTU, 59; overview of, 46–48; on precarious employment, 55; on precarious labor movement, 60; on *samboilbae*, 107; at State-of-the-Nation Sit-in Protest, 38–39; support role of, 95; on Urban Industrial Mission (UIM), 110
Kim, Il-rhan (Kim Il-lan), 212
Kim, Jin-suk (Kim Chin-suk), 45, 90, 120–26, 132, 133, 227, 237–38
Kim, Jisoo M., 113, 115
Kim, Ju-ik, 120–21
Kim, Ki-ch'un, 101
Kim, Kyŏng-bong, 51
Kim, Kyŏng-suk, 68–70, 71
Kim, Seungha (Kim Sŭng-ha), 1, 2, 117, 131–35, 139–40, 142, 146
Kim, So-yeon (Kim So-yŏn), 98–99, 101–2, 126–27, 128, 129, 130, 142, 236
Kim, To-hyŏn, 106
Kim, Young-oh (Kim Yŏng-o), 99, 100–101
Kim, Young Sam (Kim Yŏng-sam), 21
Kim-gun, 67–68
King, Martin Luther, Jr., 96
Kiryung Electronics: employment violations of, 127–29; high-altitude protest (*kogong nongsŏng*) of, 24; hunger strike against, 98–99;

moving of, 129; *och'et'uji* at, 104; protesting by, 7
Kiryung Electronics Workers' Union: agreement with, 128–29; high-altitude protest (*kogong nongsŏng*) of, 126; hunger strike of, 101–2; interviews with, 28; labor campaign of, 126; persistence of, 144–45; resilience of, 145; solidarity hunger strike of, 127
kogong nongsŏng (high-altitude protest). *See* high-altitude protest (*kogong nongsŏng*)
"Kogong'yŏjido," 91–92
Konkuk University Medical Center, 67–68
Koo, Hagen, 19, 256n47
Korea Electric Power Corporation (KEPCO), 147–48, 163
Korea Federation for Environmental Movement, 264–65n14
Korean Confederation of Trade Unions (KCTU): coalitions in, 67; homophobia in, 64; interviews with, 28; mass assemblies of, 199; membership of, 60; multiyear campaign of, 60; nationwide general strike of, 199; opposition to Nonregular Worker Protection Act by, 56; precarious workers' movement marginal status in, 60; pressure on, 56; protesting by, 157; reorganization of, 59–60; social-movement know-how of, 215–16; solidarity of, 58
Korean Metal Workers' Union, 84
Korean National Police Agency, 218
Korean Peasants League (KPL), 216
Korean Railroad Corporation (KORAIL), 1–2, 133, 135

296 INDEX

Korean Railroad Workers' Union, 140–41

Korean Solidarity against Precarious Work, 38–39, 46–47, 48–49, 94–95

Korean Synthetic Fiber, 254n17

Korean Teachers and Education Workers Union, 206

Korean Train Express (KTX), 98, 131–32

Korean Train Express (KTX) Crew Workers' Union: award for, 70; decision reversal regarding, 4; femininity of, 140–41; gendered spaces of social reproduction and, 138–41; high-altitude protest (*kogong nongsŏng*) of, 6; interviews with, 28; loss of life in, 3–4; media attention on, 140; overview of, 131–35; participation decline of, 133; persistence of, 144–45; photo of, 7, 137; place-based protest (*nongsŏng*) of, 81; poster for, 135; prayer protests of, 4; procession with full prostration (*och'et'uji*) of, 6–7, 134–35; prolonged protest of, 48; protesting types of, 4; religious support for, 133–34; resilience of, 145; solidarity as radical dependency for, 131–35; strike of, 1

Korean Women Workers Association, 65, 69

Korea Telecom (KT) Contract Workers' Union, 47–49, 250n16

Korea Times (newspaper), 186

Kotef, Hagar, 210

KT Mokdong Data Center, 94

Kumi Industrial Complex, 83, 254n17

Kuŭi Station, 67

Kwak, Chae-kyu, 121

Kwak, EKyeong (Kwak I-kyŏng), 40, 45, 64–67, 213, 216

Kwanghwamun area, 192, 195, 201–2

Kwanghwamun Billboard Occupation: Candlelight Protests as compared to, 44; characteristics of, 44; decompression following, 40–41; defeat in, 42; duration of, 48; ground-level protest camp for, 37–39; overview of, 35–37; photo of, 36; treatment of protesters during, 39; workers in, 249n1

Kwanghwamun Square: counterhegemonic resistance at, 229; description of, 40; features of, 194–95; following *Sewol* disaster, 40, 41; funeral procession at, 214–15; impeachment decision of Park Geun-hye at, 184–85; significance of, 40

Kwanghwamun Station, 194

kwangjang (public square), 194–211, 241

Kwon, Jong Bum, 200

Kwon, Okja (Kwŏn Ok-cha), 53–54, 70, 131

Kyŏngbok Palace, 195

Kyŏnggi Province, 217

labor: disavowing, 42–46; disputes, 6; laborers as despised, 23; literature regarding, 23; politics, of grief and death, 68–70; redefining priorities of organized, 56–61; of refusal, 14; repression, 21; rights, as human rights, 22; statistics regarding, 177–78. *See also* employment

LaDuke, Winona, 182

Larkin, Brian, 151

Lawyers for a Democratic Society, 133

Lee, Chang-kun (Yi Ch'ang-gŭn), 62, 90

INDEX

Lee, Ching Kwan, 8
Lee, Han-yeol (Yi Han-yŏl), 61, 197, 198
Lee, Hyo-sin (Yi Hyo-sin), 217
Lee, In-geun (Yi In-kŭn), 48, 51–52, 249n1, 250n4
Lee, Myung-bak (Yi Myŏng-bak), 161–62, 195, 201, 207–11
Lee, Namhee, 193, 234
Lee, Taeho: on city hall, 197; civic activism of, 200; fines of, 211; on *kwangjang* (public square), 184, 188; one-person protest of, 208–9; at People's Solidarity for Participatory Democracy (PSPD), 200–201, 202; on police barricades, 207; on protesting, 196–97, 198–99; on Sampoong Department Store tragedy, 200–201
Lefebvre, Henri, 187
legal-identification system, 173
Lesbians and Gays Support the Miners, 65
leukemia, 86–87, 254n20, 254n21
Lewis, Sara E., 108
LGBTQ+, 64, 173
Life and Peace Division, 159
Lim, Jae-chun (Im Chae-ch'un), 51
livelihoods, degrading quality of, 12–13
logic of elimination, 233
long-term struggle or fight (*changgi t'ujaeng*), 196–97, 241
Lopez, Patricia J., 181

madang (outdoor courtyard), 218
Mahmood, Saba, 73–74
Mandela, Nelson, 96
March First independence movement, 197
Maria, Sister: focus of, 153–54; leadership of, 147, 149–50, 159, 163; overview of, 154–61; on police, 169–70; on politics of copresence, 165–72; on protesting schedule, 163; reflexivity of, 171; relational processes of, 151; on *samboilbae,* 107, 108; on *Sewol* disaster activism, 163–64; solidarity activism and, 161–65; on visibility of nuns, 182
marital status, discrimination regarding, 128
Massey, Doreen, 14, 118, 187–88, 222, 228
mass protesting, as megaevents, 211–21
Mater 2-10 (Hwang), 235–36
McGranahan, Carole, 232
Melamed, Jodi, 22
Melucci, Albert, 150
Mexico, 145
Meyer, David S., 225–26
militant unionism, 2, 21
militarized sexual slavery, 203
military, in binary gender system, 173
Millar, Kathleen M., 16
minbok, 103
minjung (the people) movement, 43, 214, 234
Miryang encampment, 82, 147–50
Miryang grandmothers, 148–49, 163
misogyny, 172
Moon, Gyu-hyeon (Mun Kyu-hyŏn), Father, 107–8
Moon, Jae-in (Mun Chae-in), 3, 35, 43, 100–101, 224
Moon, So-ri (Mun So-ri), 231
Moore, Barrington, 73
moral economies, protest repertoires and, 71
Mount Ch'ŏnsŏng, 98

movement activists with student-government backgrounds (*undongkwŏn*), 194, 242

movement actors, amplification role of, 76

movement reflexivity, 172–77

multidirectional memory, 116, 235

Myŏngdong Cathedral of Seoul, 110, 156–57, 199

Myung-bak *sansŏng*, 207

Na, Young-Jung Tari, 173

najunge [later] incident, 65

Nam, Hwasook Bergquist, 23, 96, 120–21

National Assembly, 93–94, 217–18

National Emergency Committee of University Students, 217

National Labor Relations Committee, 49

National Labor Standards Act (1953), 21

National Museum of Korean Contemporary History, 195

National Police Agency, 200

National Security Law (Hong Kong, 2020), 225

Neely, Abigail H., 181

neo-Fascism, 225

neoliberalism, 21–22, 268–69n31

Nepalese migrant workers, 157

Niemöller, Martin, 269n34

#NoDAPL movement, 233

No More Deaths campaign, 86

nongovernmental organizations (NGOs), 47

nongsŏng (place-based protest). *See* place-based protest (*nongsŏng*)

nongsŏng (prolonged protest), 47–48, 57–58, 227, 241

Nonregular Worker Protection Act, 56, 57

numbers, 77, 78

nuns: in Catholic Priests' Association for Justice (CPAJ), 63; at *chujŏm*, 164–65; corporeal presence of, 163; following International Monetary Fund (IMF) crisis, 161; greetings of, 158; at hunger strikes, 97–98; Life and Peace Division of, 159; at Miryang encampment, 149–50; Miryang grandmothers and, 148–49, 163; organizational structures of, 161, 166–67; photo of, 155, 164; police and, 169–70; politics of copresence and, 165–72; positionality of, 171; protesting policies of, 163–64; relationalities of, 158; *samboilbae* of, 108–9; sociality of, 158–59; social-justice organizing by, 159–60; solidarity of, 154–55, 171–72; with Ssangyong Motor Union, 167–69. *See also* Maria, Sister

occupation protest (*chŏmgŏ nongsŏng*), 241

Occupy Wall Street, 224–25

och'et'uji (procession with full prostration). *See* procession with full prostration (*och'et'uji*)

Oh, Min-Gyu (O Min-gyu), 45, 55, 57, 58

Oh, Se-hoon (O Se-hun), 201

Oh, Su-yŭng, 49–50

Oido Station, 105

one-person protest (*irinsiwi*), 241

Open the Kwangjang campaign (2004), 202

ordinary affects, 118

ordinary space, transformative power of, 119. *See also* space

Organization for Economic Cooperation and Development (OECD), 17, 178

organizer, 210

outdoor courtyard (*madang*), 218

Pak, Chun-ho, 90

Pak, T'ae-yŏn, 69

Parasite (film), 19

Park, Chung Hee (Pak Chŏng-hŭi), 114, 262n20

Park, Geun-hye (Pak Kŭn-hye), 2–3, 20, 32, 40, 161–62, 184, 185, 224

Park, Hyun Ok, 20

Park, Jong-chul (Pak Chong-ch'ŏl), 197

Park, Kyoung-seok (Pak Kyŏng-sŏk), 106

Park, Rae-gun (Pak Rae-kun), 211

Park, Sunyoung, 114–15

Park, Won-soon (Pak Wŏn-sun), 218–19

People's Committee for the *Sewol*-Ferry Tragedy, 45

People's Rally, 192–93, 213–14

People's Solidarity for Participatory Democracy (PSPD): activism of, 200–201; campaign for judicial reform by, 265n19; demands of, 202; interviews with, 28; lawsuit of, 207–8; origin of, 194, 264–65n14; social-movement knowhow of, 215

People's Solidarity for Social Progress, 59

performance art, 114–15

performance/performance protesting: characteristics of, 72;

embodiment in, 11; examples of, 76; function of, 13; at Kwanghwamun Square, 40; as lived experience of injustice, 73; multidirectional memory and, 116; overview of, 73; significance of, 145; solidarity in, 75–76, 226. *See also specific protests*

place-based protest (*nongsŏng*): comparison of, 180; critical emotional event in, 81; defensive nature of, 89; defined, 79; demarcation of, 82; historical meaning of, 79–80; homemaking in, 81–82; interventions in, 81; maintaining, 82; outdoor benefits of, 88; overview of, 6, 79–89; plans for, 80–81; as protest camp, 81–82; as protest spectacle, 81; in public places, 80–81; of SHARPS, 87–88; solidarity at, 82; supplies and equipment for, 81; violence in, 81. *See also* protest camp; specific protests

place making: claims in, 229; example of, 184–88; impacts of, 220; in labor of refusal, 14; place defined in, 187–88; throwntogetherness of, 228; work of, 187

planters, 84

Poamae Park, 198–99

police: at anti-US-beef rally, 207; barricading practices of, 129, 207; death of Baek Nam-ki and, 65–66; death of Lee Han-yeol and, 61, 197; death of officer of, 162; death of Pak T'ae-yŏn and, 69; death of Park Jong-chul and, 197; harassment by, 192–93; against Korean Confederation of Trade Unions

300 **INDEX**

police (*cont.*)
(KCTU), 199; lightness of policing protests by, 200; military force of, 35, 62, 63, 65–66, 68, 81, 94, 95, 124, 208; noise disturbance and, 210; nuns and, 150, 169–70; photo of, 164; police-line of, 210; protest against, 23; at protest camps, 83–84, 138, 167; restriction of bodily movement by, 37, 91, 104, 209–10; student protesters *versus,* 197; surveillance usage by, 210; uniforms of, 200
political affect, 12–15, 31
political-claims making, 11
political dignitaries, 78
political martyrs, 9
political prisoners, 225
politics of copresence, 165–72
politics of time, 234
Post-it memorial, 68, 114
postcolonial phenomenon, 193
poverty, 17
Power, Emma R., 182
prayer services, 109–13
precarious, irregular, nonregular employment (*pijŏnggyujik*): abandonment of, 46; challenges of, 55; changing public understanding of, 55–56; characteristics of, 37; defined, 241; discrimination against, 44; disposability of, 37, 47; firings of, 37, 47; growth of, 46; as isolated, 61; *kap-ŭl* discourse and, 54–55; marginal status of, 60; neglect of, 46; *nongsŏng* function and, 57; Nonregular Worker Protection Act and, 56; overview of, 17–18, 19; as part of "lower class," 54; precarity of, 70;

prolonged strikes of, 47; revolution and instability in, 55; social death of, 70; statistics regarding, 61; strike against, 1; as subordinate party, 54; union-forming by, 47; unprotection of, 44. *See also specific companies*
precarity: capitalist unconscious and, 20; examples of, 70; fighting, 46–56; gender and, 22; as labor's disavowal, 21; as life-depriving system, 13; neoliberal, 146; overview of, 12; refusal of, 15, 45; resistance against, 32; as shaping worker-led protests, 44; social conditions of domination and, 22; as social death, 45, 70; as structure of feeling, 16–17; understanding, 15–20
press conference, for high-altitude protest (*kogong nongsŏng*), 39
Pride (2014 film), 65
privatization, precarity and, 16
procession protesting/procession with full prostration (*och'et'uji*): defined, 241; devotion in, 130; of Kiryung Electronics Workers' Union, 129; of Korean Train Express (KTX) Crew Workers' Union, 134–35; mindfulness in, 130; overview of, 6–7, 67–68, 102–9; process of, 130; reflection in, 74; self-reflection from, 129–30; spacious, flexible mind in, 130. *See also* protesting
prolonged protest (*nongsŏng*), 47–48, 57–58, 227, 241
protection, as selective, 44
protective accompaniment, 150
protest affects, 125, 133

INDEX   301

Protestant Christians, 162

protest camp: of Asahi Glass In-House Subcontracting Workers Union, 82–84, 85–86; basic needs in, 138, 139; building of, 85; characteristics of, 85, 88; of comfort women, 206; comparison of, 180; conditions of, 82–83; division of labor in, 85; friendship in, 139; guidelines and procedures in, 138; highest level of, 88; of Korean Train Express (KTX) Crew Workers' Union, 138–41; place-based protest (*nongsŏng*) as, 81–82; registering, 87–88; role delegation for, 85–86; of SHARPS, 87–88; as storage facility, 86; street-level, 88–89; supplies for, 85; support for, 206; thoughtfulness regarding, 88; time schedule for, 85–86; types of, 180; upkeep and cleaning of, 85; women's role in, 86

protesting: affinities in, 9; bonding in, 9; causes of, 81; concerns regarding, 224; contentious performances in, 10; culture in, 10; desperation in, 7–9; disavowal in, 15; dividends from, 45; documentary evidence against, 148; emotions in, 10–11; evolution of, 76–77; forms of, 2; gender hierarchy in, 173–74; high-altitude, 6, 8, 24, 35; hope in, 230; as illegal, 198; interactional dynamics in, 8; interdisciplinary literature regarding, 11; legislation regarding, 210; masculinity in, 132–33; as megaevents, 211–21; motivations in, 9; as national pastime, 224; notification system for, 218–19;

outdated tactics of, 43; overview of, 32–33; packing up from, 41–42; paradox of, 226; photo of, 7, 24, 198; placards of, 5; power of, 9–10; prayer, 4; as public-facing strategy, 9; purpose of, 45; reimagining history in, 234–35; relational processes of, 11; risks regarding, 225; sleeping during, 136–38; solidarity in, 13; as stereotypical, 231; types of, 4, 30–31, 42; visibility of, 234. *See also specific types and protests*

protest struggle to the capital (*sanggyŏng t'ujaeng*), 115–16, 216, 241

public art, 40, 41, 229

public assembly, 202–7. *See also specific cases*

public mourning, 213–15

public religion, 109–13

public square (*kwangjang*), 194–211, 241

Puch'ŏn Women Workers' Association, 69

Puig de la Bellacasa, Maria, 152, 160

p'ungmul drummers, 264n11

pushing the limits, 72–73

P'yŏngt'aek, 63, 64, 162, 208, 217

Pyŏngyang rubber factory strikes, 23

Queenmaker (2023 drama series), 231–32

queer activism, 64–65

racism, 4

radical dependency, 131–35, 141–44, 146

radical hope, 268n19

radical socialist humanism, 165

Red Devil sports fans, 201–2
reflection, in ritual, 74
refusal, 12–15, 231–36
regular or standard employment
(*chŏnggyujik*), 17–18, 37, 241. *See
also* employment
relational power, spatial praxis of,
118–19
relay hunger strike, 101. *See also*
hunger strike
religious leadership, 78, 97–98, 118,
133–34
religious organizations, influence of,
256n47
religious solidarity, decline of, 63. *See
also* solidarity
repertoire, protest: amplification of,
77; changes to, 113–14; characteristics of, 35, 37; contradictions in,
72, 77–78; feelings in, 72; function
of, 11, 230; as habitual, 73; history
of, 113–16; innovation of, 109–13;
interior life of, 75; memory of,
113–16; moral economies and, 71;
necessity of, 227; outcomes of,
228; overview of, 76–78, 113–16;
relations in, 72; sacrifice and
suffering in, 35, 37; in shaping
how movements move, 12–15;
solidarity in, 13–14, 75–76; study
of, 25–29; of use of workers'
bodies, 22; variations to, 114; as
weavers of memory, 227–28
research activist (*yŏngu hwaldongga*),
241
resilience, solidarity in, 125–31
revolutionary humanism, 165–66
revolutionary uprisings, 9
Rhee, Maria Chol-soon (I Ch'ŏl-sun),
69–70
right to have rights, 6

"right to the city," 188–94, 202–7
ritual: adaptations of, 109–13;
characteristics of, 73–74; defined,
73; as embodied pedagogy, 74;
examples of, 76; multidirectional
memory and, 116; reflection in, 74;
significance of, 145; as weavers of
memory, 227–28
Roh, Moo-hyun (No Mu-hyŏn), 21, 43,
56, 162, 208, 210
Rothberg, Michael, 116
Ryu, Eunsook (Ryu Ŭn-suk), 153–54,
174–77, 178–81, 182–83, 220

Saemangŭm Restoration Project, 103
Salzinger, Leslie, 132–33
samboilbae (procession with three
steps and a bow), 102–9, 241
Sampoong Department Store tragedy
(1995), 200–201
Samsung Department Store, 265n18
Samsung Electronics, 87
Samsung Group, 18
Samsung leukemia, 86–87, 254n20
Samsung Semiconductor, 86–87,
254n21
Sandoval, Chela, 25
sanggyŏng t'ujaeng (protest struggle
to the capital), 115–16, 216, 241
Sarangbang Group for Human
Rights, 153, 174, 176–77
Sears, Alan, 150
security, 34, 42
Sejong Cultural Center for the
Performing Arts, 195
Sejong Hotel Union, 249n1
self-employment, 18
self-learning method, 251n18
self-sacrifice, mobilizing force of,
61–68
Seoul Administrative Court, 217

Seoul Central Station, 1, 2, 4, 81, 134, 137

Seoul City Hall, 64, 192, 195, 197–98, 202, 230

Seoul High Court, 50

Seoul Human Rights Film Festival, 177

Seoul National University, 197

Seoul National University Hospital, 229

Seoul Peace Market, 61

Seoul Queer Culture Festival, 65, 219

Seoul train station, 195, 200

settler colonialism, 233

Sewol disaster movement: Blue House and, 209; Catholic mass following, 155; denial of access in, 209; effects of, 66; hunger strike against, 99; march for, 185; nun's activism following, 163–64; overview of, 20, 40; public art for, 40, 41, 215, 229; support following, 95

Sewol Movement Committee, 95

sexism, 172

sexual harassment, 172

Shah, Nayan, 97

Sharpe, Christina, 147, 153

shipbuilding, union movement in, 120–21

sidewalk, prayers on, 109–13

Simone, AbdouMaliq, 151, 182

Simpson, Audra, 14, 232, 233

Sisi, Abdel Fattah el-, 225

Sister J (2020 documentary film), 52

sleeping, for protesters, 136–38

social classes, deprivation and loss in, 19

social death, 45, 70–71

social inequality, 4

social media, 37–38, 124

social-movement causes, 13

social-movement infrastructure, 150–54, 175

social-movement know-how, 215–21

social movements, planning and organization for, 14

social movement theory, 8–9, 10–11, 12–15

social reproduction, 138–41

social suffering, 31–32

social trauma, *Sewol* disaster as, 20

solidarity: activism, 161–65; camp, 37–38, 41–42 (*See also* protest camp); in caring infrastructure, 161–65, 228; as catalytic force, 118; cleavages in, 43; conjuring, 118; defined, 14; as defining feature of protest, 13–14; demonstrating, 122; elements of, 227, 228; examples of, 230; external, 153; function of, 15, 31; in hunger strike, 97, 101, 127; importance of, 117–18, 226–31; as lifeline, 130–31; as paradoxical, 147; in performance, 75–76, 226; at place-based protest (*nongsŏng*), 82; as political affect, 12–15, 119; power of, 131; as productive, 15; as protective accompaniment, 268n13; in protest repertoire, 13–14, 75–76; as radical dependency, 131–35, 146; relational politics of, 145; as relational space, 228; religious, 63; in resilience, 125–31; in street prayer protesting, 78; team, 123; through death, 61–68; urgency of, 122; of women, 227; "You are me" messaging for, 68

Solidarity against Disability Discrimination, 106

solidarity caravan, 124–25

Solidarity for LGBT Human Rights Korea, 64

Solidarity for the Right to Mobility, 105

solidarity hunger strike (*tongjo tansik*), 101, 241. *See also* hunger strike (*tansik*)

Solnit, Rebecca, 220

sŏnbae/hubae culture, 172–73

Sŏn Buddhists, 162

Sŏngsu Bridge, 201

sŏnsaeng-nim (teacher), 176

South Africa, precarity in, 17

South Korea: contention in, 26–27; economic challenges of, 17; geopolitical dominance in, 193; illiberal democracy of, 21; income inequality statistics in, 17; infrastructure of, 195; Japanese colonial rule of, 23; as most overworked nation, 177–78; poverty statistics in, 17; precarity in, 17; presidencies in, 161–62; rebuilding of democracy in, 193–94

space: abstract, 187; for capitalism, 187; defined, 228; demanding right to, 230; experience of, 187; as political, 210; as product of interrelations, 118; as resource, 188; significance of, 187; transforming relations in, 230

Spain, 145

spatial politics, 14, 79–80, 184, 186–87, 221

speculation, making space for, 160

Squid Game (2021 drama series), 19, 62

Ssangyong Motor Union: Catholic Mass during protest of, 164, 167–68; death and, 61–63, 67; G-Voice alliance with, 64–65; nuns and, 167–69; as part of labor aristocracy, 63; photo of, 136; political formation of, 63–64; protest camps of, 84; protesting by, 51; religious support for, 111–13; solidarity with, 104; violence against, 208

Standing Rock Sioux, 233

Star Chemical/FineTek, 90, 125

State-of-the-Nation (siguk) Sit-in Protest, 37–38

Statue of Peace, 204–7

sticky bonds, of *samboilbae,* 108

street prayer protesting, 78

strike: of Korean Confederation of Trade Unions (KCTU), 199; of Korean Train Express (KTX) Crew Workers' Union, 1–2; length discussion of, 131; photo of, 3; as prolonged, 47; Pyŏngyang rubber, 23; type of, 23. *See also* protesting

striking workers, vilification of, 62

structures of feeling, repertoire as, 5

student activism, 173, 197

subway system, disability activism at, 106

suffering: in hunger strikes, 96–98 (*See also* hunger strike); images of, 115; purpose in, 55; sacrifice and, 13, 35, 43, 70, 73, 129; social, 20, 31; solidarity in, 105, 161; support in, 168; worthiness in, 77

suicide, 8, 9, 121

Sukyŭng sŭnim, 103

sulbang (drinking room), 178–79, 183

Summers Effler, Erika, 10–11

supermarket workers, *nongsŏng* of, 79–80

supporters, 31, 76, 77, 82, 94–95. *See also* care/caring infrastructure

Supporters for the Health and Rights of People in the Semiconductor Industry (SHARPS), 86–88
Supreme Court of Korea, 4, 50–51, 133
surrender, refusing, 30

Tadiar, Neferti X. M., 6, 237
Taech'uri Village, 162
T'aegŭkki Rallies, 28, 185–86, 241
Taehangno District, 200
Taehanmun of the Tŏksu Palace, 84, 112–13, 167–68
tangsaja: as driving force, 102; examples of, 74–75; forming of, 74–75; interactional dynamics of, 31; performance and ritual role of, 76; in political legal studies, 74; protest repertoire of, 30; pushing the limits by, 72
tansik (hunger strike). *See* hunger strike *(tansik)*
T'apgol Park, 200
Tarrow, Sydney, 8
Taylor, Diana, 11, 25, 72, 73, 75, 226
Terminal High Altitude Area Defense system, 220
Thailand, 145
Thatcher, Margaret, 65
the people *(minjung)* movement, 43, 214, 234
386 Generation, 43, 250n7
throwntogetherness, 188
Tibetan Buddhism, 103, 108
Tilly, Charles, 10, 76–77
time, politics of, 234
tongjo tansik (solidarity hunger strike), 101, 241. *See also* hunger strike *(tansik)*
Tongyang Cement Union, 249n1
tractors, in protest movement, 216–17

trade unions, militancy of, 43
trauma, following protesting, 62
Tronto, Joan C., 152, 236
t'ujaeng (fight or struggle), 242
Tŭngch'on-dong neighborhood (Seoul), 51
twip'uri (postactivity debrief), 178, 242
Twitter, 123–24

undongkwŏn (movement activists with student-government backgrounds), 194, 242
unions, 6. *See also specific unions*
United Nations Educational, Scientific, and Cultural Organization (UNESCO) Memory of the World Register, 208–9
United States: American dream in, 16–17; Black Lives Matter movement in, 225; #NoDAPL movement in, 233; precarity in, 16–17; racism function in, 4; Terminal High Altitude Area Defense system of, 220
unity, in protest performance, 77. *See also* solidarity
unprotected life, as bare life, 44
Urban Industrial Mission (UIM), 110, 111, 256n48
Uri Party, 56
Uses and Management of the Seoul Square, 202
US-ROK Free Trade Agreement (2008), 207
US-ROK Status of Forces Agreement, 202

vilification, of striking workers, 62
violence, 81, 124, 185–86, 192–93, 208. *See also* police

Voss, Kim, 225
vulnerable, labor oppression of, 4–5

wages, 18–19, 67
weavers of memory, 227–28
Wednesday demonstrations, 203–7
white nationalism, 225
willful politics of refusal, 231–36
Williams, Raymond, 5
Wilson Gilmore, Ruth, 1, 4, 15, 146, 184, 186–87
witnesses, emotions of, 129
women: diverse backgrounds of, 131–32; as home study tutors, 49–50; in hunger strikes, 96; labor oppression of, 4–5; in labor resistance, 23; legibility problem of, 133; marital status discrimination of, 128; in precarious, irregular, nonregular employment (*pijŏnggyujik*), 46–47; in protest camps, 86; protesting by, 23–24, 227; solidarity of, 227; wage statistics of, 18–19; as weavers of memory, 227–28
Women's Labor Movement Award, 69
Won Buddhists, 162
Wonpoong Woolen Textile, 69

working poor, 19–20
World Cup games (2002), 201–2
World Cup Stadium shopping complex, 59
World Trade Organization, 250n16
worthiness, 77–78, 98
WUNC protest performance, 77–78

YH Trading Company, 68–70, 100
YH Union, 68–70
Yŏ, Min-hŭi, 49–50
Yŏido Park, 198, 199
Yongsan, 208
Yongsan Ch'amsa, 162, 212
Yongsan Garrison, 162
yŏngu hwaldongga (research activist), 241
yongyŏk kkangp'ae (employer-hired thugs), 242
Yonsei University, 197
Yoon, Suk Yeol (Yun Sŏk-yŏl), 224
Yoosung Union, 104
Yu, Heung-hee (Yu Hŭng-hŭi), 72, 74, 126–27, 129, 130, 142
Yu, Myŏng-ja, 49
Yulee, Jiwoon, 122
Yun, Aelim, 46–47, 49

Zacchaeus, Father, 4, 133–34